Residential Design Using
Autodesk® Revit® Architecture 2012

Daniel John Stine

ISBN: 978-1-58503-680-6

PUBLICATIONS

Schroff Development Corporation

www.SDCpublications.com

Schroff Development Corporation
P.O. Box 1334
Mission KS 66222
(913) 262-2664
www.SDCpublications.com

Publisher: Stephen Schroff

Trademarks:

Autodesk®, AutoCAD®, Maya®, mental ray®, Revit®, 3ds Max® are registered trademarks or trademarks of Autodesk, Inc., and/or its subsidiaries and/or affiliates in the USA and/or other countries.

All other trademarks are trademarks of their respective holders.

Examination Copies:

Books received as examination copies are for review purposes only and may not be made available for student use. Resale of examination copies is prohibited.

Electronic Files:

Any electronic files associated with this book are licensed to the original user only. These files may not be transferred to any other party.

FOREWORD

To the Student:

This book has been written with the assumption that the reader has no prior experience using Autodesk® Revit® Architecture. The intent of this book is to provide the student with a well-rounded knowledge of tools and techniques for use in both school and industry.

The book consists of a series of tutorials which primarily focus on the development of a single project. When you finish the book you will have learned how to document and model all of the major aspects of a residential project. This includes floor plans, interior and exterior elevations, wall and building sections, door and room finish schedules and organizing drawings on sheets for printing.

The DVD has several videos that supplement the book. Studying these videos along with the book will help the reader to better understand Autodesk Revit Architecture features. The book and videos will also help prepare for the Autodesk Revit Architecture Associate's Certification Exam, see Appendix B for more information.

Be sure to check out the additional material on the DVD. There you will find chapters introducing computers, SketchUp and Autodesk Revit Architecture content creation as well as site design.

To the Instructor:

This book was designed for the architectural student using Autodesk Revit Architecture 2012. Throughout the book, the student develops a single family residence. The drawings start with the floor plans and develop all the way to photo-realistic renderings similar to the one on the cover of this book.

Throughout the book many Autodesk Revit Architecture tools and techniques are covered while creating the house model. Also, in a way that is applicable to the current exercise, industry standards and conventions are covered. Access to the internet is required for some exercises.

Each chapter concludes with a self-exam and review questions. The answers to the self-exam questions are provided, but review question answers are not (they can only be found in the Instructor's Guide available from the publisher).

Since its initial release in 2005, this book has been updated every year for the latest version of Autodesk Revit Architecture. The printed text has always been available for the fall term.

An Instructor's Resource Guide is available for this book. It contains:
- Answers to the questions at the end of each chapter
- Example images of each exercise to be turned in (can be used to grade students work)
- Outline of tools and topics to be covered in each lesson's lecture
- Suggestions for additional student work (for each lesson)
- Author's direct contact information

Errata:

Feel free to check the publisher's website for any errors or typo's found in this book after it went to the printer. Simply browser to www.SDCpublications.com, and then browser to the page for this title. Click the **View/Submit errata** link in the upper right corner of the page. If you find an error, please submit it so we can correct it in the next edition.

You may contact the publisher with comments or suggestions at **schroff@schroff.com**.
Please do not email with Autodesk Revit Architecture questions unless they relate to a problem with this book

About the Author:

Dan Stine is a registered Architect with twenty years of experience in the architectural field. He currently works at LHB (a 160 person multidiscipline firm: www.LHBcorp.com) in Duluth, Minnesota as the CAD Administrator, providing training, customization and support for two regional offices. Mr. Stine has presented at Autodesk University (au.autodesk.com) and this June in California will also be presenting two sessions at the first ever Revit Technology Conference (revitconference.com.au/rtc2011us).

Dan has worked in a total of four firms. While at these firms, he has participated in collaborative projects with several other firms on various projects (including Cesar Pelli, Weber Music Hall – University of Minnesota - Duluth). Dan is a member of the *Construction Specification Institute* (CSI) and the *Autodesk Developer Network* (ADN) and also teaches *AutoCAD* and *Autodesk Revit* classes at Lake Superior College, for the Architectural Technology program; additionally, he is a Certified Construction Document Technician (CDT). Mr. Stine has also written the following textbooks (published by SDC Publications):

- *Commercial Design using Revit Architecture 2012*
- *Design Integration using Revit 2012 (Architecture, Structure and MEP)*
- *Residential Design using AutoCAD 2012*
- *Commercial Design using AutoCAD 2012*
- *Chapters in Architectural Drawing (with co-author Steven H. McNeill, AIA, LEED AP)*
- *Interior Design using Hand Sketching, SketchUp and Photoshop (also with Steven McNeill)*

Mr. Stine is the Assistant Cub Master for *Boy Scouts of America* Pack 3043 in Duluth, MN. He likes to spend time with his family, camping, watching movies, fishing and much more! Dan also enjoys riding his bicycle, along the shoreline of Lake Superior, to work when there is no snow on the ground. The total ride distance is only 4 miles but the elevation gain is over 500 feet. Luckily the uphill part is after work!

Thanks:

I could not have done this without the support from my family: Cheri, Kayla and Carter.

Thanks to Kurt Jankofsky for his time and attention to detail in reviewing the 2011 manuscript.

Many thanks go out to Schroff Development Corporation for making this book possible!

TABLE OF CONTENTS

DVD Content

Notes:

Introduction
Sketching Exercises:

This introduction chapter is meant to compliment the lessons learned in this book. Several hand sketching concepts and exercises are provided to help the student learn to make to most out of both digital and "analog" design techniques.

Introduction I-1:
Introduction

Hand Sketching in a Digital World

Even with the modern power of the computer and design software (which is also covered in this textbook), the designer must have the ability to sketch by hand and think three-dimensionally.

The very first thoughts of a designer, when working on a new project, involve quickly sketching those thoughts onto paper. The process involves several iterations and overlays before the first line is drawn on a computer. These sketches usually take just a few minutes each and are not typically to scale but are proportionally accurate (something that a good designer has learned to do with practice).

Hand sketching is also useful at client meetings and out in the field (where the computer is not always handy or convenient). The architect can sketch possible revisions directly on a set of blueprints (which were printed from computer generated drawings). This represents the best use of time, as all the decision makers are present (who would not want to wait for the computer to load, the project file to load, and the designer to meticulously go through all the steps required by the software to explore various solutions to the problem at hand). Once the meeting is over, the revision sketch can be brought back to the office where the drawings can be updated.

Therefore, the next several pages serve as a primer for the development of your fundamental CAD skills you will learn in this textbook. You are encouraged to work through this introductory chapter and this author believes it will indirectly aid in your thought process as it relates to learning CADD. Of course, if you have previously studied this type of material you may simply skip ahead to Chapter 1. (Hey, this is not a pass if your instructor assigned it!)

Some additional "bonus" material on Engineering Graphics has been provided in an appendix chapter at the end of this text. Make sure you take a look at the DVD for a draft version of a *Roof Study Workbook* provided for your use in conjunction with this textbook.

Lineweights

In this introductory section you will spend some time sketching various building forms. This will give you practice drawing various lines (i.e., weights and styles). The lines drawn will help convey the depth of the image (which is important in both hand and computer drawings; here are a few concepts to keep in mind:

- The perimeter of major building masses should have a heavy line to make it punch out from the surrounding image.
- When buildings have multiple "major elements" the lineweights should vary. Two building dormers at the same elevation should be the same lineweight, but the lines should get lighter as they step back (i.e., away from the viewer).
- The next heaviest lines should be between materials (e.g., lap siding to brick) and around elements like windows and doors. These lines will also get lighter as they step back into the image.
- The lightest lines will be the ones which represent the various building materials (e.g., shingles, siding, brick, etc.).

ROOF PLAN VIEW

Lines get lighter as the building steps back

Lightest linework (material patterns)

Medium linework (around windows & doors)

Darkest linework (closest to viewer)

EXTERIOR

Tools Used for the Task...

The lineweights discussed in the sketch above are achieved by using various types of pencils. In general, the softer pencils draw heavier lines and the harder ones create lighter lines. Here is a brief description of the most common pencils and tools used for this type of freehand sketching.

This photo shows several tools which aid in the creation of hand sketches, not everything is needed to get started, but the cost is relatively cheap so it is not that difficult to obtain these items. Below is a list of the items pictured (no specific brand will be suggested):

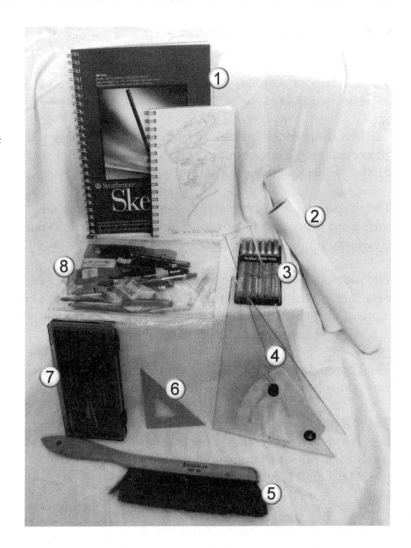

1. *Sketch books*: come in several sizes; small ones are great for carrying around.
2. *Tracing paper (bumwad)*: lightweight and highly transparent; allows for quick overlay sketching.
3. *Ink pen set*: for crisp "final" linework.
4. *Clear plastic straight edge and adjustable triangle*: nice for setting up a few construction lines.
5. *Dusting brush*: to sweep away the eraser crumbs.
6. *Triangle*
7. *Drawing set*: for creating circles and dividing needs.
8. *Pencil sack*: see below.

The image to the left shows the basic tools required to create a decent architectural freehand sketch. Just about everything shown can be purchased in a "starter kit" at any art supply store or website. The items shown to the left (from left to right) are: Eraser, Sharpener, Blending Sticks, Tip Pointer, Mechanical Pencil, (2) Charcoal Pencils; Soft and Medium, (4) Graphite Pencils; HB, 2B, 4B, and 6B, and a Graphite Stick.

One technique this author uses to quickly distinguish between the pencils (which are lying in a cluster and are all the same color) is to add colored tape to the end of the pencils.

TIP: *Make sure you sharpen the end opposite the hardness markings so you can tell the pencils apart after they have been sharpened a few times.*

The **blending sticks** are used to basically smudge the graphite on the paper into a solid gray/black area. This is useful when creating shades and shadows as well as transitions on curved surfaces, to name a few uses.

The **tip pointer** is basically several pieces of sandpaper on a stick. This is a convenient surface on which to rub your pencil tip back and forth to quickly sharpen the tip or create a chisel type tip for special effects.

The **mechanical pencil** can accept "lead" inserts of various types. However, it is ideal to have one mechanical pencil for each "lead" type you use. This system allows you to use more of the "lead" because the mechanical pencil can hold smaller pieces, whereas a wooden pencil becomes hard to use when it gets too small.

The **charcoal pencils** are useful for making very heavy black lines on the paper. Charcoal is very soft so the tips need to be sharpened often.

The **ink pens** are great for crisp consistent lines. However, the result is more permanent than pencil, but when using special paper (like Mylar) and special erasers, you can erase them.

The **graphite pencils** are the primary tool for architectural freehand sketching. You will typically start with the harder pencils (HB and 2B) and then embellish with the softer, darker pencils (4B and 6B).

Sketch Book

The ability to sketch is one that is developed over time and with lots of practice. One way to practice is by using a sketch book. Sketch books can be purchased at any art supply store or website. They come in many shapes and sizes (make sure the paper is acid free so your sketches will last for many years). With a sketch book and a small sack of pencils, you can practice just about anywhere. Just sitting in the waiting room at the doctor's office, you can practice sketching the space, working on perspective, lineweight and detail. Your sketches do not (and should not) always be about architecture. You can practice on anything and everything. One of the examples below is a quick drawing of a BMX bike in action!

SKETCH BOOK (PENCIL)

SKETCH WITH BLENDING

CHARCOAL SKETCH

Do You Have the Time?

One of the largest obstacles to becoming a talented artist is time. Like anything in life, you have to spend a certain amount of time honing your skills, be it a sport, an instrument, or in this case, sketching. Try and spend a few minutes each day sketching something/anything. Pay attention to textures, shades and shadows and perspective. With less time than you think you will get it.

Work or Play?

Everyone should enjoy what they do for a living. Try not to approach sketching from the perspective that you have to do this to get a grade or make lots of money at work. When you focus on doing something with a 110% attitude the grade and money will likely follow. With this attitude you are more likely to retain what you are studying and be prepared to apply it when needed… **so have fun**! You may, in the end, discover sketching is not for you; not all designers are great sketching artists.

Introduction I-2:
Freehand Sketching From Photos

The Grid System

The art of freehand sketching buildings is something that comes with practice. You are not expected to produce great works of art in this exercise. Rather, you should be focusing on lineweights and roof styles and forms. Therefore, to aid in sketching the buildings in this exercise, a grid system has been superimposed over each image. Directly below each image is a blank grid that is the exact same size as the image above. The student should use the blank grid as reference lines and points relative to the grid over the image above. This will aid in drawing the correct perspective and proportions for each image (again, allowing more emphasis to be placed on lineweights and observation of roof styles).

This type of exercise is meant for beginners – sketching, as stated above, to get you thinking about how lines move around relative to each other on the page. You should quickly move away from this type of sketching as it would be a crutch to reaching your full potential, and will likely create rigid, uninteresting drawings. Regardless, this is a great place to start...

Here is a sample of what you should expect to complete at a minimum. Notice the heavy points that have been added to highlight the concept of using the grid as an aid (you do not have to actually add the points in your sketches). If you have time, try sketching in some of the site context with a light pencil.

If you have a sketch book you should try sketching a few real-world buildings; the eye/hand coordination is pretty much the same as looking up at a photo on paper! Don't forget to have fun and give yourself some quality time to do a good job!

Notes:

Freehand Sketching From Photos - 1

Sketch the major forms of the building, plus the doors and windows. If you have time you can add additional detail like siding, roofing and site context.

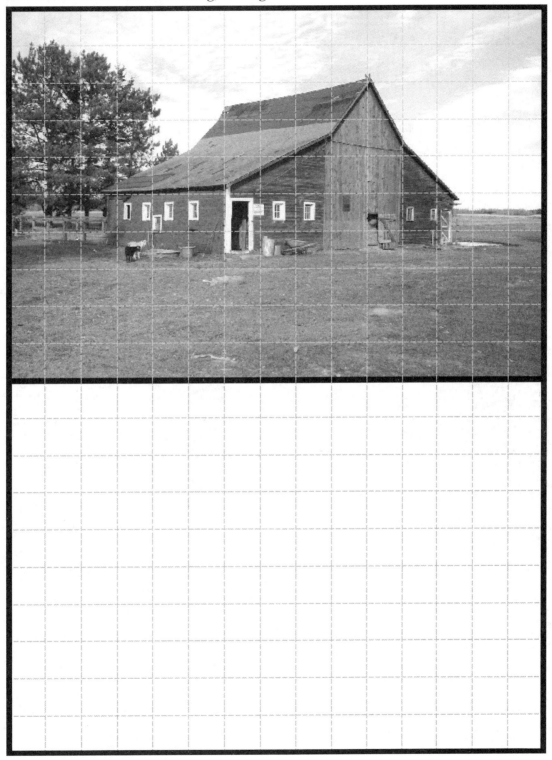

Name: _____   Date: _____

Notes:

Freehand Sketching From Photos - 2

Sketch the major forms of the building, plus the doors and windows. If you have time you can add additional detail like siding, roofing and site context.

Name: _____   Date: _____

Notes:

Freehand Sketching From Photos - 3

Sketch the major forms of the building, plus the doors and windows. If you have time you can add additional detail like siding, roofing and site context.

Name: _____   Date: _____

Notes:

Freehand Sketching From Photos - 4

Sketch the major forms of the building, plus the doors and windows. If you have time you can add additional detail like siding, roofing and site context.

Name: _____ Date: _____

Notes:

Freehand Sketching From Photos - 5

Sketch the major forms of the building, plus the doors and windows. If you have time you can add additional detail like siding, roofing and site context.

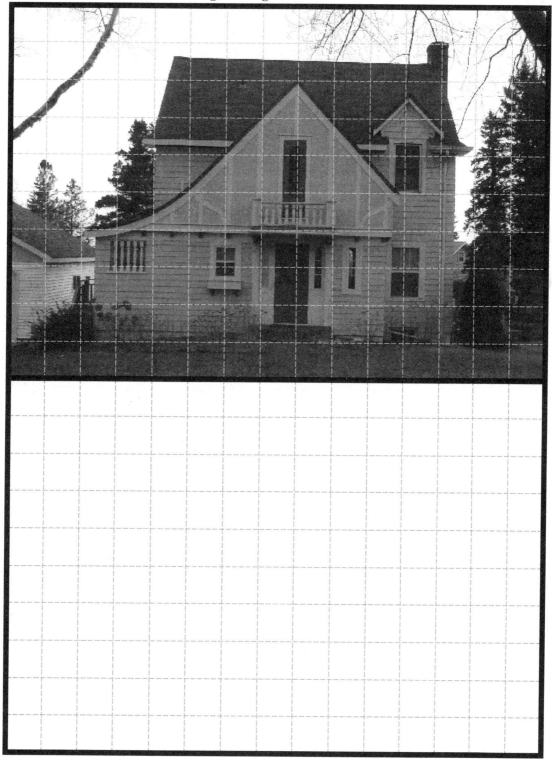

Name: _____ Date: _____

Notes:

Introduction I-3:
Surveying and Sketching Objects

Architects and designers often need to visit an existing facility, for which they have been commissioned to remodel or design an addition, and take detailed measurements and notes. There are many "tricks of the trade" involved in such an endeavor. Some are as simple as knowing the size of common building materials like ceiling tiles, floor tiles, concrete block and bricks, which allows the person surveying existing conditions to quickly get space dimensions simply by counting tiles or courses. For example, flipping ahead in this *Introduction* you will see a bench made from concrete block (pg. I-40). Knowing that the scored blocks are 8"x8", you can count the squares and add them up. Also, another photo of a hallway (page I-44) shows 2'x2' ceiling tile and 12" floor tile. The hallway is three ceiling tiles wide or 6 floor tiles wide; thus, 3x2' = 6' (using the ceiling tiles) and 6x12" = 6' (using the floor tiles). It is still a good idea to physically measure the walls, but this gives you a "common sense" way to double-check your numbers, which is very important (especially if the project site is hours away from your office!)

Another great tool in the toolbox for people checking existing conditions is a **laser tape measure**. This tool can aid in quick measurements and in some cases you can get distances difficult or impossible to acquire without a ladder or lift. For example, a stairwell might not have a location in which you and another person can stand next to each wall with a traditional tape measure. However, a laser tape measure can not only do this, but you can even do it by yourself (i.e., without a helper) as sketched in the image above.

In addition to sketching the building itself, you often need to take an inventory of items within each space. In some cases the items will be relocated to a new space, or you may need to know what kind of furniture or equipment is used in a space. For example, a bedroom might have a bed, night stands, dresser, etc.; or a banker's work room might have cabinets, copier, money counter, shredder, etc. These items are needed to aid in designing a space for a particular client, making sure the room is large enough, the correct proportions, has the proper electrical power supplied and the ideal heating and cooling being delivered (computers give off a lot of heat, for example).

Notes:

This page is provided for you to copy and survey the various pieces of furniture drawn in this textbook. You should not have any problem finding these at home or at a friend's/family's home. This will help you get a feel for the actual size of these objects and allow you to explore the art of sketching things in approximately the correct proportions. The sketches do not need to be to scale, but the different views should align via the grid paper (see example on previous page).

Top sketch	Isometric sketch
Front elevation sketch	Side elevation sketch

Item surveyed: _____ Overall dimensions (WxDxH): _____

Top sketch	Isometric sketch
Front elevation sketch	Side elevation sketch

Item surveyed: _____ Overall dimensions (WxDxH): _____

Name: _____ Date: _____

Notes:

Introduction I-4:
Sketching Floor Plans

When beginning to design a residence, one often sketches very rough floor plans on grid paper. This allows the designer to explore several design solutions without the time and exacting accuracy attributed to a CAD program. Such sketches are able to show adjacencies (i.e., which room is next to which room), circulation and room/building proportions.

The grid paper is used to quickly sketch to scale; you decide what one square is equal. For example, each square in the floor plan sketch on the next page is one foot square. Thus, all one has to do to determine the dimensions of a room is to count the number of squares in each direction. If the building were larger, one square might be equal to two feet or you might need to use larger grid paper. Designers with many years experience can sketch plans, elevations and details almost to scale without the aid of grid paper.

After the first few sketches, and the various spaces have been accounted for, you can use tracing paper (a.k.a., onion skin or bumwad). This highly transparent paper allows one to quickly create another design option based on another drawing (or drawings).

The image at the top of the next page shows a sheet of tracing paper with several "first thoughts" sketches quickly poured out on paper to capture the thoughts that are flowing through the designer's mind. The various portions of the sketch have been numbered and itemized below for your understanding.

Outline of items numbered in sketch on next page:
1. **Site plan:** No meaningful design can begin without understanding the context in which it will coexist. Important elements have been identified such as views ('+' means good view); buildable area per zoning; north and sun (for passive solar design consideration); existing structures and vegetation.

2. **Bubble diagrams:** The first pass at organizing spaces within a building is to think about their location relative to the site (for views, noise, etc.) and adjacencies to other spaces. The bubble diagram is just that – bubbles that abstractly represent spaces in relation to each other.

3. **Building sections:** Quick thoughts on vertical relationships; what areas are two-storied, vaulted ceilings, etc.

4. **Single line floor plans:** These are not to scale and may not even be proportionately accurate, but they capture one's early ideas so that they may be refined later with grid paper.

PRELIMINARY FLOOR PLAN
DEVELOPMENT ON TRACING PAPER

Looking at one of the bedrooms from the floor plan sketches you can see it is 13′-0″ wide (count 13 squares) by 16′-0″ (count 16 squares). Of course, from this you can also derive the square footage of the space: 13x16=**208**sf.

Once an acceptable design is developed you can then start to draw the plan in Autodesk® Revit® Architecture, using accurate dimensions as well as adding doors and windows.

TRY IT: Looking at the sketched plans on the next two pages, count the squares and write the dimensions and square footage for each room. Also add the overall building dimensions. The blank page that follows will give you the opportunity to sketch a few of your own floor plan designs!

PORTION OF FLOOR PLAN
SKETCH ON GRID PAPER

LIVING ROOM

ENTRY

FAMILY ROOM

CLO.

FORMAL DINING

KITCHEN

FAMILY DINING

BATH

STAIR

CLO.

MUD ROOM

GARAGE

Name:

Date:

When sketching the second floor plan you should start by aligning the exterior walls. The easiest way to do this is to sketch them at the same exact location as the common walls on the first floor plan (i.e., relative location on the grid paper).

Name: Date:

Tear this page out, make copies, and create a few different floor plan designs using the same number of spaces and square footage as the floor plans on the previous two pages (which are the plans used in this text); be sure the two floors align! Remember, one square is a foot wide in each direction.

Name:	Date:

Notes:

Introduction I-5:
Sketching Elevations – Two Point Perspective

Two-point perspective drawings are two-dimensional drawings that represent three-dimensional objects or scenes. As the name implies, there are two points (referred to as vanishing points or *VP*) which establish the perspective lines and which are both relative to a horizon line (*HL*). The object being depicted has three primary types of lines:

- *Perspective lines* (which always converge at the vanishing points).
- *Vertical lines* (which are always truly vertical to the page).
- *Angled lines* (which are usually drawn by "connecting-the-dots" via linework fully developed from the previous two line types.

Two-point perspective drawings are primarily meant for rectilinear objects. For example, a uniform series of city blocks can be sketched much easier than an 'organic' shaped suburban development.

The concepts covered can be applied to more detailed embellishments, such as windows and siding, sidewalks and driveways, or fences and garages.

Below are the three primary types of perspective created by Architects and Interior Designers [*from left to right*]: one-point, two-point and three-point perspectives. You will study one and two-point perspectives in this section.

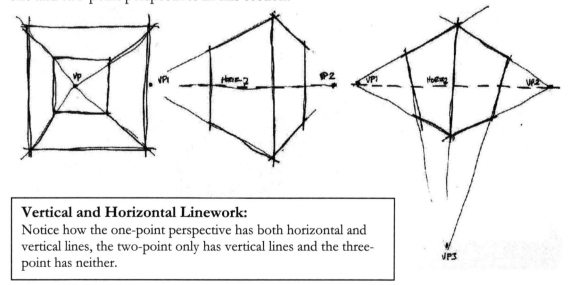

Vertical and Horizontal Linework:
Notice how the one-point perspective has both horizontal and vertical lines, the two-point only has vertical lines and the three-point has neither.

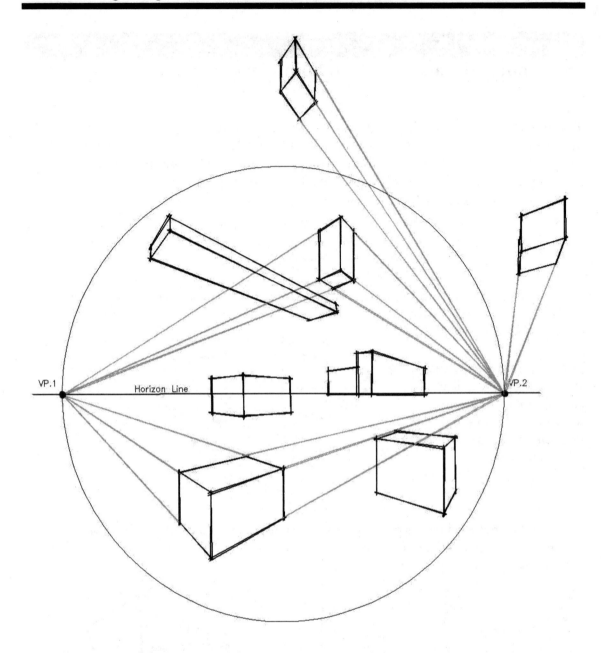

You should take a moment to notice a few things in the image above: 1) all lines are either vanishing or perfectly vertical; 2) anything drawn outside of an imaginary circle (actually shown here) is too distorted and should be avoided; 3) objects completely below the horizon are as viewed from the top and objects completely above are as viewed from below. You can quickly create rectilinear objects in any shape or size by sketching the vanishing lines and vertical lines as shown!

TRY IT: Make a few copies of the following page and try sketching some rectangular shapes similar to those shown in the image above. Try and create your own variations on this theme.

Name:_____

Date: _____

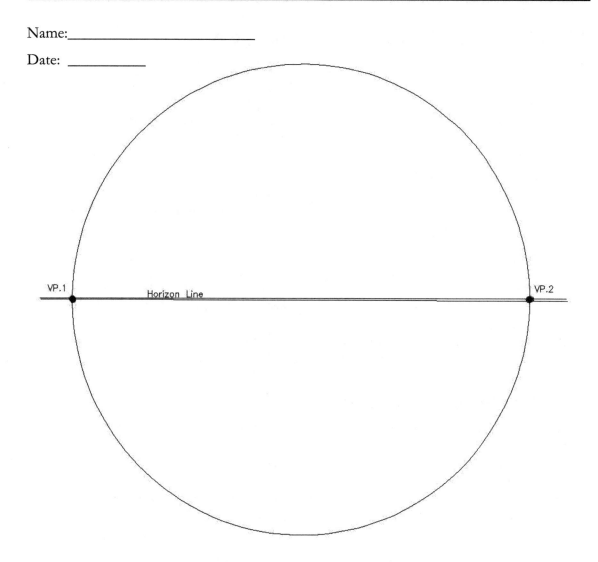

VP.1   Horizon Line   VP.2

Two-Point Perspective

The following exercise will walk you through the steps required to develop a two-point perspective of the exterior of a residence. This exercise will have similar features to that of the home designed in this textbook. You are encouraged to follow along on a

separate piece of paper and then sketch one or two views of the project in this book. The exact dimensions and proportions do not really matter at this time as you are focusing on the mechanics of perspective drawings. Try drawing this freehand first and then try again using a straight edge.

The following steps relate to the 'lettered' and then 'numbered' sketches on the following page:

Main Building With Gable Roof – Image A

This first step is simply sketching a basic box with a gable roof element dropped on top. You should try to make your sketch as similar as possible in terms of proportions; the vertical centerline (centered between the two vanishing points) has been added to aid in this.

1. Vertical line just to the right of the 'centerline' with equal portions above and below the *Horizon Line*. (See one vertical line, marked with a #1.)
2. Connect-the-dots: draw four lines from the *VP's* to the top and bottom of the vertical line as shown. (See the four lines marked with a #2.)
3. Draw two vertical lines to define the overall size of the main building.
4. Draw an 'X' and a vertical line at its intersection to discern the midpoint of the gable end of the building.

   NOTE: *It is not the midpoint of the bottom edge of the building; confirm this with a scale.*

5. Draw the ridge line of the roof: a line from *VP.1* to the vertical line sketched in the previous step. (The location of this line determines the pitch of the roof; higher = steeper.)
6. Connect-the-dots: draw lines to create the gable roof edges.
7. Lightly sketch the hidden portions of the building as shown.

Bisecting the Building – Image B

Here you will learn how to find the exact middle of the building. This will help in locating the cross-gable in the next image/task.

1. Sketch an 'X' on the bottom plane of the building.
2. Draw a perspective line from *VP.2* which passes through the 'X'.
3. Sketch three vertical lines as shown. (The vanishing line just drawn helps establish the starting point on the front and back face of the building.)
4. Connect-the-dots: from the intersection of the roof and three vertical lines.

   FYI: *The two visible bisecting lines have an arrow at the top and bottom in this image and the next one to make them stand out... these lines will eventually be erased.*

Adding Cross-Gable Entry – Image C

Next you will sketch in the "bump out" on the front of the building which is similar to the project you are working on in this book.

1. This perspective line (*from VP.1*) determines how far "out" the "bump" will be.
2. Draw two vertical lines a certain distance apart and approximately centered on the main building. (You will learn to be more precise later.)
3. Draw two perspective lines (*from VP.2*) to establish the bottom edges.
4. Draw a vertical line up to the roof edge – from the intersection of the perspective line just drawn and the bottom front edge of the main building.
5. Do the same as step 3 to establish the top edges (*from VP.2*).
6. Draw this perspective line (*from VP.1*) to verify the top-front edge is correct.
7. Use the 'X' method to discern the center of the gable wall.
8. Sketch the ridge line of the entry roof; the location determines roof slope.
9. Connect-the-dots: the remaining valley lines can be easily drawn.

All lines should be sketched very lightly and the visible lines can be made darker at the end, as well as erasing the unneeded reference lines and hidden lines.

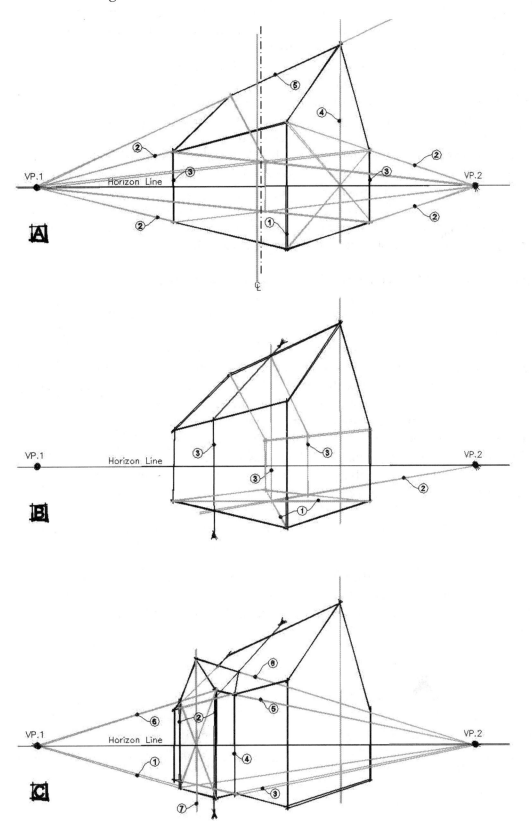

Centered and Symmetrical Addition – Image D

The following steps show you how to make an extrusion off the main building which is symmetrical. You cannot measure in from each side an equal distance because things get closer together as you approach the vanishing points.

1. The first line (*from VP.2*) will determine how large the extrusion (or addition) will be from the main mass of the residence.
2. Here you will basically extend the front and back bottom (i.e., grade) line out to the previous line drawn. (Sketch lightly as these lines will be erased.)
3. Draw an 'X' in the large, flat, rectangle just created.
4. Now you will draw a vanishing line (*from VP.2*) near the building. The intersection of this line and the 'X' lines will establish the front and back wall locations for the addition (which will be drawn in the next step).
5. Draw two lines (*from VP.1*) so that they pass through the intersection of the 'X' (from step 3) and the perspective line (from step 4), and terminate these lines at the perspective line (drawn in step 1) as shown in Image D.

Completing the Massing of the Addition – Image E

Now that the footprint of the addition is sufficiently developed, you can create the remaining linework.

1. Draw four vertical lines as shown.
2. Draw a perspective line, if needed (i.e., if you erased the previous one you drew) from *VP.2* to the roof edge of the main building; this assumes the roof edge of the addition will align with the main building and not be lower. (Simply swinging this perspective line down a bit would allow for this change.)
3. Draw two vanishing lines (*from VP.1*) through the line drawn in the previous step and the vertical lines at the main building (drawn in step 1).
4. Finding the middle of the gable end of the main building, you can sketch the roof slope lines. This is done in conjunction with the next step which locates the ridge line.
5. Draw the ridge line (*from VP.1*).
6. Find the middle of the gable end of the addition and finish sketching the sloped roof edges.

At this point you have developed the main masses of your structure. Now you can erase the reference lines and hidden lines, and then darken the remaining lines. Another option is to use tracing paper and a soft pencil to sketch a new image based on the 'visible' lines of your original sketch.

Again, you may use these techniques to add windows, siding, trim, chimneys, and such. Here is another good use for tracing paper (also referred to as bumwad or onion skin paper which comes on a roll and pieces are ripped off as needed): you can sketch different window and siding options on the tracing paper, thus not needing to start from scratch with the base model every time!

If you really want to develop your sketching skills you should try to draw some non-architectural objects. This will help you create more lively architectural renderings!

Dividing Spaces

The following technique can be used to divide a space into equal pieces. You can, of course, repeat this process to even further divide a space already divided. The graphic below pretty much speaks for itself; you start with any rectilinear face and sketch an 'X' from which you can project lines from its center point.

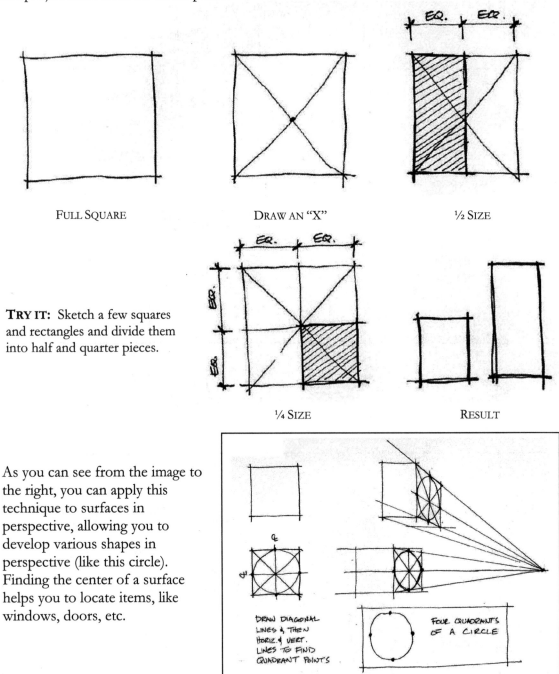

FULL SQUARE   DRAW AN "X"   ½ SIZE

TRY IT: Sketch a few squares and rectangles and divide them into half and quarter pieces.

¼ SIZE   RESULT

As you can see from the image to the right, you can apply this technique to surfaces in perspective, allowing you to develop various shapes in perspective (like this circle). Finding the center of a surface helps you to locate items, like windows, doors, etc.

DRAW DIAGONAL LINES & THEN HORIZ. & VERT. LINES TO FIND QUADRANT POINTS

FOUR QUADRANTS OF A CIRCLE

TRY IT: Add a few circles to your boxes drawn within the large circle; remember to start with the 'X'.

Repeating Spaces in Perspective

The following steps walk through the process of repeating a shape equally as it moves towards the vanishing point. This is how you might sketch railroad tracks or a picket fence. In this example you will be applying this concept to an interior elevation of base cabinets.

Adding additional spaces of equal size:
1. Sketch an 'X' in a rectangular space (a square in this example).
2. Add a horizontal line which passes through the center of the 'X'
3. Draw a diagonal line from the upper left, so that is passes through the intersection of the horizontal line (from the previous step) and the right edge of the square; continue this angle until you hit the bottom edge of the square. (You need to extend the top and bottom lines as shown.)
4. Sketch a new vertical line where the diagonal line meets the bottom horizontal line.
5. Repeat this process for additional segments.

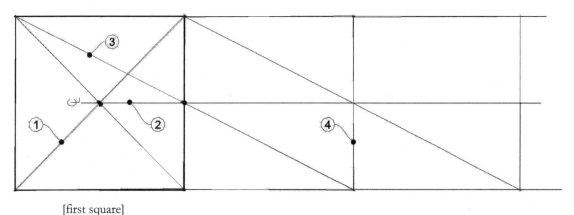

[first square]

Now you can apply this technique to surfaces that are in perspective. You can use the techniques described on the following page to finish the image which has been started for you below.

FYI: *Make a few photocopies if you think you need to try it more than once. Also you can enlarge the image that way.*

I-37

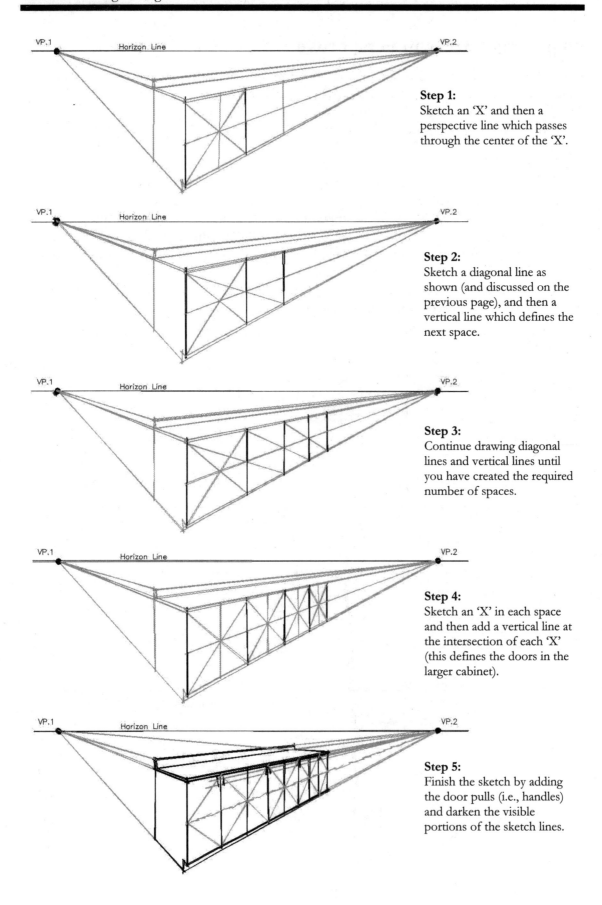

Step 1:
Sketch an 'X' and then a perspective line which passes through the center of the 'X'.

Step 2:
Sketch a diagonal line as shown (and discussed on the previous page), and then a vertical line which defines the next space.

Step 3:
Continue drawing diagonal lines and vertical lines until you have created the required number of spaces.

Step 4:
Sketch an 'X' in each space and then add a vertical line at the intersection of each 'X' (this defines the doors in the larger cabinet).

Step 5:
Finish the sketch by adding the door pulls (i.e., handles) and darken the visible portions of the sketch lines.

Sketching Two-Point Interior Perspectives

The process of creating two-point exterior perspectives can easily be applied to creating interior perspectives.

NOTE: *The distance between the vanishing points (VP.1 and VP.2) will determine how close (or far away) and how distorted the perspective will be. Also, by making the interior perspective somewhat symmetrical about the horizon (meaning an equal portion of the drawing exists both above and below the HL) the drawing will feel like you are standing within the image and not as if you where in an airplane or as an ant!*

The perspective below is of the small portion of the floor plan shown to the right. Notice how the wall with the window does not align with the wall of the smaller room beyond. Also, the ceiling of the smaller room matches the height of the wall opening that leads into it, thus there is no line at the back side of the open/wall.

TRY IT: Create 2-point perspectives from the plans below and from this book.

Below is a photo of a bench at an inter-city bus stop made of burnished concrete block. This provides a good real world example of a three-point perspective. (Straightening the vertical lines would make it two-point.)

TRY IT: Set up a horizon line and two vanishing points on a separate piece of paper. Sketch the bench utilizing the two vanishing points and vertical lines. You will have to lightly sketch a few hidden lines to locate certain points. You should also utilize the techniques just covered to create equally spaced blocks as they move back towards the horizon.

This sketch shows how you can use the technique of creating additional, equally sized spaces, as previously covered. This method is not limited to only one direction. Notice how one space is skipped to create a void. Compare this sketch to the top portion of the bench directly above.

Introduction I-6:
Sketching Elevations – One Point Perspective

Now that you have taken a look at sketching two-point perspectives, you will now shift your attention to developing one-point perspectives. A number of concepts covered in the development study of two-point perspectives also apply to one-point, so it would be helpful if you have previously studied that section of this *Introduction* chapter.

The sketch below shows a simple example of a one-point perspective. The partial floor plan sketch below the perspective is the basis of the sketch. Using this technique, you can quickly create a sketch that helps you to visualize the space three-dimensionally. From here you might adjust the floor plan or add color and present it to your client for their approval.

Floor Plan

The Basic Components of a One-Point Perspective

The process of creating a one-point perspective is described on the following page. The mechanics are very simple and do not take much time to master (like anything it just takes practice).

Establishing Depth In Your Perspective

The page after the next shows how to develop a three-dimensional grid which can be used to more accurately sketch items in perspective (in terms of depth from the viewer). This is a very rigid process and often only used for more formal presentation drawings.

NOTE: *The location of the Diagonal Point (DP) will establish the depth of the view; when positioned correctly, the view will have the proper feeling of scale and proportions.*

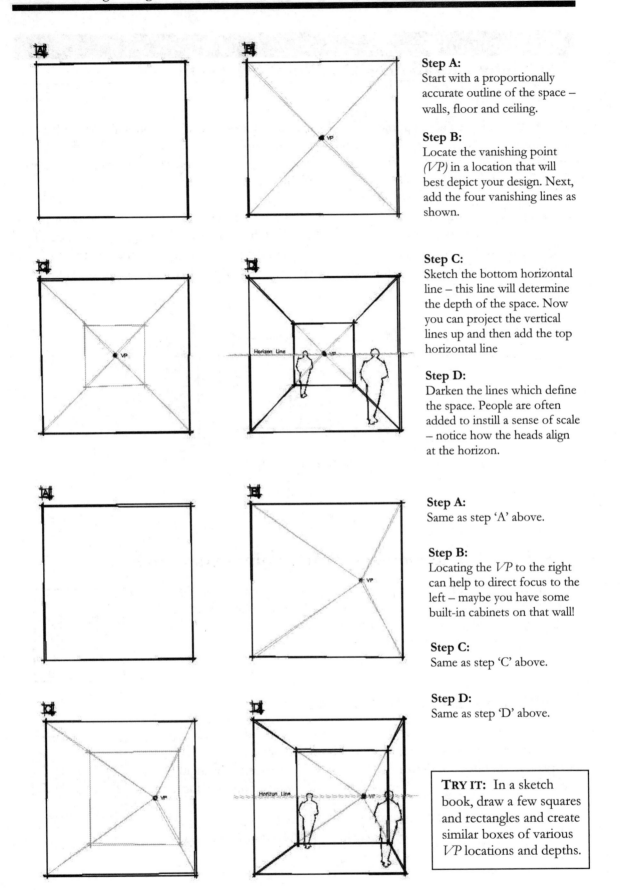

Step A:
Start with a proportionally accurate outline of the space – walls, floor and ceiling.

Step B:
Locate the vanishing point *(VP)* in a location that will best depict your design. Next, add the four vanishing lines as shown.

Step C:
Sketch the bottom horizontal line – this line will determine the depth of the space. Now you can project the vertical lines up and then add the top horizontal line

Step D:
Darken the lines which define the space. People are often added to instill a sense of scale – notice how the heads align at the horizon.

Step A:
Same as step 'A' above.

Step B:
Locating the *VP* to the right can help to direct focus to the left – maybe you have some built-in cabinets on that wall!

Step C:
Same as step 'C' above.

Step D:
Same as step 'D' above.

> **TRY IT:** In a sketch book, draw a few squares and rectangles and create similar boxes of various *VP* locations and depths.

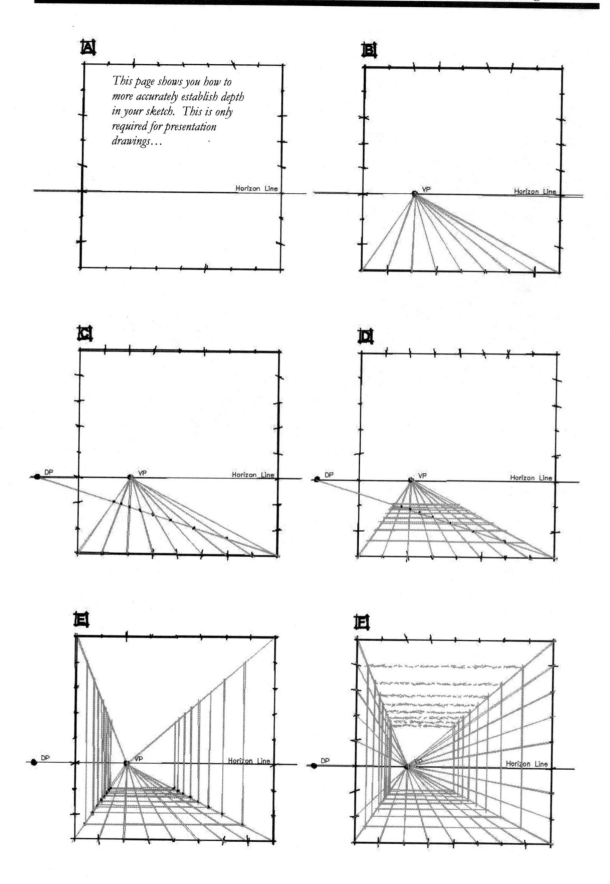

A

This page shows you how to more accurately establish depth in your sketch. This is only required for presentation drawings...

Horizon Line

B

VP

Horizon Line

C

DP · VP Horizon Line

D

DP VP Horizon Line

E

DP VP Horizon Line

F

DP VP Horizon Line

The photo to the left shows a hallway which should help you see how a one point perspective relates to the real world.

TRY IT: Try sketching this image in a sketch book or on some scrap paper. Establish a vanishing point and add the various perspective lines, the horizontal lines and the vertical lines. Notice the pattern in the flooring, the ceiling and the wall at the end of the hallway.

Vanishing point lines derived from a photo…

Equally Dividing a Line…

Here is a tip for equally dividing a line: Say you need eight equal spaces like the third line below. If you start at one end and try working your way to the other end you will almost never end up with equally spaced segments (it is too hard to judge how big the segments should be). The trick is to divide and conquer. Start with one tick in the middle (it may not be perfect but you will get very close). Next, you can divide each half in half (see the second line below). You continue this process until you have the desired number of segments; *this only works for even numbered segments.*

TRY IT: Try sketching several lines and then divide them into even numbered segments. Just focus on eyeing the center point for each segment about to be divided. Sketch light lines in case you need to make adjustments.

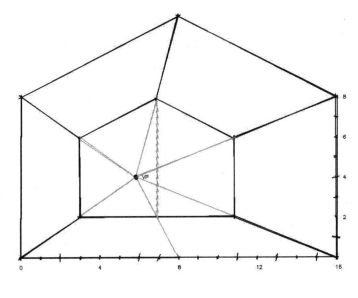

Developing a One-Point Perspective

Read though the following steps and then try them with the "starter" image that follows:

1. Sketch the five perspective lines from *VP* to corners.
2. Add the horizontal line; its location will define the depth of the space.
3. Sketch two vertical lines.
4. Locate the center of the back wall with a perspective line, and then add a vertical line up to the ridge line.
5. Connect-the-dots: add the last two sloped lines at the back edge of the roof.

[See floor plan below.]

1. Sketch perspective lines to define door width and location.
2. Locate height on adjacent wall.
3. Then project over onto back wall.
4. Add vertical lines as shown.

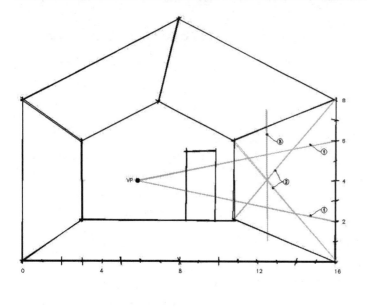

Now you will add a pair of windows to the east wall:

1. Add the two perspective lines to determine the window head and sill locations.
2. Sketch an 'X' to find the center of the wall.
3. Add a vertical line at center of wall.

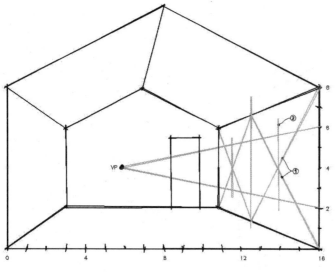

You know the window is 4' wide and the wall in this view is 8' wide (see plan view on previous page), thus you can divide the spaces as previously covered:

1. Sketch 'X's in the two spaces.
2. Add a vertical line of the intersection of each 'X'.
3. You now have the extents of the window defined and can be darkened for clarity.

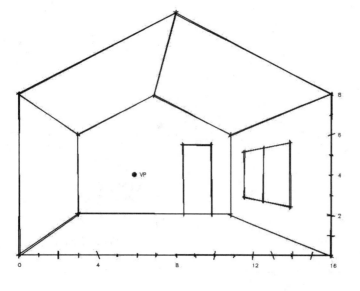

Next you will try this yourself as well as add a few more items and use a different vanishing point to better see the difference.

Name:_____

Date: _____

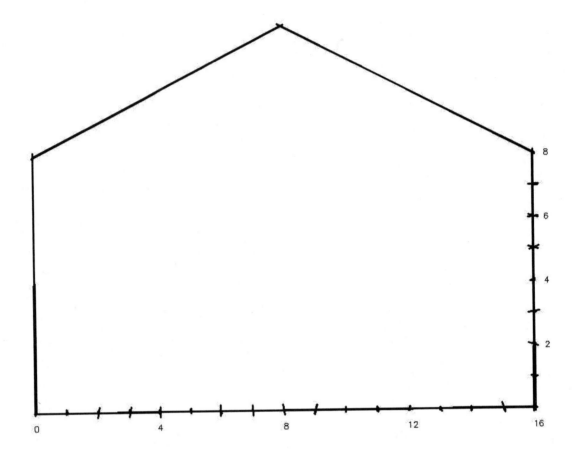

TRY IT: Use the image above as a starting point to create the same perspective as covered on the previous pages. Don't forget to make a few copies if you think you might need a few practice runs. Also, follow the following comments:

1. Add a vanishing point *(VP)* more to the right to create a unique view.

2. Add the door and window per the examples above and the floor plan.

3. Also add the following items:
    a. 2'x4' skylight.
    b. Add 3 cabinets to the left wall (2'-0"x2'-0"x3'-0" high).
    c. Sketch a 4'x8' rug centered on the room.

TIP: You can print out your CAD building sections and turn them into one point perspectives quickly for client meetings!

Notes:

Introduction I-7:
Sketching Plans – One Point Perspective

Once you have learned to create one-point interior elevations you can easily apply that technique to creating one-point floor plans. This type of perspective drawing allows you to quickly think about the design of an entire room, rather than just one corner (i.e., two walls).

Your CAD files can be used to help create the one-point perspective or they may be created after the perspective depending on the designers preferred workflow.

Simply sketch the footprint of the room, pick a vanishing point *(VP)* and then project the walls up and add features. See the next page for examples on various *VP* locations and how it affects the resultant perspective.

Plan or Elevation and VP Location...

You need to think about the information you want to convey in your one-point perspective before you start drawing. You could find you have wasted a lot of time if you get started too quickly, without thinking through to your desired result. If you want to highlight a lot of detail on the wall, then you should do a perspective from an elevation vantage point; or if you want to show overall relationships and circulation, you should create a plan-type perspective.

In the example below, you see a rough sketch of a kitchen floor plan (on the left) and (3) plan-type and (3) elevation-type one-point perspectives. Notice the various vanishing point *(VP)* locations and what they show and don't show.

TRY IT: Using the kitchen room layout in the CAD section of this textbook, add cabinets and appliances similar to those shown in the sketched plan above. Create one floor plan perspective and one elevation type perspective. Try to find the best vanishing points for each view that best portray the kitchen design.

Below is an example of the melding of a digital CAD drawing and a hand sketch. Simply print out a floor plan or building section, lay a piece of tracing paper over it, and begin producing a one-point perspective. Picking the vanishing point is very important; you want to make sure no major features are hidden. Once the vanishing point has been established you can then project lines from the *VP* through the various corners within the floor plans. The first line you draw to represent the top-of-wall will dictate all others via the "connect-the-dots" process.

This concept even works for 3D programs like Revit Architecture. You can print out an exterior perspective of the building and then hand sketch various siding and window options quickly without having to meticulously layout each in an exacting BIM program.

TRY IT: When you get to the point in the textbook where you have finished developing the floor plans, you can print either the first or second floor out on a printer and try sketching a one-point perspective over the top of it.

Notes:

Lesson 1
Getting Started With Revit Architecture 2012:

This chapter will introduce you to Autodesk® Revit® Architecture 2012. You will study the User Interface and learn how to open and exit a project and adjust the view of the drawing on the screen. It is recommended that you spend an ample amount of time learning this material, as it will greatly enhance your ability to progress smoothly through subsequent chapters.

Exercise 1-1:
What is Revit Architecture 2012?

What is Autodesk Revit Architecture used for?

Autodesk Revit (Architecture, Structure and MEP) is the world's first fully parametric building design software. This revolutionary software, for the first time, truly takes architectural computer aided design beyond simply being a high tech pencil. Revit is a product of Autodesk, Inc., makers of AutoCAD®, 3DS Max®, Maya® and many other popular design programs.

What is a parametric building modeler?

Autodesk Revit Architecture is a relatively new program designed from the ground up using state-of-the-art technology. The term parametric describes a process by which an element is modified and an adjacent element(s) is automatically modified to maintain a previously established relationship. For example, if a wall is moved, perpendicular walls will grow, or shrink, in length to remain attached to the related wall. Additionally, elements attached to the wall will move, such as wall cabinets, doors, windows, air grilles, etc.

Revit stands for **Rev**ise **Inst**antly; a change made in one view is automatically updated in all other views and schedules. For example, if you move a door in an interior elevation view, the floor plan will automatically update. Or, if you delete a door, it will be deleted from all other views and schedules. You can even delete a door from the door schedule and the drawings will instantly be revised to reflect the change.

A major goal of Autodesk Revit Architecture is to eliminate much of the repetitive and mundane tasks traditionally associated with CAD programs allowing more time for design, coordination and visualization. For example: all sheet numbers, elevation tags and reference bubbles are updated automatically when changed anywhere in the project. Therefore it is difficult to find a miss-referenced detail tag.

The best way to understand how a parametric model works is to describe the Autodesk Revit Architecture project file. A single Autodesk Revit Architecture file contains your entire building project. Even though you mostly draw in 2D views, you are actually drawing in 3D.

In fact, the entire building project is a 3D model. From this 3D model you can generate 2D elevations, 2D sections and perspective views. Therefore, when you delete a door in an elevation view you are actually deleting the door from the 3D model from which all 2D views are generated and automatically updated.

Another way in which Revit is a parametric building modeler is that **parameters** can be used to control the size and shape of geometry. For example, a window model can have two *parameters* set up which control the size of the window. Thus, from a window's properties it is possible to control the size of the window without using any of the drawing modify tools such as *Scale* or *Move*. Furthermore, the *parameter* settings (i.e., width and height in this example) can be saved within the window model (called a *Family*). You could have the 2′ x 4′ settings saved as "Type A" and the 2′ x 6′ as "Type B". Each saved list of values is called a *Type* within the *Family*. Thus, this one double-hung window *Family* could represent an unlimited number of window sizes! You will learn more about this later in the book.

Window model size controlled by parameters *Width* and *Height*

What about the different "flavors" of Revit?

Revit comes in three different "flavors": Architecture, Structure and MEP (which stands for Mechanical, Electrical and Plumbing). Any "flavor" of Revit can open and edit the same Revit Project file or content (aka families). The only requirement is that each "flavor" of Revit be the same version; for example: Autodesk Revit Architecture 2012, Autodesk Revit Structure 2012 and AutoCAD Revit MEP 2012.

The tutorials in this textbook only require Autodesk Revit Architecture. You can download the free 30 trial from autodesk.com. Students may download a free 13 month version of all three "flavors" of Revit at www.students.autodesk.com.

Revit model of an existing building, with architecture, structural, mechanical, plumbing and electrical all modeled.

Image courteous of LHB, Inc.   www.LHBcorp.com

Now is as good a time as any to make sure the reader understands that Revit is not, nor has it ever been, backwards compatible. This means there is no *Save-As* back to a previous version of Revit. Also, an older version of Revit cannot open a file, project or content, saved in a newer format. So make sure you consider what version your school or employer is currently standardized on before upgrading any projects or content.

Why use Revit?

Many people ask the question, why use Revit versus other programs? The answer can certainly vary depending on the situation and particular needs of an individual or organization.

Generally speaking, this is why most companies use Revit:

- Many designers and drafters are using Revit to streamline repetitive drafting tasks and focus more on designing and detailing a project.
- Revit is a very progressive program and offers many features for designing buildings. Revit is constantly being developed and Autodesk provides incremental upgrades and patches on a regular basis; Revit 2012 was released about a year after the previous version.
- Revit was designed specifically for architectural design and includes features like:
  o Mental Ray's Photo Realistic Renderer
  o Phasing (which makes Revit a 4D tool)
  o Pantone digital color
  o Vectoral Shadows (real-time shadows)
  o Design Options
  o Conceptual Energy Analysis

32bit versus 64bit?

Starting in the 2009 version of Revit, a 64bit version of the software is available. This allows the software to take full advantage of hardware that, for the most part, has now been 64bit for a few years. One of the biggest advantages is access to more than 3GB of RAM. Many BIM stations have 8GB of RAM to handle large projects. It should be pointed out that most computers come with a 32bit operating system (e.g., MS Windows XP, MS Windows Vista or MS Windows 7); however, each has a 64bit version which cost a little more. The 64bit version of Revit looks the same and creates a model identical to one created in the 32bit version of Revit. Either version of Revit will work fine for this textbook.

A few basic Revit concepts:

The following is meant to be a brief overview of the basic organization of Revit as a software application. You should not get too hung up on these concepts and terms as they will make more sense as you work through the tutorials in this book. This discussion is simply laying the groundwork so you have a general frame of reference on how Revit works.

The Revit platform has three fundamental types of elements:
- Model Elements
- Datum Elements
- View-Specific Elements

Model Elements

Think of *Model Elements* as things you can put your hands on once the building has been constructed. They are typically 3D, but can sometimes be 2D. There are two types of *Model Elements*:

- **Host Elements** (walls, floors, slabs, roofs, ceilings) – Tools vary depending on the "flavor" of Revit (e.g., Revit Architecture has a Ceiling tool whereas Revit Structure does not).

- **Model Component** (Stairs, Doors, Furniture, Beams, Columns, Pipes, Ducts, Light Fixtures, Model Lines) – Options vary depending on the "flavor" of Revit (e.g., Revit MEP has a Duct tool whereas Revit Architecture and Revit Structure do not).

    o Some *Model Components* require a host before they can be placed within a project. For example, a window can only be placed in a host, which could be a wall, roof or floor depending on how the element was created. If the host is deleted, all hosted or dependent elements are automatically deleted.

Model Elements
Windows & Doors; require a host

Host Elements
Roof, Wall & Floor

Model Elements
Stair & Washer/Dryer; do not require a host

Datum Elements

Datum Elements are reference planes within the building that graphically and parametrically define the location of various elements within the model. These features are available in all "flavors" of Revit. These are the three types of *Datum Elements*:

- **Grids**
  - o Typically laid out in a plan view to locate structural elements such as columns and beams, as well as walls. Grids show up in plan, elevation and section views. Moving a grid in one view moves it in all other views as it is the same element. (See the next page for an example of a grid in plan view).

- **Levels**
  - o Used to define vertical relationships, mainly surfaces that you walk on. They only show up in elevation and section views. Many elements are placed relative to a *Level*; when the *Level* is moved those elements move with it (e.g., doors, windows, casework, ceilings). **WARNING:** If a *Level* is deleted, those same "dependent" elements will also be deleted from the project!

- **Reference Planes**
  - o These are similar to grids in that they show in up in plan and elevation or sections. They do not have reference bubbles at the end like grids. Revit breaks many tasks down into simple 2D tasks which result in 3D geometry. *Reference Planes* are used to define 2D surfaces on which to work within the 3D model. They can be placed in any view, either horizontally or vertically.

View-Specific Elements

As the name implies, the items about to be discussed only show up in the specific view in which they are created. For example, notes and dimensions added in the architectural floor plans will not show up in the structural floor plans. These elements are all 2D and are mainly communication tools used to accurately document the building for construction or presentations.

- **Annotation elements** (text, tags, symbols, dimensions)
  - o Size automatically set and changed based on selected drawing scale

- **Details** (detail lines, filled regions, 2D detail components)

Grids

Dimensions

Text

Tags
(Door & Room)

Symbol
(North Arrow)

Filled Region
(Cross Hatch)

File Types (and extensions):

Revit has four primary types of files that you will work with as a Revit user. Each file type, as with any Microsoft Windows based program, has a specific three letter file name extension; that is, after the name of the file on your hard drive you will see a period and three letters. They are:

.RVT	Revit project files; the file most used (also for backup files)
.RFA	Revit family file; loadable content for your project
.RTE	Revit template; a project starter file with office standards preset
.RFT	Revit family template; a family starter file with parameters

The Revit platform has three fundamental ways in which to work with the elements (for display and manipulation):

- Views
- Schedules
- Sheets

The following is a cursory overview of the main ideas you need to know. This is not an exhaustive study on views, schedules and sheets.

Views

Views, accessible from the *Project Browser* (see page 5-4), is where most of the work is done while using Revit. Think of views as slices through the building, both horizontal (plans) and vertical (elevations and sections).

- **Plans**
  - A *Plan View* is a horizontal slice through the building. You can specify the location of the cut plane which determines if certain windows show up or how much of the stair is seen. A few examples are: architectural floor plan, reflected ceiling plan, site plan, structural framing plan, HVAC floor plan, electrical floor plan, lighting [ceiling] plan, etc. The images below show this concept; the image on the left is the 3D BIM. The middle image shows the portion of building above the cut plane removed. Finally, the last image on the right shows the plan view in which you work and place on a sheet.

- **Elevations**
  - Elevations are vertical slices, but where the slice lies outside the floor plan as in the middle image below. Each elevation created is listed in the *Project Browser*. The image on the right is an example of a South exterior elevation view, which is a "live" view of the 3D model. If you select a window here and delete it, the floor plans will update instantly.

- **Sections**
    - Similar to elevations, sections are also vertical slices. However, these slices cut through the building. A section view can be cropped down to become a wall section or even look just like an elevation. The images below show the slice, the portion of building in the foreground removed, and then the actual view created by the slice. A setting exists, for each section view, to control how far into that view you can see. The example on the right is "seeing" deep enough to show the doors on the interior walls.

- **3D and Camera**
    - In addition to the traditional "flattened" 2D views that you will typically work in, you are able to see your designs more naturally via 3D and Camera views. A 3D view is simply a non-perspective 3D view of the project viewed from the exterior. A Camera view is a true perspective view; cameras can be created both in and outside of the building. Like the 2D views, these 3D/Camera views can be placed on a sheet to be printed. Revit provides a number of tools to help explore the 3D view, such as Section Box, Steering Wheel, Temporary Hide and Isolate, and Render.

      The image on the left is a 3D view set to "shade mode" and has shadows turned on. The image on the right is a camera view set up inside the building; the view is set to "hidden line" rather than shaded, and the camera is at eyelevel.

Schedules

Schedules are lists of information generated based on content that has been placed, or modeled, within the project. A schedule can be created, such as the door schedule example shown below, that lists any of the data associated with each door that exists in the project. Revit allows you to work directly in the schedule views. Any change within a schedule view, is a change directly to the element being scheduled. Again, if a door were to be deleted from this schedule, that door would be instantly deleted from the project.

	DOOR				FRAME		DETAIL				FIRE	HDWR	
DOOR NUMBER	WIDTH	HEIGHT	MATL	TYPE	MATL	TYPE	HEAD	JAMB	SILL	GLAZING	RATING	GROUP	
1000A	3' - 8"	7' - 2"	WD		HM		11/A8.01	11/A8.01					
1046	3' - 0"	7' - 2"	WD	D10	HM	F10	11/A8.01	11/A8.01 SIM				34	
1047A	6' - 0"	7' - 10"	ALUM	D15	ALUM	SF4	6/A8.01	6/A8.01	1/A8.01 SIM	1" INSUL		2	CARD READER N. LEAF
1047B	6' - 0"	7' - 2"	WD	D10	HM	F13	12/A8.01	11/A8.01 SIM			60 MIN	85	MAG HOLD OPENS
1050	3' - 0"	7' - 2"	WD	D10	HM	F21	8/A8.01	11/A8.01		1/4" TEMP		33	
1051	3' - 0"	7' - 2"	WD	D10	HM	F21	8/A8.01	11/A8.01		1/4" TEMP		33	
1052	3' - 0"	7' - 2"	WD	D10	HM	F21	8/A8.01	11/A8.01		1/4" TEMP		33	
1053	3' - 0"	7' - 2"	WD	D10	HM	F21	8/A8.01	11/A8.01		1/4" TEMP		33	
1054A	3' - 0"	7' - 2"	WD	D10	HM	F10	8/A8.01	11/A8.01		1/4" TEMP	.	34	
1054B	3' - 0"	7' - 2"	WD	D10	HM	F21	8/A8.01	11/A8.01		1/4" TEMP	.	33	
1055	3' - 0"	7' - 2"	WD	D10	HM	F21	8/A8.01	11/A8.01		1/4" TEMP	.	33	
1056A	3' - 0"	7' - 2"	WD	D10	HM	F10	9/A8.01	9/A8.01			20 MIN	33	
1056B	3' - 0"	7' - 2"	WD	D10	HM	F10	11/A8.01	11/A8.01			20 MIN	34	
1056C	3' - 0"	7' - 2"	WD	D10	HM	F10	20/A8.01	20/A8.01	-		20 MIN	33	
1057A	3' - 0"	7' - 2"	WD	D10	HM	F10	8/A8.01	11/A8.01			20 MIN	34	
1057B	3' - 0"	7' - 2"	WD	D10	HM	F30	9/A8.01	9/A8.01		1/4" TEMP	20 MIN	33	
1058A	3' - 0"	7' - 2"	WD	D10	HM	F10	9/A8.01	9/A8.01			.	33	

DOOR AND FRAME SCHEDULE

Sheets

You can think of sheets as the pieces of paper on which your views and schedules will be printed. Views and schedules are placed on sheets and then arranged. Once a view has been placed on a sheet, its reference bubble is automatically filled out and that view cannot be placed on any other sheet. The settings for each view, called "view scale," control the size of the drawing on each sheet; view scale also controls the size of the text and dimensions.

Exercise 1-2:
Overview of the Revit User Interface

Revit is a powerful and sophisticated program. Because of its powerful feature set, it has a measurable learning curve, though its intuitive design makes it easier to learn than other CAD programs. However, like anything, when broken down into smaller pieces, we can easily learn to harness the power of Revit. That is the goal of this book.

This section will walk through the different aspects of the User Interface (UI). As with any program, understanding the user interface is the key to using the program's features.

Application Menu, *Purple R*

Quick Access Toolbar (QAT)

RIBBON: *Tabs*

RIBBON: **(Temporary)** *Contextual Tab*

Info Center

RIBBON: *Panel*

RIBBON: *Tool*

Options Bar

Type Selector, *on Properties Palette*

Properties Palette

Drawing Window

Project Browser

View Control Bar

Navigation Bar

Context Menu

Status Bar

FIGURE 1-2.1 Revit User Interface

The Revit User Interface:

TIP: See the DVD for a more in-depth look at the User Interface.

Application Menu:

Access to *File* tools such as *Save, Plot, Export* and *Print* (both hardcopy and electronic printing). You also have access to tools which control the Revit application as a whole, not just the current project, such as *Licensing* and *Options*.

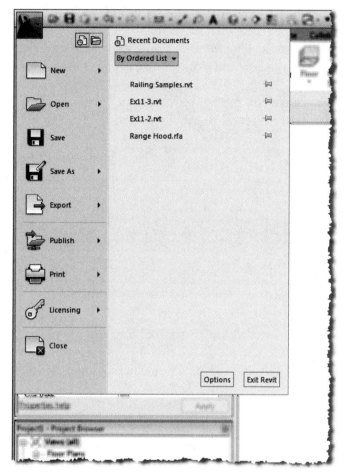

Recent and Open Documents:

These two icons (from the *Application* menu) toggle the entire area on the right to show either the recent documents you have been in (icon on the left) or a list of the documents you currently have open.

In the *Recent Documents* list you click a listed document to open it. This saves time as you do not have to click *Open → Project* and browse for the document (*Document* and *Project* mean the same thing here). Finally, clicking the "Pin" keeps that project from getting bumped off the list as additional projects are opened.

In the *Open Documents* list the "active" project you are working in is listed first, clicking another project switches you to that open project.

The list on the left, in the *Application Menu* shown above, represents three different types of buttons: *button, drop-down button* and *split button*. Save and Close are simply **buttons**. Save-As and Export are **drop-down buttons**, which means to reveal a group of related tools. If you click or hover your cursor over one of these buttons, you will get a list of tools on the right. Finally, **split buttons** have two actions depending on what part of the button you click on; hovering over the button reveals the two parts (see bottom image to the right). The main area is the most used tool; the arrow reveals additional related options.

Button

Drop-down Button

Split Button

Quick Access Toolbar:

Referred to as *QAT* in this book, this single toolbar provides access to often used tools (*Open*, *Save*, *Undo*, *Redo*, *Measure*, *Tag*, etc.). It is always visible regardless of what part of the *Ribbon* is active.

The *QAT* can be positioned above or below the *Ribbon* and any command from the *Ribbon* can be placed on it; simply right-click on any tool on the *Ribbon* and select *Add to Quick Access Toolbar*. Moving the *QAT* below the *Ribbon* gives you a lot more room for your favorite commands to be added from the *Ribbon*. Clicking the larger down-arrow to the right reveals a list of common tools which can be toggled on and off.

Some of the icons on the *QAT* have a down-arrow on the right. Clicking this arrow reveals a list of related tools. In the case of *Undo* and *Redo*, you have the ability to undo (or redo) several actions at once.

Ribbon – Home Tab:

The *Home* tab on the *Ribbon* contains most of the tools needed to model a building, essentially the things you can put your hands on when the building is done.

Each tab starts with the *Modify* tool, i.e., the first button on the left. This tool puts you into "selection mode" so you can select elements to modify. Clicking this tool cancels the current tool and unselects elements. With the *Modify* tool selected you may select elements to view their properties or edit them.

The *Ribbon* has three types of buttons, *button*, *drop-down button* and *split*, as covered on the previous page. In the image above you can see the *Wall* tool is a **split button**. Most of the time you would simply click the top part of the button to draw a wall. Clicking the down-arrow part of the button, for the *Wall* tool example, gives you the option to draw a *Wall*, *Structural Wall*, *Wall by Face*, *Wall Sweep*, and a *Reveal*.

TIP: *The Model Text tool is only for placing 3D text in your model, not for adding notes!*

Ribbon – Annotate Tab:

To view this tab, simply click the label "Annotate" near the top of the *Ribbon*. This tab presents a series of tools which allow you to add notes, dimensions and 2D "embellishments" to your model in a specific view, such as a floor plan, elevation, or section. All of these tools are **view specific**, meaning a note added in the first floor plan will not show up anywhere else, not even another first floor plan; for instance, a first floor electrical plan.

Notice, in the image above, that the *Dimension* panel label has a down-arrow next to it. Clicking the down-arrow will reveal an **extended panel** with additional related tools.

Finally, notice the *Component* tool in the image above; it is a **split button** rather than a *drop-down button*. Clicking the top part of this button will initiate the *Detail Component* tool. Clicking the bottom part of the button opens the fly-out menu revealing related tools. Once you select an option from the fly-out, that tool becomes the default for the top part of the split button for the current session of Revit (see image to right).

Ribbon – Modify Tab:

Several tools which manipulate and derive information from the current model are available on the *Modify* tab. Additional *Modify* tools are automatically appended to this tab when elements are selected in the model (see the *Modify* contextual tab on the next page).

> ***TIP:*** *Do not confuse the Modify tab with the Modify tool when following instructions in this book.*

Ribbon – View Tab:

The tools on the *View* tab allow you to create new views of your 3D model; this includes views that look 2D (e.g., floor plans, elevations and sections) as well as 3D views (e.g., isometric and perspective views).

The *View* tab also gives you tools to control how views look: everything from what types of elements are seen (e.g., Plumbing Fixture, Furniture or Section Marks) as well as line weights.

> *NOTE: Line weights can be controlled on a view by view basis or at a project wide level.*

Finally, notice the little arrow in the lower-right corner of the *Graphics* panel. When you see an arrow like this you can click on it to open a dialog box with settings that relate to the panel's tool set (*Graphics* in this example). Hovering over the arrow reveals a tooltip which will tell you what dialog box will be opened.

Ribbon – Modify Contextual Tab:

The *Modify* tab is appended when certain tools are active or elements are selected in the model; this is refereed to as a *contextual tab*. The first image, below, shows the *Place Wall* tab which presents various options while adding walls. The next example shows the *Modify Walls* contextual tab which is accessible when one or more walls are selected.

Place Wall contextual tab – accessible when the Wall tool is active.

Modify Walls contextual tab – accessible when a wall is selected.

Ribbon – Customization:

There is not too much customization that can be done to the *Ribbon*. One of the only things you can do is pull a panel off the *Ribbon* by clicking and holding down the left mouse button. This panel can be placed within the *drawing window* or on another screen if you have a dual monitor setup.

The image above shows the *Build* panel, from the *Home* tab, detached from the *Ribbon* and floating within the drawing window. Notice that the *Insert* tab is active. Thus, you have constant access to the *Build* tools while accessing other tools. Note that the *Build* panel is not available on the *Home* tab as it is literally moved, not just copied.

When you need to move a detached panel back to the *Ribbon* you do the following: hover over the detached panel until the sidebars show up and then click the "Return panels to ribbon" icon in the upper right (identified in the image above).

FYI: *Whenever the resolution of your monitor is too low or you don't have the Revit application maximized on the screen the buttons may be modified to take up less room on the Ribbon; typically the words are removed. Compare the image to the right with the Build panel above.*

Ribbon – States:

The *Ribbon* can be displayed in one of four states:

- Full Ribbon (default)
- Minimize to Tabs
- Minimize to Panel Tiles
- Minimize to Panel Buttons

The intent of this feature is to increase the size of the available drawing window. It is recommended, however, that you leave the *Ribbon* fully expanded while learning to use the program. The images in this book show the fully expanded state. The images below show the other three options. When using one of the minimized options you simply hover (or click) your cursor over the Tab or Panel to temporarily reveal the tools.

Minimize to Tabs

Minimize to Panel Tiles

Minimize to Panel Buttons

Ribbon – References in this Book:

When the exercises make reference to the tools in the *Ribbon* a consistent method is used to eliminate excessive wording and save space. Take a moment to understand this so that things go smoothly for you later.

Throughout the textbook you will see an instruction similar to the following:

> 23. Select **Home → Build → Wall**

This means, click the ***Home*** tab, and within the ***Build*** panel, select the ***Wall*** tool. Note that the *Wall* tool is actually a split button, but a subsequent tool was not listed so you are to click on the primary part of the button. Compare the above example to the one below:

> 23. Select **Home → Build → Wall → Structural Wall**

The above example indicates that you should click the down-arrow part of the *Wall* tool in order to select the *Structural Wall* option.

Thus the general pattern is this:

Tab → Panel → Tool → drop-down list item

Tab: This will get you to the correct area within the *Ribbon*.

Panel: This will narrow down your search for the desired tool.

Tool: Specific tool to select and use.

Drop-down list item: This will only be specified for drop-down buttons and sometimes for split buttons.

The image below shows the order in which the instructions are given to select a tool; note that you do not actually click the panel title.

Options Bar:

This area dynamically changes to show options that compliment the current operation. The *Options Bar* is located directly below the *Ribbon*. When you are learning to use Revit you should keep your eye on this area and watch for features and options appearing at specific times. The image below shows the *Options Bar* example with the *Wall* tool active.

Properties Palette – Element Type Selector:

Properties Palette; nothing selected

The *Properties Palette* provides instant access to settings related to the element selected or about to be created. When nothing is selected, it shows information about the current view. When multiple elements are selected, the common parameters are displayed.

The *Element Type Selector* is an important part of the *Properties Palette*. Whenever you are adding elements or have them selected, you can select from this list to determine how a wall to be drawn will look, or how a wall previously drawn should look (see image to right). If a wall type needs to change, you never delete it and redraw it; you simply select it and pick a new type from the *Type Selector*.

Type Selector; Wall tool active or a Wall is selected

The **Selection Filter** drop-down list below the *Type Selector* lets you know the type and quantity of the elements currently selected. When multiple elements are selected you can narrow down the properties for just one element type, such as *wall*. Notice the image to the right shows four walls are in the current selection set. Selecting **Walls (4)** will cause the *Palette* to only show *Wall* properties even though many other elements are selected (and remain selected).

The width of the *Properties Palette* and the center column position can be adjusted by dragging the cursor over that area. You may need to do this at times to see all the information. However, making the *Palette* too wide will reduce the useable drawing area.

Selection Filter; multiple elements selected

The *Properties Palette* should be left open; if you accidentally close it you can reopen it by **View → Window → User Interface → Properties**.

Project Browser:

The *Project Browser* is the "Grand Central Station" of the Revit project database. All the views, schedules, sheets and content are accessible through this hierarchical list. The image to the left shows the seven major categories; any item with a "plus" next to it contains sub-categories or items.

Double-clicking on a View, Legend, Schedule or Sheet will open it for editing. Right-clicking will display a pop-up menu with a few options such as *Delete* and *Copy*.

Like the *Properties Palette*, the width of the *Project Browser* can be adjusted. When the two are stacked above each other, they both move together.

The *Project Browser* should be left open; if you accidentally close it, by clicking the "X" in the upper right, you can reopen it by:
View → Window → User Interface → Project Browser.

The *Project Browser* and *Properties Palette* can be repositioned on a second monitor, if you have one, when you want more room to work in the drawing window.

Status Bar:

This area will display information about the current command or list information about a selected element. The right hand side of the *Status Bar* shows the number of elements selected. The small funnel icon to the left of the selection number can be clicked to open the *Filter* dialog box, which allows you to reduce your current selection to a specific category. For example, select the entire floor plan, and then filter it down to just the doors. This is different than the *Selection Filter* in the *Properties Palette* which keeps everything selected.

Unchecking **Press & Drag** prohibits Revit from automatically starting to move an element directly below your cursor when you click and drag the mouse.

The two drop-down lists towards the center of the *Status Bar* control **Design Options** and **Worksets**. The latter is not covered in this book but *Design Options* are. *Worksets* relate to the ability for more than one designer to be in the model at a time.

Drawing Window:

This is where you manipulate the Building Information Model (BIM). Here you will see the current view (plan, elevation or section), schedule or sheet. Any changes made are instantly propagated to the entire database.

View Control Bar:

This is a feature which gives you convenient access to tools which control each view's display settings (i.e., scale, shadows, detail level and graphics style). The important thing to know is that these settings only affect the current view, the one listed on the *Application Title Bar*. All of these settings are available in the *Properties Palette*, but this toolbar cannot be turned off like the *Properties Palette* can.

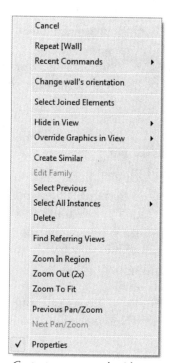

Context Menu:

The *context menu* appears near the cursor whenever you right-click on the mouse. The options on that menu will vary depending on what tool is active or what element is selected.

Elevation Marker:

This item is not really part of the Revit UI, but is visible in the drawing window by default via the various templates you can start with, so it is worth mentioning at this point. The four elevation markers point at each side of your project and ultimately indicate the drawing sheet on which you would find an elevation drawing of each side of the building. All you need to know right now is that you should draw your floor plan generally in the middle of the four elevation markers that you will see in each plan view; DO NOT delete them as this will remove the related view from the *Project Browser*.

Context menu example with a wall selected

This concludes your brief overview of the Revit user interface. Many of these tools and operations will be covered in more detail throughout the book.

Exercise 1-3:
Open, Save and Close an Existing Project

To *Open* **Revit Architecture 2012**:

Start → All Programs → Autodesk → Autodesk Revit Architecture 2012

FYI: Your icon may not say "x64"; this is not a problem.

Or double-click the Revit icon from your desktop.

This may vary slightly on your computer; see your instructor or system administrator if you need help.

Autodesk Revit Architecture 2011

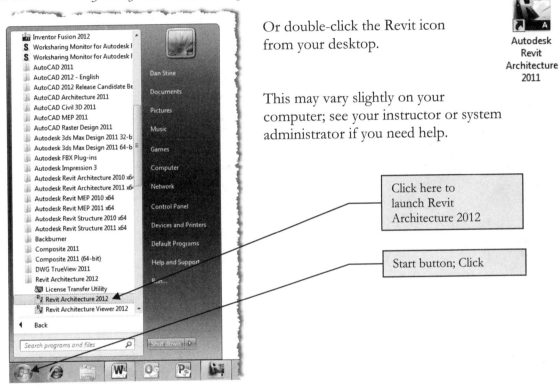

Click here to launch Revit Architecture 2012

Start button; Click

FIGURE 1-3.1 Starting Revit

Open an Existing Revit Project:

By default, Revit will open in the *Recent Files* window, which will display thumbnails of recent projects you have worked on. Clicking on the preview will open the project.

1. Click the **Open** link (see the image to the right).

You may click open under *Project* or on the *Quick Access Toolbar*.

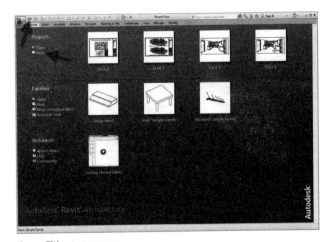

Recent Files startup screen

Next you will open an existing Revit project file. You will select a sample file provided on the DVD that came with this book.

2.   Click the drop-down box at the top of the *Open* dialog (Figure 1-3.2). Browse to your DVD drive; the drive letter will vary from computer to computer.

> ***TIP:*** *If you cannot locate the DVD that came with this textbook, you can substitute any Revit file you can find; try clicking on the Training Files shortcut on the left if needed.*

> ***TIP:*** *The training folder may not contain any files depending on how Revit was installed on your computer. You can access the files on Autodesk's website (www.autodesk.com).*

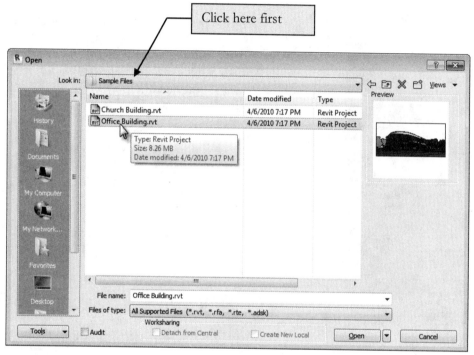

FIGURE 1-3.2 Open dialog; DVD contents shown

3.   Select the file named **Office Building.rvt** and click **Open**.

FYI: *Notice the preview of the selected file. This will help you select the correct file before taking the time to open it.*

The *Office Building.rvt* file is now open and the last saved view is displayed in the drawing window (Figure 1-3.3). This is the project shown on Page 1-3 displaying Revit's photo-realistic rendering capabilities.

FIGURE 1-3.3 Sample file "Office Building.rvt"

The *Application Menu* lists the projects and views currently open on your computer (Figure 1-3.4).

4. Click **Application Menu →**
   Open Documents (icon)
   (Figure 1-3.4).

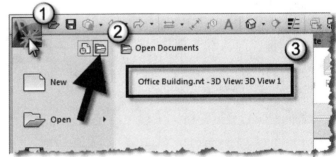

Notice that the *Office Building.rvt* project file is listed. Next to the project name is the name of a view open on your computer (e.g., floor plan, elevation).

Figure 1-3.4 Application Menu: Open Documents view

Additional views will be added to the list as you open them. Each view has the project name as a prefix. The current view, the view you are working in, is always at the top of the list. You can quickly toggle between opened views from this menu by clicking on them.

You can also use the *Switch Windows* tool on the *View* tab; both do essentially the same thing.

Switch
Windows

Open Another Revit Project:

Revit lets you open more than one project at a time.

5. Click **Open** from the *Quick Access Toolbar.*

6. Per the instructions previously covered, browse to the **DVD**.

7. Select the file named **Church Building.rvt** and click **Open** (Figure 1-3.5).

   TIP: If you cannot locate the DVD that came with this textbook, substitute one of the training files.

FIGURE 1-3.5 Sample file "Church Building.rvt"

8. Click **Open Documents** from the *Application* menu (Figure 1-3.6).

Notice that the *Church Building.rvt* project is now listed along with a view: Floor Plan: Level 1.

Try toggling between projects by clicking on *Office Building.rvt – 3D View: 3D View 1.*

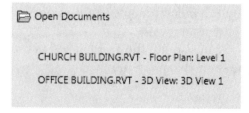

FIGURE 1-3.6 Open Documents

Close a Revit Project:

9. Select **Application menu** → **Close**; click **No** if prompted to save.

This will close the current project/view. If more than one view is open for a project, only the current view will close. The project and the other opened views will not close until you get to the last open view.

10. Repeat Step 9 to close the other project file.

If you have not saved your project yet, you will be prompted to do so before Revit closes the view. **Do not save at this time**. When all open project files are closed, you will find yourself back in the *Recent Files* screen, which is where you started.

Saving a Revit Project:

At this time we will not actually save a project.

To save a project file, simply select *Save* from the *Quick Access Toolbar*. You can also select *Save* from *Application Menu* or press *Ctrl + S* on the keyboard.

You should get in the habit of saving often to avoid losing work due to a power outage or program crash.

You can also save a copy of the current project by selecting **Save As** from the Application Menu. Once you have used the *Save As* command you are in the new project file and the file you started in is then closed.

Closing the Revit Program:

Finally, from the *Application* menu select **Exit Revit**. This will close any open projects/views and shut down Revit. Again you will be prompted to save, if needed, before Revit closes the view. **Do not save at this time**.

You can also click the "X" in the upper right corner of the *Revit Application* window.

Exercise 1-4:
Creating a New Project

Open **Autodesk Revit Architecture**.

Creating a New Project File:

The steps required to set up a new Revit Architecture model project file are very simple. As mentioned earlier, simply opening the Revit program starts you in the *Recent Files* window.

To manually create a new project (maybe you just finished working on a previous assignment and want to start the next one):

1. Select **Application menu → New → Project**.

    NOTE: If you select the New *link in the* Recent Files *startup screen, a new project is quickly setup using the default template. This is not recommended as this template is lacking content, views and sheets.*

After clicking *New → Project* you will get the ***New Project*** dialog box (Figure 1-4.1).

FIGURE 1-4.1 New Project dialog box

The *New Project* dialog box lets you specify the template file you want to use, or not use a template at all. You can also specify whether you want to create a new project or template file.

2. Leave the **default.rte** *template file* selected. You need to click in the textbox and "arrow key" to the right to see the template file name, and leave *Create new* set to **Project** (Figure 1-4.1).

3. Click **OK**. You now have a new unnamed project file.

To name an unnamed project file you simply *Save*. The first time an unnamed project file is saved you will be prompted to specify the name and location for the project file.

4. Select **Application menu** → **Save** from the *Menu Bar*.

5. Specify a **name** and **location** for your new project file.
    Your instructor may specify a location or folder for your files if in a classroom setting.

What is a Template File?

A template file allows you to start your project with specific content and certain settings preset the way you like or need them.

For example, you can have the units set to Imperial or Metric. You can have the door, window and wall families you use most loaded and eliminate other less often used content. Also, you can have your company's title block preloaded and even have all the sheets for a project set up.

A custom template is a must for design firms using Revit and will prove useful to the student as he or she becomes more proficient with the program.

Be Aware:
It will be assumed from this point forward that the reader understands how to create, open and save project files. Please refer back to this section as needed. If you still need further assistance, ask your instructor for help.

Exercise 1-5:
Using Zoom and Pan to View Your Drawings

Learning to *Pan* and *Zoom* in and out of a drawing is essential to accurate and efficient drafting and visualization. We will review these commands now so you are ready to use them with the first design exercise.

Open **Revit Architecture**.

You will select a sample file from the DVD that came with this textbook.

1. Select **Open** from the *Quick Access Toolbar*.

2. Browse to the **DVD** (usually the D drive, but this can vary).

3. Select the file named **Church Building.rvt** and click **Open** (Figure 1-5.1).

    TIP: *If you cannot locate the DVD that came with this textbook, substitute any of the training files that come with Revit.*

FIGURE 1-5.1 Church Building.rvt project

If the default view that is loaded is not **Floor Plan: Level 1**, double-click on **Level 1** under **Views\Floor Plans** in the *Project Browser*. Level 1 will be bold when it is the active or current view in the drawing window.

Using Zoom and Pan Tools:

You can access the zoom tools from the ***Navigation Bar***, or the *scroll wheel* on your mouse.

The *Zoom* icon contains several *Zoom* related tools:
- The default (i.e., visible) icon is *Zoom in Region*, which allows you to window an area to zoom into.
- The *Zoom* icon is a **split button**.
- Clicking the down-arrow part of the button reveals a list of related *Zoom* tools.
- You will see the drop-down list on the next page.

Zoom In

4. Select the top portion of the *Zoom* icon (see image to right).

5. Drag a window over your plan view (Figure 1-5.2).

Selection window: Pick two diagonal points, that is, two opposite corners, to define the window.

FIGURE 1-5.2 Zoom In window

You should now be zoomed in to the specified area (Figure 1-5.3).

FIGURE 1-5.3 Zoom In results

Zoom Out

6. Click the down-arrow next to the zoom icon (Figure 1-5.4). Select **Previous Pan/Zoom**.

You should now be back where you started. Each time you select this icon, you are restoring a previous view state. Sometimes you have to select this option multiple times if you did some panning and multiple zooms.

Take a minute and try the other *Zoom* tools to see how they work. When finished, click **Zoom to Fit** before moving on.

FIGURE 1-5.4 Zoom Icon drop-down

Default 3D View

Clicking on the *Default 3D View* icon, on the *QAT*, loads a 3D View. This allows you to quickly switch to a 3D view.

7. Click on the **Default 3D View** icon.

8. Go to the **Open Documents** listing in the *Application Menu* and notice the *3D View* and the *Floor Plan* view are both listed at the bottom.

Open Documents

Church Building.rvt - 3D View: {3D}

Church Building.rvt - Floor Plan: Level 1

> **REMEMBER:** *You can toggle between views here.*

9. Click the **Esc** key to close the *Application* menu.

ViewCube

The *ViewCube* gives you convenient view control over the 3D view. This technology has been implemented in many of Autodesk's programs to make the process seamless for the user.

10. You should notice the ***ViewCube*** in the upper right corner of the drawing window (Figure 1-5.5). If not, you can turn it on by clicking *View → Windows → User Interface → ViewCube*.

> **TIP:** *The ViewCube only shows up in 3D views.*

Hovering your cursor over the *ViewCube* activates it. As you move about the *Cube* you see various areas highlight. If you click, you will be taken to that highlighted area in the drawing window. You can also click and drag your cursor on the *Cube* to "roll" the model in an unconstrained fashion. Clicking and dragging the mouse on the disk below the *Cube* allows you to spin the model without rolling. Finally, you have a few options in a right-click menu, and the **Home** icon, just above the *Cube*, gets you back to where you started if things get disoriented!

11. Give the *ViewCube* a try, then click the **Home** icon when you are done.

FIGURE 1-5.5 ViewCube

> **REMEMBER:** *The home icon only shows up when your cursor is over the ViewCube.*

Navigation Wheel

Similar to the *ViewCube*, the *Navigation Wheel* aids in navigating your model. With the *Navigation Wheel* you can walk through your model, going down hallways and turning into rooms. Revit has not advanced to the point where the doors will open for you; thus, you walk through closed doors or walls as if you where a ghost!

The *Navigation Wheel* is activated by clicking the upper icon on the *Navigation Bar*.

Unfortunately, it is way too early in your Revit endeavors to learn to use the *Navigation Wheel*. You can try this in the chapter on creating photorealistic renderings and camera views. You would typically use this tool in a camera view.

Figure 1-5.6 Navigation Wheel

12. **Close** the *Church Building* project **without** saving.

Using the Scroll Wheel on the Mouse

The scroll wheel on the mouse is a must for those using BIM software. In Revit you can *Pan* and *Zoom* without even clicking a zoom icon. You simply **scroll the wheel to zoom** and **hold the wheel button down to pan**. This can be done while in another command (e.g., while drawing walls). Another nice feature is that the drawing zooms into the area near your cursor, rather than zooming only at the center of the drawing window. Give this a try before moving on. Once you get the hang of it, you will not want to use the icons. The only thing you cannot do is *Zoom to Fit* so everything is visible on the screen.

Exercise 1-6:
Using Revit's Help System

This last section of your introductory chapter will provide a quick overview of Revit Architecture's *Help System*. This will allow you to study topics in more detail if you want to know how something works beyond the introductory scope of this textbook.

1. Click the **round question mark** icon in the upper-right corner of the screen.

You are now in Revit's *WikiHelp* site (Figure 1-6.1). This is a website which opened in your web browser. This window can be positioned side-by-side with Revit which is especially nice if you have a dual-screen computer system. This interface requires a connection to the internet. As a website, Autodesk has the ability to add and revise information at any time, unlike files stored on your hard drive. This also means that the site can change quite a bit, potentially making the following overview out of date. If the site changes, just follow along as best you can for the next two pages.

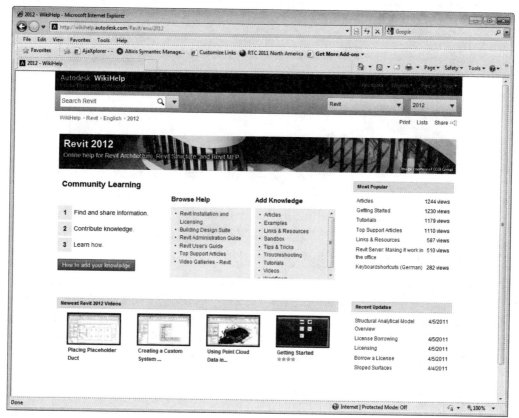

FIGURE 1-6.1 Autodesk WikiHelp site

In the upper left you can search the *Help System* for a word or phrase. You may also click any of the links to learn more about the topic listed. The next few steps will show you how to access the *Help System's* content on the Revit user interface, a topic you have just studied.

2. In the *Browse Help* section, select **Revit User's Guide**.

3. Click the first link in the search results list; it should be **User Interface**.

Notice the tree structure on the left. You can use this to quickly navigate the User's Guide.

4. On the left, click the plus symbols for: **Revit User's Guide → Introduction to Revit → User Interface** and then click directly on **Ribbon**.

You now see information about the *Ribbon* as shown in the image below. Notice additional links are provided below on the current topic. You can use the browser's *Back* and *Forward* buttons to move around in the *Help System*.

FIGURE 1-6.2 Help window; Ribbon overview

Next, you will try searching the Revit *Help System* for a specific Revit feature. This is a quick way to find information if you have an idea of what it is you are looking for.

5. In the upper-left corner of the current *Help System* web page, click in the *Search* textbox and enter **gutter**.

6. Press **Enter** on the keyboard.

The search results are shown in Figure 1-6.3. Each item is a link which will take you to information on that topic.

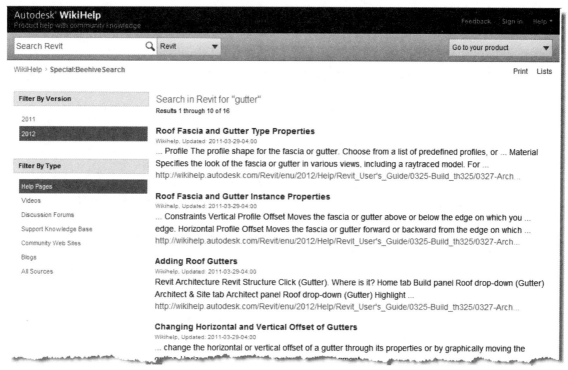

FIGURE 1-6.3 Help search results

The *Help System* can be used to complement this textbook. It is a reference resource, not a tutorial. As you are working though the tutorials in this book, you may want to use the *Help System* to fill in the blanks if you are having trouble or want more information on a topic.

What is a Wiki?

A Wiki site is a special type of website where anyone can add information to the site. This makes the potential knowledgebase very large. Anyone who sees a mistake in the steps or instructions provided can make a change. Additionally, a person with specific expertise can add additional information which will help other users. This is similar to the popular information website Wikipedia. For more information about Autodesk's WikiHelp site and how users such as you may add to and edit the content, visit:
http://wikihelp.autodesk.com/training/enu/wiki_guidelines.

Self-Exam:

The following questions can be used as a way to check your knowledge of this lesson. The answers can be found at the bottom of this page.

1. The *View* tab allows you to save your project file. (T/F)

2. You can zoom in and out using the wheel on a wheel mouse. (T/F)

3. Revit is a parametric architectural design program. (T/F)

4. A _____ file allows you to start your project with specific content and certain settings preset the way you like or need them.

5. In the Revit user interface, projects are viewed in the _____ window.

Review Questions:

The following questions may be assigned by your instructor as a way to assess your knowledge of this section. Your instructor has the answers to the review questions.

1. The *Options Bar* dynamically changes to show options that compliment the current operation. (T/F)

2. Revit is strictly a 2D drafting program. (T/F)

3. The Projects/Views listed in the *Open Documents* list allow you to see which Projects/Views are currently open. (T/F)

4. When you use the *Pan* tool you are actually moving the drawing, not just changing what part of the drawing you can see on the screen. (T/F)

5. Revit was not originally created for architecture. (T/F)

6. The icon with the floppy disk picture ( ) allows you to _____ a project file.

7. Clicking on the _____ next to the *Zoom* icon will list additional zoom tools not currently shown in the *View* toolbar.

8. You do not see the *ViewCube* unless you are in a _____ view.

Lesson 2
Lake Cabin: FLOOR PLAN:

In this lesson you will get a down and dirty overview of the functionality of Autodesk® Revit® Architecture. We will cover the very basics of creating the primary components of a floor plan: Walls, Doors, Windows, Roof, Annotation and Dimensioning. This lesson will show you the amazing "out-of-the-box" powerful, yet easy to use, features in Autodesk Revit Architecture. It should get you very excited about learning this software program. Future lessons will cover these features in more detail while learning other editing tools and such along the way.

Exercise 2-1:
Walls

In this exercise we will draw the walls, starting with the exterior. Read the directions carefully, everything you need to do is clearly listed.

Rough Sketch of Lake Cabin Plan:

This sketch is just to give you an idea of what you will be creating in this chapter (Figure 2-1.1).

FIGURE 2-1.1 Lake Cabin Sketch

Exterior Walls:

1. Start a new project named **Lake Cabin**. *See Lesson 1 on creating a new project.*

2. Click **Home → Build → Wall**
   (i.e., the upper part of the icon, not the down-arrow part). See Figure 2-1.2.

Notice that the *Ribbon, Options Bar* and *Properties Palette* have changed to show options related to drawing walls. Next you will modify those settings.

FIGURE 2-1.2 Wall tool

3. Modify the *Ribbon* and *Options Bar* to the following (Figure 2-1.3):
   a. *Change Element Type (via the Element Type Selector):* Click the down-arrow and select **Generic – 12"**.
   b. *Height:* Change the height from 20'-0" to **9'-0"**.
   c. *Location Line:* Set this to **Finish Face: Exterior**.

FIGURE 2-1.3 Ribbon, Options Bar and Type Selector

You are now ready to draw the exterior walls in the *Level 1* view.

4. In the drawing window, **click** in the upper left corner.

   TIP: Remember to draw within the four elevation marks (see the image to right).

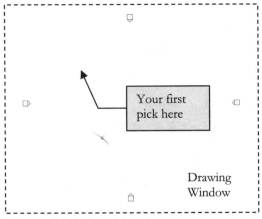

FIGURE 2-1.4 First pick point

5. Start moving the mouse to the right. **Click** when the wall is **48'-0"** long and horizontal.

Notice as you move the mouse Revit dynamically displays a length and an angle. If you want a horizontal line you move the mouse straight across the screen. A dashed line and a tooltip will appear when the line is snapped to the horizontal (Figure 2-1.4).

FIGURE 2-1.5 Horizontal tooltip displayed

TIP: If your mouse moved a little when you clicked and the wall is not exactly 48'-0", simply click on the dimension and type 48 and press Enter. You do not need to type the foot symbol.

You are now ready your second wall.

6. Start moving your mouse straight down, or South, until the dashed line and tooltip appear (indicating a vertical line); type **26** and press **Enter**.

TIP: Once the wall is drawn the temporary dimension will say 25'-6" as it is to the wall centerline on the north corner.

Typing the length allows you to accurately input a length without having to spend a lot of time setting the mouse in just the right position. However, you can still adjust the dimension after the wall is drawn.

7. Draw the other two exterior walls.

Interior Walls:

The same tool is used to draw both interior and exterior walls.

8. Select the *Wall* tool and modify the **Ribbon, Options Bar** and **Properties Palette** to the following:
    a. *Type Selector:* Click the down-arrow and select **Generic – 5"**.
    b. *Location Line:* Set this to **Wall Centerline**.

9. Drawing a wall between bedrooms: *Snap* (you will see a triangle symbol appear before clicking) to the midpoint of the east wall (Figure 2-1.6). Do not click the second point yet; see the next step to finish the wall.

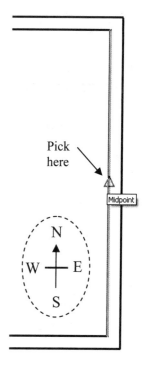

FIGURE 2-1.6 Interior wall start point

10. While moving the mouse to the West (left) and snapped to the horizontal plane, type **20 2 1/2**.

   TIP: Type the length as shown; you don't need a dash, the foot or the inch symbol as they are assumed here. You do need two spaces – after the feet and before the fraction.

11. Draw the vertical wall to close off the bedrooms. Revit allows you to do this with one wall segment by selecting your points in a particular way. See **Figure 2-1.7** for a graphical description of this process; press **Esc** twice to unselect the new wall (first Esc pressed) and cancel the *Wall* command (second Esc pressed).

FIGURE 2-1.7 Draw wall with object tracking

12. **One More Step:** Draw the two interior walls for the bathroom to complete the interior walls; dimensions are to center of walls (Figure 2-1.1).

13. **Save** your project (*Lake Cabin.rvt*) via the *QAT*.

Exercise 2-2:
Doors

In this exercise you will add doors to your cabin floor plan.

1. Open **Lake Cabin.rvt** created in Exercise 2-1.

FIGURE 2-2.1 Door tool

Placing Doors:

2. Click **Home → Build → Door** (Figure 2-2.1).

Notice that the *Ribbon*, *Options Bar* and *Properties Palette* has changed to show options related to doors. Next you will modify those settings.

The *Type Selector* indicates the door style, width and height. Clicking it lists all the doors loaded into the current project.

FIGURE 2-2.2 Door type selected

The default template project that you started from has several sizes for a single flush door. Notice that the there are two standard heights in the list. The 80″ (6′-8″) doors are the standard residential height and the 84″ (7′-0″) doors are the standard commercial door height.

3. Change the *Type Selector* to **36″ x 80″**; see Figure 2-2.2.

4. Move your cursor over a wall and position the door as shown in **Figure 2-2.4**. Notice that the swing of the door changes depending on what side of the wall your cursor is favoring (Figure 2-2.4).

5. Click to place the door and Revit will automatically trim the wall.

6. While the door is still selected, click on the *change swing (control arrows)* symbol to make the door swing against the wall (Figure 2-2.3).

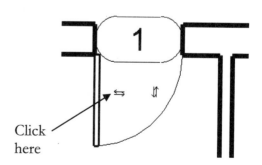

Click here

FIGURE 2-2.3 Changing door swing

FIGURE 2-2.4 Dynamic graphical info during door insertion

Revit allows you to continue inserting doors until you select a different tool from the *Ribbon* or press *Esc*.

7. Insert the doors into the bedrooms as shown in **Figure 2-1.1**. The exact position is not important in this exercise.

8. Change the *Type Selector* to **30" x 80"**.

9. Insert a door into the bathroom.

Notice that door types recently used are listed at the bottom of the list (Figure 2-2.5).

FIGURE 2-2.5 Door Element Types

Deleting Doors:

Next you will learn how to delete a door. This process will work for most objects (i.e., walls, windows, text, etc.) in Revit.

10. Insert a door between the two bedrooms, any size.

11. Press the **Esc** key twice.

TIP: You can also click the Modify icon located on the left of every tab on the Ribbon. **Modify**

12. Click on the door you just inserted, between bedrooms, and press the **Delete** key on your keyboard.

13. **Save** your project (*Lake Cabin.rvt*).

Exercise 2-3:
Windows

In this exercise you will add windows to your cabin floor plan.

1. Open **Lake Cabin.rvt** created in Exercise 2-2.

Placing Windows:

2. Click **Home → Build → Window** (Figure 2-3.1).

FIGURE 2-3.1 Window tool

Again, notice that the *Ribbon, Options Bar* and *Properties Palette* have changed to show options related to windows. Next you will modify those settings.

The *Type Selector* indicates the window style, width and height. Clicking the *Type Selector* lists all the windows loaded in the current project.

3. Change the *Type Selector* to **36" x 72"** (Figure 2-3.2).

FIGURE 2-3.2 Window options

4. Move your cursor over a wall and place two windows as shown in **Figure 2-3.3**. Notice, as you move your cursor near a wall, that the position of the window changes depending on what side of the wall your cursor is favoring.

5. With the Window tool still active, change the *Type Selector* to **24" x 72"**.

6. Place the other four windows in the living room area as shown in **Figure 2-1.1**. Again, in this exercise we are not concerned with the exact placement of the windows.

7. Change the *Type Selector* to **24" x 48"**.

8. Place the remaining five windows: two in each bedroom and one in the bathroom, as shown in **Figure 2-1.1**.

9. **Save** your project (*Lake Cabin.rvt*).

FIGURE 2-3.3 Two large windows

Object Snap Symbols:

By now you should be well aware of the snaps that Revit suggests as you move your cursor about the drawing window.

If you hold your cursor still for a moment while a snap symbol is displayed, a tooltip will appear on the screen. However, when you become familiar with the snap symbols you can pick sooner. (Figure 2-3.4)

The TAB key cycles through the available snaps near your cursor.

The keyboard shortcut turns off the other snaps for one pick. For example, if you type SE (snap endpoint) on the keyboard while in the Wall command, Revit will only look for an endpoint for the next pick.

Finally, typing SO (snaps off) turns all snaps off for one pick.

See Exercise 3-2 for more information.

Symbol	Position	Keyboard Shortcut
✕	Intersection	SI
☐	Endpoint	SE
△	Midpoint	SM
○	Center	SC
✕	Nearest	SN
⌐	Perpendicular	SP
Ω	Tangent	ST

FIGURE 2-3.4 Snap Reference Chart

Exercise 2-4:
Roof

You will now add a simple roof to your lake cabin.

1. Open **Lake Cabin.rvt** created in Exercise 2-3 (if necessary).

Sketching a Roof:

2. Click **Home → Build → Roof** (click the bottom part of the button); a fly-out menu will appear (Figure 2-4.1).

FIGURE 2-4.1 Roof tool

The fly-out prompts you for the method you want to use to create the roof.

3. Click **Roof by footprint**.

When Revit detects an issue that might not be appropriate, a warning is displayed. In this case you see *Roof is on the Lowest... Level* warning.

Revit notices that you are on Level 1 and asks you if you want to move the roof another level. In our case we want to move it to Level 2 (Figure 2-4.2).

FIGURE 2-4.2 Roof is on the Lowest Level prompt

4. Make sure **Level 2** is selected and click **Yes** (Figure 2-4.2).

You are still on Level 1, but Revit will move the roof to Level 2 once you are finished drawing it. The entire model is grayed out at the moment because you are in "Sketch Mode;" when finished sketching, the roof and everything will return to normal. You will not see the roof as it will be above the current view (i.e., Level 1); you will learn more about this on the next page.

Also notice the *contextual tab* **Create Roof Footprint** has temporarily been added to the *Ribbon*, which has design options relative to the roof (Figure 2-4.3) as with the *Options Bar* directly below the *Ribbon*.

FIGURE 2-4.3 Roof sketch options on the *Ribbon* and *Options Bar*

5. Pick each of the exterior walls to specify the roof footprint.
   Be sure to pick the exterior side of the wall.

6. Click **Finish Edit Mode** via the green checkmark on the *Ribbon*.

You should be on Level 1. You can see this in the *Project Browser*, as Level 1 is bold.

7. To see the roof click the **Default 3D View** icon on the *QAT* (Figure 2-4.4).

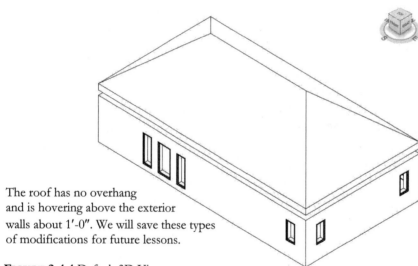

The roof has no overhang and is hovering above the exterior walls about 1'-0". We will save these types of modifications for future lessons.

FIGURE 2-4.4 Default 3D View

8. Click the **X** in the upper right corner of the drawing window to close the current view (3D). This will close the 3D view but not the project or the Level 1 view.

> **NOTE:** *Clicking the X on the Title Bar closes Revit.*

Closing a View

Exercise 2-5:
Annotation and Dimensions

Adding text is very simple in Revit. In this exercise we will add labels to each room in our lake cabin floor plan. We will also place two dimensions.

Placing Text:

1. Open **Lake Cabin.rvt** created in Exercise 2-4, if not already open.

2. Make sure your current view is **Level 1**. The word "Level 1" will be bold under the heading *Floor Plans* in your *Project Browser*. If Level 1 is not current, simply double-click on the "Level 1" text in the *Project Browser* (Figure 2-5.1).

3. Select **Annotate → Text → Text**; do not select *Model Text* from the Home tab of the *Ribbon*.

   WARNING: *Do not use the Model Text tool icon the Home tab; this is 3D text and not for notes.*

Once again, notice the *Ribbon* has changed to display some text options; all of this falls under a *contextual tab* named *Modify | Place Text* (Figure 2-5.2).

FIGURE 2-5.1 Project Browser

FIGURE 2-5.2 Ribbon: contextual tab for Text tool

The *Type Selector* indicates the text size. From this *Contextual Ribbon* you can also place text with arrow lines, or leaders, and set the text alignment, Left justified, Centered or Right justified. We will not adjust these settings at this time.

4. You will now place the words "Living Room". **Click** within the living room area to place the text (Figure 2-5.3).

5. Type **Living Room**, then click somewhere in the plan view to finish the text.

You may notice that the text seems too large. This is a good time to explain what the text height is referring to in the *Type Selector (i.e., ¼" Arial)*. The text height, in the *Properties Palette*, refers to the size of the text on a printed piece of paper. For example, if you print your plan you should be able to place a ruler on the text and measure ¼" in height when the text is set to ¼" in the *Type Selector*.

This can be a complicated process in other CAD programs; Revit makes it very simple. All you need to do is change the *View Scale* for **Level 1** and Revit automatically adjusts the text and annotation to match that scale. Currently our *View Scale* is set to ⅛" = 1'-0"; we want the *View Scale* to be ¼" = 1'-0". With the *View Scale* set to ⅛" = 1'-0" our text is twice as big as it should be. Next you will change the *View Scale* for Level 1.

FIGURE 2-5.3 Placing text

In the lower-left corner of the drawing window, on the *View Control Bar*, click on the text of the listed scale (i.e., ⅛″ = 1′-0″).

6. In the pop-up menu, which lists several standard scales, select **¼″ = 1′-0″** (Figure 2-5.4).

You should now notice that your text and even your door and window tags are half the size they used to be (Figure 2-5.5).

You should understand that this scale adjustment only affected the current view (i.e., Level 1). If you switched to Level 2 you would notice it is still set to ⅛″ = 1′-0″. This is nice because you may, on occasion, want one plan at a larger scale to show more detail.

7. Finally, using the *Text* tool, place a room name label in each room as shown in **Figure 2-1.1** and **Figure 2-5.5** below.

8. **Save** your project.

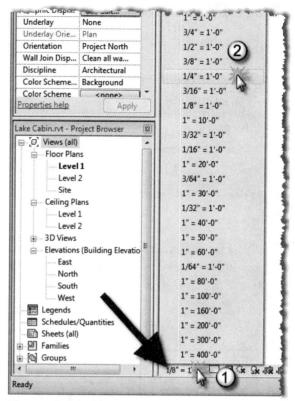

FIGURE 2-5.4 Changing View Scale

FIGURE 2-5.5 Floor Plan with text at ¼″ = 1′-0″

Place Dimensions:

To finish this exercise you will place two overall plan dimensions.

Aligned

9. Select **Annotate → Dimension → Aligned** (see icon to right).

10. On the *Options Bar*, change the drop-down list that says *Wall centerlines* to **Wall faces**. This option will allow you to dimension to the outside face of your building, as you would normally do when dimensioning the overall footprint of your building.

11. Place a dimension by selecting two walls and then clicking a third point to specify where the dimension line should be located relative to the walls (Figure 2-5.6).

FIGURE 2-5.6 Placing Dimensions

12. Place one more dimension indicating the depth of the building.

The *Dimension* tool, as just used, places permanent dimensions; they can be deleted however. Revit also provides a tool to list a dimension but not actually place a permanent dimension; this is called the **Measure** tool. The *Measure* tool is convenient when you simply want to know what a dimension is but do not need to document it for the construction drawings.

13. **Save** your project.

Exercise 2-6:
Printing

The last thing you need to know to round off your basic knowledge of Revit is how to print the current view. Printing will be covered in more detail later in the text; this section will just brush over the surface of the process.

Printing the Current View:

1.   Select **Application Menu → Print** (hover) **→ Print**.

2.   Adjust your settings to match those shown in **Figure 2-6.1**.

   - Select a printer from the list that you have access to.
   - Set *Print Range* to: **Visible portion of current window**

FIGURE 2-6.1 Print dialog

3.   Click on the **Setup** button to adjust additional print settings.

4.   Adjust your settings to match those shown in **Figure 2-6.2**.

   - Set Zoom to: **Fit to page**.

FIGURE 2-6.2 Print Settings dialog

5. Click **OK** to close the *Print Setup* dialog and return to *Print*.

6. Click **No** if you get the following prompt (Figure 2-6.3).

FIGURE 2-6.3 Save Print Settings prompt

7. Click the **Preview** button in the lower left corner. This will save paper and time by verifying the drawing will be correctly positioned on the page (Figure 2-6.4).

8. Click the **Print** button at the top of the preview window.

9. Click **OK** to print to the selected printer.

> **FYI:**
> Notice you do not have the option to set the scale (i.e., ⅛″ = 1′-0″). If you recall from our previous exercise the scale is set in the properties for each view.
>
> If you want a quick half-scale print you can change the zoom factor to 50%. You could also select **Fit to Page** to get the largest image possible but not to scale – which is selected above as this plan will not fit on 8½″ x 11″ (letter) sized paper at ¼″ = 1′-0″.

Printer versus Plotter?

Revit can print to any printer or plotter installed on your computer.

A **Printer** is an output device that uses smaller paper (e.g., 8½″x11″ or 11″x17″). A **Plotter** is an output device that uses larger paper; plotters typically have one or more rolls of paper ranging in size from 18″ wide to 36″ wide. A roll feed plotter has a built-in cutter that can, for example, cut paper from a 36″ wide roll to make a 24″x36″ sheet.

FIGURE 2-6.4 Print Preview

Plotter with three paper rolls

Color **printer**/copier

Self-Exam:

The following questions can be used as a way to check your knowledge of this lesson. The answers can be found at the bottom of the page.

1.   The *Measure* tool is used to dimension drawings. (T/F)

2.   Revit will automatically trim the wall lines when you place a door. (T/F)

3.   Snap will help you to draw faster and more accurately. (T/F)

4.   A 6'-8" door is a standard door height in _____ construction.

5.   While using the *Wall* tool, the height can be quickly adjusted on the

       _____ bar.

Review Questions:

The following questions may be assigned by your instructor as a way to assess your knowledge of this section. Your instructor has the answers to the review questions.

1.   The *View Scale* for a drawing/view is set by clicking the scale listed on the *View Control Bar*. (T/F)

2.   Dimensions are placed with only two clicks of the mouse. (T/F)

3.   The relative size of text in a drawing is controlled by the *View Scale*. (T/F)

4.   You can quickly switch to a different view by double-clicking on that view's label in the *Project Browser*. (T/F)

5.   You cannot select which side of the wall a window is offset to. (T/F)

6.   The _____ key cycles through the available snaps near your cursor.

7.   Which specific *Roof* tool did you use in this chapter?   _____

8.   While in the *Door* tool you can change the door style and size via the

       _____ _____ within the *Properties Palette*.

9.   When plotting, you must tell Revit the desired scale (i.e., ⅛" = 1'-0", ¼" = 1'-0", etc.), while in the *Plot* dialog box. (T/F)

10.   The *Quick Access Toolbar* has a tool which gives you quick access to a 3D view of your model. (T/F)

Lesson 3
Overview of Linework and Modify Tools:

It may seem odd to you that, in a revolutionary 3D design program, you will begin by learning to draw and edit 2D lines and shapes. However, any 3D object requires, at a minimum, detailed information in at least two of the three dimensions. Once two dimensions are defined, Autodesk® Revit® Architecture can begin to automate much of the third dimension for you. Many building components and features will require you to draw the perimeter using 2D lines.

Many of the edit tools that are covered in this lesson are the same tools that are used to edit the 3D building components.

Exercise 3-1:
Lines and Shapes

Drawing Lines

You will draw many 2D lines in Autodesk Revit Architecture, typically in what is called *Sketch* mode. Two dimensional lines in Autodesk Revit Architecture are extremely precise drawing elements. This means you can create very accurate drawings. Lines, or any drawn object, can be as precise as 8 decimal places (i.e., 24.999999999) or 1/256.

Autodesk Revit Architecture is a vector based program. That means each drawn object is stored in a numerical database. When geometry needs to be displayed on the screen, Autodesk Revit Architecture reads from the project database to determine what to display on the screen. This ensures that the line will be very accurate at any scale or zoom magnification.

A raster based program, in contrast to vector based, is comprised of dots that infill a grid. The grid can vary in density, and is typically referred to as resolution (e.g., 600x800, 1600x1200, etc.). This file type is used by graphics programs that typically deal with photographs, such as Adobe Photoshop. There are two reasons this type of file is not appropriate for Computer Aided Design (CAD) programs:

- A raster based line, for example, is composed of many dots on a grid, representing the line's width. When you zoom in, magnifying the line, it starts to become pixilated, meaning you actually start to see each dot on the grid. In a vector file you can "infinitely" zoom in on a line and it will never become pixilated because the program recalculates the line each time you zoom in.

- A CAD program, such as Revit, only needs to store the starting point and end point coordinates for each wall, for example; the dots needed to draw the wall are calculated on-the-fly for the current screen resolution. Whereas a raster file has to store each dot that represents the full length and width of the line, or lines in the wall example. This can vary from a few hundred dots to several thousand dots, depending on the resolution, for the same line.

The following graphic illustrates this point:

Vector vs. Raster Lines

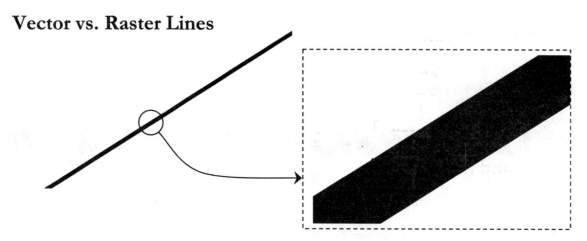

FIGURE 3-1.1 Vector Line Example
File Size: approx. 33kb

FIGURE 3-1.1A Vector Line Enlarged 1600%

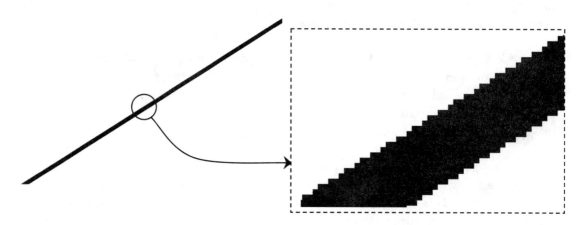

FIGURE 3-1.2 Raster Line Example
File Size: approx. 4.4MB

FIGURE 3-1.2A Raster Line Enlarged 1600%

The Detail Lines Tool:

You will now study the *Detail Lines* tool.

    1. **Open** Revit.

Each time you start Revit, you are in the *Recent Files* view. This view is closed automatically when a new or existing project is opened.

    2. Start a new project: select **Application Menu → New → Project** and then click **OK** to start a new project based on the default template.

The drawing window is set to the *Level 1 Floor Plan* view. The 2D drafting will be done in a drafting view. Next you will learn how to create one of these views.

    3. Select **View → Create → Drafting View**
(Remember: this means *Tab → Panel → Icon* on the *Ribbon*.)

Drafting
View

    4. In the *New Drafting View* dialog box, type **Ex 3-1** for the *Name* and set the *Scale* to **3/4″ = 1′-0″** by clicking the down-arrow at the right (Figure 3-1.3).

FIGURE 3-1.3 New Drafting View dialog

You are now in the new view and the *Project Browser* will contain a category labeled *Drafting Views (Detail)*. Here, each *Drafting View* created will be listed.

    5. In the *Project Browser*, click the plus symbol next to the label **Drafting Views (Detail)**; this will display the *Drafting Views* that exist in the current project (Figure 3-1.4).

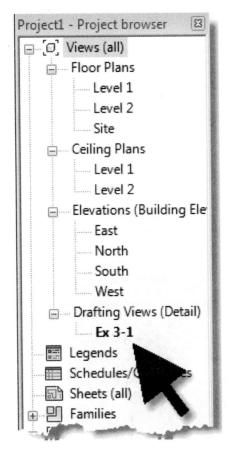

FIGURE 3-1.4 Project Browser: Drafting Views

You are now ready to start looking at the *Detail Lines* tool:

6. Select the **Annotate** tab on the *Ribbon*.

7. On the *Detail* panel, select **Detail Line** (Figure 3-1.5).

   TIP: *Do not use the "Model Line" tool on the Home tab.*

8. **Draw a line** from the lower left corner of the screen to the upper right corner of the screen, by simply clicking two points on the screen within the drawing window.

   NOTE: *Do not drag or hold your mouse button down; just click (Figure 3-1.6).*

After clicking your second point, you should notice the length and the angle of the line are graphically displayed; this information is temporary and will disappear when you move your cursor.

FIGURE 3-1.5 Annotate tab

You should also notice that the *Detail Line* tool is still active, which means you could continue to draw additional lines on the screen.

9. After clicking your second point, select the **Modify** tool from the left side of the *Ribbon*.

Modify

Selecting *Modify* cancels the current tool and allows you to select portions of your drawing for information or editing. Revit conveniently places the *Modify* tool in the same location on each tab so it is always available no matter which tab on the *Ribbon* is active.

TIP: Pressing the Esc key twice reverts Revit back to Modify mode.

Did You Make a Mistake?

Whenever you make a mistake in Revit you can use the **UNDO** command, via the *QAT*, to revert to a previous drawing state. You can perform multiple UNDO's all the way to your previous *Save*.

Similarly, if you press Undo a few too many times, you can use **REDO**.

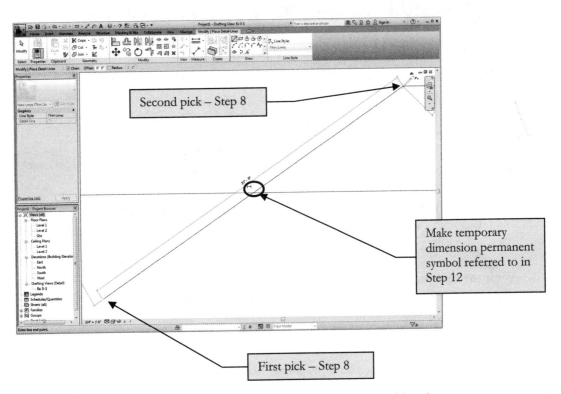

FIGURE 3-1.6 Your first detail line; exact dimensions are not important at this point.

Notice in the image above, that while the *Detail Line* tool is active, the *Modify | Place Detail Line* contextual tab is shown. As soon as you click the *Modify* button or press Esc, the tab reverts back to the basic *Modify* tab.

This constitutes your first line! However, as you are probably aware, it is not a very accurate line as far as length and angle are concerned. Your line will likely be a different length due to where you picked your points and the size and resolution of your monitor.

Typically you need to provide information such as length and angle when drawing a line; you rarely pick arbitrary points on the screen as you did in the previous steps. Revit allows you to get close with the on-screen dimension and angle information. Most of the time you also need to accurately pick your starting point. For example, how far one line is from another or picking the exact middle point on another line.

Having said that, however, the line you just drew still has precise numbers associated with its length and angle; this information is displayed after the line is drawn. The dimension and angle information is displayed until you begin to draw another line or select another tool. You can also select the line. While the dimensions are still visible, they can be used to modify the length and angle of the line; you will try that later.

10. If not already selected, click the **Modify** tool from the *Ribbon.*

Notice that the temporary dimensions have disappeared.

While you are in *Modify* mode, you can select lines and objects in the current view.

11. Now **select the line** by clicking the mouse button with the cursor directly over the line.

FYI: *Always use the left button unless the right button is specifically mentioned.*

Notice that the temporary dimensions have returned.

The following step shows how to make a temporary dimension permanent:

If, at any point, you want to make a temporary dimension permanent, you simply click the "make this temporary dimension permanent" symbol near the dimension. You will try this now.

12. With the diagonal line still selected, click the "make this temporary dimension permanent" symbol near the dimension (Figure 3-1.6).

13. Select **Modify** to unselect the line.

The dimension indicating the length of the line is now permanent (Figure 3-1.7). The value of your dimension will not be the same as the one in this book as the size of your monitor and the exact points picked can vary greatly.

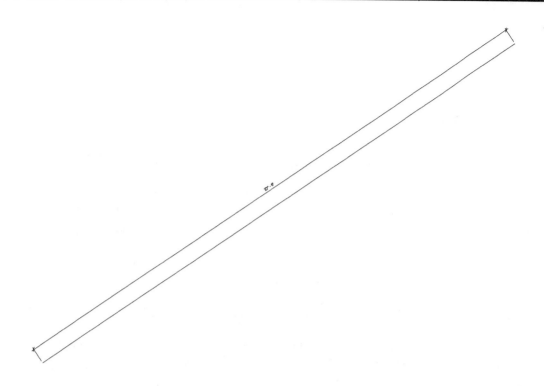

FIGURE 3-1.7 Temp dimension converted to permanent dimension

The following shows how to change the length of the line:

Currently, the line is approximately 20 - 30′ long (27′-6″ in Figure 3-1.7). If you want to change the length of the line to 22′-6″, you select the line and then change the dimension text, which in turn changes the line length. This can also be done with the temporary dimensions; the key is that the line has to be selected. You will try this next.

FYI: Your detail line length will vary slightly depending on the size and resolution of your computer monitor. This also assumes you have not performed any zooming, including spinning the wheel button on your mouse. If your line is way off you should Undo or start over so the next several steps work out as intended.

14. In *Modify* mode, select the diagonal line.

15. With the line currently selected, click on the dimension-text.

A dimension-text edit box appears directly over the dimension, within the drawing window. Whatever you type as a dimension changes the line to match.

16. Type **22 6** (i.e., 22 *space* 6) and press **Enter** (Figure 3-1.8).

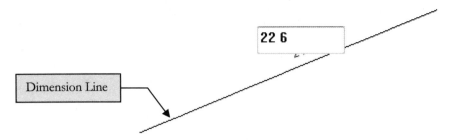

FIGURE 3-1.8 Editing dimension to change line length

You should have noticed the line changed length. Revit assumes that you want the line to change length equally at each end, so the midpoint does not move. Try changing the dimension to 100′ and then Undo.

Locking Dimensions:

Revit allows you to *Lock* a dimension, which prevents the dimension and line length from changing. You will investigate this now to help avoid problems later.

    17. Make sure the line is *not* selected; to do this press Esc or click *Modify*.

    18. Select the dimension, not the line, and note the following about the selected dimension (Figure 3-1.9).

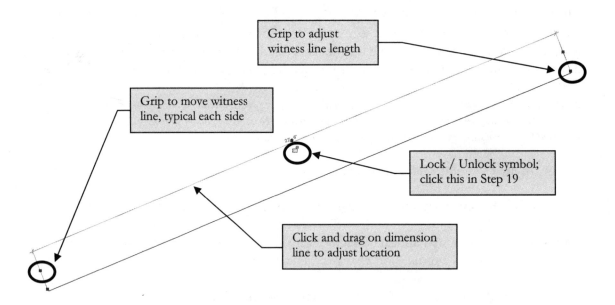

FIGURE 3-1.9 Selected dimension

19. Click on the **Lock/Unlock** padlock symbol to lock the dimension (Figure 3-1.9).

The dimension is now locked. Again, this means that you cannot change the dimension OR the line, though you can move it. The dimension is attached to the line in such a way that changing one affects the other. Next you will see what happens when you try to modify the dimension while it is locked.

Any time the line or dimension are selected you will see the lock or unlock symbol in the locked position.

FYI: Clicking the dimension's padlock icon anytime it is visible will toggle the setting between locked and unlocked.

20. Select **Modify** to unselect the *Dimension*.

21. Select the line (not the dimension).

22. Click on the dimension text and attempt to modify the line length to **21′**.

As you can see, Revit will not let you edit the text.

Even though your current view is showing a relatively small area, i.e., your *Drafting View,* it is actually an infinite drawing board.

In architectural CAD drafting, everything is drawn true to life size, or full-scale, ALWAYS! If you are drawing a building, you might draw an exterior wall that is 600′-0″ long. If you are drawing a window detail, you might draw a line that is 8″ long. In either case you are entering that line's actual length.

You could, of course, have an 8″ line and a 600′-0″ line in the same *Drafting View.* Either line would be difficult to see at the current drawing magnification (i.e., approximately 22′ x 16′ area; also recall that your diagonal line is 22′-6″ long). So, you would have to zoom in to see the 8″ line and zoom out to see the 600′-0″ line. Next you will get to try this.

When the diagonal line is selected, notice the *Properties Palette* lists the type of entity selected (i.e., Lines), the *Style* (i.e., Thin Lines) and the *Length* (i.e., 22′-6″). See Chapter 1 for more information on the *Properties Palette* and how to open it if you accidentally closed it.

FIGURE 3-1.10 Properties Palette with diagonal line selected

Draw an 8″ Line:

The next steps will walk you through drawing an 8″ horizontal line. Revit provides more than one way to do this. You will try one of them now.

23. Select **Annotate** → **Detail** → **Detail Line**.

24. Pick a point somewhere in the upper left corner of the drawing window.

25. Start moving the mouse towards the right, and generally horizontal until you see a dashed reference line extending in each direction of your line appear on the screen, as in Figure 3-1.11.

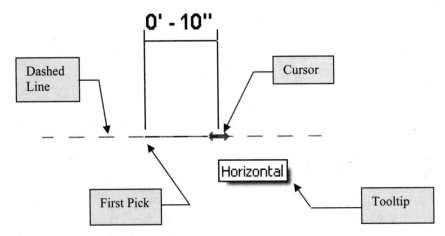

FIGURE 3-1.11 Drawing a line with the help of Revit

TIP: *You will see a dashed horizontal line and a tooltip when the line is horizontal.*

As you move the mouse left and right, you will notice Revit displays various dimensions that allow you to quickly draw your line at these often used increments. See the next exercise to learn more about how to control the increments shown.

26. With the dashed line and *tooltip* visible on the screen, take your hand off the mouse, so you do not accidentally move it, and type: **8″** and then press **Enter**.

   TIP: *Remember, you have to type the inch symbol; Revit always assumes you mean feet unless you specify otherwise. A future lesson will review the input options in more detail.*

You have just drawn a line with a precise length and angle!

27. Use the **Measure** tool to verify it was drawn correctly. Click *Modify* → *Measure* → *Measure (down arrow)* → *Measure Between Two References*

28. Use the **Zoom In Region** tool to enlarge the view of the 8″ line; via the *Navigation Bar* (image to right).

29. Now use the **Zoom to Fit** or **Previous Pan/Zoom** tools so that both lines are visible again.

Draw a 600′ Line:

30. Select the **Detail Line** tool and pick a point in the lower right corner of the drawing window.

31. Move the cursor straight up from your first point so that the line snaps to the vertical and the dashed line appears (Figure 3-1.12).

32. With the dashed line and *tooltip* visible on the screen, take your hand off the mouse so you do not accidentally move it; type: **600** and then press **Enter**.

> **TIP #1:** *Notice this time you did not have to type the foot symbol (′).*

FIGURE 3-1.12 Drawing another Detail Line; 600′-0″ vertical line – lower right

> **TIP #2:** *You do not need to get the temporary dimension close to reading 600′; the temporary dimension is ignored when you type in a value.*

33. Press the **Esc** key twice to exit the *Detail Line* tool and return to the *Modify* mode.

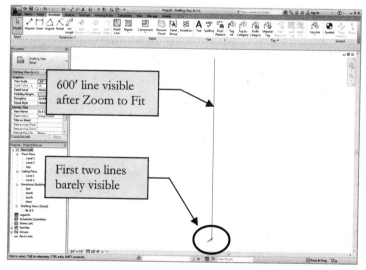

600′ line visible after Zoom to Fit

First two lines barely visible

Because the visible portion of the drawing area is only about 16′ tall, you obviously would not expect to see a 600′ line. You need the change the drawing's magnification by zooming out to see it.

34. Use **Zoom to Fit** to see the entire drawing (Figure 3-1.13).

FIGURE 3-1.13 Detail view with three lines

Drawing Shapes:

Revit provides several tools to draw common shapes like squares, rectangles, circles and ellipses. These tools can be found on the *Ribbon* while the *Detail Line* tool is active. You will take a look at *Rectangle* and *Circle* now.

Creating a Rectangle:

35. Use **Previous Pan/Zoom**, or *Zoom Region*, to get back to the original view where the diagonal line spans the screen.

36. Select the **Detail Line** tool.

Notice the *Ribbon, Options Bar* and *Properties Palette* have changed to show various options related to *Detail Lines* (Figure 3-1.14).

FIGURE 3-1.14 Place Detail Lines Tab on Ribbon

37. Select the **Rectangle** tool from the *Ribbon*.

   TIP: Hover your cursor over the icon to see tooltip until you learn what tools the icons represent.

38. Pick the "**first corner point**" somewhere near the lower center of the drawing window (Figure 3-1.15).

Notice the temporary dimensions are displaying a dimension for both the width and height. At this point you can pick a point on the screen, trying to get the dimensions correct before clicking the mouse button. If you do not get the rectangle drawn correctly, you can click on each dimension-text and change the dimension while the temporary dimensions are displayed; see the next two steps for the rectangle dimensions.

39. Draw a 2'-8" x 4'-4" rectangle using the temporary dimensions displayed on the screen; if you do not draw it correctly do the following:

   a. Click the dimension-text for the horizontal line, then type **2'-8"** and then press **Enter**.

   b. Type **4'-4"** and then press **Enter** for the vertical dimension.

FIGURE 3-1.15 Drawing with Rectangle added

Creating a Circle:

40. With the *Detail Line* tool active, select **Circle** from the *Ribbon* (Figure 3-1.16).

41. You are now prompted to pick the center point for the circle; pick a point approximately as shown in (Figure 3-1.15).

FIGURE 3-1.16 Detail Line shapes

You should now see a dynamic circle and a temporary dimension attached to your cursor, which allows you to visually specify the circle's size. Move your mouse around to see that you could arbitrarily pick a point on the screen to create a quick circle if needed, then proceed to Step 42 where you will draw a circle with a radius of 1'-6⅝".

42. Type **1 6 5/8** and then press **Enter** (Figure 3-1.17).

FIGURE 3-1.17   Drawing with Circle added

Notice in the image above the *Detail Line* is still active because the *contextual tab,* **Modify |**
Place Detail Lines, is visible and the *Status Bar* is prompting to "Click to enter circle
center". You need to press **Esc** or click *Modify* to cancel the command; clicking another
command will also cancel the current command.

43. **Select the circle** and notice a temporary
    dimension appears, indicating the circle's radius.
    Press **Esc** to unselect it (Figure 3-1.18).

    *TIP: This temporary dimension can be used to change the radius
    of the circle while the circle is selected.*

44. **Save** your project as "**ex3-1.rvt**".

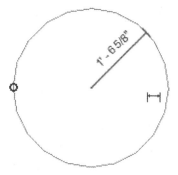

FIGURE 3-1.18
Circle selected

Exercise 3-2:
Snaps

Snaps are tools that allow you to accurately pick a point on an element. For example: when drawing a line you can use *Object Snap* to select, as the start-point, the endpoint or midpoint of another line or wall.

This feature is absolutely critical to drawing accurate technical drawings. Using this feature allows you to be confident you are creating perfect intersections, corners, etc. (Figure 3-2.1).

Object Snaps Options:

You can use *Object Snaps* in one of two ways.

o "Normal" mode
o "Temporary Override" mode

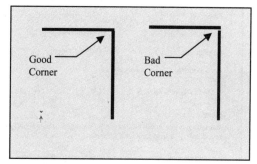

FIGURE 3-2.1 Typical problem when *Snaps* are not used

"Normal" *OSNAP* mode is a feature that constantly scans the area near your cursor when Revit is looking for user input. You can configure which types of points to look for.

NOTE: *The term "normal" is not a Revit term, rather it is simply a description used in this book to differentiate this portion of the Snaps feature from the Temporary Override portion discussed next.*

Using a "Temporary Override" *Object Snap* for individual pick-points allows you to quickly select a particular point on an element. This option will temporarily disable the other *Object Snap* settings, which means you tell Revit to just look for the endpoint on an object, for the next pick-point only, rather than the three or four types being scanned for by the "normal" *Object Snaps* feature.

Overview of the Snaps Dialog Box:

Revit provides a *Snaps* dialog box where you specify which *Object Snaps* you want enabled. Next you will take a look at it.

1. Open project **Ex3-1** and select **Manage → Settings → Snaps**.

Snaps

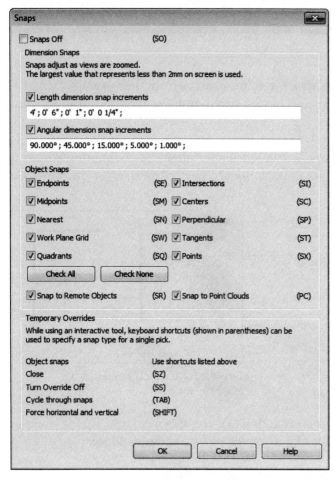

FIGURE 3-2.2 Snaps dialog box; default settings

You should now see the *Snaps* dialog box (Figure 3-2.2). Take a minute to study the various settings that you can control with this dialog box. Notice the check box at the top that allows you to turn this feature off completely.

Dimension Snaps

This controls the automatic dimensions that Revit suggests when you are drawing. Following the given format you could add or remove increments. If you are zoomed in close, only the smaller increments are used.

Object Snaps

This controls the "normal" *Object Snaps* that Revit scans for while you are drawing. Unchecking an item tells Revit not to scan for it anymore. Currently, all *Object Snaps* are enabled (Figure 3-2.2).

Temporary Overrides

This area is really just information on how to use Temporary Overrides.

While drawing you will occasionally want to tell Revit you only want to *Snap* to an Endpoint for the next pick. Instead of opening the *Snaps* dialog and un-checking every *Object Snap* except for Endpoint, you can specify a *Temporary Override* for the next pick. You do this by typing the two letters, in parentheses, in the *Object Snaps* area of the *Snaps* dialog (Figure 3-2.2).

2. Make sure the *Snaps Off* option is unchecked in the upper-left corner of the dialog box; this turns Snaps completely off.

3. Click on the **Check All** button to make sure all *Snaps* are checked.

4. Click **OK** to close the *Snaps* dialog box.

Understanding Snap Symbols:

Again, you should be well aware of the *Object Snap* symbols that Revit displays as you move your cursor about the drawing window, while you are in a tool like *Wall* and Revit is awaiting your input or pick-point.

If you hold your cursor still for a moment, while a snap symbol is displayed, a tooltip will appear on the screen. However, when you become familiar with the snap symbols you can pick sooner, rather than waiting for the tooltip to display (Figure 3-2.3).

The TAB key cycles through the available snaps near your cursor.

Finally, typing **SO** turns all snaps off for one pick.

Symbol	Position	Keyboard Shortcut
✕	Intersection	SI
☐	Endpoint	SE
△	Midpoint	SM
○	Center	SC
✕	Nearest	SN
┗	Perpendicular	SP
♋	Tangent	ST

FIGURE 3-2.3 Snap symbols

FYI: The Snaps shown in Figure 3-2.2 are for Revit in general, not just the current project. This is convenient; you don't have to adjust to your favorite settings for each Project or View, existing or new.

Setting Object Snaps:

You can set Revit to have just one or all Snaps running at the same time. Let us say you have Endpoint and Midpoint set to be running. While using the *Wall* tool, you move your cursor near an existing wall. When the cursor is near the end of the wall you will see the Endpoint symbol show up, when you move the cursor towards the middle of the line you will see the Midpoint symbol show up.

The next step shows you how to tell Revit which Object Snaps you want it to look for.

5. First you will save a new copy of your project.

6. Select **Application Menu → Save-As → Project** and name the project **ex3-2.rvt**.

7. As discussed previously, open the ***Snaps*** dialog box.

8. Make sure only the following *Snaps* are checked:
   a. Endpoints
   b. Midpoints
   c. Centers
   d. Intersections
   e. Perpendicular

9. Click **OK** to close the dialog box.

For More Information:

For more on using Snaps, search Revit's *Help System* for **Snaps**. Then double-click **Snap Points** or any other items found by the search.

Now that you have the *Snaps* adjusted, you will give this feature a try.

10. Using the ***Detail Line*** tool, move your cursor to the lower-left portion of the diagonal line (Figure 3-2.4).

11. Hover the cursor over the line's endpoint (without picking); when you see the *Endpoint* symbol you can click to select that point.

Just So You Know

It is important that you see the *OSNAP* symbol before clicking. Also, once you see the symbol you should be careful not to move the mouse too much.

These steps will help to ensure accurate selections.

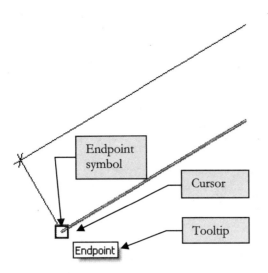

FIGURE 3-2.4 Endpoint SNAP symbol visible

While still in the Detail Line tool you will draw lines using *Snaps* to sketch accurately.

12. Draw the additional lines shown in **Figure 3-2.5** using the appropriate *Object Snap*, changing the selected Snaps as required to select the required points.

TIP #1: At any point while the Line tool is active, you can open the SNAP dialog box and adjust its settings. This will not cancel the Line command.

TIP #2: Also, remember you can press Tab to cycle through the various snap options below or near your cursor.

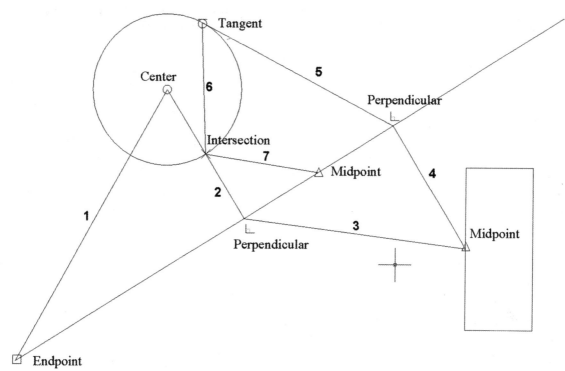

FIGURE 3-2.5 Lines to draw and Snap to use

13. **Save** your project.

You drawing might look slightly different depending on where you drew the rectangle and circle in the previous steps.

This is a Residential Example?

OK, this is not really an architectural example yet. However, the point here is to focus on the fundamental concepts and not architecture just yet.

Save Reminders:

Revit is configured to remind you to save every 30 minutes so you do not lose any work (Figure 3-2.6).

It is recommended that you do not simply click *Cancel*, but do click the **Save the project** option.

FIGURE 3-2.6 Save reminder

Exercise 3-3:
Edit Tools

The *edit tools* are used often in Revit. A lot of time is spent tweaking designs and making code and client related revisions.

Example: you use the *design tools* (e.g., Walls, Doors, Windows) to initially draw the project. Then you use the *edit tools* to *Move* a wall so a room becomes larger, *Mirror* a cabinet so it faces in a different direction, or *Rotate* the furniture per the owner's instructions.

FIGURE 3-3.1 Modify panel

You will usually access the various edit tools from the Modify menu *or* Modify contextual tab on the *Ribbon*. You can probably visualize what most of the commands do by the graphics on the icons; see Figure 3-3.1. When you hover over an icon, the tool name will appear. The two letters shown to the right is its keyboard shortcut; pressing those two keys, one at a time, activates that tool.

In this exercise you will get a brief overview of a few of the edit tools by manipulating the tangled web of lines you have previously drawn.

1. **Open** project **ex3-2.rvt** from the previous lesson.

2. **Save-As** "**ex3-3.rvt**".

FYI: You will notice that instructions or tools that have already been covered in this book will have less "step-by-step" instruction.

Delete Tool:

It is no surprise that the *Delete* tool is a necessity; things change and mistakes are made. You can *Delete* one element at a time or several. Deleting elements is very easy; you select the elements, and then pick the *Delete* icon. You will try this on two lines in your drawing.

3. While holding the **Ctrl** key, select the lines identified in **Figure 3-3.2**.

   TIP: See the section below Figure 3-3.2 on Selecting Entities.

4. Select **Delete** from the *Ribbon* (or press the **Delete** key on the keyboard).

The lines are now deleted from the project.

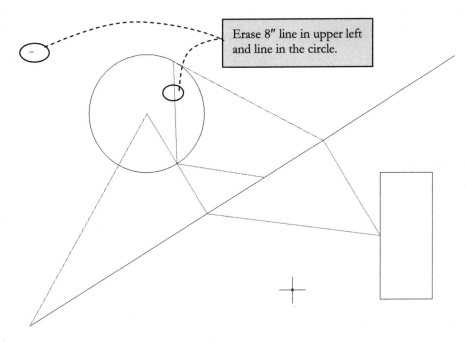

Erase 8″ line in upper left and line in the circle.

FIGURE 3-3.2 Lines to be erased

Selecting Objects:

At this time we will digress and take a quick look at the various techniques for selecting entities in Revit. Most tools work the same when it comes to selecting elements.

When selecting entities, you have two primary ways to select them:
- o Individually select entities one at a time
- o Select several entities at a time with a window

You can use one or a combination of both methods to select elements when using the *Copy* tool.

<u>Individual Selections:</u>
When prompted to select entities to copy or delete, for example, you simple move the cursor over the element and click; holding the **Ctrl**, key you can select multiple objects. Then you typically click the tool you wish to use on the selected items. Press **Shift** and click on an item to subtract it from the current selection set.

Continued on next page

<u>Window Selections</u>:
Similarly, you can pick a *window* around several elements to select them all at once. To select a *window*, rather than selecting an object as previously described, you select one corner of the *window* you wish to define. That is, you pick a point in "space" and hold the mouse button down. Now, as you move the mouse you will see a rectangle on the screen that represents the windowed area you are selecting; when the *window* encompasses the elements you wish to select, release the mouse.

You actually have two types of windows you can select. One is called a **window** and the other is called a **crossing window**.

Window:
This option allows you to select only the objects that are completely within the *window*. Any lines that extend out of the *window* are not selected.

Crossing Window:
This option allows you to select all the entities that are completely within the *window* and any that extend outside the *window*.

Using Window versus Crossing Window:
To select a *window* you simply pick and drag from left to right to form a rectangle (Figure 3-3.3a).

Conversely, to select a *crossing window*, you pick and drag from right to left to define the two diagonal points of the window (Figure 3-3.3b).

Selecting a chain of lines (hover, tab, click):
Revit provides a quick and easy way to select a chain of lines, that is, a series of lines (or walls) whose endpoints are perfectly aligned. You simply hover your cursor over one line so it highlights, then press the Tab key once, and then click the mouse button. This trick can be used to quickly select all the exterior walls on a building, for example.

Turning off **Press & Drag** on the *Status Bar* helps to avoid accidentally clicking directly on an element and moving it rather than starting the intended first corner of a selection window.

Remember, all these draw, modify and select tools have direct application to working with Revit's 3D building components, not just the 2D geometry being covered in this chapter.

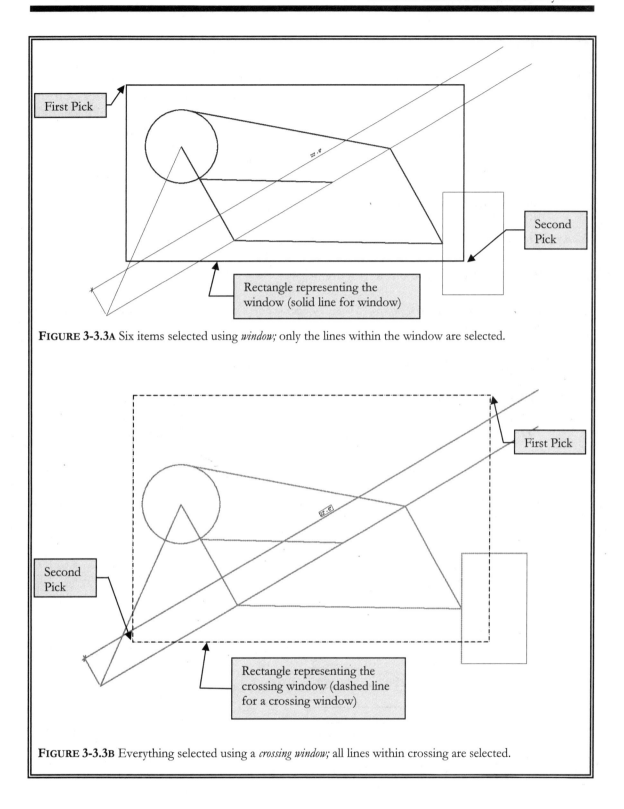

FIGURE 3-3.3A Six items selected using *window;* only the lines within the window are selected.

FIGURE 3-3.3B Everything selected using a *crossing window;* all lines within crossing are selected.

Copy Tool:

The *Copy* tool allows you to accurately duplicate an element(s). You select the items you want to copy and then pick two points that represent an imaginary vector, which provides both length and angle, defining the path used to copy the object. You can also type in the length if there are no convenient points to pick in the drawing. You will try both methods next.

5. **Select the circle**.

6. Select **Copy** from the *Ribbon*.

Notice the prompt at the bottom: Click to enter move start point.

7. Pick the **center** of the **circle** (Figure 3-3.4).

> *FYI: You actually have three different Snaps you can use here: Center, Endpoint and Intersection. All occur at the exact same point.*

Notice the prompt at the bottom: Click to enter move end point.

8. Pick the **endpoint** of the angled line in the lower left corner (Figure 3-3.4).

> *FYI: If you want to make several copies of the circle, select* Multiple *on the* Options Bar.

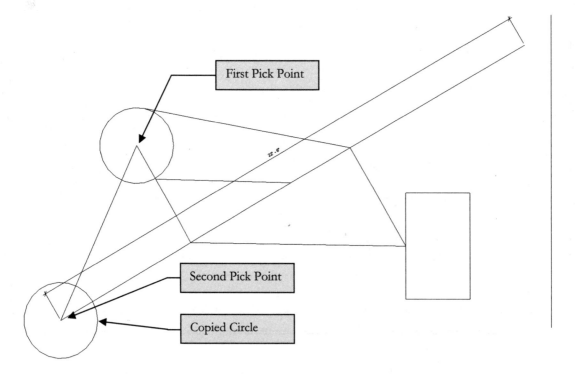

FIGURE 3-3.4 Copied circle; also indicates points selected

9. **Select the rectangle** *(all four lines).*

    TIP: Try the "hover, tab, click" method discussed on page 3-22.

10. Select **Copy**.

11. Pick an arbitrary point on the screen. In this scenario it makes no difference where you pick; you will see why in a moment.

At this point you will move the mouse in the direction you want to copy the rectangle, until the correct angle is displayed, and then type in the distance, rather than picking a second point on the screen.

12. Move the mouse towards the upper right until 45 degrees displays, then type **6'** and then press **Enter** (Figure 3-3.5).

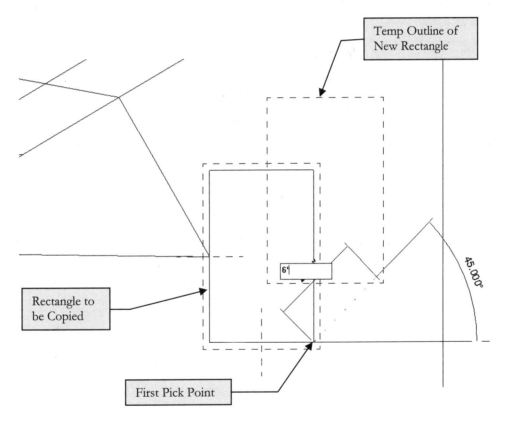

FIGURE 3-3.5 Copying rectangle; angle set visually and distance typed in

NOTE: Your drawing may look a little different than this one because your drawing is not completely to scale.

Move Tool:

The *Move* tool works exactly like the *Copy* tool except, of course, you move the element(s) rather than copy it. Given the similarity to the previous tool covered, the *Move* tool will not be covered now. You are encouraged to try it yourself; just Undo your experiments before proceeding.

Rotate Tool:

With the *Rotate* tool, you can arbitrarily or accurately rotate one or more objects in your drawing. When you need to rotate accurately, you can pick points that define the angle, assuming points exist in the drawing to pick, or you can type a specific angle.

Rotate involves the following steps:
- Select element(s) to be rotated
- Select *Rotate*
- Determine if the Center of Rotation symbol is where you want it.
  - If you want to move it:
    - Simply drag it, or
    - Click *Place* on the *Options Bar*
- Select a point to define a reference line and begin rotation.
- Pick a second point using one of the following methods:
  - By selecting other objects or using the graphic angle display *or*
  - You can type an angle and press **Enter**.

13. **Select the new rectangle** you just copied *(all four lines)*.

14. Select **Rotate** on the *Ribbon*.

Notice that the "Center of Rotation" grip, by default, is located in the center of the selected elements. This is the point about which the rotation will occur. See Figure 3-3.6.

You will not change the "Center of Rotation" at this time.

15. Pick a point directly to the right of the "Center of Rotation" grip; this tells Revit you want to rotate the rectangle relative to the horizontal plane (Figure 3-3.6).

Now, as you move your mouse up or down, you will see the temporary angle dimension displayed. You can move the mouse until the desired angle is displayed and then click to complete the rotation, or you can type the desired angle and then press **Enter**. If you recall, the *Snaps* dialog box controls the increments of the angles that Revit displays; they are all whole numbers. So if you need to rotate something 22.45 degrees, you must type it as Revit will never display that number as an option.

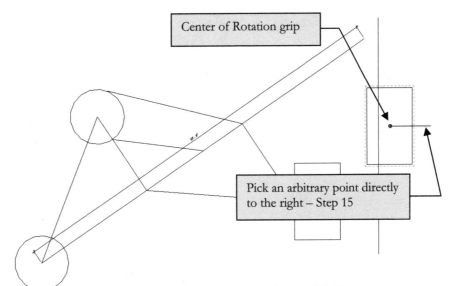

FIGURE 3-3.6 Rotate tool; first step – select lines and then click Rotate

16. Move the mouse up and to the left until 90 degrees is displayed and then click to complete the rotation (Figure 3-3.7).

FIGURE 3-3.7 Rotate tool; last step – select angle visually or type angle

The previous steps just rotated the rectangle 90 degrees counter-clockwise about its center point (Figure 3-3.8).

17. Select the **Undo** icon.

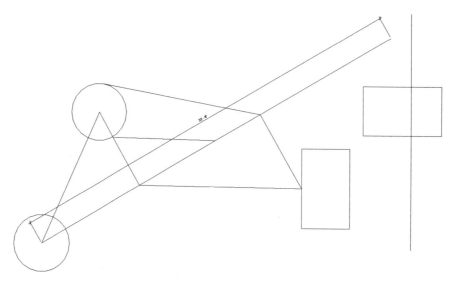

FIGURE 3-3.8 Rotate tool; rectangle rotated about its center point

Now you will do the same thing, except with a different angle and "Center of Rotation".

18. **Select the rectangle** and then pick **Rotate**.

19. Click and drag the "Center or Rotation" grip to the left and *Snap* to the midpoint of the vertical line (Figure 3-3.9).

20. Pick a point to the right, creating a horizontal reference line.

21. Start moving your mouse downward, then type **22.5** and then press **Enter** (Figure 3-3.10).

The rectangle is now rotated 22.5 degrees in the clockwise direction (Figure 3-3.11).

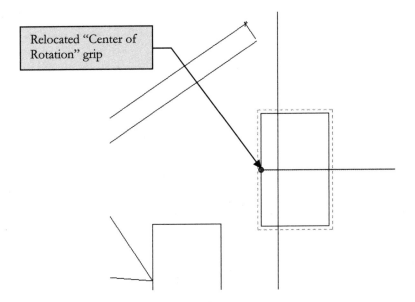

Relocated "Center of Rotation" grip

FIGURE 3-3.9 Rotate tool; relocated Center of Rotation grip

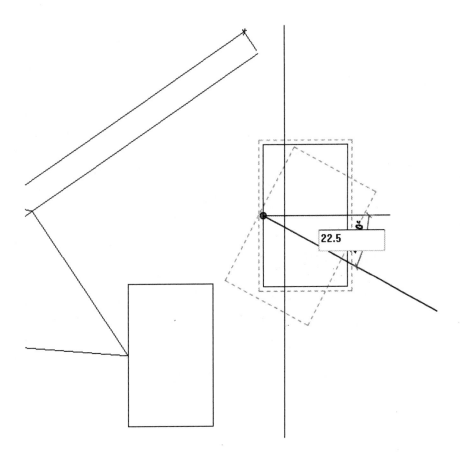

22.5

FIGURE 3-3.10 Rotate tool; typing in exact angle

FIGURE 3-3.11 Rotate tool; rectangle rotated 22.5 degrees

Scale Tool:

The *Scale* tool has steps similar to the *Rotate* tool. First you select what you want to scale or resize, specify a scale factor and then you pick the base point. The scale factor can be provided by picks on the screen or entering a numerical scale factor (e.g., 2 or .5, where 2 would be twice the original size and .5 would be half the original size).

Next you will use the *Scale* tool to adjust the size of the circle near the bottom.

Before you resize the circle, you should use the *Modify* tool/mode to note the **diameter** of the circle. Select the circle and view its temporary dimensions. After resizing the circle, you will refer back to the temporary dimensions to note the change. This step is meant to teach you how to verify the accuracy and dimensions of entities in Revit.

22. Select the bottom circle.

23. Select the **Scale** icon from the *Ribbon*.

On the *Options Bar* you will specify a numeric scale factor of .5 to resize the circle to half its original size.

24. Click **Numerical** and then type **.5** in the textbox *(see the Options Bar above)*.

You are now prompted: **Click to enter origin** on the *Status Bar*. This is the base point about which the circle will be scaled; see examples in Figure 3-3.13 on the next page.

25. Click the center of the circle.

You just used the *Scale* tool to change in the size of the circle from 1'-6 5/8" to 9 5/16" radius. A Scale Factor of .5 reduces the entities to half their original scale (Figure 3-3.12).

Selecting the Correct Center of Rotation *(Base Point)*:

You need to select the appropriate *Center of Rotation*, or Base Point, for both the *Scale* and *Rotate* commands to get the results desired. A few examples are shown in Figure 3-3.13. The dashed line indicates the original position of the entity being modified. The black dot indicates the base point selected.

FIGURE 3-3.12 Resize circle; notice it is half the size of the other circle

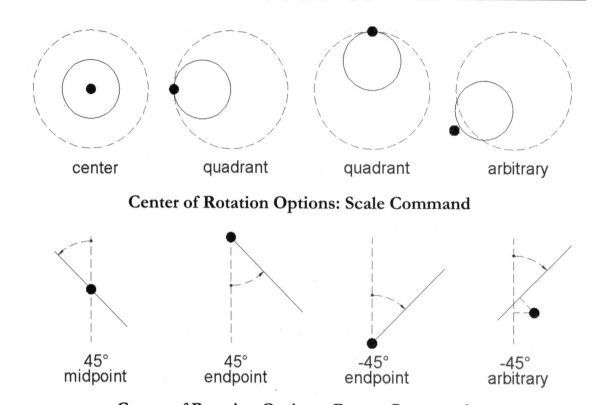

Center of Rotation Options: Scale Command

Center of Rotation Options: Rotate Command

FIGURE 3-3.13 Center of Rotation Options and the various results

This will conclude the brief tour of the *Edit* tools. Do not forget, even though you are editing 2D lines, the edit tools work the same way on 3D elements such as walls, floors, roofs, etc. Exception: you cannot *Scale* walls, doors, etc.; these objects have to be modified by other methods. You would not typically change the door thickness when changing its width and height as would happen if you could use the *Scale* tool on it.

As you surely noticed, the *Modify* panel on the Ribbon has a few other tools that have not been investigated yet. Many of these will be covered later in this book.

26. **Save** the project. Your project should already be named "ex3-3.rvt" per Step 2 above.

Carter Residence

Exercise 3-4:
Annotations

Annotations, or text and notes, allow the designer and technician to accurately describe the drawing. Here you will take a quick look at this feature set.

Annotations:

Adding annotations to a drawing can be as essential as the drawing itself. Often the notes describe a part of the drawing that would be difficult to discern from the drawing alone.

For example: a wall framing drawing showing a bolt may not indicate, graphically, how many bolts are needed or at what spacing. The note might say *"5/8" anchor bolt at 24" O.C."*

Next you will add text to your drawing.

1. **Open** project **ex3-3.rvt** from the previous lesson.

2. **Save-As "ex3-4.rvt"**.

3. Use **Zoom** if required to see the entire drawing, except for the 600' line which can run off the screen.

4. Select **Annotate → Text → Text**.

   Note that the *Model Text* tool on the *Home* tab is only for drawing 3D text – *Drafting Views* are only 2D so that command is not even an option currently.

Text

From the *Text* icon tooltip (see image to the right) you can see that the keyboard shortcut for the *Text* tool is **TX**. Thus, at any time you can type T and then X to activate the *Text* tool; if you have another command active, Revit will cancel it.

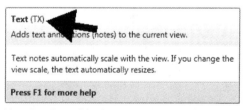

Text icon's tooltip (hover cursor over icon)

Experienced and efficient designers use a combination of keyboard shortcuts and mouse clicks to save time. For example, while your left hand is typing TX, your right hand can be moving toward the location where you want to insert the text. This process is generally more efficient than switching between tabs on the *Ribbon* and clicking icons, or fly-out icons which require yet another click of the mouse.

Notice the current *prompt* on the *Status Bar* at the bottom of the screen; you are asked to "Click to start text or click and drag rectangle to create text wrapping text". By clicking on the screen you create one line of text, starting at the point picked, and press **Enter** to create additional lines. By clicking and dragging a rectangle you specify a window, primarily for the width, which causes Revit to automatically move text to the next line. When the text no longer fits within the window it is pushed below, or what is called "text wrapping" (Figure 3-4.1).

FIGURE 3-4.1 Status Bar while Text tool is active

You should also notice the various text options available on the *Ribbon* while the *Text* tool is active (Figure 3-4.2). You have two text heights loaded from the template file you started with, text justification icons (Left, Center, Right) and the option to attach leaders, or pointing arrows, to your drawings. The *Text* tool will be covered in more detail later in this book.

FYI: The text heights shown (i.e., ¼", 3/32" via Type Selector) are heights the text will be when printed on paper, regardless of the view scale.

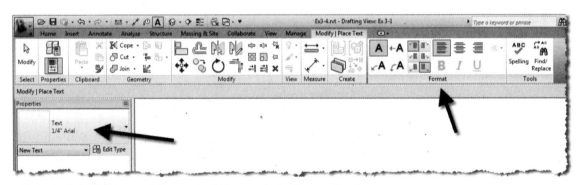

FIGURE 3-4.2 Ribbon and Properties Palette with the Text tool active

5.   Pick a point in the upper left portion of the view as shown in Figure 3-4.3.

6.   Type "**Learning Revit Architecture is fun!**"

7.   Click anywhere in the view, except on the active text, to finish the *Text* command; pressing **Enter** will only add new lines.

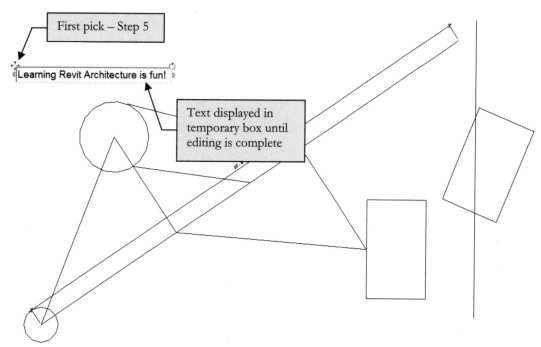

FIGURE 3-4.3 Text tool; picking first point and typing text.

As soon as you complete the text edit, the text will still be selected and the *Move* and *Rotate* symbols will be displayed near the text; this allows you to more quickly *Move* or *Rotate* the text after it is typed (Figure 3-4.4).

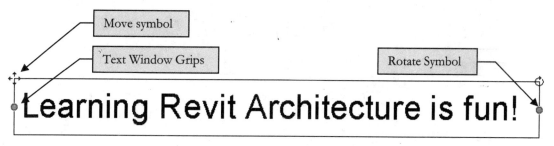

FIGURE 3-4.4 Text tool; text typed with Move and Rotate symbols showing.

8. Finish the *Text* tool completely by pressing *Modify* or clicking in the drawing.

TIP: Notice that the text is no longer selected and the symbols are gone; the contextual tab also disappears on the Ribbon.

Your text should generally look similar to Figure 3-4.5.

9. Print your drawing; refer back to page 2-15 for basic printing information. Your print should fit the page and look similar to Figure 3-4.5.

10. **Save** your project.

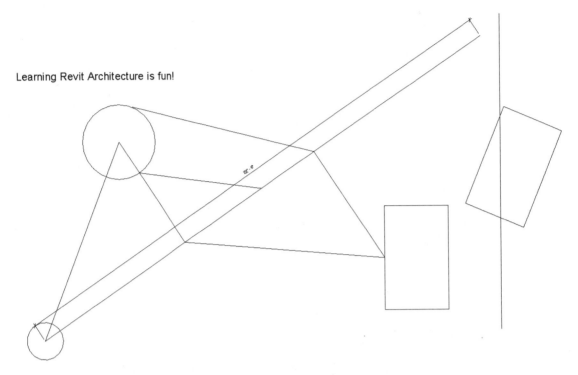

Learning Revit Architecture is fun!

FIGURE 3-4.5 Text tool; text added to current view

Carter Residence

Images courtesy of LHB
www.LHBcorp.com

Self-Exam:

The following questions can be used as a way to check your knowledge of this lesson. The answers can be found at the bottom of the page.

1. Revit is only accurate to three decimal places. (T/F)

2. The triangular shaped Snap symbol represents the Midpoint snap. (T/F)

3. You can move or rotate text via its modify symbols when text is selected. (T/F)

4. Use the _____ tool to duplicate objects.

5. When selecting objects, use the _____ _____ to select all the objects in the selection window and all objects that extend through it.

Review Questions:

The following questions may be assigned by your instructor as a way to assess your knowledge of this section. Your instructor has the answers to the review questions.

1. Revit is a raster based program. (T/F)

2. The "Center of Rotation" you select for the *Rotate* and *Scale* commands is not important. (T/F)

3. Entering 16 for a distance, actually means 16'-0" to Revit. (T/F)

4. Use the *Detail Line* tool, with _____ selected on the *Ribbon*, to create squares.

5. You can change the height of the text from the *Type Selector*. (T/F)

6. Pressing the _____ key cycles you through the snap options.

7. Where do the two predefined text heights come from? _____

8. Specifying degrees with the *Rotate* tool, you must type the number when Revit does not display the number you want, the increments shown on-screen are set in the

    _____ dialog box.

9. List all the Snap points available on a circle (ex. Line: endpoint, midpoint,

    nearest) _____.

10. The Snaps Off option must not be checked in the Snaps dialog box too automatically and accurately select snap points while drawing. (T/F)

Notes:

Lesson 4
Drawing 2D Architectural Objects:

This lesson is meant to give you practice drawing in Autodesk® Revit® Architecture; while doing so you will become familiar with the various shapes and sizes of the more common symbols used in a residential design.

Do not forget that learning to draw 2D is important in Autodesk Revit Architecture. You often define 3D items, like walls, in 2D floor plans, while Autodesk Revit Architecture takes care of the third dimension automatically. Additionally, you will often want to embellish a view with 2D lines; for example, the exterior elevation, which is a 2D projection of a 3D model.

If you have used other design programs, like AutoCAD or AutoCAD Architecture, these lessons will help you understand the different way to draw using Autodesk Revit Architecture, a more visual or graphic based input system.

Each drawing will be created in its own *Drafting View*.

For some of the symbols to be drawn, you will have step-by-step instruction and a study on a particular tool that would be useful in the creation of that object. Other symbols to be drawn are for practice by way of repetition and do not provide step by step instruction.

Do NOT draw the dimensions; they are for reference only.

Exercise 4-1:
Sketching Rectilinear Objects

Overview:

All the objects you will draw in this exercise consist entirely of straight lines, either orthogonal or angular.

As previously mentioned, all the objects MUST BE drawn in SEPERATE *Drafting Views*. Each object will have a specific name provided, which is to be used to name the *Drafting View*. All views will be created in one Project file which should be saved in your personal folder created for this course.

view name: **Bookcase**

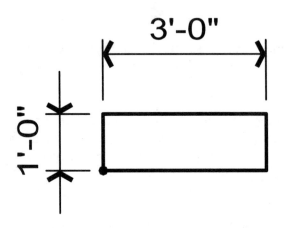

This is a simple rectangle that represents the size of a bookcase.

1. **Open** a new project; **Save** the project as **Ex4-1.rvt**.

2. Create a new *Drafting View* named Bookcase (Figure 4-1.1) *(from the View tab)*.

3. Select **Detail Line** from the *Annotate* tab.

By default, the current line thickness is set to *Thin Lines*. You can see this on the *Ribbon* when the *Detail Line* tool is active. You will change this to *Medium* next.

4. Set the line thickness to **Medium Lines** (Figure 4-1.2; also see image to the right).

> *NOTE: Use this setting for all the drawings in this chapter.*

5. Click the **Rectangle** button on the *Ribbon* (Figure 4-1.2).

6. **Draw a rectangle**, per the dimensions shown above, generally in the center of the drawing window.

> *TIP: You should be able to accurately draw the rectangle using the temporary dimensions; if not, click on the dimension text to change it.*

FIGURE 4-1.1 New Drafting View dialog

FIGURE 4-1.2 Ribbon and Options Bar; Medium Lines and Rectangle selected

view name: **Coffee Table**

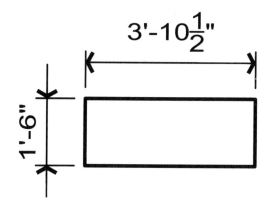

7. Create a new *Drafting View*.

   NOTE: *This step will be assumed for the rest of the drawings in this exercise.*

8. Similar to the steps listed above, plus the suggestions mentioned below, create the coffee table shown to the left.

Draw the rectangle as closely as possible using the visual aids; you should be able to get the 1'-6" dimension correct. Then click on the text for the temporary horizontal dimension and type in 3'-10 1/2".

Entering fractions: the 3'-10½" can be entered in one of four ways.

o	3 10.5	*Notice there is a space between the feet and inches.*
o	3 10 1/2	*Two spaces separate the feet, inches and fractions.*
o	0 46.5	*This is all in inches; that is 3'-10½" = 46.5".*
o	46.5"	*Omit the feet and use the inches symbol.*

view name: **Desk-1**

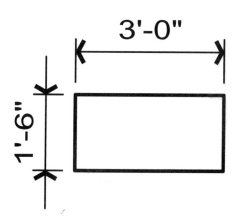

9. Draw the *Desk* in its own view, similar to the steps outlined above.

TIP: *You should double-check your drawing's dimensions using the Measure tool. Pick the icon from the Modify tab and then pick two points. A temporary dimension will display.*

4-3

view name: **Night Table**

Obviously you could draw this quickly per the previous examples. However, you will take a look at copying a *Drafting View* and then modifying an existing drawing.

You will use the *Move* tool to stretch the 3'-0" wide desk down to a 1'-6" wide night table.

First you will look at *Drafting Views* and how they are organized in the *Project Browser*, and then you will copy the *Desk-1 Drafting View* to start the *Night Table* drawing/view.

10. Locate the **Drafting Views** section in the *Project Browser* and expand it by clicking on the "plus" symbol.

Notice that the three views you previously created are listed (Figure 4-1.3). The *Desk-1* view is shown with bold text because it is the current view. All *Drafting Views* are listed here and can be renamed, copied or deleted at anytime by right-clicking on the item in the list. You will copy the *Desk-1* view next.

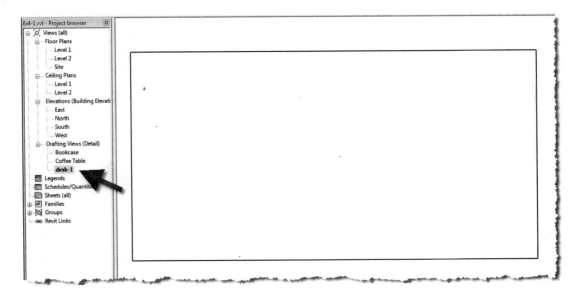

FIGURE 4-1.3 Project Browser: Drafting Views section expanded

11. Right-click on the *Desk-1* view (Figure 4-1.4).

Next you will select *Duplicate with Detailing* which will copy the *View* and the *View's* contents, whereas the *Duplicate* option will only copy the *View* and its settings but without any line work.

12. Select **Duplicate View →
    Duplicate with Detailing** from the pop-up menu (Figure 4-1.4).

You now have a new View named *Copy of Desk-1* in the *Drafting Views* list. This *View* is open and current.

Figure 4-1.4 Drafting Views list –
Right click on Desk-1 view for menu

13. Right-click on the new view name, ***Copy of Desk-1***, and select **Rename** from the pop-up menu.

14. Type **Night Table** and then click **OK** (Figure 4-1.5).

FIGURE **4-1.5** Rename View dialog – Night Table entered

You are now ready to modify the copy of the *Desk-1* linework. You will use the *Move* tool to change the location of one of the vertical lines, which will cause the two horizontal lines to stretch with it. Autodesk Revit Architecture *Detail Lines* automatically have a parametric relationship to adjacent lines when their endpoints touch them.

15. Select the vertical line on the right and then click the **Move** icon on the *Ribbon*.

16. Pick the midpoint of the vertical line, then move the mouse 1'-6" to the left and click again (Figure 4-1.6).

> **Step 1:**
> Select line and then click the Move icon

1'-6"

> **Step 3:**
> Move to left 1'-6" with Horiz. snap and click

> **Step 2:**
> Click the midpoint of the vertical line

FIGURE 4-1.6 Move tool used to stretch a rectangle

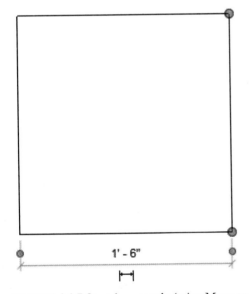

1' - 6"

FIGURE 4-1.7 Stretch rectangle (using Move tool)

The rectangle is now resized, or stretched, to be half its original width.

You will notice that the horizontal lines automatically adjusted.

Revit assumes a special relationship between a line being edited and any line whose endpoint is directly touching it.

TIP: *You can select "Disjoin" on the Options Bar while in the Move command if you don't want other lines to move or stretch with it. You will not do that here though.*

17. **Save** your project.

view name: **Dresser-1**

18. Draw the dresser using the following tip:

    TIP: *Simply draw two rectangles. Move the smaller rectangle into place using the Move tool and Snaps.*

view name: **Dresser-2**

19. Draw this smaller dresser.

view name: **Desk-2**

20. Draw this desk in the same way you drew *Dresser-1*.

view name: **File Cabinet**

21. Draw this file cabinet.

view name: **Chair-1**

22. Draw this chair per the following tips:

Draw the 2′x2′ square first, and then draw three separate rectangles as shown to the right. Move them into place with *Move* and *Snaps*. Next, delete the extra lines so your drawing looks like the one shown on the left. Pay close attention to the dimensions!

view name: **Sofa**

23. *Duplicate* and *Rename* the *Chair-1* view to start this drawing.

TIP: See the next page for more information on creating this drawing.

You can create the *Sofa* in a similar way that you created the *Night Table*; that is, you will use the *Move* tool. Rather than selecting one vertical line, however, you will select all the lines on one side of the chair.

You can select all the lines on one side in a single step, rather than clicking each one individually while holding the Ctrl key. You will select using a *window* selection, not a *crossing window* selection.

24. **Select** all the lines on the right side (Figure 4-1.8).

TIP: Pick from left to right for a window *selection.*

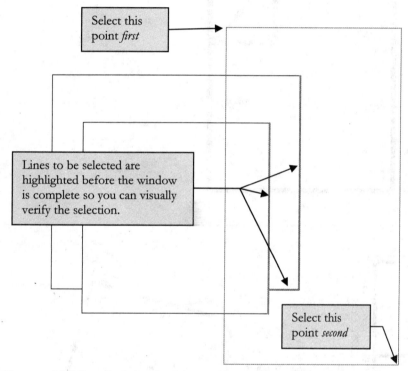

Select this point *first*

Lines to be selected are highlighted before the window is complete so you can visually verify the selection.

Select this point *second*

FIGURE 4-1.8 Stretch chair using Move tool

25. Use the ***Move*** tool to extend the chair into a sofa.

TIP: The difference between the chair width and the sofa width is the distance the lines are to be moved.

You have just successfully transformed the chair into a sofa! Do not forget to *Save* often to avoid losing work. Also, use the *Measure* tool to verify your drawing's accuracy.

view name: **Bed-Double.dwg**

26. Draw this bed using lines and rectangles; the exact sizes of items not dimensioned are not important.

FIGURE 4-1.9 Floor Plan example using similar furniture to that drawn in this exercise.

Image courtesy of Stanius Johnson Architects
www.staniusjohnson.com

Exercise 4-2:
Sketching Objects With Curves

Similar to the previous exercise, you will draw several shapes; this time the shapes will have curves in them.

You will look at the various commands that allow you to create curves, like *Arc*, *Circle* and *Fillet*.

Again, you will not draw the dimensions as they are for reference only; each drawing should be drawn in its own *Drafting View*. Name the view with the label provided.

Finally, you can ignore the black dot on each of the drawings below. This dot simply represents the location from which the symbol would typically be inserted or placed.

view name: **Laundry-Sink**

This is a simple rectangle that represents the size of a laundry sink, with a circle that represents the drain.

1. **Open** a new Revit project and name it **Ex4-2.rvt**.

2. Draw the rectangle shown; refer to Exercise 4-1 for more information.

3. Use the **Measure** tool to verify the size of your rectangle.

Next you will draw a circle for the drain. The drain needs to be centered left and right, and 5" from the back edge. The following steps will show you one way in which to do this.

4. Select the **Detail Line** tool from the *Annotate* tab.

5. Select the **Circle** icon from the *Ribbon* (Figure 4-2.1).

FIGURE 4-2.1 Sketch Options for detail lines

6. Pick the midpoint of the top line (Figure 4-2.2).

   FYI: This is the center of the circle.

7. Type **0 1** for the radius and press **Enter** (0 1 = 0' – 1").

   FYI: This creates a 2" diameter circle.

FIGURE 4-2.2 Creating a circle and moving it into place.

At this point you may get an error indicating the "Element is too small on screen" (Figure 4-2.3). This is supposed to prevent a user, like yourself, from accidentally drawing a very small line when you click the mouse twice right next to each other or trying to change the dimension to a previously drawn line to something less than 1/32". If you get this error, you simply zoom in on your drawing more so the circle is more prominently visible on the screen.

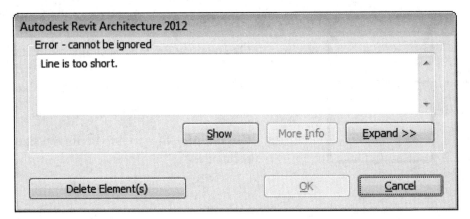

FIGURE 4-2.3 Revit error message when creating the circle IF you are zoomed out too far

8. If you did get the error message just described, click *Cancel*, *Zoom In* and then draw the circle again.

9. Select the circle and then the **Move** tool.

10. **Move** the circle straight down 5" (Figure 4-2.2).

That's it! Do not forget to save your *Ex4-2* project often.

view name: Dryer

Here you will draw a dryer with rounded front corners. This, like all the other symbols in this lesson, is a plan view symbol, as in "viewed from the top."

11. Draw a 30"x26" Rectangle.

12. Use the ***Measure*** tool to verify your dimensions.

Next, you will draw the line that is 2½" from the back of the dryer. You will draw the line in approximately the correct position and then use the temporary dimensions to correct the location.

13. Select the **Detail Line** tool and then pick a point approximately 3"down from the upper-left corner; a temporary dimension will be displayed before you click your mouse button (Figure 4-2.4).

14. Complete the horizontal line by picking a point perpendicular to the vertical line on the right (Figure 4-2.4).

15. With the temporary dimensions still displayed, click the text for the 0'-3" dimension, type **0 2.5** and then press **Enter** (Figure 4-2.5).

16. Click ***Modify*** to clear the selection and make the *Temporary Dimensions* go away.

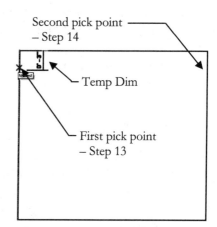

FIGURE 4-2.4 Drawing a line

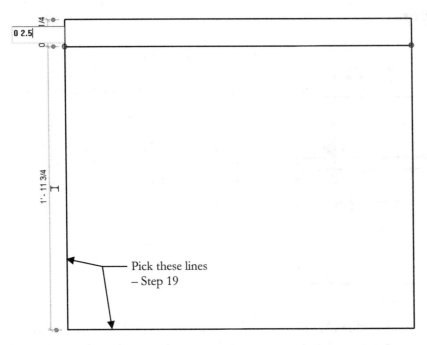

FIGURE 4-2.5 Adjusting new lines position via temporary dimensions

Next you will round the corners. You still use the *Detail Line* tool, but use a *Draw* option called *Fillet Arc*, pronounced "Fill it". You will try this next.

17. With the ***Detail Lines*** tool active, select the **Fillet Arc** *Draw* option on the *Ribbon* (Figure 4-2.6).

18. Check **Radius** and enter **0′ 2″** in the text box on the *Options Bar* (Figure 4-2.6).

FIGURE 4-2.6 Ribbon and Options Bar; options for Detail Lines in Fillet mode

19. Pick the two lines identified in Figure 4-2.5.

The intersection of the two lines is where the arc is placed; notice the two lines you picked have been trimmed back to the new *Fillet Arc*.

20. Repeat the previous step to **Fillet** the other corner.

view name: **Washer**

This drawing is identical to the *Dryer* except for the door added to the top. You can duplicate the *Dryer Drafting View* to get a jump start on this drawing.

To draw the door you will use the **Offset** option, which is part of the *Detail Line* tool.

The ***Offset*** tool is easy to use; to use it you:
o   Select the *Detail Line* tool
o   Select the *Pick Lines* icon on the *Ribbon*
o   Enter the *Offset* distance on the *Options Bar*
o   Select near a line, and on the side to offset

21. Select the ***Detail Line*** tool.

22. Select the **Pick Lines** icon on the *Ribbon* (Figure 4-2.7).

FIGURE 4-2.7 Ribbon and Options Bar: options for Detail Lines in Pick Lines mode

Note that the *Pick Lines* icon toggles you from *Draw* mode to *Pick Lines* mode. The *Pick Lines* mode allows you to use existing linework to quickly create new linework. You should notice the available options on the *Options Bar* have changed after selecting *Pick Lines*; you can switch back by selecting the *Draw* icons on the *Ribbon* (Figure 4-2.7).

23.   Enter **0' 6"** for the *Offset* distance (Figure 4-2.7).

Next you will need to select a line to offset. Which side of the line you click on will indicate the direction the line is offset. Revit provides a visual reference line indicating which side the line will be offset to and its location based on the offset distance entered.

Without clicking the mouse button, move your cursor around the drawing and notice the visual reference line. Move your mouse from side-to-side over a line to see the reference line move to correspond to the cursor location.

24. **Offset** the left vertical line towards the right.

> *TIP: Make sure you entered the correct offset distance in the previous step (Figure 4-2.8).*

You will need to look at the washer drawing and the dryer drawing dimensions to figure out the door size.

25. **Offset** the other three sides; your sketch should look like Figure 4-2.9.

26. Use the ***Fillet Arc*** sketch mode, in the *Detail Line* tool, to create a 1″ radius on the four corners.

27. Click ***Modify*** to finish the current command.

Figure 4-2.8 Offset left vertical line towards the right 6″

FIGURE 4-2.9 All four lines offset inward to create outline for washer door

All four corners should now be rounded off.

28. Draw a small 4″x1″ rectangle to represent the door handle. Draw it anywhere. Then using *Snaps*, move it to the midpoint of the bottom door edge, and then move the handle 2″ up.

29. **Save** your project. Make sure the view name is *Washer*.

> *TIP: Revit also provides an Offset tool on the Modify tab of the Ribbon. The steps required are very similar to those just described.*

view name: **Range**

Now you will draw a kitchen *Range* with four circles that represent the burners.

In this exercise you will have to draw temporary lines, called *construction lines*, to create reference points needed to accurately locate the circles. Once the circles have been drawn, the construction lines can be erased.

30. Draw the range with a 2″ deep control panel at the back; refer to the steps described to draw the dryer if necessary.

31. Draw the four construction lines shown in Figure 4-2.10. Use the **Ref Plane** tool on the *Home* tab.

32. Draw two 9½″ Dia. circles and two 7½″ Dia. circles using the intersection of the construction lines to locate the centers of the circles (Figure 4-2.10).

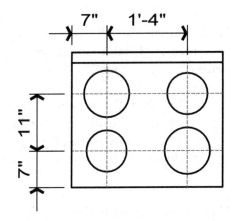

FIGURE 4-2.10 Range with four temporary construction lines (shown dashed for clarity)

TIP: Refer back to the Laundry-Sink for sketching circles.

33. **Erase** the four **Ref Plane** lines (construction lines).

34. **Save** your project.

TIP:
When using the Measure *tool, you can select* Chain *on the* Options Bar *to have Revit calculate the total length of several picks. For example, you can quickly get the perimeter of a rectangle by picking each corner. Notice, as you pick points, the* Total Length *is listed on the* Options Bar.

view name: **Chair-2**

Now you will sketch another chair. You will use *Detail Line* with *Offset* and the *Arc* settings.

First you will draw the arc at the perimeter.

35. Select *Detail Line* and then **Center – Ends Arc** from the *Ribbon* (Figure 4-2.1).

Notice on the *Status Bar* you are prompted to "**Click to enter arc center**".

36. *First Pick*: Pick a point somewhere in the middle of a new *Drafting View* named *Chair-2* (Figure 4-2.11).

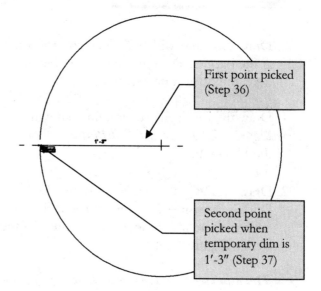

First point picked (Step 36)

Second point picked when temporary dim is 1'-3" (Step 37)

You are now prompted, on the *Status Bar* "**Drag arc radius to desired location**".

37. *Second Pick*: Move the cursor towards the left, while snapped to the horizontal, until the temporary dimension reads **1'-3"** (Figure 4-2.11).

FIGURE 4-2.11 Sketching an arc; picking second point

> **NOTE:** *As you can see, Revit temporarily displays a full circle until you pick the second point. This is because Revit does not know which direction the arc will go or what the arc length will be. The full circle allows you to visualize where your arc will be (Figure 4-2.11).*

38. *Third Pick*: Move the cursor to the right until the arc is 180 degrees and snapped to the horizontal again (Figure 4-2.12).

> **TIP:** *Notice that your cursor location determines on which direction or side the arc is created; move the cursor around before picking the third endpoint to see how the preview arc changes on screen.*

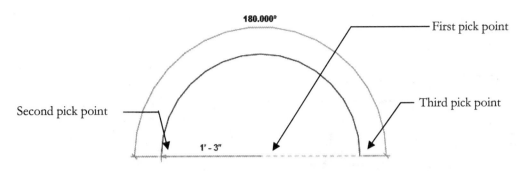

FIGURE 4-2.12 Pick points for arc command

Next you will draw the three *Detail Lines* to complete the perimeter of the chair.

39. Draw two vertical lines **1'-3"** long; attached to the arc endpoints.

   TIP: Do not forget to use Medium Lines *when sketching detail lines; if you forgot you can select the lines, while in* Modify *mode, and select* Medium Lines *from the* Element Type Selector *on the* Ribbon.

40. Draw the **2'-6"** line across the bottom.

Notice the radius is 1'-3". You did not have to enter that number because the three points you picked were enough information for Revit to determine it automatically.

If you had drawn the three lines in Steps 39 and 40 before the arc, you would not have had the required center point to pick while creating the arc. However, you could have drawn a temporary horizontal line across the top to set up a center pick that would allow you to draw the circle in its final location; or even better, use the **Start-End-Radius** *Detail Line* option.

You have now completed the perimeter of the chair.

41. Use the ***Offset*** tool to offset the arc and two vertical lines the required distance to complete the sketch.

42. **Save** your project.

view name: **Love-Seat**

You should be able to draw this *Love-Seat* without any further instruction. Use the same radius as *Chair-2*.

You can create the drawing using a combination of the following tools:
- o *Detail Line*
- o *Fillet Arc*
- o *Offset*
- o *Move*

view name: **Tub.dwg**

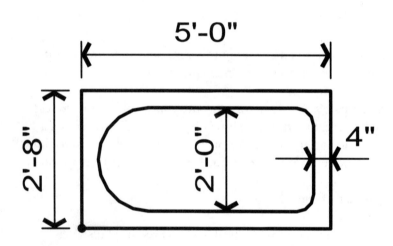

Now you will draw a bathtub. You will use several commands previously covered.

You will use the following tools:
- o *Detail Line*
- o *Fillet Arc*
- o *Offset*
- o *Move*

You may also wish to draw one or more construction lines to help locate things like the large radius, although it can be drawn without them.

view name: **Lav-1**

Draw this lavatory per the following specifications:

- o Larger arcs shown shall have a 2½″ radius
- o Smaller arcs shown shall have a 1″ radius, outside corners
- o Sides and Front of sink to have 1½″ space, offset
- o Back to have 4″ space, offset
- o Small rectangle to be 4½″x1″ and 1½″ away from the back
- o 2″ Dia. drain, 8″ from back

view name: **Lav-2**

Next you will draw another lavatory. This time you will use the *Ellipse* tool.

43. Create a new *Drafting View.*

44. Select *Detail Lines* and then **Ellipse** from the *Options Bar* (Figure 4-2.1).

Notice the *Status Bar* prompt: "**Click to enter ellipse center**".

45. Pick near the middle of the screen.

46. With the cursor snapped to the vertical, point the cursor straight down and then type **0 9.5**; press **Enter.**

   NOTE: 9½″ is half the HEIGHT, which is 1′-7″.

Now you need to specify the horizontal axis of the ellipse.

47. Again, snapping to the horizontal plane, position the cursor towards the right then type **0 11** and then press the **Enter** key.

   NOTE: 11″ is half the width: 1′-10″.

That's all it takes to draw an ellipse!

48. **Copy** the ellipse vertically downward **3½″** (Figure 4-2.13).

Next you will use the *Scale* tool to reduce the size of the second ellipse. To summarize the steps involved:

- Select the ellipse to be resized
- Select the *Scale* icon
- Pick the origin
- Pick the opposite side of the ellipse
- Enter a new value for the ellipse.

FIGURE 4-2.13   Ellipse copied downward 3½″

49. Select the lower ellipse.

50. Select the **Scale** icon on the *Ribbon,* on the *Modify* tab.

Notice the *Status Bar* prompt: "**Pick to enter origin**". The origin, or base point, is a point on, or relative to, the object that does not move.

51. *First Pick:* Pick the top edge, midpoint, of the selected ellipse (Figure 4-2.14).

52. *Second Pick:* Pick the bottom edge, midpoint, of the same ellipse (Figure 4-2.14).

53. Type **1 2** (i.e., 1′-2″) and press **Enter**; this will be the new distance between the two points picked.

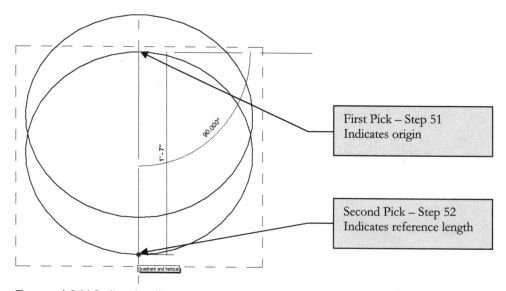

First Pick – Step 51
Indicates origin

Second Pick – Step 52
Indicates reference length

FIGURE 4-2.14 Scaling the ellipse

Next you need to draw the faucet and drain. As it turns out, the faucet and drain for *Lav-1* are in the same position relative to the middle and back (black dot). So to save time, you will *Copy/Paste* these items from the *Lav-1* drafting view into the *Lav-2* view.

54. Open **Lav-1** *Drafting View*.

55. Select the entire *Lav-1* sketch.

56. Pick **Modify | Lines → Clipboard → Copy** while the *Lav-1* linework is selected.

57. Switch back to the *Lav-2* view and press **Ctrl + V** on the keyboard. Press both keys at the same time.

58. Pick a point to the side of the *Lav-2* sketch (Figure 4-2.15).

59. Select the faucet, the small rectangle, and the drain, the circle.

> *TIP: Use a* window *selection, picking from left to right.*

60. Select the **Move** tool; pick the middle/back of the *Lav-1* sketch and then pick the middle/back of the *Lav-2* sketch.

> *NOTE: These two points represent the angle and distance to move the selected items.*

61. **Erase** the extra *Lav-1* linework from the *Lav-2* view.

You should now have the faucet and drain correctly positioned in your *Lav-2* view.

FIGURE 4-2.15 Lav-2 view: moving items from copied sketch

view name: **Sink-1**

Draw this lavatory per the following specifications:

- ○ 2" space, offset at sides and front
- ○ 3" Dia. Circles centered in sinks
- ○ 2" rad. for Fillets
- ○ 1½" Dia. at faucet spaces; 3½" apart

view name: **Water-Closet**

You should be able to draw this symbol without any help.

TIP: Draw a construction line from the Origin (i.e., black dot) straight down 11" (2'-4" – 1'-5" = 11"). This will give you a point to pick when drawing the ellipse.

view name: **Tree**

62. Draw one large circle and then copy it similar to this drawing.

63. Draw one small 1" diameter circle at the approximate center.

64. **Save** your project.

view name: **Door-36**

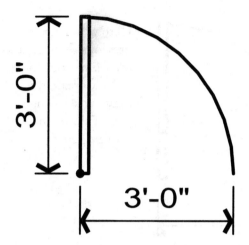

This symbol is used to show a door in a floor plan. The arc represents the path of the door as it opens and shuts.

A symbol like this, 90 degrees open, helps to avoid the door conflicting with something in the house like cabinets or a toilet. Existing doors are typically shown open 45 degrees so it is easier to visually discern new from existing.

Revit has an advanced door tool, so you would not actually draw this symbol very often. However, you may decide to draw one in plan that represents a gate in a reception counter or one in elevation to show a floor hatch. Refer back to Figure 4-1.9 for a floor plan example with door symbols.

65. Draw a **2"x3'-0" rectangle**.

66. Draw an arc using **Center – Ends Arc**; select the three points in the order shown in Figure 4-2.16.

   TIP: *Be sure your third pick shows the cursor snapped to the horizontal plane.*

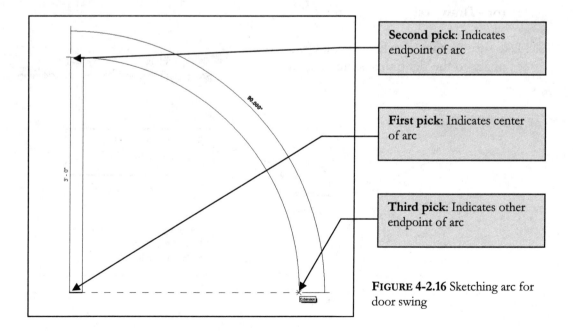

FIGURE 4-2.16 Sketching arc for door swing

view name: **Door2-36**

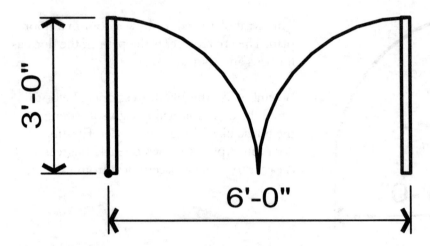

Here you will use a previous drawing and the *Mirror* tool to quickly create this drawing showing a pair of doors in a single opening.

67. Right-click on **Door-36** view label in the *Project Browser*, select "**Duplicate with detailing**" from the pop-up menu.

68. **Rename** the new *Detail View* **Door2-36**.

Next you will mirror both the rectangle and the arc. By default, Revit wants you to select a previously drawn line to be used as the "axis of reflection", but you do not have a line that would allow you to mirror the door properly to the left, so you have to pick the "*Draw Mirror Axis*" option on the *Ribbon*.

69. Select the rectangle and the arc, use a *crossing window* by picking from right to left, and then pick the **Modify | Lines → Modify → Mirror - Draw Axis** tool from the *Ribbon*.

70. Make sure *Copy* is checked on the *Options Bar*. See image to the right; this is the default.

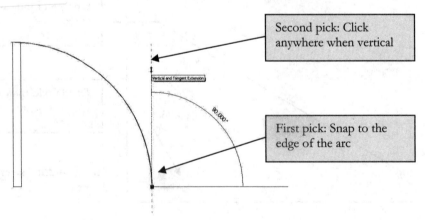

Second pick: Click anywhere when vertical

First pick: Snap to the edge of the arc

FIGURE 4-2.17 Creating axis of reflection

Notice the *Status Bar* is prompting you to **"Pick Start Point for Axis of Reflection"**.

71. Pick the two points shown in **Figure 4-2.17**.

At this point the door symbol, the rectangle and arc, is mirrored and the *Mirror* tool is done.

72. Select **Modify** to end the command and unselect everything.

73. **Save** your project as "Ex4-2.rvt".

view name: **Clg-Fan-1**

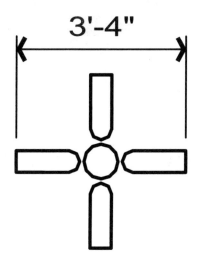

You will use the *Array* command while drawing this ceiling fan.

The *Array* command can be used to array entities in a rectangular pattern (e.g., columns on a grid) or in a polar pattern (i.e., in a circular pattern).

You will use the polar array to rotate and copy the fan blade all in one step!

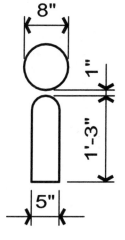

74. Start a new drawing and create the portion of drawing shown in the figure to the right.

75. Select the fan blade and then select **Array** from the *Ribbon*.

Similar to the *Rotate* tool, you will relocate the *Center of Rotation Symbol* to the center of the 8″ circle. This will cause the fan blade to array around the circle rather than the center of the first fan blade.

76. Click *Radial* on the *Options Bar* and then click and *drag* the **Rotation grip** to the center of the 8″ circle (or click the *Place* button on the *Options Bar*), make sure Revit snaps to the center point before clicking (see Figure 4-2.19).

77. Make the following changes to the *Options Bar* (Figure 4-2.18).

FIGURE 4-2.18 Array options on the Options Bar

78. After typing the angle in the *Options Bar*, press **Enter**.

You should now see the three additional fan blades and a temporary array number. This gives you the option to change the array number if desired.

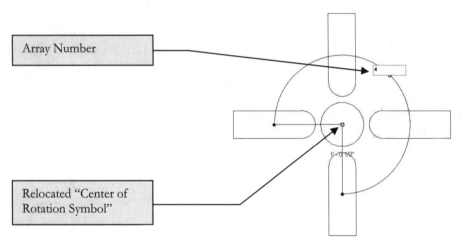

FIGURE 4-2.19 Arraying fan blades

79. Click **Modify** to complete the *Array* and finish the ceiling fan.

Because you left *Group and Associate* checked on the *Options Bar* when you created the array, you can select any part of a fan blade and the array number will appear, like a temporary dimension, and allow you to change the number. You can select *Ungroup* from the *Options Bar* to make each item individually editable as if you had drawn everything from scratch.

80. **Save** your project.

FYI: You can export each Drafting View to a file and import it back into any project file. It can then be placed as a symbol into floor plans. This would make for smaller files on large projects, such as a large hospital complex. The major downside is that you would not see anything in your 3D views for furniture. Thus, you will not likely use these for your Revit plans, but you will be able to utilize every skill learned in this section!

Self-Exam:

The following questions can be used as a way to check your knowledge of this lesson. The answers can be found at the bottom of the page.

1. Revit does not allow you to copy *Detail Views*. (T/F)

2. Entering 4 3.25 in Revit means 4'-3¼". (T/F)

3. Reference Planes (aka, construction lines) are useful drawing aids. (T/F)

4. Use the _____ tool to sketch an oval shape.

5. When you want to make a previously drawn rectangle wider you would use

    the _____ tool.

Review Questions:

The following questions may be assigned by your instructor as a way to assess your knowledge of this section. Your instructor has the answers to the review questions.

1. Use the *Offset* option to quickly create a parallel line(s). (T/F)

2. If Revit displays an error message indicating a line is too small to be drawn, you simply zoom in more and try again. (T/F)

3. Use the _____ command to create a reverse image.

4. With the *Move* tool, lines completely within the selection window are actually only moved, not stretched. (T/F)

5. You can relocate the "center of rotation" when using *Radial Array* (T/F)

6. Occasionally you need to draw an object and then move it into place to accurately locate it. (T/F)

7. The _____ is an option within the *Detail Line* tool which allows you create a rounded corner where two lines intersect.

8. When using the *Mirror* tool, you occasionally need to draw a temporary line that represents the *Axis of Reflection*. (T/F)

9. Which line style was required to be selected in the *Type Selector*, in the *Properties Palette*, for all the linework in this Lesson? _____

10. In the *Detail Line* tool, how many options allow you to draw arcs? _____

Notes:

Lesson 5
Residence: FLOOR PLAN (First Floor):

In this lesson you will draw the first floor plan of a single family residence. The project will be further developed in subsequent chapters. It is recommended that you spend adequate time on this lesson as later lessons build upon this one.

Be sure to check out the videos on the DVD for more information on modeling walls, doors and windows using Autodesk® Revit® Architecture.

Exercise 5-1:
Project Setup

The Project:

You will model a two-story residence located in a suburban setting. Just to the North of the building site is a medium sized lake. For the sake of simplicity, the property is virtually flat.

The main entry is from the South side of the building. You enter the building into a large foyer. The second floor has a railing that looks down onto the foyer.

This building is not meant to meet any particular building code. It is strictly a tool to learn how to use Autodesk Revit Architecture 2012. Having said that, however, there are several general comments as to how codes may impact a particular part of the design; each must be verified with your local rules and regulations.

Creating the Project File:

A Building Information Model (BIM), as previously mentioned, consists of a single file. This file can be quite large. For example, the prestigious architectural design firm SOM used Autodesk Revit Architecture to design the Freedom Tower in New York. As you can imagine, a skyscraper would be a large BIM file, whereas a single family residence would be much smaller.

Large databases are just starting to enter the architectural design realm. However, banks, hospitals, etc. have been using them for years, even with multiple users!

When Autodesk Revit Architecture is launched, the *Recent Files* view is loaded. Template files have several items setup and ready to use (e.g., some wall, door and window types). Starting with the correct template can save you a significant amount of time.

Autodesk Revit Architecture provides a handful of templates with particular project types in mind. They are *Commercial, Construction* and *Residential.*

In this exercise you will use the *Residential* template. It has several aspects of the project file pre-setup and ready for use. A few of these items will be discussed momentarily.

As your knowledge in Revit increases, you will be able to start refining a custom template, which probably originated from a standard template. The custom template will have things like a firm's title block and a cover sheet with abbreviations, symbols etc. all setup and ready to go.

Next you will create a new project file.

1. Select ***Application Menu → New → Project***.

   You are now in the *New Project* dialog box. Rather than clicking **OK**, which would use a stripped-down default template, you will select **Browse** so you can select a specialized template (Figure 5-1.1).

FIGURE 5-1.1 New Project dialog

2. Click the **Browse...** button.

3. Select the template named **Residential-Default.rte** from the list of available templates (Figure 5-1.2).

4. Click **Open** to select the highlighted template file.

5. Click **OK** to complete the *New Project* dialog.

FIGURE 5-1.2 Choose Template dialog

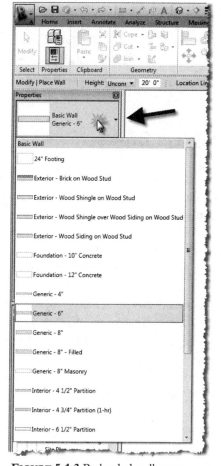

You have just set up a project file that you will use for the **remainder of this book**, so be sure you selected the correct template file!

Next, you will take a look at the predefined wall types that have been loaded with the template file.

6. Select **Home → Build → Wall**.

7. Click the ***Type Selector*** down-arrow on the *Properties Palette* (Figure 5-1.3).

Wall Types:

Notice the wall types that have been preloaded as part of the *Residential* template. These wall types are many of the types of walls one would expect to find on a typical residential construction project.

FIGURE 5-1.3 Preloaded wall types

The walls are mostly wood stud walls; both interior and exterior. If you look at the *Default* or *Commercial* templates, you will see mostly metal stud and concrete block (CMU) wall types.

Additionally, the thicknesses of materials can vary between commercial and residential; this is also accounted for in the templates. For example, gypsum board is typical ⅝" thick on commercial projects whereas it is usually only ½" on residential work.

To reiterate the concept, consider the following comparisons between a typical commercial interior wall and a typical residential interior wall.

- Typical Commercial Wall
    - ⅝" Gypsum Board
    - 3⅝" Metal Stud
    - ⅝" Gypsum Board
        - Total thickness: **4⅞"**

- Typical Residential Wall
    - ½" Gypsum Board
    - 2x4 Wood Stud (3½" actual)
    - ½" Gypsum Board
        - Total Thickness: **4½"**

Project Browser:

Take a few minutes to look at the *Project Browser* and notice the views and sheets that have been set up via the template file you selected (Figure 5-1.4).

Many of the views that you need to get started with the design of a residence are set up and ready to go.

Practically all the sheets typically found on a residential project have been created; see Figure 5-1.4 under the *Sheets (all)* heading of the *Project Browser*. Also, notice the sheets with a plus symbol next to them. These are sheets that already have views placed on them. You will study this more later, but a view, such as your *East Elevation* view, is placed on a sheet at a scale you select. This means your title block sheets will have printable information as soon as you start sketching walls in one of your plan views.

FIGURE 5-1.4 Project Browser: various items preloaded

Project Information:

Revit provides a dialog to enter the basic project information, such as client name, project address, etc. Next you will enter this information.

8. Select **Manage → Settings → Project Information**.

Project
Information

9. Enter the *Project Information* shown in Figure 5-1.5.

FYI: For now you will enter three question marks for the date.

Project Issue Date:	**???**
Project Status:	**Preliminary**
Client Name:	**John Brown**
Project Name:	**New Residence**
Project Number:	**2012-048**

FIGURE 5-1.5 Project Information dialog

10. Click the **Edit** button next to the *Project Address* parameter (Figure 5-1.5).

11. Enter the project address shown in Figure 5-1.6.

FYI: This is the address where the house is going to be built, not the client's current address.

Enter:
2138 East Superior Street
Duluth, MN 55812

NOTE: You can enter any address you want to at this point; the address suggested is made up.

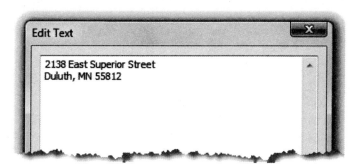

FIGURE 5-1.6 Adding Project Address (partial view)

12. Click **OK**.

13. Click the **Edit** button next to the
    Energy Data parameter (Figure 5-1.7).
    a.   Enter/select the information
         shown.

14. Click **OK**.

15. Click **OK** to close the *Project
    Information* dialog box.

FIGURE 5-1.7 Adding Energy Data (partial view)

The project information is now saved in your
Revit project database. Revit has already used
some of this information to infill in a portion
of your title block on each of your sheets.
You will verify this next.

Note that the *Energy Data* information is
mainly used by external applications or
Revit MEP to perform energy analyses like
heating and cooling loads. Using Revit in conjunction with programs like *Autodesk Green
Building Studio, Autodesk Ecotect* or *IES Virtual Environment* can help create more energy
efficient buildings because you can study the design impacts on energy consumption earlier
in the project when changes are still possible.

16. Under the **Sheets** heading, in the
    Project Browser, double-click on the
    sheet **A1 – First Floor Plan**.

17. **Zoom** in to the lower right area of
    the title block (Figure 5-1.8).

Notice that much of the information is
automatically filled in, and this is true for
every sheet!

Your project database is now set up.

18. **Save** your project as **Ex5-1.rvt**.

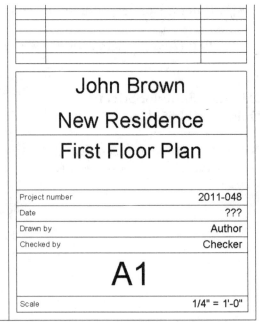

FIGURE 5-1.8 Sheet A1 – First Floor Plan: Title block with
Project Information added automatically

Exercise 5-2:
Exterior Walls

You will begin the first floor plan by drawing the exterior walls. Like many projects, early on you might not be certain what the exterior walls are going to be. So, you will start out using the generic wall styles. Then you will change them to a custom wall style, which you will create once you have decided what the wall construction is.

Often a residence is designed with a specific site in mind. However, to keep in line with most drafting and design classes, where floor plans are studied before site plans, you will develop the plans now.

Completed Plans – For Reference:

The following two images show the floor plans as they will look when you are done with this book. You should not need to use any information from these images; they are simply meant to introduce you to the project.

First Floor:
Living Room, Kitchen, Formal Dining, Coat Closet, ½ Bath, Mud Room, Garage

Second Floor:
Master Bath & Bedroom, Two Bedrooms,
Bathroom, Linen Closet, Office

Adjust Wall Settings:

1. Switch to *First Floor* view; select **Wall** from the *Home* tab.

2. Make the following changes to the wall options within the *Ribbon, Options Bar* and *Properties Palette* (Figure 5-2.1):
    - *Wall style:* **Basic Wall: Generic – 8"**
    - *Height:* **Unconnected**
    - *Height:* **19' 0"**
    - *Location Line:* **Finish Face; Exterior**
    - *Chain:* **checked**

FIGURE 5-2.1 Ribbon and Option bar – Wall command active

Draw the Exterior Walls:

3. **Draw** the walls shown in Figure 5-2.2. Make sure your dimensions are correct. Use the *Measure* tool, on the *QAT,* to double check your dimensions. Center the building between the elevation tags (see Figure 1-2.1). Move the elevation tags as needed by selecting the square part of the tag and using the Move tool (do not delete them).

NOTE: If you draw in a clockwise fashion, your walls will have the exterior side of the wall correctly positioned. You can also use the spacebar to toggle which side the exterior face is on.

TIP: In the Options Bar, while you are in the Wall tool, you can click Chain to continuously draw walls. When Chain is not selected you have to pick the same point twice: once where the wall ends and again where the next wall begins

FIGURE 5-2.2 Exterior walls

Modifying Wall Dimensions:

Now that you have the exterior walls drawn, you might decide to adjust the building size for masonry coursing if you have a concrete block foundation, or subtract square footage to reduce cost.

Editing walls in Revit is very easy. You can select a wall and edit the temporary dimensions that appear, or you can use the *Move* tool to change the position of a wall. Any walls whose endpoints touch the modified wall are also adjusted (i.e., they grow or shrink) automatically.

Next, you will adjust the dimensions of the walls just drawn. You will assume the house will have a concrete block (CMU) foundation.

4. Click **Modify** and then select the far left wall (Figure 5-2.3).

Clicking *Modify* cancels the current command and de-selects everything. Sometimes you have to press it twice to completely clear everything.

5. Select the temporary dimensions text (35'-0") and then type **34 8** (Figure 5-2.3).

> **FYI:** *Remember you do not need to type the foot or inch symbol; the space distinguishes between them.*

FIGURE 5-2.3 Editing wall dimensions

> **TIP:** *Whenever you want to adjust the model via temporary/permanent dimensions, you need to select the object you want to move first and then select the text, or number, of the temporary or permanent dimension.*

6. In the lower right corner of the floor plan, select the wall shown in Figure 5-2.4.

7. Edit the 4'-4" dimension to **4'-0"**.

> **TIP:** *Just type 4 and press Enter; Revit will assume feet when a single number is entered.*

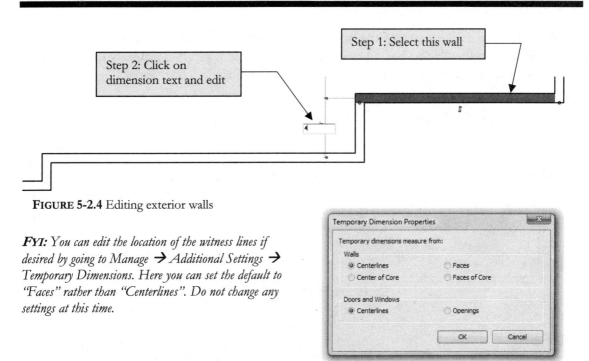

FIGURE 5-2.4 Editing exterior walls

FYI: You can edit the location of the witness lines if desired by going to Manage → Additional Settings → Temporary Dimensions. Here you can set the default to "Faces" rather than "Centerlines". Do not change any settings at this time.

TIP:
Concrete blocks (or CMU) come in various widths, and most are 16″ long and 8″ high. When drawing plans, there is a simple rule to keep in mind to make sure you are designing walls to coursing. This applies to wall lengths and openings within CMU walls.

Dimension rules for CMU coursing in floor plans:
- *e′*-0″ or *e′*-8″   where *e* is any even number (e.g., 6′-0″ or 24′-8″)
- *o′*-4″   where *o* is any odd number (e.g., 5′-4″)

Using the Align Tool with Walls:

Revit has a tool called *Align* that allows you to quickly make one element align with another. You will make the South wall of the garage align with the wall you just modified. After they are aligned, you will *Lock* the relationship so the two walls will always move together, which is great when you know you want two walls to remain aligned but might accidentally move one, maybe while zoomed in and you cannot see the other wall.

8. Select the **Modify → Modify → Align** icon.

Notice the *Status Bar* is asking you to select a reference line or point. This is the wall, or linework, that is in the correct location; the other wall(s) will be adjusted to match the reference plane.

9. Select the exterior face of the horizontal wall you just modified. Set *Prefer* to **Wall Faces** on the *Options Bar* (Figure 5-2.5). You should notice a temporary dashed line appear on screen. This will help you to visualize the reference plane.

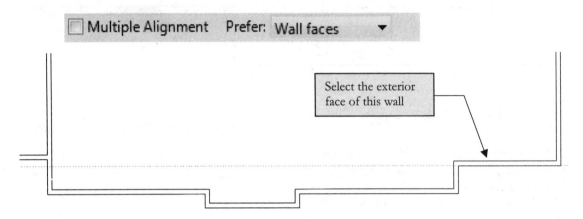

Notice the *Status Bar* is prompting you to select an entity to align with the temporary reference plane.

10. Now, select the exterior face of the South garage wall (Figure 5-2.6).

FIGURE 5-2.6 Align tool: select wall(s) to be aligned

Note that if you would have selected the interior face of the wall that side of the wall would have aligned with the reference plane rather than the exterior, as it did. If you made a mistake, click *Undo* and try it again.

Also, notice that you have a padlock symbol showing. Clicking the padlock symbol will cause the alignment relationship to be maintained, a parametric relationship. Next you will lock the alignment relationship and experiment with a few edits to see how modifying one wall affects the other.

11. Click on the **padlock** symbol (Figure 5-2.6).

The padlock symbol is now in the locked position.

12. Click **Modify** to unselect the walls.

13. Select the garage wall identified in Figure 5-2.6.

Next you will make a dramatic change so you can clearly see the results of that change on both locked walls.

14. Change the 4'-0" dimension to **20'-0"** (Figure 5-2.7).

Notice that both walls moved together (Figure 5-2.7). Also notice that when either wall is selected, the padlock is displayed, which helps in identifying "locked" relationships while you are editing the project. Whenever the padlock symbol is visible, you can click on it to unlock it, or remove the aligned relationship.

FIGURE 5-2.7 Wall edit: Both walls move together

Next you will make a few more wall modifications, on your own, to get the perimeter of the building to masonry coursing.

15. Modify wall locations by selecting a wall and modifying the temporary dimensions; the selected wall will move to match Figure 5-2.8; do not draw the dimensions at this time.

   TIP: Make sure you use the Measure *tool to verify all dimensions before moving on!*

   TIP: Clicking the grip on the witness line of a Temporary Dimension causes the witness line to toggle locations on the wall (i.e., exterior face, interior face and center). You can also drag the grip to a different wall.

FIGURE 5-2.8 Exterior walls with final dimensions

Changing a Wall Type:

In the next several steps, you will learn how to change the generic walls into a more refined wall type. Basically, you select the wall(s) you want to change and then you pick a different wall type from the *Type Selector* on the *Properties Palette*. Remember, the *Ribbon*, *Options Bar* and *Properties Palette* are context sensitive, which means the wall types are only listed in the *Type Selector* when you are using the *Wall* tool or you have a wall selected.

16. Select all the walls in your *First Floor* plan view.

> ***TIP:*** *You can select all the walls at once: click and drag the cursor to select a window. Later in the book you will learn about "Filter Selection" which also aids in the selection process.*

FIGURE 5-2.9 Type Selector

17. From the *Type Selector* on the *Properties Palette*, select **Exterior – Wood Shingle over Wood Siding on Wood Stud** (Figure 5-2.9).

18. Click **Modify** to unselect the walls.

If you zoom in on the walls, you can see their graphic representation has changed a little. It would have changed a lot, of course, if you had selected a brick and CMU cavity wall. But you typically try to start with a wall closest to the one you think you will end up with, though you may never even have to change the wall type.

Even though the wall did not change much graphically in this plan view, it did change quite a bit. In a 3D view, which you will look at in a moment, the wall now has siding and trim! The image to the right is a snapshot of the 19'-0" tall wall you now have in your model.

Next, you will create a custom wall type for the walls around the garage. You will need a wall type similar to the one you just selected, but with 2x4 studs rather than 2x6's. You will start by making a copy of the existing wall type and then modify the copy.

Create a Custom Wall Type:

As previously mentioned, Revit provides several predefined wall styles, from wood studs with gypsum board to concrete block and brick cavity walls. However, you will occasionally need a wall style that has not yet been predefined by Revit. You will study this process next.

First, you will take a close look at the predefined wall type you are using for the exterior walls.

19. With the *Wall* tool selected, pick the wall type: **Exterior – Wood Shingle over Wood Siding on Wood Stud**, from the *Type Selector* drop-down list (Figure 5-2.9).

20. Click the **Edit Type** button on the *Properties Palette*.

21. You should be in the *Type Properties* dialog box (Figure 5-2.11).

FIGURE 5-2.10 Edit Type button

22. Click the **Edit** button next to the *Structure* parameter (Figure 5-2.11).

FIGURE 5-2.11 Type Properties

23. Finally, you are in the *Edit Assembly* dialog box. This is where you can modify existing wall types or create new ones. Click **<<Preview** to display a preview of the selected wall type (Figure 5-2.12).

Here, the *Edit Assembly* dialog box allows you to change the composition of an existing wall or to create a new wall.

Things to notice (Figure 5-2.12):

- The exterior side is labeled at the top and interior side at the bottom.

- You will see horizontal lines (i.e., *Layers*) identifying the core material. The core material can be used to place walls and dimension walls. For example, the *Wall* tool will let you draw a wall with the interior or exterior core face as the reference line. On an interior wall you might dimension to the face of stud rather than to the finished face of gypsum board; this would give the contractor the information needed for the part of the wall he will build first.

- Each row is called a *Layer*. By clicking on a *Layer* and picking the **Up** or **Down** buttons, you can reposition materials within the wall assembly.

FIGURE 5-2.12 Edit Assembly

24. Click **Cancel** to close the open dialog box.

Next, you will instruct Revit to create a new wall type which will be based on a copy of the currently selected wall type.

25. Click the **Duplicate** button (Figure 5-2.11).

26. Enter **Exterior – Wood Shingle over Wood Siding on 2x4 Wood Stud** for the new wall type name, and then click **OK** (Figure 5-2.13).

> *FYI:* Notice that you have simply added "2x4" as a descriptor; making the name distinguishable from the others. Be sure to remove the "2" at the end, which was automatically added by Revit in case you did not change the name.

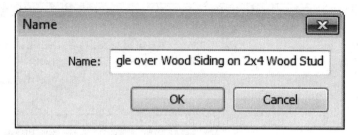

FIGURE 5-2.13 New wall type name

27. Click the **Edit** button next to the *Structure* parameter.

Next you will simply change the size of the wood stud layer and then save your changes.

28. Change the *Thickness* of the *Wood – Stud Layer* to **0′ 3 ½″**.

29. Your dialog should look like **Figure 5-2.14**. Notice the total wall thickness is listed near the top.

30. Click **OK** to close all dialog boxes.

You now have access to your newly defined wall. You can sketch new walls using the *Wall* tool or you can change existing walls to your new wall type using the *Modify* tool.

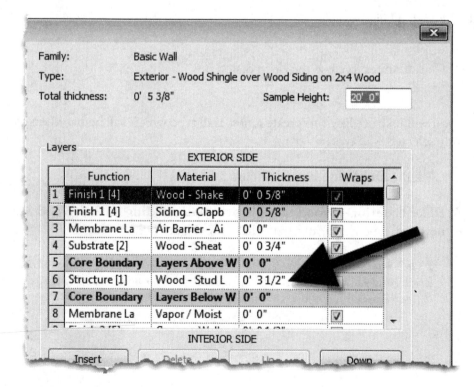

FIGURE 5-2.14 Edit Assembly; change stud size to 2x4

The next step is to change the wall type for the three walls around the garage.

31. Select the **Modify** icon from the *Ribbon*; this cancels any active commands and allows you to select objects in your model.

32. **Zoom out** so you can see the entire plan. Dragging your mouse from upper-right to lower-left, make a *crossing window* to select the three garage walls; **or** hold down **Ctrl** and click each wall.

33. With the walls selected, pick **Basic Wall: Exterior – Wood Shingle over Wood Siding on 2x4 Wood Stud** from the *Type Selector* drop down; see tip below.

You should notice the wall thickness change; the reference line (face, center, etc.) does not move. You had *Finish Face: Exterior* selected when you drew the walls; so the exterior side of the wall does not move, which is good.

TIP: If, after selecting all the walls, the Type Selector *is grayed out and the contextual tab says* Multi-Select, *you have some other type of element selected, such as text or dimensions (although you have not been instructed to draw anything but walls yet) or one of the four elevation tags. Try to find those objects and delete them, but DO NOT delete the elevation tags. You can also click on the* Filter *button, located on the Ribbon when objects are selected, and uncheck the types of elements to exclude from the current selection.*

For many of the walls, Revit can display more refined linework and hatching within the wall. This is controlled by the *Detail Level* option for each view. At the moment, making this change will only reveal the exterior sheathing, but this is helpful information. You will change the *Detail Level* for the *First Floor Plan* view now.

34. Click on the **Detail Level** icon in the lower-left corner of the drawing window (Figure 5-2.15).

35. Select **Medium**.

FYI: This view adjustment is only for the current view, as are all changes made via the View Control Bar.

FIGURE 5-2.15 Detail Level; set to medium

You may need to zoom in, but you should now see a line added for the exterior sheathing. If you did not pay close enough attention when drawing the walls originally, some of your walls may show the sheathing to the inside of the building.

TIP: *On the View tab you can select* Thin Lines *to temporarily turn off the line weights; this has no effect on plotting.*

36. Select **Modify** (or press **Esc**); select a wall. You will see a symbol appear that allows you to flip the wall orientation by clicking on that symbol (Figure 5-2.16).

Click this symbol to flip wall orientation

FIGURE 5-2.16 Selected Wall

37. Whether you need to adjust walls or not, click on the flip symbol to experiment with its operation.

TIP: *The flip symbol is always on the exterior side, or what Revit thinks is the exterior side, of the wall.*

38. If some walls do need to be adjusted so the sheathing and flip symbol are to the exterior, do it now. You may have to select the wall(s) and use the *Move* tool to reposition the walls to match the required dimensions.

TIP: *Walls are flipped about the Location Line, which can be changed via the Properties Palette. So changing the Location Line to Wall Centerline before flipping the wall will keep the wall in the same position. Be sure to change the Location Line back to Exterior Face.*

TIP: *You can use the MOVE tool on the Ribbon to accurately move walls. The steps are the same as in the previous chapters!*

Follow these steps to move an element:
- *Select the wall*
- *Click the Move icon*
- *Pick any point on the wall*
- *Start the mouse in the correct direction; do not click!*
- *Start typing the distance you want to move the wall and press Enter.*

You can see your progress nicely with a 3D view. Click the
Default 3D View icon on the *QAT*. The enlargement image
walls are shaded to make the image more clear (Figure 5-2.17).

FIGURE 5-2.17 Default 3D View;
zoomed in to detail (image on the right)

If you zoom in on the walls, you
can see how much detail Revit can
store in a wall type. By picking a few points,
you defined the wall's width, height and
exterior finish materials.

The last thing you will do in this exercise is to adjust the
height of the walls at the garage and a portion of the living
room; refer to image on the book's cover. Revit allows you
to modify the building model in any view. You will make
the wall height adjustments in the current 3D View, per the
following steps.

39. In the *3D View*, click to select the three exterior garage walls.

> **TIP:** *Holding down the Ctrl key allows you to select multiple elements, while holding down the Shift key allows for subtraction from the current selection set. The total number of selected items is listed in the lower right, on the Status Bar; make sure it is says "3".*

You will notice, similar to other views, when an element is selected in a 3D view the entire
object temporarily turns blue and becomes transparent. This helps to see which objects are
in the current selection set when several items are selected.

You should also see the *Ribbon* has been populated with options for the selected walls, just like the plan views. You will adjust the height setting in the *Properties Palette* next.

40. In the *Properties Palette*, change the *Unconnected Height* parameter to **12'-0"** and then press **Enter**.

41. Make the same height adjustment to the three exterior walls at the Eastern most portion of the living room (Figure 5-2.18).

42. Close the *3D View* and switch back to the *First Floor Plan* view.

43. Save your project as **ex5-2.rvt**.

Figure 5-2.18 Completed exercise

TIP: Holding down the Shift key while pressing the wheel button on the mouse allows you to fly around the building. You will have to experiment with how the mouse movements relate to the building orbit. Selecting an item first causes that item to remain centered on the screen during orbit.

Exercise 5-3:
Interior Walls

In this lesson you will draw the interior walls for the first floor. Using the line sketching and editing techniques you have studied in previous lessons, you should be able to draw the interior walls with minimal information.

Overview on How Plans are Typically Dimensioned:

The following is an overview of how walls are typically dimensioned in a floor plan. This information is intended to help you understand the dimensions you will see in the exercises, as well as prepare you for the point when you dimension your plans, in a later lesson.

Wood or metal stud walls are typically dimensioned to the centers of the walls. This is one of the reasons the walls do not need to be the exact thickness. Here are a few reasons why you should dimension to the center of the stud rather than to the face of the gypsum board:

o   The contractor is laying out the walls in a large "empty" area. The most useful dimension is to the center of the stud; that is where they will make a mark on the floor. If the dimension was to the face of the gypsum board, the contractor would have to stop and calculate the center of the stud, which is not always the center of the wall thickness; for example, a stud wall with one layer of gypsum board on one side and two layers of gypsum board over resilient channels on the other side of the stud.

Dimension Example
– Two Stud Walls

o   When creating a continuous string of dimensions, the extra dimensions indicating the thickness of the walls would take up an excessive amount of room on the floor plans, space that would be better used by notes.

Occasionally, you should dimension to the face of a wall rather than the center; here's one example:

o   When indicating design intent or building code requirements, you should reference the exact points/surfaces. For example, if you have uncommonly large trim around a door opening, you may want a dimension from the edge of the door to the face of the adjacent wall. Another example would be the width of a hallway; if you want a particular width you would dimension between the two faces of the wall and add the text "clear" below the dimension to make it known, without question, that the dimension is not to the center of the wall.

Dimensions for masonry and foundation walls:

- o Foundation and masonry walls are dimensioned to the nominal face and not the center. These types of walls are modular (e.g., 8"x8"x16") so it is helpful, for both designer and builder, to have dimensions that relate to the masonry wall's "coursing".

Dimension Example
– Two masonry Walls

Dimensions from a stud wall to a masonry wall:

- o The rules above apply for each side of the dimension line. For example: a dimension for the exterior foundation wall to an interior stud wall would be from the exterior face of the foundation wall to the center of the stud on the interior wall.

Again, you will not be dimensioning your drawings right away, but Revit makes it easy to comply with the conventions above.

Dimension Example
– Stud to masonry

Adjust Wall Settings:

1. Select **Wall** form the *Home* tab on the *Ribbon*.

2. Make the following changes to the wall options in the *Properties Palette* and *Options Bar* (similar to Figure 5-2.1):
   - Wall style: **Interior – 4 ½" partition**
   - Height: **Second Floor**
   - Location Line: **Wall Centerline**

Contos Residence

Image courtesy of Anderson Architects
Alan H. Anderson, Architect, Duluth, MN

Drawing the Interior Walls:

Now that you have the perimeter drawn, you will draw a few interior walls. When drawing floor plans it is good practice to sketch out the various wall systems you think you will be using; this will help you determine what thickness to draw the walls. Drawing the walls at the correct thickness helps later when you are fine-tuning things.

Although Revit provides most of the wall types required, it is a good idea for the student to understand exactly what is being drawn.

Take a moment to think about the basic interior wall in a residential project. It typically consists of the following:

- o 2x4 wood studs
  (actual size is 1½″ x 3½″)
- o ½″ gypsum board

The wall system described above is shown in Figure 5-3.1.

4 ½″

2x4 WOOD STUDS
at 16″ O.C.

ONE LAYER OF ½″
GYPSUM BOARD
EACH SIDE

FIGURE 5-3.1
Sketch – Plan view of interior wall system

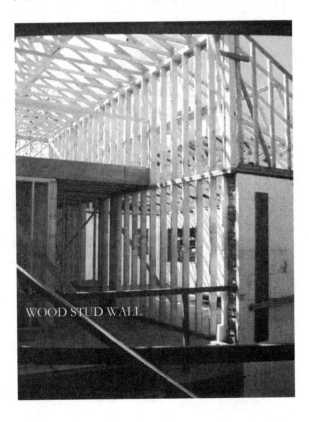

WOOD STUD WALL

All your interior walls should be drawn **4½″** <u>for each floor</u>.

Image courtesy of
Stanius Johnson Architects
Daniel's Construction, Amery WI.
Photo by Robert Aho
www.staniusjohnson.com

3. Draw a vertical wall approximately as shown in Figure 5-3.2. You will adjust its exact position in the next step.

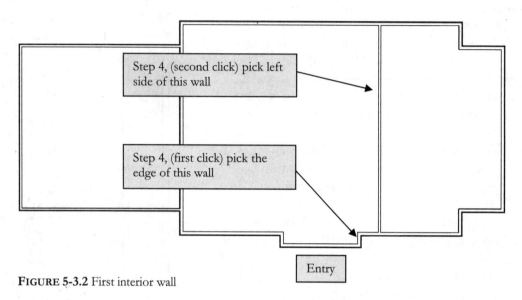

Step 4, (second click) pick left side of this wall

Step 4, (first click) pick the edge of this wall

Entry

FIGURE 5-3.2 First interior wall

4. Use the **Align** tool to align the interior wall you just drew with the edge of the exterior wall (Figure 5-3.2). Set *Prefer* to *Wall Faces* on the *Options Bar*. When you are done, the wall should look like Figure 5-3.3.

FYI: You do not need to lock this alignment.

5. Create the same wall for the West side of the entry, repeating the steps above.

Next, you will draw a handful of walls per the given dimensions. You will use the same partition type (4½″ partition).

6. Draw the interior walls shown in Figure 5-3.4; see the tips below which should help you sketch the walls more accurately.

FIGURE 5-3.3 Aligned wall

FIGURE 5-3.4 Layout dimensions for first floor interior walls

TIP - DIMENSION WITNESS LINE CONTROL:

When sketching walls, you can adjust the exact position of the wall after its initial placement. However, the temporary dimensions do not always reference the desired wall location (left face, right face, or center). You will see how easy it is to adjust a dimension's witness line location so you can place the wall exactly where you want it.

First, you will be introduced to some dimension terminology. The two "boxed" notes below are only for permanent dimensions, the others are for both permanent and temporary.

Next you will adjust the witness lines so you can modify the inside clear dimension, between the walls, in the above illustration.

When you select a wall you will see temporary dimensions, similar to the image on the next page.

TIP - DIMENSION WITNESS LINE CONTROL: (CONTINUED FROM PREVIOUS PAGE)

NOTE: Some elements do not display temporary dimensions; in that case you can usually click the "Activate Dimensions" button on the Options Bar to see them.

Clicking, not dragging, on the witness line grip causes the witness line to toggle between the location options (left face, right face, center). In the example below, the grip for each witness line has been clicked until both witness lines refer to the "inside" of the room.

Click the witness line grip until the witness line references the element location you prefer; repeat for the other side.

Selected Wall

In the above example, the temporary dimension could now be modified, which would adjust the location of the wall to a specific inside or clear dimension.

Not only can you adjust the witness line about a given element, you can also move the witness line to another element. This is useful because Revit's temporary dimensions, for a selected element, do not always refer to the desired element. You can relocate a witness line (temporary or permanent) by clicking and dragging the grip; see example below.

Result: New witness line location after dragging grip

Step 1: Selected Wall

Step 2: Drag this grip to far left

Next you will use the *Trim* tool to remove a portion of wall that is not needed.

7. Select **Trim** from the *Modify* tab.

8. Select the two walls identified in Figure 5-3.5.

   FYI: The walls can be selected in either order.

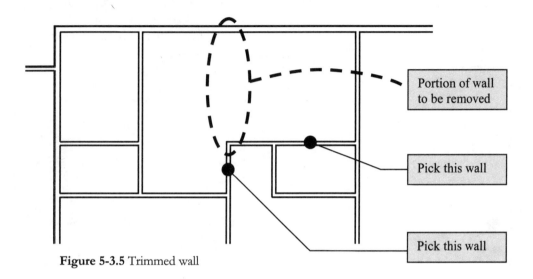

Figure 5-3.5 Trimmed wall

Modify an Existing Wall:

Next you want to change the portion of wall between the house and the garage. Currently, the wall is your typical exterior wall which includes siding on the garage side. The entire vertical wall is one element, so to only change the interior portion you will need to split the current wall, trim the corners and then draw a new interior wall.

9. **Zoom** in on the interior garage wall and select the **Modify → Modify → Split** tool.

   FYI: This will break a wall into two; when used in plan it splits the wall vertically and when used in a section a horizontal split results.

10. Pick somewhere in the middle of the wall (Figure 5-3.6a).

11. Use the **Trim** tool to trim the corners so the exterior wall only occurs at exterior conditions. Select **Unjoin Elements** (see "Warning Prompt" section on the next page).

    TIP: Select the portion of wall you wish to retain (Figure 5-3.6b).

FIGURE 5-3.6A Split wall   **FIGURE 5-3.6B** Trim wall

Additional Custom Wall Types:

Next, you will create a new interior partition type using a copy of the original exterior wall type as a starting point. It is easier to start with a wall that is similar to the one you wish to create.

Structurally, this wall could probably only require 2x4 studs. However, directly above this wall will be an exterior wall (the portion above the garage roof) that wants to have 2x6 studs to allow for adequate insulation. Additionally, you will want to insulate the interior garage wall; this helps with noise and heat loss when the large garage door is opened in -20 degree weather!

Truthfully, in this case it may be easier to start with a new wall, given the complexity of the exterior wall you are about to modify. However, this will give you a little more insight on how the exterior wall is constructed and the interworking of Revit's wall assembly.

12. Using wall type: **Exterior – Wood Shingle over Wood Siding on Wood Stud** as a starting point, create a new wall type named **Exterior – Garage Wall (Interior)**. *(Remember to click Edit Type and then Duplicate; see page 5-15.)*

13. Click the **Edit** button next to the *Structure* parameter.

Typically you will want to give walls more generic names so they can be used elsewhere in the project. Because you know this wall will only be used once, it is easier to give it a more descriptive name so it is not confused with other wall types later.

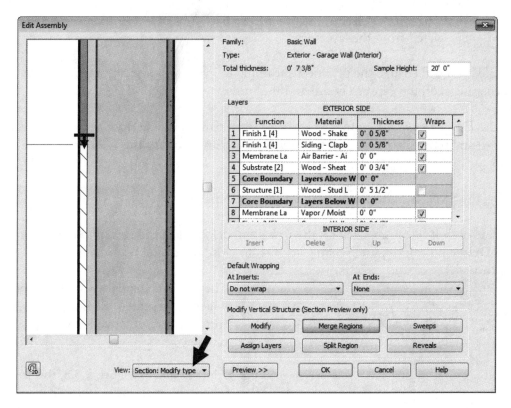

FIGURE 5-3.7 Edit Assembly dialog

The *Edit Assembly* dialog shown in Figure 5-3.7 will be modified in the following way. This is just an overview; the detailed instructions will follow:

- First, you will delete the horizontal sweeps.
  - A sweep is a closed 2D shape that is extruded along the length of a wall at a given height; a unique material can be specified.
  - This wall type currently has two sweeps (refer back to Figure 5-2.17): one at the base of the wall and another near the second floor line.

- Second, you will merge the two "vertically stacked" exterior finish layers so you can delete the exterior finish layers.
  - A layer can be split vertically into multiple regions; the exterior layer of this wall style is split into two regions. One has the material "Wood-Shakes" assigned to it and the other has "Finishes – Exterior – Siding / Clapboard" assigned to it.
  - Looking at Figure 5-3.7, you can visually see which layers are spilt vertically by looking at the Thickness column; the shaded "Thickness" cells are "vertically stacked" layers.
  - Vertically stacked layers must be *Merged* back into one region before they can be deleted from the layers list.

- Finally, you will change the plywood sheathing to gypsum board and move the air barrier between the gypsum board and the studs.

14. In the *Edit Assembly* dialog make sure the *Preview* pane is visible (*click on the <<Preview button*) and then select **Section: modify type attributes** from the *View* list (Figure 5-3.7).

15. Click the **Sweeps** button to load the *Wall Sweeps* dialog.

16. Delete both *Wall Sweeps*: click on the row number, to select the row, and then click the **Delete** button (Figure 5-3.8). Click **OK** to close the dialog box when done.

FIGURE 5-3.8 Wall Sweeps to be deleted

The two rectangular shaped sweeps, which represented the horizontal trim, are now removed from the preview section.

Also, notice in Figure 5-3.8, this is where the material is assigned to the sweep.

Next you will merge the two "vertically stacked" layers into one region. The tricky part here is that Revit will let you merge any two regions. So you need to keep an eye on the cursor and the pop-up tooltip.

17. Select the **Merge Regions** button.

18. Using the *scroll wheel* on the mouse, zoom in on the region split line at the top edge of the vertical dimension; you need to click in the *Preview* window to activate that area first (Figure 5-3.7).

19. Move your cursor over the short horizontal line and then press the **Tab** key until the cursor changes to a horizontal line with an arrow pointing downward and the tooltip states that **Layer 1 and Layer 2 will be merged** (see Figure 5-3.7), and then click.

    FYI: You can also Pan *in the Preview pane using your scroll wheel button.*

20. Individually select the *Layer* numbers 1 and 2, to select the row, and **Delete** them. This will delete the two exterior finish layers: shakes and siding.

    FYI: Watch the Preview pane while you do this.

21. Click the **Membrane Layer** row and then click the **Down** button to move the location of the air barrier within the wall.

22. Do not change the wood stud layer; leave it at 5½".

23. Change the ¾" sheathing layer by clicking in each cell in that row and then clicking the down-arrow that appears to the right; change the *Function* to **Finish 1** [4], *Material* to **Gypsum Wall Board**, *Thickness* to ½" (Figure 5-3.9).

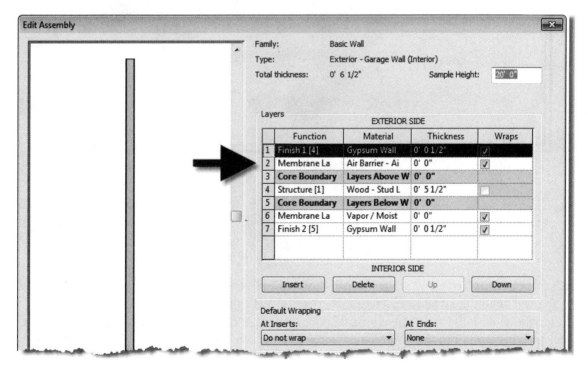

FIGURE 5-3.9 Modified edit assembly dialog

Now that you have created a new wall type, you can sketch the wall in the first floor plan view.

24. With your new wall type selected in the *Type Selector*, use the **Wall** tool to sketch a wall between the garage and the house. Set the wall *Height* to **Second Floor**.

   TIP: Set the Location Line to Finish Face: Interior *and then select the interior corner of the exterior wall.*

28' - 1 7/16"

FIGURE 5-3.10 New interior garage wall added

It is important to remember that the "flip control" symbol is displayed on the exterior side of the wall when the wall is selected; this corresponds to the *Exterior Side* and *Interior Side* designations with the wall type editor. If your symbol is on the wrong side, click it to flip the wall and the symbol to the other side. You will then have to *Move* or *Align* the wall so it is flush with the adjacent exterior wall.

25. Save your project as **Ex5-3.rvt**.

Exercise 5-4:
Doors, Openings and Windows

This lesson will take a closer look at inserting doors and windows.

Now that you have sketched the walls, you will add some doors. A door symbol indicates which side the hinges are on and the direction the door opens.

New doors are typically shown open 90 degrees in floor plans, which helps to avoid conflicts such as the door hitting an adjacent base cabinet. Additionally, to make it clear graphically, existing doors are shown open only 45 degrees.

Door symbol Example – New Door drawn with 90 degree swing

Door symbol Example – Existing Door shown with 45 degree swing

One of the most powerful features of any CAD program is its ability to reuse previously drawn content. With Revit you can insert entire door systems (door, frame, trim, etc). You drew a 2D door symbol in Lesson 4; however, you will now use Revit's powerful *Door* tool which are fully 3D.

For those new to drafting, you may find this comparison between CAD and hand drafting interesting: when hand drafting, one uses straight edges or a plastic template that has doors and other often used symbols to trace.

Hand Drafting Template – Plastic template with holes representing common residential shapes, at ¼″ = 1′-0″

Image used by permission, Timely Templates
www.timelytemplates.com

Doors in stud walls are dimensioned to the center of the door opening. On the other hand and similar to dimensioning masonry walls, doors in masonry walls are dimensioned to the face (see example below).

Door Dimension Example – Dimension to the center of the door opening

Door Dimension Example – Dimension the opening size and location

Loading Additional Door Families:

Revit has done an excellent job providing several different door families. This makes sense seeing as doors are an important part of an architectural project. Some of the provided families include bi-fold, double, pocket, sectional (garage), and vertical rolling, to name a few. In addition to the library groups found on your local hard drive, many more are available via the *Web Library* feature, which requires an internet connection.

The default template you started with *(Residential-Default.rte)* only provides four door *families*; each family contains multiple door sizes. If you want to insert other styles, you will need to load additional *families* from the library. The reason for this step is that, when you load a family, Revit actually copies the data into your project file. If every possible group was loaded into your project at the beginning, not only would it be hard to find what you want in a large list of doors, but also the files would be several megabytes in size before you even drew the first wall.

You will begin this section by loading a few additional families into your project.

1. Open project ex5-3.rvt and **Save-As ex5-4.rvt**.

2. With the *Door* tool selected, select **Load Family** on the *Ribbon* (Figure 5-4.1).

Load Family

3. Browse through the **Doors** folder for a moment. The *Doors* folder is a sub-folder of the *Imperial Library*; Revit should have taken you there by default, if not you can browse to:
    a. *XP:* C:\Documents and Settings\All Users\Application Data\Autodesk\RAC 2012\Imperial Library\ Doors.
    b. *Vista and Windows 7:* C:\ProgramData\Autodesk\RAC 2012\Imperial Library\ Doors

FIGURE 5-4.1 Load content from Library

Each file represents a *family*, each having one or more similar *Types* of varying sizes. Next you will load four door families into your project.

FIGURE 5-4.2 Door families on hard drive

4. Select **Bifold-2 Panel.rfa**, and then click **Open** (Figure 5-4.2).

As soon as you click *Open*, the selected family is copied into your current project and is available for placement.

5.   Repeat Steps 2 – 4 to load the following
     door families:
     a.   **Sliding-2 panel**
     b.   **Single-Panel 4**

TIP: If you hold the Ctrl key you can select several door files and load them at one time.

6.   In the *Project Browser*, expand the *Families* category and then *Doors* to see the loaded door families (Figure 5-4.3).

If you expand the *Doors* sub-category itself in the *Project Browser* you see the predefined door sizes associated with that group. Right-clicking on a door size allows you to rename, delete or duplicate it. To add a door size, you duplicate and then modify properties for the new item, similar to how you created a new wall.

FIGURE 5-4.3 Loaded door families

Downloading Additional Door Families from the Internet:

Now you will explore Autodesk's online content website: seek.autodesk.com. You will learn how to download a few more door families that are not available locally on your hard drive.

This content distribution site is geared toward all of Autodesk's design software. If you browse directly to the site using your web browser you can search for several types of design files, including AutoCAD and 3DS Max. However, you can also initiate a search from within Revit and automatically narrow your search down to Revit content.

7.   Switch to the **Insert** tab on the *Ribbon*.

Notice the *Autodesk Seek* panel on the
Insert tab (Figure5-4.4).

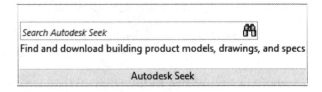

FIGURE 5-4.4 Insert tab, Seek panel

Normally you might type something such as garage door and sort through the options that appear. You are encouraged to try this on your own. In this case you will enter specific family names to gain quick access to content required for this lesson.

8. Click in the text box and enter "**Overhead-Sectional-Flush**" (Figure 5-4.5).

FIGURE 5-4.5 Insert tab, Seek panel

9. Press **Enter**.

Your default web browser is automatically opened and any matching items are listed (Figure 5-4.6). In this case there should only be one element that matches the name you entered. Of course, this website could change, so the results could vary. If this door family is not available, search for another overhead garage door.

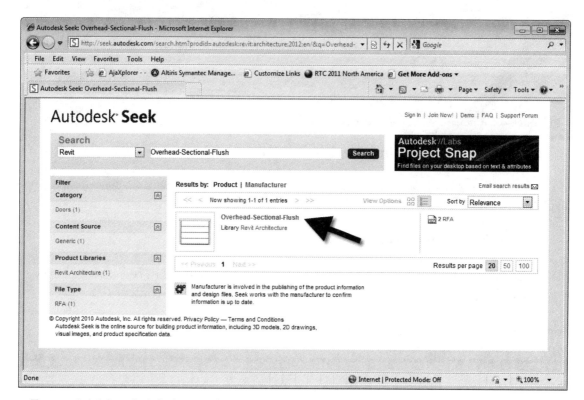

FIGURE 5-4.6 Autodesk Seek opened in web browser

10. Click "**Overhead-Sectional-Flush**" to download that family.

You now have the option to download the 2009 or the 2010 version of the family; you can download any version as long as it is not newer than the version of Revit software you are using. You will be downloading the files to your computer's hard drive. However, it is interesting to note that the content may also be dragged and dropped into an open project. For more on this, click "About i-drop" in the upper right.

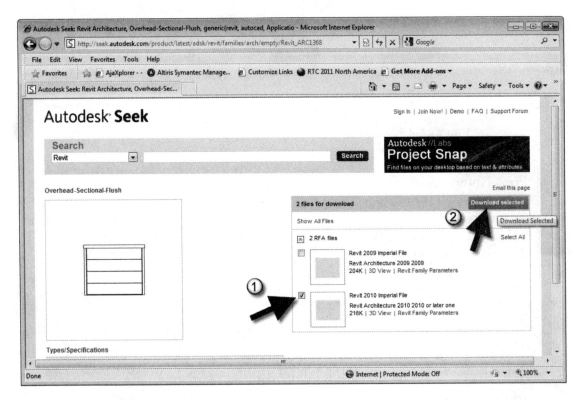

FIGURE 5-4.7 Autodesk Seek opened in web browser

    11. Check the **Revit 2010 Imperial File** check-box.

FYI: Revit can always open an older Revit file format, but never a newer one. So it is possible to load the 2009 or 2010 content, but it will take a little longer as Revit will have to upgrade it first.

    12. Click the **Download selected** button.

    13. **Check the box** and click **Accept** if you have read Autodesk's *Terms and Conditions* policy and agree to it. You must do this before downloading content.

Terms and Conditions

☑ I have read and agree to the Terms and Conditions.

Note: You need to agree to the Terms and Conditions only one time. Agreeing to the terms will place a cookie on your machine that will allow you to download content from Autodesk® Seek every subsequent time.

| Accept | Cancel |

    14. Select **Save** (Figure 5-4.8).

    15. *Save* the file to your computer's *Desktop* using the default name provided.

FYI: You will be prompted to specify a location to save the downloaded files. Make sure you pay attention to where the files are being saved so you can load them into your project later.

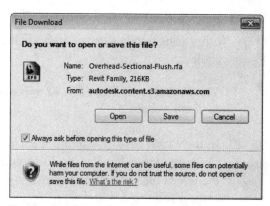

You may repeat the previous steps to load the remaining content, or enter your search text in the current *Seek* page.

16. Repeat the previous steps to download four more door families from the Web Library:
    a. **Double-Raised Panel with Sidelights**
    b. **Single-Entry 3**
    c. **Single-Pocket**
    d. **Opening-Elliptical Arch**

FIGURE 5-4.8 Web browser download prompt

Now that you have saved the door family files to the hard drive, you need to load them into your current project.

You may want to create a folder where you save all the families you download. This would make future access more convenient, especially if you did not have internet access at that time. This folder should probably not be in Revit's standard folder location as it may be difficult to migrate the data after an upgrade (i.e., sorting the custom files from the default files).

One more thing on families via the web: you have access to content via sources other than Revit. You can try an internet search with text that reads something like *"autodesk revit families."* As Revit's popularity grows, more and more product manufactures will start making families available that represent their products, thus making it easier for designers to incorporate their products into a project. For example, one can also download an extensive wall and ceiling library from United States Gypsum (USG) at www.usgdesignstudio.com. Additionally, you can visit www.augi.com (Autodesk Users Group International), or www.revitcity.com for Revit related resources and content.

Rather than loading content with the *Door* tool active, you will just use the *Load Family* tool directly from the *Insert* tab.

17. Select **Insert** → **Load From Library** → **Load Family** from the *Ribbon*.

18. Browse to the location where you saved the family files and select **Double-Raised Panel with Sidelights.rfa**, and then click **Open** (similar to Figure 5-4.2).

19. Repeat the previous two steps to load the other four families, from Step 16, into your project.

    TIP: You can press the Ctrl key and select more than one family to load.

20. In the *Project Browser*, expand the *Doors* category, under *Families*, again to verify all the doors have been loaded into your project (Figure 5-4.9)

Note that the *Opening-Elliptical Arch* does not display here; it actually shows up under *Generic Model*.

Next you will start inserting the doors into the first floor plan.

Doors
- Bifold-2 Panel
- Double-Glass 1
- Double-Raised Panel wi
- Overhead-Sectional-Flus
- Single-Entry 3
- Single-Flush
- Single-Panel 4
- Single-Pocket
- Single-Raised Panel with
- Sliding-2 panel
- Sliding-Closet

FIGURE 5-4.9 All door families loaded for this exercise

21. With the *Door* tool selected, pick **Single-Entry 3: 36" x 80"** from the *Type Selector* on the *Properties Palette*.

22. Insert one door in the North wall of the garage as shown in Figure 5-4.10.

Immediately after the door is inserted, or when the door is selected, you can click on the horizontal or vertical flip-controls to position the door as desired.

Since "Tag on placement" was selected on the *Options Bar*, Revit automatically adds a *Door Tag* near the newly inserted door. The door itself stores information about the door that can then be compiled in a door schedule. The doors are automatically numbered in the order they are placed. The number can be changed at any time to suit the designer's needs; you will do this later in the door schedule section. Most architects and designers use 1x or 1xx (i.e., 12 or 120) numbers for the first floor and 2x or 2xx numbers for the second floor door numbers.

FIGURE **5-4.10** First door placed at rear of garage

The *Door Tag* can be moved simply by clicking on it to select it, and then clicking and dragging it to its new location. You may need to press the *Tab* key to pre-highlight the tag before you can select it.

Also, with the *Door Tag* selected you can set the vertical/horizontal orientation and whether a leader should be displayed when the tag is moved; it is done via the settings on the *Options Bar*. The tag must be selected.

23. Click *Modify* and then select the newly placed door; take a moment to review the information displayed in the *Properties Palette*.

> *TIP: If the Properties Palette is not visible, simply type "pp" on the keyboard; do not press Enter.*

Notice, in Figure 5-4.11, you see the *Instance Parameters* which are options that vary with each door, e.g., *Sill Height* and *Door Number (Mark)*. These parameters control selected or to-be-created items.

The *Type Parameters* are not visible in this dialog. To be sure you want to make changes that affect all doors of that type, Revit forces you to click the *Edit Type* button and make changes in the *Type Properties* dialog. Also, in the *Type Properties* dialog, you can add additional pre-defined door sizes to the *"Single-Entry 3"* door family by clicking the *Duplicate* button, providing a new name and changing the "size" dimensions for that new *Type*.

FIGURE **5-4.11**
Properties for door

24. Finish inserting doors for the first floor (Figure 5-4.12). Use the following guidelines:

   a. Use the door styles shown in Figure 5-4.12.

   b. Doors across from each other in the *Mud Room* should align with each other.

   c. Place doors approximately as shown; exact location is not important.

   d. See the next page for information on sliding pocket doors.

   e. While inserting doors, you can control the door swing by moving the cursor to one side of the wall or the other and by using the spacebar on the keyboard.

   f. The order in which the doors are placed does not matter; this means your doors may have different numbers than the ones shown below.

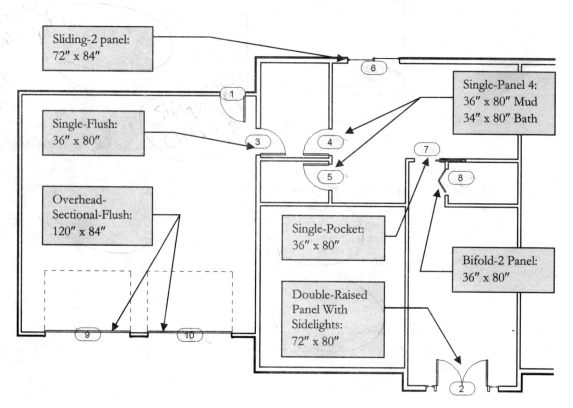

FIGURE 5-4.12 Doors to be inserted

Sliding Pocket Doors:

Sliding pocket doors are doors that slide into the wall rather than swinging open into a room. This type of door is convenient when the door will be open most of the time and you do not want, or have room for, an open door. On the other hand, if the door will be used often, like the door from the hallway into the bath room, you should use a swinging door for ease of use and long-term durability.

One important thing to keep in mind when designing a room with a sliding door: the entire width of the door is in the wall when the door is fully open. That means you need space in the wall next to the door that equals the width of the door plus a few inches depending on the manufacturer. This includes plumbing and electrical that might be in the wall.

ROUGH OPENING IN WIDTH IS 2 TIMES THE DOOR SIZE PLUS 2" (50.8mm). R.O. IN HEIGHT IS 4" (101.6 mm) MORE THAN DOOR HEIGHT.

ROUGH OPENING   FRAME INSTALLED IN ROUGH OPENING.   FRAME AND DOOR INSTALLED. READY FOR DRYWALL.

POCKET DOOR EXAMPLES – Double door and Single door photos (top); Installation illustration (bottom)

Images used by permission, KrisTrack www.kristrack.com

Insert Openings:

With the first floor doors in place, you will add three openings. An opening is similar to a door in that, when placed, it removes a portion of wall automatically creating a circulation route. Also, like doors, openings come in different predefined shapes and sizes.

One common mistake is to break a wall so the floor plan appears to have an opening. However, when a section is cut through the opening there is no wall above the opening. This is also problematic for the room tagging feature and the *Ceiling Placement* tool.

One of the keys to working successfully in Revit is to model the building project just like you would build it, because that is the way Revit is designed to work.

Next, you will place two larger openings in the walls between the *Foyer* and the *Living Room* and the *Dining Room*. A smaller opening will be placed in the wall between the *Dining Room* and the *Kitchen*. All three openings are from a family you previously loaded: *Opening-Elliptical Arch*.

The *Type Properties* dialog is shown below (Figure 5-4.13). Notice the various fields that can be filled in. For example, you could enter how much it would cost to construct an opening with an arched top in the *Cost* field.

FIGURE 5-4.13 Type Properties for: *Opening-Elliptical Arch* family

25. Select **Home → Build → Component**; just click the upper part of the icon which defaults to the *Place a Component* option, seen via down-arrow selection.

26. Place the three **openings** as shown in Figure 5-4.14.

   TIP: *Select the appropriate opening (family/type) from the Type Selector on the Properties Palette.*

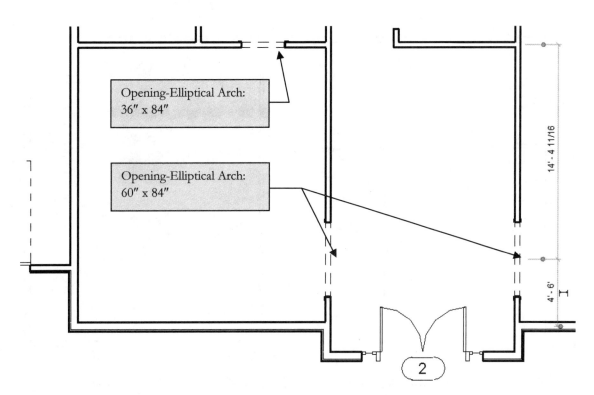

FIGURE 5-4.14 Openings placed in first floor plan

Insert Windows:

Adding windows to your project is very similar to adding doors. The template file you started from has three families preloaded into your project: Casement with Trim, Double Hung with Trim and Fixed with Trim. Looking at the *Type Selector* drop-down you will see the various sizes available for insertion. Additional families can be loaded, similar to how you loaded the doors, although your project will only use two families total and they are already loaded: *Double Hung* and *Fixed*.

27. Using the ***Window*** tool on the *Basics* tab, select **Double Hung with Trim: 36″ x 72″** in the *Type Selector*; place 9 windows total in this step.

28. Insert the windows as shown in **Figure 5-4.15**; be sure to adjust the window locations to match the dimensions shown, but do not add the dimensions. Be sure to click towards the exterior side of the wall, so the window has the proper orientation.

TIP: To edit location: Modify → select window → adjust temporary dimension witness lines → edit temporary dimension text.

FIGURE 5-4.15 (9) windows added: Double Hung with Trim: 36″ x 72″

With a window *Type*, within a family, not only is the window size pre-defined, but the vertical distance off the ground is as well. Next you will see where this setting is stored.

29. Select one of the windows that you just placed in the walls and then notice the information presented in the *Properties Palette*.

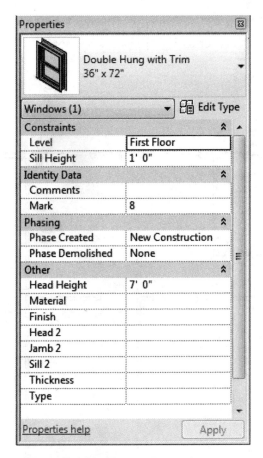

Figure 5-4.16a Element Properties

As previously discussed, this palette shows the various settings for the selected item: a window in this case (Figure 5-4.16).

As you might guess, the same size window could have more than one sill height (i.e., distance from the floor to the bottom of the window). So Revit lets you adjust this setting on a window-by-window basis; this is called an *Instance Parameter*.

Another setting you might have noticed by now is *Phase Created*. This is part of what makes Revit a 4D program; the fourth dimension is time. Again, you might have several windows that are existing and several new ones in an addition, all the same size window. Revit lets you do that!

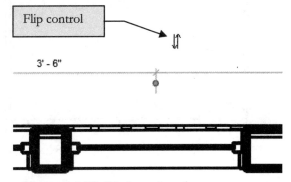

Figure 5-4.16b Window selected

Notice a Flip Control icon is shown when the window is selected, similar to doors. This icon should be on the exterior side of the wall. If not, simply click on the icon to flip the window's orientation within the wall.

30. Make sure the *Sill Height* is **1'-0"** and the **Flip Control** icon is on the exterior side of the wall; if not, change all nine windows.

Next, you will insert several double hung windows that are not as tall in the less prominent rooms, also in the *Kitchen* so cabinets will fit below the window. However, if you did place the tall windows in the *Kitchen*, you would realize it as soon as you tried to place the base cabinets and generate interior elevations or sections in the *Kitchen*. This is because the entire Revit project is one 3D database.

Compare the above mentioned conflict with traditional CAD, where the 2D elevations have nothing to do with the floor plans, sections, or interior elevations. With traditional CAD, you could draw the exterior elevations with the tall windows and place cabinets under it in plan view and then draw an interior elevation showing the cabinets and a shorter window. The windows are usually ordered and rough openings framed based on the exterior elevations. Revit helps to avoid these types of costly mistakes.

31. Insert window **Double Hung with Trim: 36″ x 48″** as shown in **Figure 5-4.17**; use *Instance Properties* to make sure the *Sill Height* is set to **3′-0″**; place 9 windows total.

FIGURE 5-4.17 (9) windows added: Double Hung with Trim: 36″ x 48″

Creating a New Window Type:

You will add four more windows to the East wall. These will be high windows, two on either side of a fireplace. Rather than using one of the predefined window sizes, you will create a new size within an existing family.

These windows will be fixed, non-operable, so you will be adding a new type to the *Fixed with Trim* family.

32. Select the **Window** tool and then select the **Edit Type** button on the *Properties Palette*.

33. Set the *Family* drop-down to **Fixed with Trim** and then set the *Type* drop-down to **36″ x 24″** (Figure 5-4.18). **Do not select the Double Hung window!**

   FYI: *You could have selected this in the* Type Selector *before clicking the* Edit Type *button.*

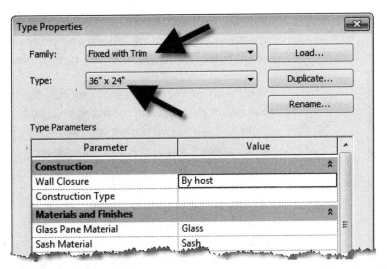

FIGURE 5-4.18 Type Properties – *Family*: Fixed with Trim; *Type*: 36″ x 24″

34. Click the **Duplicate** button.

35. Enter **36″ x 20″** for the name and then click **OK**.

You are now viewing the *Type Properties* for the new 36″ x 20″ type you just created. However, the name has nothing to do with actually changing the window size. You will do this next.

36. Change the *Height* parameter to **1′-8″**.

37. Change the *Default Sill Height* to **5′-4″**. *(This makes the top of all your windows align at 7′-0″.)*

38. Click **OK** to close the *Type Properties* dialog.

39. Add the windows as dimensioned in Figure 5-4.20.

FIGURE 5-4.19 Type Properties: New predefined window size

You are probably wondering where the windows are? They are tagged and you can select them. However, they are not visible.

With your project being a 3D model, Revit has to cut through the model as a certain elevation when generating the plan view. The default *Cut Plane* is 4'-0" above the floor line.

As you should recall, the sill of the new window type you just created is 5'-4" (Figure 5-4.19). If it is not, you should select the 36"x20" windows and adjust the sill height in the *Properties Palette*.

So the window occurs above the cut line. The windows will show up just fine in elevation and section views. Next you will see where the *Cut Plane* is set for each plan view.

POWER TIP: If you want the windows to be visible, or a high stair landing to show, you can create a Plan Region, *which allows you to override the cut plane within the selected area. See Help for more on this.*

FIGURE 5-4.20
First floor plan: last four windows added

40. Click the **Modify** tool on the *Ribbon* to unselect elements and cancel any active commands. This will cause the *Properties Palette* to show information about the current view.

41. Scroll down, in the *Properties Palette*, and select **Edit** next to *View Range*.

Notice the *Cut Plane* is set to 4'-0" (Figure 5-4.21). Try changing it and closing the dialog to see the various effects it has on your *Floor Plan* view; look at the stairs and the high windows.

Be sure to set the *Cut Plane* back to 4'-0" before proceeding.

42. Click **OK** to close the *View Range* dialog box.

FIGURE 5-4.21 View Range properties

Cleaning House:

As previously mentioned, you can view the various *Families* and *Types* loaded into your project via the *Project Browser*. The more families and types you have loaded the larger your file is, whether or not you are using them in your project. Therefore, it is a good idea to get rid of any door, window, etc., that you know you will not need in the current project. You do not have to delete any at this time, but this is how you do it:

Figure: Project Browser

- In the *Project Browser*, navigate to Families → Windows → Fixed. Right-click on **36″ x 48″** and select **Delete**.

Another reason to delete types is to avoid mistakes. As you have seen, loading a door family brings in 6′-8″ and 7′-0″ tall doors. On a residential project you would rarely use 7′-0″ tall doors, so it would be a good idea to delete them from the project so you don't accidentally pick them.

That concludes the exercise on adding doors, openings and windows to the first floor plan.

Exercise 5-5:
Adding a Fireplace

The last thing you will do in this lesson is to add a fireplace to the *Living Room*. Creating a fireplace is beyond the scope of this introductory book, so you will download one from the *Web Library* (http://seek.autodesk.com).

1.   Using techniques previously described to download doors from *Seek* (page 5-39), download the following items:
   a.   **Mantel 1** (Figure 5-5.1)
   b.   **Masonry Chimney-Wall** (Figure 5-5.1)

Mantel 1   Masonry Chimney-Wall

FIGURE 5-5.1 Seek content – download: Mantel and Chimney

2.   **Load** the downloaded families into your project (see page 5-41).

You are now ready to place the fireplace in the first floor plan.

3.   With the *First Floor Plan* view current, select **Home → Build → Component** from the *Ribbon*.

4.   From the *Type Selector*, pick **Masonry Chimney-Wall : Chimney**.

The chimney will be looking for a wall to be inserted into; this is a *wall hosted family*. When your cursor is near a wall, you will see a "ghost" chimney to help you visually place the element; when the cursor is not near a wall, Revit does not display the "ghost" image because it is not a valid location to place the selected element.

Try moving the cursor around the plan for a minute. Notice, again, that when the cursor is near a wall you see the "ghost" image and the image orients itself with the wall (e.g., vert., horiz., angled). When the element encounters another element placed within a wall, you will see a small circle with a diagonal line through it indicating the two elements cannot overlap. Furthermore, the element flips to the side of the wall the cursor is on. Try moving the cursor from one side of the wall to the other and observe the image flip back and forth.

5. Move your cursor to the middle portion of the easternmost wall, between the high windows; with your cursor on the exterior side of the wall, click to place the fireplace.

6. Adjust the temporary dimensions so the chimney is centered on the wall (Figure 5-5.2).

Next you will place the mantel in the plan view. This is less automatic as it does not attach to the wall. So you will insert the mantel in the middle of the living room, rotate it and then move it into place.

FIGURE 5-5.2 Chimney added

7. Use the **Component** tool to insert **Mantel 1:80″ x 58¾″** into the middle of the *Living Room*.

8. Select the *Mantel* and use the **Rotate** tool to rotate the mantel 90 degrees in the clockwise direction.

TIP: You could have also pressed the spacebar during placement in step 7 and then skipped step 8.

FIGURE 5-5.3 3D view of mantel

9. With the *Mantel* still selected, use the **arrow keys** on your keyboard to "nudge" the element into place, or try using the *Align* tool (Figure 5-5.4)

10. Take a minute to look at the *3D View* of all that you have completed so far (Figure 5-5.5 and image below).

Fireplace

Mantel

11. **Save** your project as **Ex5-5.rvt**.

FIGURE 5-5.4 Mantel added in plan view

FIGURE 5-5.5 3D View of completed chapter

Self-Exam:

The following questions can be used as a way to check your knowledge of this lesson. The answers can be found at the bottom of the page.

1. The *Options Bar* allows you to select the height at which your wall will be drawn. (T/F)

2. It is not possible to draw a wall with the interior or exterior face of the core as the reference point. (T/F)

3. Objects cannot be moved accurately with the *Move* tool. (T/F)

4. The _____ tool, on the *Ribbon*, has to be selected in order to select an object in your project.

5. A wall has to be _____ to see its flip icon.

Review Questions:

The following questions may be assigned by your instructor as a way to assess your knowledge of this section. Your instructor has the answers to the review questions.

1. Revit comes with many predefined doors and windows. (T/F)

2. The *Project Information* dialog allows you to enter data about the project, some of which is automatically added to sheet borders. (T/F)

3. You can delete *families* and *types* in the *Project Browser*. (T/F)

4. It is not possible to add a new window *type* to a window *family*. (T/F)

5. It is not possible to select which side of the wall a window should be on while you are inserting the window. (T/F)

6. What tool will break a wall into two smaller pieces? __Split__

7. The __Align__ tool allows you to match the surface of two adjacent walls.

8. Use the __Space__ key, on the keyboard, to flip the door swing while placing doors using the *Door* tool.

9. You adjust the location of a dimension's witness line by clicking on, or dragging, its __Grip__ .

10. The __Default__ file has a few doors, windows and walls preloaded in it.

Notes:

Lesson 6
Residence: SECOND FLOOR and BASEMENT PLANS:

In this lesson you will develop the second floor plan as well as the basement. This will involve copying objects from the first floor with some modifications along the way. You will also add stairs and dimensions to your plans. Be sure to check out the DVD video on *Stairs*.

Exercise 6-1:
View Setup and Enclosing the Shell

Discussion: Second Floor View Current Conditions

1. Switch to the **Second Floor** view under *Floor Plans* in the *Project Browser*, double-click on the view name.

You should see a plan view similar to Figure 6-1.1. The geometry you are seeing is a result of two things:

- First, the height of walls drawn on the first floor:
    i. Some of the exterior walls that you sketched in the first floor plan are 19'-0" tall.
    ii. From the elevation views, you can see that the second floor is 9'-0" above the first.
    iii. As you may recall from the last chapter, the default *View Range* – Cut Line is 4'-0" above the floor.
    iv. So, relative to the first floor, the second floor Cut Plane is 13'-0" above it (9'-0" + 4'-0").
    v. Therefore, the 19'-0" tall walls extend past the second floor Cut Plane; that is why they are bold (elements in section automatically have a heavier line weight).
    vi. The exterior walls of the garage and east living room walls are only 12'-0", which is below the Cut Plane. It is still within the *View Range* so it shows up in "elevation" or projection. Elements in *projection* (i.e., beyond the Cut Plane) have lighter lines than those in section (i.e., at the Cut Plane).

- Second, the *Underlay* feature:
    i. In the *Properties Palette* (View Properties) for the *Second Floor Plan* view you will see a parameter labeled *Underlay* (Figure 6-1.2).
    ii. This feature is currently set to *First Floor*.
    iii. The *Underlay* feature causes the selected view's walls to be displayed as light gray lines for reference.

iv. The walls shown as part of an underlay cannot be selected using a *window* selection but can be selected, and even deleted, by picking directly on a wall, or anything else.

FIGURE 6-1.1 Second Floor: initial view

You do not need to see the first floor walls at the moment, so you will turn them off.

2. In the *Properties Palette* dialog set **Underlay** to **none**. *(Click Modify first if the View Properties are not currently shown.)*

Now you should only see the exterior walls (Figure 6-1.3).

Next, you will sketch two more exterior walls to enclose the second floor. These walls only occur above the second floor line so they will only have wood shakes for siding.

FIGURE 6-1.2 View Properties: Second Floor view

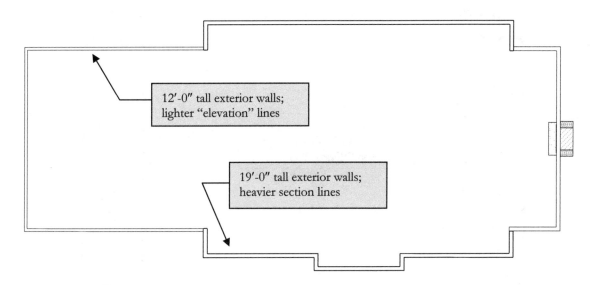

12'-0" tall exterior walls; lighter "elevation" lines

19'-0" tall exterior walls; heavier section lines

FIGURE 6-1.3 Second Floor: underlay turned off

3. Using the *Wall* tool, select **Exterior – Wood Shingle on Wood Stud** from the *Type Selector*.

If you look at the properties for this wall you will see that it is very similar to your primary exterior wall assembly. The main difference is that the vertical elements are stripped away: horizontal siding and two sweeps. You will see another wall type with just horizontal siding as well. These two walls are loaded in the template for the reason you are about to use one: as infill between the main, more complex, wall type. The image to the right shows, from left to right, horizontal siding only, shakes only and then the main wall you have previously used.

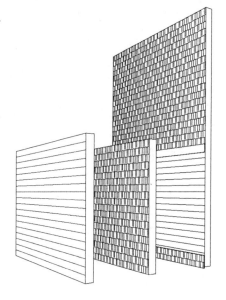

If you tried to use the wall type "Basic Wall: Exterior – Wood Shingle over Wood Siding on Wood Stud", the horizontal wood siding would start at the second floor line for any wall placed on the second floor. This is why you need a wall that just has wood shingles and no sweeps (i.e., horizontal. trim boards).

4. Draw the two walls as shown in Figure 6-1.4, using the following information:
    - Set the *Height* to **Roof** (*Options Bar*).
    - Set the *Location Line* to **Finished Face: Interior** (*Options Bar*).
    - Pick the interior side of the existing wall; press the *spacebar* if you need to flip the wall before picking the wall end point.

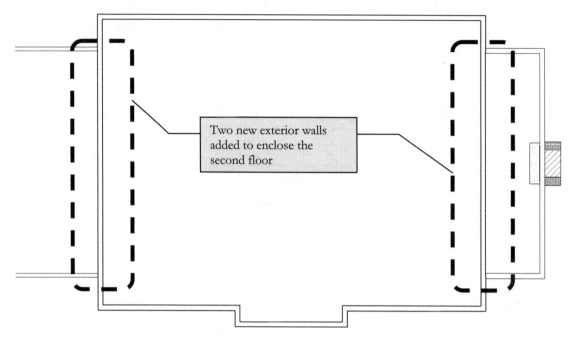

Two new exterior walls added to enclose the second floor

FIGURE 6-1.4 Second Floor: two exterior walls added

The height of the walls will change later when the roof is drawn. In fact, the height will vary as it extends up to the underside of the gable end roof; see image on the book cover.

The two walls just drawn will be supported by the second floor, which has not been drawn yet. The bottom of the walls is aligned with *Level 2* because of the view you are in.

You may have noticed that the exterior face of the wall does not appear to align perfectly with the adjacent walls. You will explore this problem and correct it in the next steps.

5. Select one of the walls just placed.

6. Click the **Edit Type** button on the *Properties Palette*.

7. In the *Type Properties* dialog, click **Edit** next to the ***Structure*** parameter.

8. Take note of the overall wall thickness and the thickness of the various layers (Figure 6-1.5A).

9. Close the dialog boxes, *Edit Assembly* and *Type Properties*, by clicking **OK**.

10. Follow the previous steps to look at the structure properties for the **Exterior – Wood Shingle over Wood Siding on Wood Stud**.

   NOTE: *The sheathing thickness is not the same (Figures 6-1.5a and b). You will change one so they both match.*

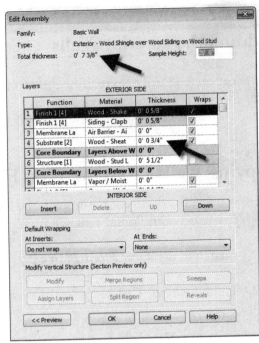

FIGURE 6-1.5A & B Comparing two walls' properties; sheathing thickness varies

11. Modify the *Sheathing* from ½″ to ¾″ for *Exterior – Wood Shingle on Wood Stud*.

12. **Save** your project as **Ex6-1.rvt**.

FYI:

Just as a reminder: the four elevation tags should not be deleted. You will study these more thoroughly later. This is what they represent:

The default template has four elevation tags shown in plan view. These symbols represent what the four preset views listed in the *Project Browser* will see. Therefore, you should always start drawing your plan in the approximate center of the four symbols. The symbols can be moved by dragging them with your mouse.

Again, do not delete these elevation tags as that will delete the actual views from the *Project Browser*.

Any view (e.g., plan, elevation or section) can be recreated but all the notes and dimensions, which are view specific, would have to be manually recreated.

Exercise 6-2:
Adding the Interior Walls

This short exercise will help reinforce the commands you have already learned. You will add walls, doors and windows to your project.

Copying Walls From the First Floor:

Often, you will have walls occur in the same location on each floor. The easiest thing to do is copy/paste between floors. You will try this now.

1. Switch to the *First Floor Plan* view.

2. Hold down the **Ctrl** key; select the four walls identified in Figure 6-2.1.

FIGURE 6-2.1 First Floor: Selected walls, (4) total, to be copied/pasted to the Second Floor

3. With the four walls selected, select **Modify | Walls → Clipboard → Copy**; this command is different than *Copy* in the *Modify* panel which only works in the current view.

Clipboard

4. Click **Modify** to unselect the first floor walls and then switch back to the ***Second Floor Plan*** view.

> ***TIP:*** *Press Ctrl + Tab to switch between open views.*

5. Select **Modify → Clipboard → Paste → Aligned to Current View** (Figure 6-2.2).

You should now see the four walls in your *Second Floor Plan* view (Figure 6-2.3).

FIGURE 6-2.2
Modify tab: Paste Aligned fly-out

Why did we not just draw these four first floor walls 19'-0" high like the exterior walls?

Simulating real-world construction is ideal for several reasons. Mostly, you can be sure exterior walls align from floor to floor. Although the four walls align, they do not necessarily have to because they are separated by floor construction, this allows one floor to later be modified easily. However, if an exterior wall is moved in any plan view, you want to make sure it moves everywhere, so these walls are drawn full height.

6. Select **Modify** to deselect the walls via the *Ribbon*.

Any time a wall is copied, or copy/pasted, any hosted elements attached to the wall(s) are copied with the wall. Next, you will delete the openings that were copied with the walls from the first floor.

7. Individually select each of the four openings and delete them

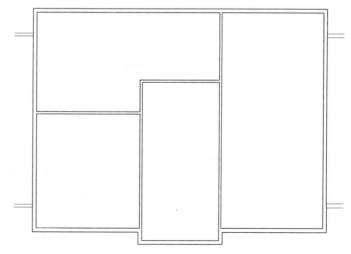

FIGURE 6-2.3 Second Floor: walls copied, doors deleted

Your first floor walls have their *top constraint* set to the second floor, so when you copied the walls from the first floor to the second floor Autodesk® Revit® Architecture automatically set the *top constraint* to the next level above the first floor: the *Roof* level. This is fine for now.

Next you will add a few more interior walls.

8. Using the **Wall** tool, draw the walls shown in Figure 6-2.4 using the following information:
   a. Wall type: **Interior – 4½″ Partition**
   b. Location Line: *use whatever is appropriate*
   c. Height: **Roof**
   d. Do not draw the dimensions at this time.
   e. Notice that one of the interior walls from Figure 6-2.3 gets extended and another gets trimmed; the walls previously created have a heavy dashed line over them (Figure 6-2.4).

FIGURE 6-2.4 Second Floor: additional walls added

Joining Geometry:

Occasionally the intersection of two walls will not clean up, so you can use the *Join Geometry* icon on the *Tools* toolbar. The steps are as follows:

- Click *Modify* → *Geometry* → *Join*.

- Select the two walls.

- That's it; the walls are joined.

Intersecting walls

Walls joined

Controlling the View Scale

The size of the dimensions and door and window tags is controlled by the *View Scale*. Each *View* has its own scale setting. To facilitate the creation of this book, the *View Scale* has been set to 3/32″ = 1′-0″ typical. At that scale, Revit makes the text and symbols larger so it is legible at the smaller scale. However, the images in this book are not to scale.

The default *View Scale* is ¼″ = 1′-0″ for the plan views, floor, ceiling and framing plans. This is good and should not be changed for this tutorial. In addition to controlling the text and symbols, it also controls the size, or scale, of that drawing on the plot sheet (i.e., one of the sheets in a set of drawings). This only makes sense seeing as *View Scale* has everything to do with what scale that view is intended to be printed at.

The *View Scale* can be controlled via the *View Properties* dialog or more conveniently on the *View Control Bar* at the bottom of the drawing window (Figure 6-2.5).

9. Save your project as **ex6-2.rvt**.

FIGURE 6-2.5
View Scale

Exercise 6-3:
Adding Doors, Openings and Windows

Do not forget to keep a backup of your files on a separate disk (i.e., flash drive, CD or DVD). Your project file should be about 8.5 MB when starting this exercise. Most computers today have a CD or DVD burner you can use to save large files. Remember, your Revit project is one large file and not many small files. You do not want anything to happen to it. Make sure you have a copy of this file in two places at all times – do this daily!

Adding More Doors

Now you will add the second floor doors and openings, but first you must load one more *door family* into your project.

1. Open project ex6-2.rvt and **Save-As ex6-3.rvt**.

2. Load the door Family **Bifold–4 Panel.rfa** into your project.

   Reminder: Click the Door tool, Load Family button (Ribbon), and then browse to the Doors sub-folder.

3. Add the doors as shown in Figure 6-3.1:
   a. Center the closet doors in the closet.

   TIP: With the inserted door selected, you can "nudge" the door using the arrow keys.

   FYI: The more zoomed in you are, the more accurate the "nudge" increments are.

Residential Door Sizes!
Doors come in many shapes and sizes.

Thickness: 1⅜", 1¾" and 2¼"
The 1⅜" door is most often used in residential construction and the 2¼" door is typically only used on exterior doors for high-end projects, i.e., big budget.

Size: ranges from 1'-0" x 6'-8" to 4'-0" x 9'-0"
The height of a residential door is usually 6'-8". This writer recently worked on a project where 7'-0" high doors were specified. The contractor was so used to the standard 6'-8" dimension; he framed all the exterior openings at 6'-8". To top it off, the exterior walls where concrete (ICF system), so the openings could not be modified. Thus, 6'-8" doors were used.

You can find more information on the internet; two examples are
   algomahardwoods.com and madawaska-doors.com
   (wood veneer door mfr.)   *(custom solid wood door mfr.)*

FIGURE 6-3.1 Second Floor; doors added

The door numbers were temporarily hidden from view for clarity. On your plans you notice that the new doors have different numbers while the windows have the same number. Why is this? It relates to industry standards for architectural drafting. Each window that is the same size and configuration has the same type number throughout the project. Each door has a unique number because doors have so many variables (i.e., locks, hinges, closer, panics, material, and fire rating). To make doors easier to find, many architectural firms will make the door number the same as the room number the door opens into. You can change the door number by selecting the tag and then clicking on the text. The door schedule will be updated automatically.

Adding More Windows:

4. Add the windows as shown in Figure 6-3.2.

    a. Verify via the *Properties Palette* that each window's *Head Height* is set to 7'-0".

        TIP: *Type* PP *if you accidentally closed the* Properties Palette.

    b. All windows are **Double Hung with Trim: 36″ x 48″** unless otherwise noted in Figure 6-3.2.

    c. Similar to the previous image, the door and window tags have been temporarily hidden from view; you will learn how to do this next.

    d. All dimensions are from the center of the window to the exterior face of wall.

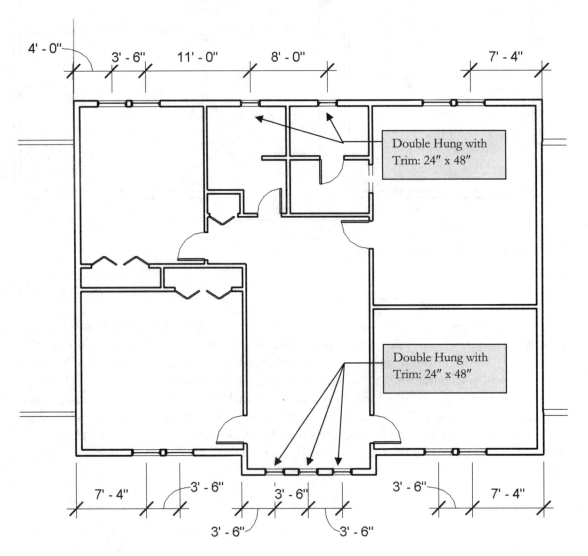

FIGURE 6-3.2 Second floor plan: windows added

Using Hide/Isolate to Control Visibility:

Now you will shift gears for a moment and look at the *Hide/Isolate* feature. This allows you to temporarily hide or isolate the selected elements or all the elements in the same category as those selected.

This feature is accessed via the *View Control Bar*, similar to the *View Scale* feature previously discussed.

5. Holding the **Ctrl** key, select one door tag and one window tag.

6. On the *View Control* bar click the **Temporary Hide/Isolate** icon (looks like sunglasses).

7. From the pop-up menu, select **Hide Category** (Figure 6-3.3).

FIGURE 6-3.3 View Control bar: Hide/Isolate selected

You should notice two things. First, all the door and window tags are gone. Second, the *Hide/Isolate* icon has a cyan background and the drawing window has a heavy cyan border around it, with text in the upper left stating "Temporary Hide/Isolate", which reminds you that some thing(s) is temporarily removed from the current view.

As implied by the feature name, the tags are temporarily hidden from view; they have not been deleted.

If you would have selected *Hide Element*, only the selected elements would have been hidden from view rather than the entire category.

To restore this temporary setting, do the following:

8. Click the **Temporary Hide/Isolate** icon again (nothing has to be selected).

9. Select **Reset Temporary Hide/Isolate** from the pop-up menu.

> **FYI:** *Hiding items does affect printing. If you close the project and reopen it the temporary override will be gone.*

All is now back to normal. Try a few other variations on this feature and observe the results. Select *Reset Temporary Hide/Isolate* before proceeding.

Apply Hide/Isolate to View:

If you temporarily hide a few elements or categories and you want those items to be permanently hidden, you can select **Apply Hide/Isolate to View** from the *Hide/Isolate* icon menu shown in Figure 6-3.3.

This feature allows you to hide (or isolate) individual items; for example, you could select a single window tag and hide it. The only way to see it again in that view is to select the **Reveal Hidden Elements** icon on the *View Control Bar* (Figure 6-3.4a).

FIGURE 6-3.4A
View Control Bar: Reveal Hidden Elements

FIGURE 6-3.4B
Ribbon: Reveal Hidden Elements panel

You should notice two things. First, all the hidden window tags are magenta and everything else is light gray. Second, the *Reveal Hidden Elements* icon has a magenta background and the drawing window has a heavy magenta border around it which reminds you that the current view settings are currently being modified.

Restoring Hidden Elements:

To restore a hidden item you first click the *Reveal Hidden Elements* (Figure 6-3.4a) icon and then select the element(s) to be restored to view. Once the item(s) is selected, you click **Unhide Element** or **Unhide Category** from the *Ribbon (Figure 6-3.4b)*. Finally, you select the *Reveal Hidden Elements* icon again to return to the normal "current view" settings.

Exercise 6-4:
Basement Floor Plan

Basement Floor Plan:

Now you will sketch the basement floor plan. Not all residences have basements; they mostly occur in cold climates where the foundation walls are deep to avoid frost heave. Once you have dug out for the deep foundation walls along the entire perimeter of the building, it does not take much more effort or resources to create a basement. Drawing a basement is the same as the other floors; you draw the exterior walls, concrete foundation walls in this case, the interior walls, etc. Once again, with the residential template that you started with being set up for the typical residential project, it should not surprise you that a typical foundation wall type is already set up and ready to be sketched; both 10″ and 12″ walls have been predefined.

1. Open your project file ex6-3.rvt and **Save As ex6-4.rvt**.

2. Switch to the **_Foundation_** floor plan view; <u>not</u> the _Basement_ plan.

You should see a grayed out representation of the first floor.

3. In _View Properties_ do the following two steps:

    a. Note the **Underlay** parameter is set to **First Floor**; if not set properly, you should change it now so _First Floor_ is the current _Underlay_.

    b. Set the **Discipline** to **Architectural**.

This underlay setting gives you an outline of your building that can be used to sketch the foundation walls.

4. Using the **_Wall_** tool, draw the foundation walls using the following information (see _Type Selector_ and _Options Bar_ image below):
    a. _Wall type:_   **Foundation – 12″ Concrete**
    b. _Location Line:_   **Finish Face: Exterior**
    c. _Depth:_   **T.O. Footing** (i.e., Top of Footing).

    > **_FYI:_** _Notice this setting on the Options Bar changes from "Height" to "Depth" when a "foundation" wall is selected!_

    d. Check **Chain** on the _Options Bar_.
    e. Start anywhere by snapping to one of the exterior corners of the _Underlay_; work in a clockwise direction.

When finished, your plan should look like Figure 6-4.1. The garage area will be slab-on-grade (i.e., no basement under it), so make sure you sketch a foundation wall between the garage and basement as shown.

FIGURE 6-4.1 Foundation Floor Plan; with First Floor Underlay turned on

5. Set the *Underlay* parameter for "Foundation" floor plan to **None** in the *Properties Palette*.

So What Exactly Did You Just Draw?

You just drew a foundation where the **top** is based on the current level, a level named Foundation in this example, and the "Depth" parameter on the *Options Bar* controls the **bottom** of the wall (T.O. Footing in this example).

The image to the right should make this concept perfectly clear (Figure 6-4.2).

FYI: *Each level datum has a corresponding floor plan view when the target is blue (as seen in the image to the right). You many not need all of these views in a set of construction documents, but they are useful for creating the Building Information Model (BIM).*

FIGURE 6-4.2
Foundation wall in section

Creating a New Foundation Wall Type:

Because the garage area is slab-on-grade, both sides of the foundation wall will have earth against them. The main basement walls act like a retaining wall because they only have earth on one side of the wall. Therefore, you will change the three exterior foundation walls, at the garage area, to 8″ concrete. You will have to create a new wall type to accommodate this need.

NOTE: *When the "Wall Function" is set to* <u>*Retaining*</u> *in the "Type Parameters" for a wall, the wall cannot be room bounding, so Room/Room Tags cannot be added.*

Disclaimer:

All dimensions and sizes shown in this book are solely for the purpose of learning to use the software. Under no circumstances should any information be assumed to be appropriate for a real-world project. A structural engineer should be consulted if you do not have adequate expertise in that area.

---

6. Select the ***Wall*** tool and then select **Foundation – 12″ Concrete** from the *Type Selector*.

7. Create a new wall type based on the current selection; name it **Foundation – 8″ Concrete**.

   REMEMBER: *Properties Palette* → *Edit Type* → *Duplicate*

8. Adjust the *Type Parameters* of the new wall so the Width is **8″**.

   FYI: *This is through* Properties Palette → Edit Type → Edit Structure.

9. Select the three exterior garage foundation walls, while holding down the Ctrl key, and then select your new wall in the *Type Selector*.

   REMEMBER: *Click* Modify *first to cancel the* Wall *tool.*

   TIP: *Hover your cursor over one wall, press Tab to highlight all three walls (a chain of walls), and then click to select all three walls at once!*

Your basement plan should look like Figure 6-4.3.

Because the *Location Line* was set to <u>Finish Face: Exterior,</u> the exterior side of the foundation wall is stationary when walls of a different width are selected; this is the desired result in this situation.

FYI: *You will add footings below the foundation walls in Exercise 10-2.*

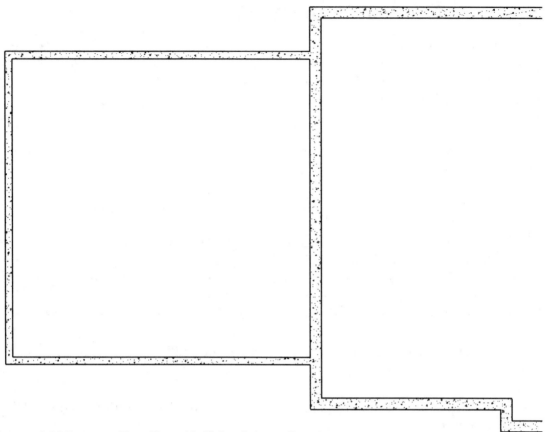

FIGURE 6-4.3 Basement Floor Plan; with 8″ foundation walls at the garage

Adding Interior Walls in the Basement:

To make things simple, for this tutorial and structurally, you will copy all the walls from the first floor to the basement. In the process of accomplishing this task you will also study the selection **Filter** function.

First you will switch to the first floor and select a large area, using a *crossing window* (i.e., picking from right to left) and then use the *Filter* function to strip the selection down to just the walls.

10. Switch to the ***First Floor*** view and select all the interior walls using a *crossing window* (Figure 6-4.4).

Everything within or passing through the *crossing window* is now selected. Next you will filter out everything except for the walls.

FIGURE 6-4.4 First Floor Plan; selecting all walls with a crossing window

11. With everything from the previous step still selected, click the **Filter** icon on the *Status Bar* (Figure 6-4.5).

FIGURE 6-4.5 Filter Selection icon

You are now in the *Filter* dialog (Figure 6-4.6). This lists all the element types or categories that are in the current selection set. When you click OK, only the items checked will be part of the current selection set.

FIGURE 6-4.6 Filter dialog

12. Uncheck everything except the **Walls** item in the *Filter* dialog (Figure 6-4.6).

13. Click **OK** to update the current select set.

TIP: Notice the number of selected items is listed in the lower right corner of the program window (image to the right). If you know you want to delete 3 doors and the count shows 4 items, you would not want to click Delete before you unselect the fourth item!

Now only the walls are selected. Next you will copy them to the *Clipboard* and then *Paste* them into the basement floor plan.

This selection technique can be used in many ways. For example, you could select all the walls and change their *Top Constraint* via the *Properties* dialog.

14. From the *Ribbon* select **Modify | Walls → Clipboard → Copy**.

15. Switch to the **Basement** view, not the Foundation view.

16. Select **Modify** on the *Ribbon*, and then **Modify → Clipboard → Paste → Aligned to Current View**.

You should get the following warning (Figure 6-4.7):

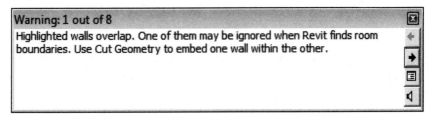

FIGURE 6-4.7 Wall placement warning

This error is indicating that the wall(s) you just placed overlaps another wall (vertically or horizontally). In this case it may be that the *Top Offset* is not set to 0″, but to 6″, which causes the wall to extend 6″ above the *Top Constraint* (which is the first floor line). So, if the first floor walls start at the first floor line, the basement walls extend up into the first floor walls by 6″, the two walls would be overlapping vertically.

If you get this warning, click the "X" in the upper right corner of the warning window; this will close it. Then select all the interior walls in the basement and make sure the *Top Offset* is set to 0″, via the *Properties Palette*; you can also check the *Base Offset* for the first floor walls.

When finished, your plan should look like Figure 6-4.8.

FIGURE 6-4.8 Walls added to the basement floor, copied from the first floor

Even though the doors were not selected, they were still copied with the walls just as before. This is fine; to save time you will leave the doors as they are.

17. **Save** your project as **ex6-4.rvt**.

Exercise 6-5:
Stairs

Next you will add stairs to your floor plans. Revit provides a powerful stair tool that allows you to design stairs quickly with various constraints specified in the *family* which was loaded with the template you started from (e.g., 7″ maximum riser).

Stair Type Parameters:

Before you draw the stair, it will be helpful to review the options available in the stair family.

1. Open ex6-4.rvt and *Save As* **ex6-5.rvt**. Open the *First Floor* plan.

2. From the *Project Browser*, expand the *Families* → *Stairs* → *Stair* (i.e., click the plus sign next to these labels).

3. Right-click on the stair type: **Residential – Closed 2 Sides**, and select the **Type Properties...** option from the pop-up menu.

You should now see the options shown in Figure 6-5.1.

Take a couple minutes to see what options are available. We will quickly review a few below.

- Tread Depth: Treads are typically 12″ deep (usually code min.) and 1″ of that depth overlaps the next tread; so only 11″ is visible in plan view. This overlap is called the *nosing*.
- Riser: This provides Revit with the maximum dimension allowed (by code, or if you want it, less). The actual dimension will depend on the floor-to-floor height.
- Stringer dimensions: These dimensions usually vary per stair depending on the stair width, run and materials, to name a few.
- Cost: Estimating placeholder.

FYI: *Closed 2 Sides (part of the name of the stair family) means there will be a wall on each side of the stair; thus a stringer will be visible above the stair.*

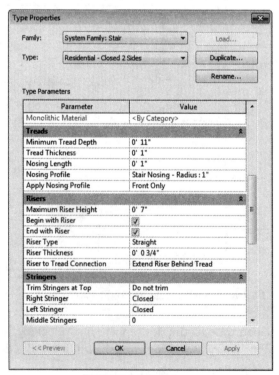

FIGURE 6-5.1 Stair type properties

Calculate Tread and Riser Size:

Although Revit automatically calculates the rise and tread dimensions for you, it is still a good idea to understand what is happening.

The *riser* is typically calculated to be as large as building codes will allow. Occasionally a grand stair will have a smaller riser to create a more elegant stair.

Similarly, the *tread* is usually designed to be as small as allowable by building codes.

The largest riser and shortest tread create the steepest stair allowed. This takes up less floor space (Figure 6-5.2). A stairway that is too steep is uncomfortable and unsafe.

Building codes vary by location; for this exercise you will use 7" (max.) for the risers and 9" (min.) for the treads.

· Codes usually require that each tread be the same size, likewise with risers.

Calculate the number and size of the risers:

>Given:
>Risers: **7"** max.   Floor to floor height: **9'-0"**.

>Calculate the number of risers:
>9'-0" divided by 7" (or 109" divided by 7") = 15.429

Seeing as each riser has to be the same size we will have to round off to a whole number. You cannot round down because that will make the riser larger than the allowed maximum (9'-0" / 15 = 7.2"). Therefore you have to round up to 16. Thus: 9'-0" divided by 16 = 6.75

So you need **16** risers that are **6¾"** each.

FIGURE 6-5.2 Stair rise/run comparison

Drawing the Stairs in Plan:

You will be drawing a U-shaped stair from the first floor to the second and an L-shaped stair from the basement to the first floor. At first, when using Revit to draw stairs, it may be helpful to manually figure out the number of risers and landings. That information will be helpful when drawing the stair. As you become more familiar with the *Stair* tool, you will not need to do those calculations to draw a stair.

To get an idea about what you are going to draw next, take a moment to look at Figure 6-5.3. The image below is at the first floor, and the "UP" label indicates where you would access the stair on the first floor. (Everything else rises from there, of course, to the second floor.)

FIGURE 6-5.3 Stair information overview

The first thing you will do, to prepare to draw the stair from the first floor to the second floor, is to draw a temporary reference line. This line will be used to accurately pick a starting point while using the *Stair* command (you will be picking a starting point near the middle of the room – next to the "UP" label in Figure 6-5.3). After the stair is drawn, you will erase the line.

You have had plenty of practice drawing lines in previous chapters, so you will be given minimal instruction on how to draw the line.

4. Make sure you are in the *First Floor Plan* view.

5. **Zoom in** to the front *Entry Foyer*.

6. Using the **Detail Line** tool from the *Annotate* tab, draw the temporary line in the *First Floor Plan* view, as shown in Figure 6-5.4.

FIGURE 6-5.4 Draw a temporary detail line

7. Click on the **Home** tab on the *Ribbon*.

8. Select **Home → Circulation → Stairs**.

9. Click on the **Edit Type** icon in the *Properties Palette* (Figure 6-5.5); note the options and click **OK**.

Railing Ramp Stairs

Circulation

FIGURE 6-5.5 Stair tool active; Select Edit Type from the Properties Palette

10. In the *Properties Palette*, make sure the *Width* is set to **3'-0"** and that *Top Level* is set to **Second Floor** (Figure 6-5.6).

11. Click the endpoint of your temporary detail line as shown in **Figure 6-5.7**; you are selecting the start point for the first step. Make sure you are snapping to the line for accuracy; a tooltip will appear stating "endpoint" before you click.

12. Pick the remaining points as shown in Figures 6-5.7, 6-5.8 and 6-5.9.

> **TIP:**
> Notice the palette to the left is the *Instance Properties* which controls selected or to-be-created instances. In this case, of course, we are talking about a to-be-created instance.
>
> Clicking the *Edit Type* button here would make changes to this stair and any others previously created. Your project does not have any previously created stairs at this time.

FIGURE 6-5.6 Stair instance properties

Notice as you draw the stairs, Revit will display the number of risers drawn and the number of risers remaining to be drawn to reach the next level, or whatever level is selected as *Top Level* in *Properties*.

If you click *Finish Stairs*, the green check mark on the *Ribbon*, before drawing all the required risers, Revit will display a warning message. You can leave the problem to be resolved later.

Pick #2: After picking the first point below, begin moving the cursor straight up; click when the label below the stairs reads "8 Risers Created, 8 Remaining."

Pick #1: Pick the endpoint of your temporary line as the starting point for the stair.

8 RISERS CREATED, 8 REMAINING

FIGURE 6-5.7 Beginning to sketch the stair

Pick #3: Move the cursor horizontally, to the right from pick #2, until Revit snaps to the wall. Make sure you see the dashed extension line before picking.

Before clicking you should see this temporary line, which indicates Revit is going to align your next pick with something, the previously drawn stair in this case.

8 RISERS CREATED, 8 REMAINING

FIGURE 6-5.8 Continuing to sketch the stair

Pick #4: Move the cursor straight down until Revit indicates "16 Risers Created, 0 Remaining."

TIP: You can move the mouse past that point; you do not need to click directly on it.

16 RISERS CREATED, 0 REMAINING

FIGURE 6-5.9 Last step in sketching the stair

13. Click the **green check mark** to *Finish* the stair on the *Ribbon* (Figure 6-5.5).

14. Erase the temporary detail line; you may need to press the Tab key (i.e., tap, not hold down) to select it rather than the stair.

Your stair should now look like Figure 6-5.10! Notice that Revit adds a break-line at the *Cut Plane* and everything above that is dashed in.

As soon as you click *Finish Stair*, Revit will automatically add the landing, creating it between the two stair runs sketched. The width of the landing will match the stair width, which is 3'-0". This is true for any stair configuration using the above method. You will see this momentarily when you sketch an L-shaped stair in the basement.

FIGURE 6-5.10 Finished stair

The second floor plan also shows this stair, but with a down arrow and no break lines because it does not pass through that view's *Cut Plane*!

Modeling the Basement Stairs:

Now you will draw the L-shaped stairs from the basement to the first floor.

To get an idea about what you are going to draw next, take a moment to look at Figure 6-5.11. The image below is at the basement level, and the "UP" label indicates where you would access the stair on the basement level. Everything else rises from there, of course, to the first floor.

15. Save your project as **ex6-5.rvt**; remember to save often.

16. Switch to the **Basement** floor plan view.

17. Select the **Stair** tool.

FIGURE 6-5.11 Stair information overview

18. In the *Properties Palette* make the following changes:

    a. Change the *Type Selector* to **Residential – Open 2 Sides**.

    b. Make sure the *Top Level* is set to **First Floor**; the *Stair* tool defaults to the next *Level* up – which is "foundation" level and not "first floor" in your case.

FYI: The properties button on the Ribbon relates to the sketch lines themselves while in the Create Stair *mode. The Properties Palette settings relate to the stair model rather than the sketch lines.*

19. Select the **Railing Type** button on the *Ribbon*.

20. Select **None** and **OK**.

21. Using the same techniques you employed to sketch the first floor stair, draw the basement stair per the information given in Figure 6-5.11.

TIP: While sketching the stairs, you can select a window (picking from left to right) around a run of stairs and move it. Also, do not forget to draw a temporary line(s) if you think it will help.

Your stair should look like Figure 6-5.12. If not, select one of the riser/tread lines and press the *Delete* key on the keyboard to erase the stair and try again. It can get a little frustrating when you are not familiar with the ins-and-outs of what Revit is doing or what information it needs to proceed. Take your time; take a break if necessary.

Next you will draw three walls next to the stair. This will close off the two open sides and the bottom of the stair.

TIP: If a stair needs to be modified at any time in the future, you do not actually have to delete the stair and start over; it is recommended above for practice. If you select a stair, you can click the Edit Sketch icon on the Ribbon to re-enter Sketch mode for that stair.

FIGURE 6-5.12 Finished basement stair

22. Using the **Wall** tool, draw the three interior walls as shown in **Figure 6-5.13**.

- Use the standard interior wall you used for the other floors.

  TIP #1: You can select one and see what type it is in the Type Selector.

  TIP #2: You can also select a wall and right-click, and then select "Create Similar" from the pop-up menu to add another wall of the type selected.

- Click the *Chain* option.

- Set *Location Line* to one of the finished wall faces.

- *Top Constraint* set to: **First Floor**.

- Click the inside points of the stair. Press the *spacebar* if needed to flip the wall so it is created outside of the stair footprint.

- Draw the third wall under the stair, at the fifth riser line.

FIGURE 6-5.13 Three walls added at stairs

A cutaway 3D view of your model looks something like this; you will learn to do cutaway views later in the book.

You should notice two things about this 3D view:

First: The basement wall you just added extends through the basement stair. You will fix that in the building sections lesson.

Second: No floors have been drawn yet. You will draw floor systems in the next chapter.

23. **Save** your project.

FIGURE 6-5.14 3D view of stair

FYI: Normally you would not rename your project file. You do it here in the book for grading and restore options, should things get really corrupted.

Make sure to examine the stair sample file available on Autodesk's online content library (seek.autodesk.com – search for "Revit samples" and select the stair option). You can download this file and see examples of several different stair types side-by-side (see image below). You can select one and view its properties to see how it was done. You can also Copy/Paste one into your project; select your stair, and then select the newly imported type(s) from the *Type Selector*. The partial view of the sample file, shown below, has open riser, single stringer, no stringer, spiral...

FIGURE 6-5.15 Partial view of sample stair file from Revit's website

Modify the Building's Floor-to-Floor Height:

You will not need to do this for this tutorial, but you can modify the building's floor-to-floor height (or Level). The reasons for doing this vary. Some examples might be to make the building shorter or taller, to accommodate ductwork in the ceilings or the depth of the floor structure; the longer the span, the deeper the structure. The default floor-to-floor height in the template file you started from is 9'-0", which is fine for this project. However, should you want to change this for another project, here is how to do it:

- Open any exterior elevation from the *Project Browser*.

- Change the floor-to-floor height to be 12'-0" for each level; in this example, to the right.

- Select the floor elevation symbol, and then select the text displaying the elevation. You should now be able to type in a new number. Press Enter to see the changes. Notice the windows move because the sill height has not been changed (Figure A).

FIGURE A Exterior elevation: modifying Level 3 elevation

- The floor-to-floor height is a good thing to figure out, when possible, before drawing the stairs, as it affects the number of risers and treads required, not to mention floor area.

Exercise 6-6:
Dimensions

Next you will add dimensions to your floor plans. Revit provides a powerful dimension tool that allows you to quickly dimension drawings. This process is much easier than other CAD programs. Revit has a dimension style all setup and ready to use, which works for most designers. Furthermore, the size of the text and ticks are tied to the *View Scale* feature to make sure the dimensions always print at the correct size. For example, a dimension's text and ticks would get twice as big just by changing the *View Scale* from ¼″ = 1′-0″ to ⅛″ = 1′-0″. You will try this in a moment.

Industry standard dimensioning conventions were covered in the previous lesson. You may want to take a minute and review that information (see page 5-23).

Drawing dimensions in Revit involves the following steps:

- Select the *Aligned* dimension tool from the *Annotate* tab.

- *Ribbon*, *Options* Bar and *Type Selector*:
  - Select one of the predefined styles from the *Type Selector*.
  - Select the kind of dimension you want: Linear, Angular, Radial, Arch Length.
  - Tell Revit what part of the wall you want to dimension to: Wall centerlines, Wall Face, Center of Core, Face of Core; this can change for each side of a dimension's line.

- Select two, or more, walls to dimension between.

- Select a location for the dimension line.

Adding Dimensions to the First Floor Plan:

1. Open ex6-5.rvt and **Save-As ex6-6.rvt**.

2. Switch to the *First Floor Plan* view.

3. **Zoom in** on the North wall of the garage.

4. Select the **Annotate → Dimension → Aligned** tool.

Notice the *Ribbon, Options Bar* and *Type Selector* changes to give you control over the various options mentioned above (Figure 6-6.1).

FIGURE 6-6.1 Ribbon, Option Bar and Type Selector: Dimension tool active

5. Set the *Type Selector* to **Linear – 3/32" Arial**.

6. Click the **Edit Type** button on the *Properties Palette*.

Notice the various properties you can adjust for the selected dimension type (Figure 6-6.2).

Creating a new, custom, dimension type is the same as for walls, doors, etc.; just click the *Duplicate* button, provide a name and then adjust the properties.

All the dimensions you see here are multiplied by the *View Scale*. For example, the 3/32" text is multiplied by 48 when the *View Scale* is set to ¼" = 1'-0"; thus, the text is 4½" tall in ¼" drawings. When the ¼" view is placed on a *Sheet*, Revit automatically scales the view down 1/48. At this point the text is 3/32" again. This

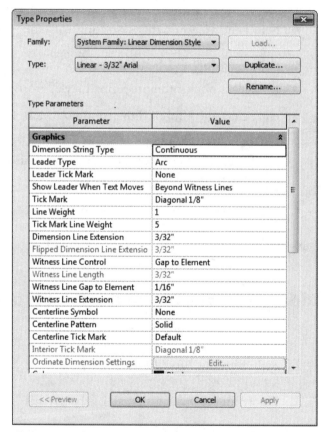

FIGURE 6-6.2 Properties: for selected dimension type

makes the view actually a ¼" = 1'-0" on the *Sheet*, which is actual sheet size – say 22" x 34". Finally, all this is changed automatically whenever the *View Scale* is changed: dimension and text size as well as the *View* size on sheets! You will learn about *Sheets* later in the book.

7. Click **OK** to close the dialog box.

The Aligned dimension tool allows you to place dimensions by picking walls. You will try this now.

8. Next, select **Wall Faces** on the *Options Bar* (Figure 6-6.1).

9. Draw your first dimension by clicking the three points as identified in **Figure 6-6.3**.

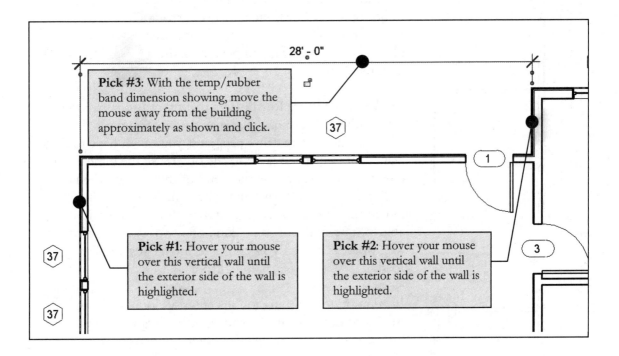

FIGURE 6-6.3 First Floor plan: first dimension added

FYI: In the figure above (6-6.3), you can select points 1 and 2 in the opposite order as well.

10. Dimension the rest of the North exterior wall as shown in Figure 6-6.4 You may not be able to read the dimensions in the image provided, but you can still determine the number of dimensions required and Revit provides the dimension text anyway. See the next page for dimension comments.

Once you have drawn one dimension, as in Step 11, the remaining dimensions in that "string" should align with the first. Revit helps you make the third pick (as in Figure 6-6.3) by automatically snapping to the previous dimension when you move your cursor to it.

You can add a "string" of dimensions by simply clicking on parallel walls. When done, click somewhere away from any Revit elements to position and finish the dimension string. To edit a string of dimensions after it has been placed, simply select it and pick the **Edit Witness Lines** tool on the *Ribbon*.

Edit
Witness Lines
Witness Lines

Yet another feature Revit offers that other programs do not is the ability to automatically snap to the center of a door or window opening. In other programs you might have to draw a line from one door jamb to the other, use the dimension command to snap to the midpoint of the line and then delete it. Then you are left with dimensions that just look like they dimension to the center. Remember, Revit's dimensions are able to modify the drawing, kind of a two-way road if you will, whereas other CAD programs are mostly a one-way road.

In addition to snapping to the center of doors and windows, Revit will also snap to the jambs; depending on where your mouse is relative to the element being dimensioned.

You will notice that Revit does not care if a dimension's witness line overlaps a door or window tag. The tags need to be selected and moved manually, individually or in groups.

Next you will dimension the west side of the building.

FIGURE 6-6.4
First Floor: rotated 90 degrees
to increase image size in book

11. Dimension the West exterior walls and openings as shown in **Figure 6-6.5**.

> **TIP:**
> If you click on this dimension, you can drag its grip to the left to shorten the witness line. Revit will still reference the correct wall.

FIGURE 6-6.5 First Floor: dimensions added to the West wall

The last two images in the exercise give you an idea of what each dimension type which was loaded with the residential template looks like. Similar to other elements in Revit, you can select a dimension and verify what type it is by looking at the *Type Selector* on the *Properties Palette*. Also, you can change the type by selecting the desired type from the *Type Selector*.

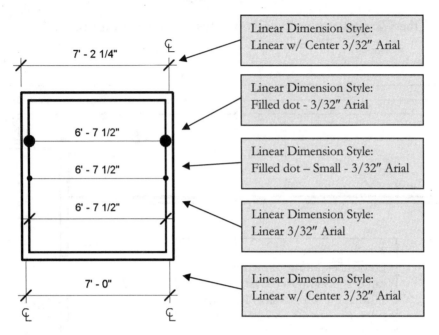

FIGURE 6-6.6 Dimension type comparison

FIGURE 6-6.7 Dimension type comparison

This should be enough for you to understand how to dimension your plans. If you want more practice, you can dimension the rest of the *First Floor Plan*, and then the other two floors; your instructor may require this. See Revit's *Help System* if you want to dig in a little deeper in to Revit's dimensioning options.

12. **Save** your Project as **ex6-6.rvt**.

Self-Exam:

The following questions can be used as a way to check your knowledge of this lesson. The answers can be found at the bottom of the page.

1. The default settings for the floor plan view shows the walls for the floor below. (T/F)

2. The size of dimension text and arrows are set by the *View Scale* feature. (T/F)

3. You should start drawing your floor plan generally centered on the default elevation marks in a new project. (T/F)

4. You can use the *Align* tool to align one wall with another. (T/F)

5. Where do you change the maximum riser height? _____

Review Questions:

The following questions may be assigned by your instructor as a way to assess your knowledge of this section. Your instructor has the answers to the review questions.

1. It is not possible to copy/paste elements from one floor to another and have them line up (with the original objects). (T/F)

2. Revit's dimension tool can snap to the middle of a door opening without the need to draw a temporary line to snap to. (T/F)

3. Each Revit view is saved as a separate file on your hard drive. (T/F)

4. You select the part of the wall to be deleted when using the *Trim* tool. (T/F)

5. You cannot "finish stair" if you have not drawn all the treads or risers that are required between the two specified levels. (T/F)

6. What parameter should be set to none, in the *View Properties* dialog, if you

   do not want to see the walls from the floor below? __underlay__

7. The __View__ __Scale__ controls the size of dimensions and text, plus the scale that view is placed on a sheet.

8. You can use the __Filter__ tool to quickly select a certain type of element from a large group of selected objects.

9. The number of __Risers__ remaining is displayed while sketching a stair.

Notes:

Lesson 7
Residence: ROOF:

This lesson will look at some of the various options and tools for designing a roof for your building. You will also add skylights. Be sure to check out the video on Roofs located on the DVD.

Exercise 7-1:
Roof Design Options (Style, Pitch and Overhang)

In this lesson you will look at the various ways to use the *Roof* tool to draw the more common roof forms used in architecture today.

Start a New Autodesk® Revit® Architecture Project:

You will start a new project for this lesson so you can quickly compare the results of using the *Roof* tool.

1. Start a new project using the **default.rte** template.

2. Switch to the **North** elevation view and rename the level named *Level 2* to **T.O. Masonry**. This will be the reference point for your roof. Click **Yes** to rename corresponding views automatically.

    TIP: Just select the Level *datum and click on the level datum's text to rename.*

3. Switch to the *Level 1 Floor Plan* view.

Drawing the Buildings:

4. Set the Level 1 *"Detail Level"* to **medium**, so the material hatching is visible within the walls.

    TIP: Use the View Control Bar at the bottom.

5. Using the *Wall* tool with the wall *Type* set to "**Exterior - Brick on Mtl. Stud**," draw a **40'-0" x 20'-0"** building (Figure 7-1.1).

    FYI: The default Wall height is OK; it should be 20'-0".

Be sure to draw the building
within the elevation tags.

> **TIP:** *You can draw the building
> in one step if you use the*
> Rectangle *option on the Ribbon,*
> *while using the* Wall *tool.*

Elevations tags – (4) are shown which
correspond to the (4) elevation views
listed in the *Project Browser*.

FIGURE 7-1.1 Bldg. and Elev. tags

You will copy the building so that you have a total four buildings. You will draw a different
type of roof on each one.

6.   Drag a window around the walls to select them. Then use the **Array** command to set
     up four buildings **35'-0" O.C.** (Figure 7-1.2). See the *Array Tip* below.

> **TIP:** *Zoom in and make
> sure the brick is on the
> exterior side of the wall. If
> not, you can select each wall
> and click its* flip *icon.*
>
> **ARRAY TIP:** *Select the
> first building, select Array,
> and then, just like the
> Copy command, define a
> copy 35' to the right; then
> enter the number of copies.*

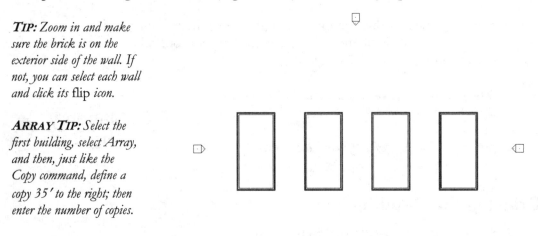

FIGURE 7-1.2 Four buildings

7.   Select all of the buildings and click **Ungroup**
     from the *Ribbon*.

Ungroup

Hip Roof:

The various roof forms are largely defined by the *"Defines slope"* setting. This is displayed in the *Options Bar* while the *Roof* tool is active. When a wall is selected and the *"Defines slope"* option is selected, the roof above that portion of wall slopes. You will see this more clearly in the examples below.

8.   Switch to the **T.O. Masonry** *Floor Plan* view.

9.   Select the **Home → Build → Roof** *(down-arrow)* **→ Roof by Footprint** tool.

10. Set the overhang to **2'-0"** and make sure **Defines slope** is selected (checked) on the *Options Bar*.

11. Select the four walls of the West building, clicking each wall one at a time.

   TIP: Make sure you select towards the exterior side of the wall; notice the review line before clicking.

12. Click **Finish Edit Mode** (i.e., the green checkmark) on the *Ribbon* to finish the *Roof* tool.

13. Click **Yes** to attach the roof to the walls.

14. Switch to the **South** elevation (Figure 7-1.3).

FIGURE 7-1.3 South elevation – Hip roof

You will notice that the default wall height is much higher than what we ultimately want. However, when the roof is drawn at the correct elevation and you attach the walls to the roof, the walls automatically adjust to stop under the roof object. Additionally, if the roof is raised or lowered later, the walls will follow; you can try this in the South elevation view by simply using the *Move* tool. ***REMEMBER:*** *You can make revisions in any view.*

15. Switch to the **3D** view using the icon on the *QAT* (Figure 7-1.4).

> You can change the "model graphics style" to **Shading with Edges** if you would like. Select the *Visual Style* icon on the *View Control Bar* at the bottom.

FIGURE 7-1.4 3D view – hip roof

Gable Roof:

16. Switch back to the **T.O. Masonry** view (not the ceiling plan for this level).

17. Select the **Roof** tool, and then **Roof by Footprint**.

18. Set the overhang to **2'-0"** and make sure **Defines slope** is selected (checked) on the *Options Bar*.

19. Only select the two long (40'-0") walls.

20. **Uncheck** the **Defines slope** option.

21. Select the remaining two walls (Figure 7-1.5).

22. Pick the **green checkmark** on the *Ribbon* to finish the roof.

23. Select **Yes** to attach the walls to the roof.

24. Switch to the **South** elevation view (Figure 7-1.6).

FIGURE 7-1.5 Gable – plan view

FIGURE 7-1.6 South elevation – gable roof

25. Switch to the **3D** view (Figure 7-1.7).

Notice the wall extends up to conform to the underside of the roof on the gable ends.

FYI: *You may be wondering why the roofs look odd in the floor plan view. If you remember, each view has its own cut plane. The cut plane happens to be lower than the highest part of the roof – thus, the roof is shown cut at the cut plane. If you go to Properties Palette → View Range (while nothing is selected) and then adjust the cut plane to be higher than the highest point of the roof, then you will see the ridge line.*

FIGURE 7-1.7 3D view – gable roof

Shed Roof:

26. Switch back to the **T.O. Masonry** view.

27. Select the **Roof** tool, and then **Roof by Footprint**.

28. Check **Defines slope** on the *Options Bar*.

29. Set the overhang to **2'-0"** on the *Options Bar*.

30. Select the East wall (40'-0" wall, right-hand side).

31. Uncheck **Defines slope** in the *Options Bar*.

32. Select the remaining three walls (Figure 7-1.8).

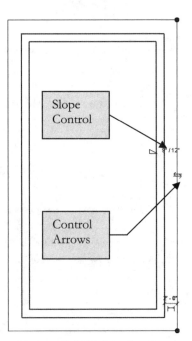

FIGURE 7-1.8 Selected walls

33. Set the **Slope**, or roof pitch, to 3/12 (Figure 7-1.9) on the *Properties Palette*.

34. Click **Apply** on the *Properties Palette*.

35. Pick the **green checkmark** on the *Ribbon* to finish the roof.

36. Select **Yes** to attach the walls to the roof.

FIGURE 7-1.9
Properties for Roof tool

FYI: *You can also change the slope of the roof by changing the Slope Control text (see Figure 7-1.8); just select the text and type a new number.*

TIP: *You can use the Control Arrows, while the roof line is still selected, to flip the orientation of the roof overhang if you accidentally selected the wrong side of the wall and the overhang is on the inside of the building.*

37. Switch to the **South** elevation view (Figure 7-1.10).

FIGURE 7-1.10 South elevation – shed roof

38. Switch to the **Default 3D** view (Figure 7-1.11).

FIGURE **7-1.11** Default 3D view – shed roof

Once the roof is drawn, you can easily change the roof's overhang. You will try this on the shed roof. You will also make the roof slope in the opposite direction.

39. In **T.O. Masonry** view, Select **Modify** from the *Ribbon*, and then select the shed roof.

40. Click **Edit Footprint** from the *Ribbon*.

Edit Footprint

41. Click on the East roof sketch-line to select it.

42. Uncheck **Defines slope** from the *Options Bar*.

43. Now select the West roofline and check **Defines slope**.

If you were to select the green check mark now, the shed roof would be sloping in the opposite direction. But, before you do that, you will adjust the roof overhang at the high side.

44. Click on the East roofline again, to select it.

45. Change the overhang to **6'-0"** in the *Options Bar*.

Changing the overhang only affects the selected roofline.

46. Select the **green check mark**.

47. Switch to the South view to see the change (Figure 7-1.12).

FIGURE 7-1.12 South elevation – shed roof (revised)

Thus you can see it is easier to edit an object than to delete it and start over. Just remember you have to be in sketch mode (i.e., *Edit Sketch*) to make changes to the roof. Also, when a sketch line is selected, its properties are displayed in the *Properties Palette*. That concludes the shed roof example.

Flat Roof:

48. Switch back to the **T.O. Masonry** *Floor Plan* view.

49. Select **Home → Roof → Roof by Footprint**.

50. Set the overhang to **2'-0"** and make sure **Defines slope** is not selected (i.e., un-checked) in the *Options Bar*.

51. Select all four walls.

52. Pick the **green check mark**.

53. Select **Yes** to attach the walls to the roof.

FIGURE 7-1.13 South elevation – flat roof

54. Switch to the South elevation view (Figure 7-1.13).

55. Also, take a look the **Default 3D view** (Figure 7-1.14).

FIGURE 7-1.14 Default 3D view – flat roof

56. Save your project as **ex7-1.rvt**.

Want More?

Revit has additional tools and techniques available for creating more complex roof forms. However, that is beyond the scope of this book. If you want to learn more about roofs, or anything else, take a look at one of the following resources:

- Revit **Web Site** (www.autodesk.com)
- Revit **Newsgroup** (potential answers to specific questions)
  www.augi.com; www.revitcity.com; www.autodesk.com; www.revitforum.org
- Revit **Blogs** information from individuals (some work for Autodesk and some don't)
  www.revitoped.com, insidethefactory.typepad.com

Exercise 7-2:
Gable Roof

The template file you started with already has a *Roof Plan* view created. You can think of this as the top plate height for your wall. This *Roof Plan* view creates a working plane for the *Roof* tool. After creating a high roof, over the two story areas, you will create a *Low Roof* view and design roofs over the one story areas: garage and portion of the family room.

Create Gable Roof:

1. Open ex6-6.rvt and **Save As ex7-2.rvt**.

2. Switch to the ***Roof Plan*** view.

Your image should look something like Figure 7-2.1. The walls you can see in the *Roof Plan* view were created in Lesson 5; the specified height extends into the *Roof Plan's View Range*. Whereas the two walls you cannot see were created on the second floor, in Lesson 6, and the specified height does not extend up into the *Roof Plan's View Range*. This does not really matter because, as you will see in a moment, you have enough information visible to create the footprint of the roof; also, you will *Attach* the walls to the roof, just like the previous exercises, which causes them to conform to the underside of the roof.

Because the walls do not connect, neither will the overhang lines you will be sketching. Before you can "finish" a roof sketch, you must have the entire perimeter of the roof drawn with line endpoints connected. Revit allows you to sketch additional lines and use tools like *Trim* to complete the perimeter of the roof sketch.

3. Select the ***Roof*** tool from the *Home* tab.

4. Select ***Roof by Footprint*** from the drop-down menu.

5. Make sure ***Pick Walls*** is selected on the *Ribbon*.

FIGURE 7-2.1 Roof Plan; initial view

First you will specify the roof overhang for the entire roof.

6. Set the *Overhang* to **1'-6"** on the *Options Bar*.

You only need to select four walls to define the extents of the gable roof you are about to create. However, the perimeter will not be closed after selecting the four walls.

7. With *Defines slope* selected on the *Options Bar*, select the two walls as shown in Figure 7-2.2; make sure the overhang lines are on the exterior side of the building.

    TIP: *Use the flip control icon while the line is still selected if your overhang is on the wrong side (i.e., interior).*

8. With *Defines slope* NOT selected on the *Options Bar*, select the two walls as shown in Figure 7-2.2; make sure the overhang lines are on the exterior side of the building.

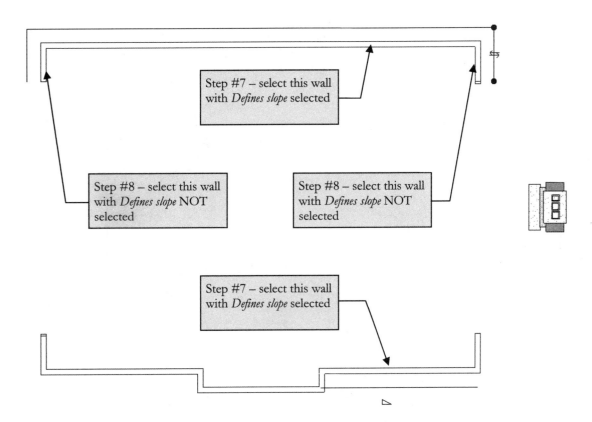

9. Change the roof pitch, or *Slope*, to **8″** on the *Properties Palette* (Figure 7-2.3).

10. Click **Apply**.

Note that the four walls, just selected, can be selected in any order. Of course it would be easier to select all the sloping edges first and then all the non-sloping edges second. That way you do not have to keep toggling the *Defines slope* option on and off.

Next you will use the *Trim* tool to close the perimeter of the roof footprint. Many of your 2D drafting skills learned early in this book can be applied to this type of *Sketch* mode.

Finally, notice the roof type is set to **Generic – 12″** as seen in the image to the right. This can be modified similar to walls via the *Edit Type* button.

FIGURE 7-2.3 Roof Properties

11. Select **Modify** from the *Ribbon*.

12. Select the **Trim** icon from the contextual tab on the *Ribbon*, and then select the roof lines that are not yet connected to make them connected (Figure 7-2.4).

FIGURE 7-2.4 Roof Plan; entire roof perimeter defined

Now that the roof footprint is complete you can finish the roof.

13. Select the **green checkmark** from the *Ribbon*.

14. Click **Yes** to attach the walls (Figure 7-2.5).

FIGURE 7-2.5 Roof Plan; attachment warning

15. Switch to your **Default 3D** view.

Your project should look like Figure 7-2.6. Notice that the walls that were visible in the *Roof Plan* view are now attached to the roof. The East and West walls that have not been attached can be attached manually.

FIGURE 7-2.6 3D View; gable roof added

16. While in the 3D view, select the East wall that has not been attached to the roof yet. Notice how the wall is transparent when selected.

17. Select the **Attach Top/Base** button from the *Ribbon*; then **select the roof** (Figure 7-2.7).

18. Repeat the previous two steps with the West wall.

> *TIP: Click in the upper left corner of the Front face of the ViewCube to quickly view that side of the building (see image to right).*

FIGURE 7-2.7 3D View; wall attached to roof

Main Entry Gable:

Next you will draw the gable roof element over the main entry.

You can modify the existing roof to add this design feature.

19. Switch back to the ***Roof Plan*** view.

20. Select the existing **roof**, and then ***Edit Footprint*** from the *Ribbon*.

21. Select ***Pick Walls*** and then make sure the overhang is still **1'-6"** and the pitch is **8"/12"**.

22. Edit the roof sketch to look like Figure 7-2.8.

TIP: *Use the* Split *and* Trim *tools to modify the existing sketch.*

Two vertical lines are set to *Defines slope*

FIGURE 7-2.8 Edit roof sketch

23. Select the **green checkmark** to finish the roof.

NOTE: *If you get any errors, make sure all the "defines slope" sketch lines have the same slope.*

This is where the power of Revit really begins to shine. As you can see in the *Roof Plan* view (Figure 7-2.9 below), Revit was able to interpret the sketch using the *Pitch* and *Defines slope* information to create the proper roof, complete with ridgelines and valleys.

Next you will change the *View Range* of the *Roof* view so you can see the low roof, which will be added in the next exercise.

24. Select **Edit** next to *View Range* in the *Properties Palette* (make sure nothing is selected in the model first).

25. Change both *Bottom* and *View Depth* to **Unlimited**.

26. Click **OK**.

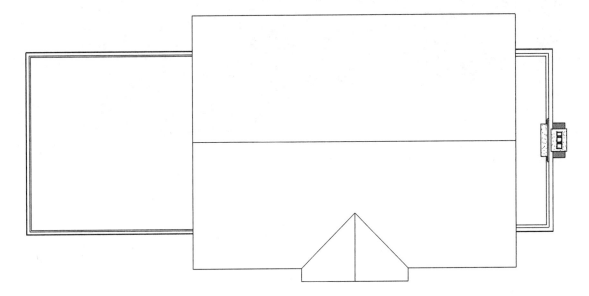

FIGURE 7-2.9 Site plan view; revised roof created

27. Switch to the ***Default 3D*** view.

When finished, your 3D view should look like Figure 7-2.10.

TIP:
Custom fascias, gutters and soffits are beyond the scope of this tutorial. However, you can take a look at the Help system for more information on this.

After reviewing the Help system, try adding these techniques to your Revit project.

This entry roof element could have been drawn as a separate element. This would be useful if the fascia/eaves did not align, for example.

FIGURE 7-2.10 3D view; Entry roof element added

28. Save your project as **Ex7-2.rvt**.

TIP: You have probably figured this out by now: the last view open when you close will be the current view the next time the project is opened.

Exercise 7-3:
Low Roof Elements

In this exercise you will add the lower roof elements, which will involve adding a new level datum for reference.

Create a New Level:

1. Open ex7-2.rvt and **Save As ex7-3.rvt**.

2. Open the **South** elevation view.

3. Click **Home → Datum → Level** from the *Ribbon*.

4. Draw a *Level* symbol at the top of the low exterior walls, at elevation 12′-0″. Draw the symbol so both ends align with the other symbols below and above it (Figure 7-3.1).

> **TIP:** *Hover your cursor over the top of the garage wall (do not click). Next, move your cursor towards the left and pick two points across from each other horizontally, picking from left to right.*

FIGURE 7-3.1 South elevation; new level added

Notice that Revit automatically names the level and creates a floor plan and reflected ceiling plan views with the same name (Figure 7-3.2). Next, you will rename the *Level* datum.

5. Press **Esc** or select **Modify** from the *Ribbon*.

6. Now select the *Level* symbol you just created in the drawing window.

FIGURE 7-3.2 South elevation; new level added (named Level 8 in this example)

7. With the *Level* symbol selected, **drag the small circle grip** near the target symbol (see image below) to the right. This will relocate all the level targets away from the building.

8. With the *Level* symbol still selected, click on the text to rename the level label. Press *Undo* if you accidentally click an icon and change the level position; you may need to zoom in to click the text.

9. Change the label to **Low Roof** (Figure 7-3.3).

FIGURE 7-3.3 South elevation; renaming a level datum

10. Click **Yes** when prompted to rename corresponding views (Figure 7-3.4).

Notice the *Low Roof* label is now listed in the *Floor Plans* and *Ceiling Plans* sections of the *Project Browser*.

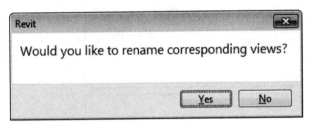

FIGURE 7-3.4 Rename prompt

Add another gable roof:

11. Open the newly created **Low Roof Floor Plan** view.

    TIP: *You may want to close the Ceiling Plan views so you don't accidentally click on them*

12. Select the **Roof** tool (down-arrow) from the *Ribbon*.

13. Select **Roof by footprint** from the drop-down list.

14. Set the overhang to **1'-6"** on the *Options Bar*.

15. You are now prompted to select exterior walls to define the footprint. Select ONLY the three wall segments that define the *Living Room* area per **Figure 7-3.5**. Only the horizontal sketch lines are to be *Defines slope* as shown.

    REMEMBER: *Pick the exterior side of the walls.*

You will notice in Figure 7-3.5 that there is one section that still needs to be sketched to close the footprint or outline.

Only the two horizontal lines should *Define slope*

Draw line (shown as dashed here) – Step 17

Pick the three walls with dots (large black dots are not in Revit) – Step 15

FIGURE 7-3.5 Low Roof plan view; adding roof

16. Select the **Lines** tool from the *Ribbon* (Figure 7-3.6).

17. Draw the line to create a complete rectangle (i.e., footprint), making sure you use *Snaps* to accurately snap to the endpoints of the lines already present (Figure 7-3.5). Use *Trim* if needed.

18. Change the *Slope* to **8" / 12"** in the *Properties Palette*.

19. Click **Apply** in the *Properties Palette*.

FIGURE 7-3.6 Roof sketch options

Again, this will make the roof pitch 8/12, which means for every 12" of horizontal run, the roof will *rise* 8" vertically.

20. Now click the **green checkmark** from the *Ribbon* to finish the roof.

21. Click **Yes** when prompted to attach the highlighted walls to the roof (Figure 7-3.7).

FIGURE 7-3.7 Prompt

You will now see a portion of the roof in your plan view. The cutting plane is 4'-0" above the floor level, so you are seeing the roof thickness in section at 4'-0" above the *Low Roof* level (Figure 7-3.8 on next page).

- Switch to an elevation view to see the roof, the South elevation, shown in Figure 7-3.9.

- You can also switch to the **Default 3D** view to see the roof in isometric view.

FIGURE 7-3.9 South elevation

After looking at the roof you have created, switch back to the plan view: **Low Roof.** You will now add a roof over the garage.

FIGURE 7-3.8 Low Roof plan view

22. **Zoom in** on the garage area.

23. Select the *Roof* tool and click *Roof by Footprint*.

24. With *Defines slope* checked in the *Options Bar*, pick the two horizontal walls: North and South (Figure 7-3.10).

25. Uncheck *Defines slope*, select the West wall, and then use the *Line* tool to sketch a line to close the footprint, as shown in Figure 7-3.11. Be sure to use *Snaps* to accurately draw the enclosed area.

26. Make sure the *Slope* is set to **8"/12"** and then select the **green checkmark** from the *Ribbon* (Figure 7-3.6).

27. Click **Yes** when prompted to attach the highlighted walls to the roof (Figure 7-3.7).

FIGURE 7-3.10 Low Roof plan view at garage

28. Switch to the **South** elevation view (Figure 7-3.11).

FIGURE 7-3.11 South elevation view; garage roof added

The 3D model is shown shaded and has *Ambient Shadows* turned on (Figure 7-3.12).

Revit content is setup to make glass in windows and curtain walls transparent.

FIGURE 7-3.12 Shaded model

Changing to a Hip Roof:

Now that you have drawn the roof, you will see what is involved to modify the gable roof to a hip roof. In the first exercise in this Lesson, you learned how to create a hip roof from scratch. Here you will modify a previously drawn gable roof into a hip roof.

29. Switch to the **Roof Plan** view.

30. Click on the main roof element to select it.

> **TIP:** *Select one of the lines at the perimeter of the roof.*

31. Select **Edit Footprint** from the *Ribbon*.

Edit
Footprint

32. Select the vertical line on the left.

33. With the left vertical line selected, check **Defines slope** on the *Options Bar*.

34. Repeat these steps for the right vertical line.

Your screen should look like Figure 7-3.13.

FIGURE 7-3.13 Roof Plan; vertical lines set to *Defines slope*

35. Select the **green check mark** from the *Ribbon*.

36. Switch to the ***South*** exterior elevation view.

You now have a hip roof. However, there is a little problem with the lower roofs; they do not properly intersect. This could be a problem when it rains!

FIGURE 7-3.14 South Elevation; main roof changed to a hip roof

37. Switch to the ***Default 3D*** view.

38. Select **Modify → Geometry → Join/Unjoin Roof** tool from the *Ribbon*.

39. ***Join*** the lower roof over the garage to the upper roof.

> ***TIP:*** *Select the edge of the low roof and then select the face of the upper roof, which will be the face you wish to extend the roof to. Hover your cursor over the icon on the ribbon to see the extended tooltip for more information.*

40. Now ***Join*** the low roof over the *Living Room* with the upper roof.

Your model should look similar to Figure 7-3.15.

FIGURE 7-3.15 3D view; low roofs joined to upper roof

Here you can see that the bottoms of the roofs, to be joined, do not have to align with each other.

After looking at the two roof options, the client decides they like the gable option so you will change it back. Do not simply click *Undo*; the next steps will show you how to *Unjoin* the roof.

    41. Switch to the ***Roof Plan*** view.

    42. Select **Modify → Geometry → Join/Unjoin Roof**.

This tool, as its name implies, allows you to both *Join* and *Unjoin* roof elements. To *Unjoin*, you simply click on a line that has been created by a *Join* and the entire *Join* will go away.

    43. Select the valley line as shown in **Figure 7-3.16**.

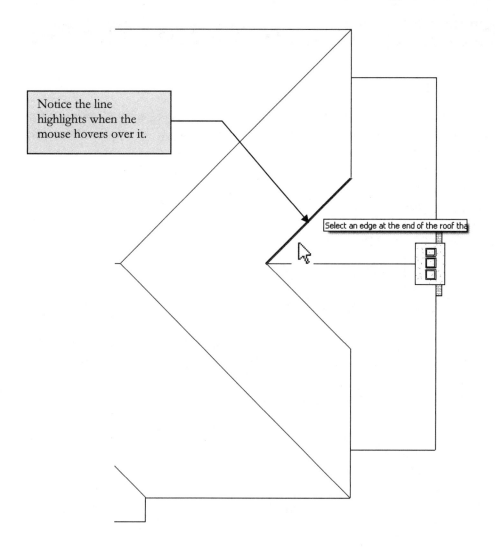

Notice the line highlights when the mouse hovers over it.

Select an edge at the end of the roof tha

FIGURE 7-3.16 Roof plan; Unjoining the lower roof from the upper roof

As soon as you click the valley line, the roof in unjoined.

44. Repeat this process to *Unjoing* the West lower roof.

45. Change the hip roof back to a gable using the techniques previously covered.

When finished, your 3D view should look like 7-3.12 again.

46. **Save** your project.

Exercise 7-4:
Skylights

This short exercise covers inserting skylights in your roof. The process is much like inserting windows. In fact, Revit lists the skylight types with the window types, so you use the *Window* tool to insert skylights into your project.

Inserting Skylights:

You will place the skylights in an elevation view.

1. Load project file **ex7-3.rvt**.

Load Family

2. Switch to the **North** elevation view.

3. Select the **Window** tool and use the *Load Family* icon to import the *skylight* family (skylight.rfa) into the current project; it can be found in the *Windows* folder.

4. Select **Skylight: 24″ x 27″** from the *Type Selector*.

You are now ready to place skylights in the roof. Revit will only look for roof objects when placing skylights; this is what is called a *roof hosted family*, so you do not have to worry about a skylight ending up in a wall.

5. Roughly place two skylights as shown in Figure 7-4.1.

> *FYI: This can be done directly in the elevation view.*

FIGURE 7-4.1 North elevation, skylights added

6. Press **Esc** or click the **Modify** tool to cancel the *Window* tool.

Next, you will want to align the skylights with each other.

7. Switch to the **East** elevation view.

8. Select one of the visible skylights.

You should now have the skylight selected and see the reference dimensions that allow you to adjust the exact location of the object. Occasionally, the dimension does not go to the point on the drawing that you are interested in referencing from. Revit allows you to adjust where those temporary dimensions reference.

9. Click and drag the grip shown in Figure 7-4.2 to (wait until it snaps) the ridge of the main roof (Figure 7-4.3).

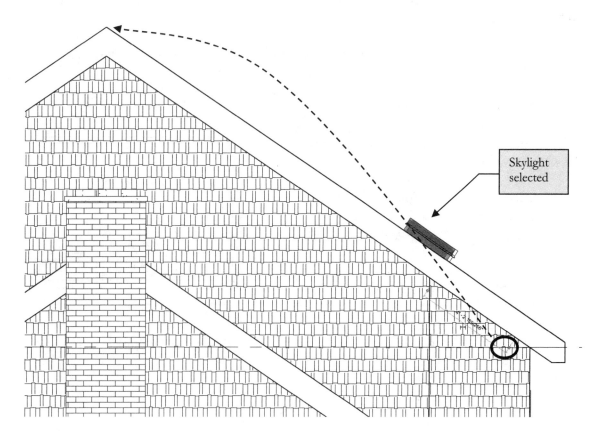

FIGURE 7-4.2 East elevation; temporary dimension shown after selecting the skylight.

10. Click on the dimension text and change the text to **18'-0"**.

    NOTE: This will adjust the position of the skylight relative to the ridge.

11. Select the other skylight and adjust it to match the one you just revised.

FIGURE 7-4.3 East elevation; temp dimension witness line adjusted.

Your skylights now align vertically on the roof. The same step would allow you to align the skylight horizontally.

12. Use the temporary dimensions to center the skylight over the second floor windows that are below it, on the North elevation.

13. **Zoom in** on one of the skylights

The number may vary; it is not a problem if it does vary.

14. Select the skylight. You should see a symbol appear near the bottom of the tag; this is the *Move* icon (Figure 7-4.4).

15. Drag on the *Move* icon to position the skylight tag so the tag does not overlap the skylight (Figure 7-4.5).

This can be done with any tag (i.e., Door tag, Room tag, etc.).

FIGURE 7-4.4 Enlarged view of skylight

16. Adjust the other skylight tag. As you reposition these tags, you may see a reference line appear indicating the symbol will automatically align with an adjacent symbol.

REMEMBER: The size of the tag is based on the View Scale setting.

Take a minute to look at your shaded 3D view and try changing the view so you can see through the skylight glass into the space below (Figure 7-4.6).

17. **Save** as **ex7-4.rvt**.

FIGURE **7-4.5** Enlarged skylight view – revised

FIGURE **7-4.6** Shaded skylight view

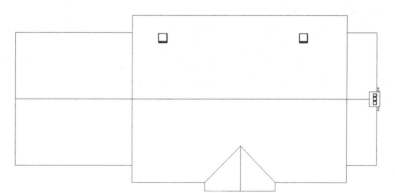

FIGURE **7-4.7** Roof plan

Reference material: Roof position relative to wall

The remaining pages in this chapter are for reference only and do not need to be done to your model. You are encouraged to study this information so you become more familiar with how the *Roof* tool works.

The following examples use a brick and concrete wall example. The image below shows the *Structure* properties for said wall type. Notice the only item within the *Core Boundary* section is the *Masonry – Concrete Block* (i.e., CMU) which is 7⅝″ thick (nominally 8″). Keep this in mind as you read through the remaining material.

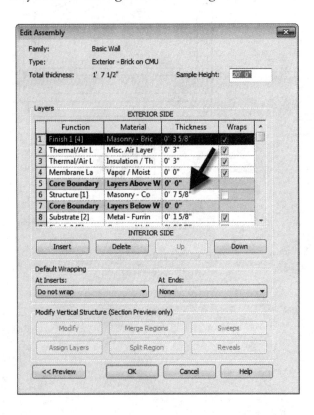

The following examples will show you how to control the position of the roof system relative to the wall below, both vertically and horizontally. The roof properties that dictate its position basically involve relationships between three things: the **Level Datum**, the exterior **Wall System** and the bottom edge of the **Roof System**. There are several other properties (e.g., pitch, construction, fascia, etc.) related to the roof that will not be mentioned at the moment so the reader may focus on a few basic principles.

The examples on this page show a sloped roof sketched with *Extend into wall (to core)* enabled and the *Overhang* set to 2'-0". Because *Extend into wall (to core)* was selected, the bottom edge of the roof is positioned relative to the *Core Boundary* of the exterior wall rather than the finished face of the wall. See the discussion about the wall's *Core Boundary* on the previous page.

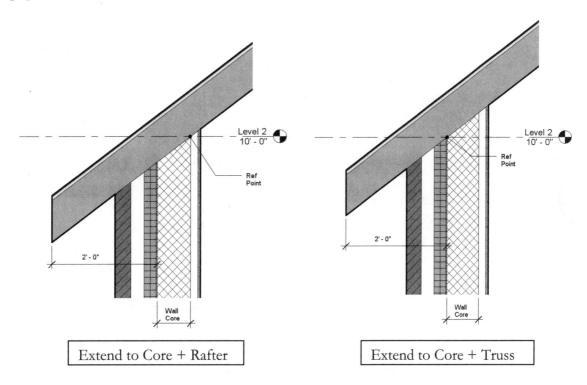

Extend to Core + Rafter   Extend to Core + Truss

Revit Roof Properties under Consideration:

Extend Into Wall:
(To Core)
This option was *checked* on the *Options Bar* while sketching the roof.

Rafter Or Truss:
This option is an *Instance Parameter* of the roof object; the example on the above left is set to *Rafter* and the other is set to *Truss*.

NOTE: The Extend into Wall (to core) *option affects the relative relationship between the wall and the roof, as you will see by comparing this example with the one on the next page.*

Base Level:
Set to *Level 2*: By associating various objects to a level, it is possible to adjust the floor elevation (i.e., *Level Datum*) and have doors, windows, floors, furniture, roofs, etc., all move vertically with that level.

Base Offset:
From Level
Set to *0'-0"*. This can be a positive or negative number which will be maintained even if the level moves.

The examples on this page show a sloped roof sketched with *Extend into wall (to core)* NOT enabled and the *Overhang* set to 2'-0". Notice that the roof overhang is derived from the exterior face of the wall (compared to the *Core Boundary* face on the previous example when *Extend into wall* was enabled).

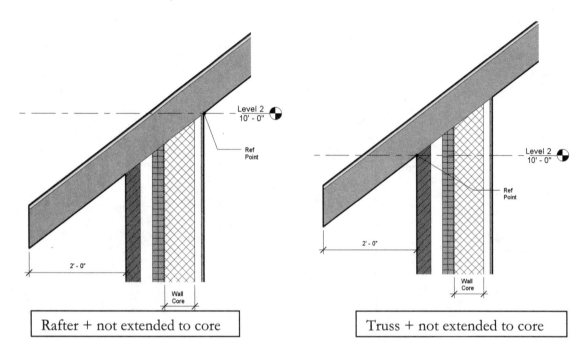

Rafter + not extended to core

Truss + not extended to core

Revit Roof Properties under Consideration:

Extend Into Wall:
(To Core)

This option was *NOT checked* on the *Options Bar* while sketching the roof.

Rafter Or Truss:

This option is an *Instance Parameter* of the roof object; the example on the above left is set to *Rafter* and the other is set to *Truss*.

NOTE: The Extend into wall (to core) *option affects the relative relationship between the wall and the roof, as you will see by comparing this example with the one on the previous page.*

Base Level:

Set to *Level 2*. By associating various objects to a level, it is possible to adjust the floor elevation (i.e., *Level Datum*) and have doors, windows, floors, furniture, roofs, etc., all move vertically with that level.

Base Offset:
From Level

Set to *0'-0"*. This can be a positive or negative number which will be maintained even if the level moves.

As you can see from the previous examples, you would most often want to have *Extend to wall (to core)* selected while sketching a roof because it would not typically make sense to position the roof based on the outside face of brick or the inside face of gypsum board, for commercial construction.

Even though you may prefer to have *Extend to wall (to core)* selected, you might like to have a 2'-0" overhang relative to the face of the brick rather than the exterior face of concrete block. This can be accomplished in one of two ways:

(A) You can modify the overhang, while sketching the roof, to include the wall thickness that occurs between the face of wall and face of core: 2'-0" + 9⅝" = 2'-9⅝". See the image to the right.

(B) The second option is to manually edit the sketch lines. You can add dimensions while in *Sketch* mode, select the sketch line to move, and then edit the dimension. The dimension can also be *Locked* to maintain the roof edge position relative to the wall. When you finish the sketch the dimensions are hidden.

Energy Truss:

In addition to controlling the roof overhang, you might also want to control the roof properties to accommodate an energy truss with what is called an *energy heal*, which allows for more insulation to occur directly above the exterior wall).

To do this you would use the *Extend into wall (to core)* + *Truss* option described above and then set the *Base Offset from Level* to 1'-0" (for a 1'-0" energy heal). See the image and the *Properties Palette* shown on the next page.

Many other properties and techniques exist which one can use to develop the roof for a project, things like the *Rafter Cut* and *Fascia Depth* which control the fascia design. Also, you can apply a sweep to a roof edge to add a 1x fascia board around the building. These are intermediate to advanced concepts and will not be covered here.

This concludes the study of the *Roof* tool!

Self-Exam:

The following questions can be used as a way to check your knowledge of this lesson. The answers can be found at the bottom of the page.

1. You do not have to click the *green check mark* to finish a roof. (T/F)

2. The wall below the roof automatically conforms to the underside of the roof when you join the wall to the roof. (T/F)

3. The roof overhang setting is available from the *Options Bar*. (T/F)

4. To create a gable roof on a building with four walls, two of the walls should not have the _____ option checked.

5. Is it possible to change the reference point for a temporary dimension that is displayed while an element is selected? (Y/N)

Review Questions:

The following questions may be assigned by your instructor as a way to assess your knowledge of this section. Your instructor has the answers to the review questions.

1. When creating a roof using the *"create roof by footprint"* option, you need to create a closed perimeter. (T/F)

2. The *Defines slope* setting be changed after the roof is finished. (T/F)

3. Skylights need to be rotated to align with the plane, or pitch, of the roof. (T/F)

4. Skylights have the glass transparent in shaded views. (T/F)

5. While using the **Roof** tool, you can use the ___Trim___ tool from the *Ribbon* to fill in the missing segments to close the perimeter.

6. You use the _Base Offset From Level_ parameter to adjust the vertical position of the roof relative to the current working plane (view).

7. While using the *Roof* tool, you need to select the _Modify_ tool from the *Ribbon* before you can select a roofline for modification.

8. You need to use the _Control Arrows_ to flip the roofline when you pick the wrong side of the wall and the overhang is shown on the inside.

9. The _Join/Unjoin Roof_ from the *Modify* tab (on the *Ribbon*) allows you to extend one roof element over, and into, another.

10. Changing the name of a level tag (in elevation) causes Revit to rename all the corresponding views (plan, ceiling, etc.) if you answer yes to the prompt. T

SELF-EXAM ANSWERS:
1 - F, 2 – T, 3 – T, 4 – defines slope, 5 – Y

Notes:

Lesson 8
Residence: FLOOR SYSTEMS AND REFLECTED CEILING PLANS:

In this lesson you will learn to create floor structures and reflected ceiling plans.

Even though you currently have floor levels defined, you do not have an object that represents the mass of the floor systems. You will add floor systems with a hole for the stair.

Ceiling systems allow you to specify the ceiling material by room and the height above the floor. Once the ceiling has been added, it will show up in section views. Sections are created later in this book.

Be sure to view the videos on modeling floors and ceilings located on the DVD. Many of the videos cover additional material not found in the book.

Exercise 8-1:
Floor Systems

Similar to other Autodesk® Revit® Architecture elements, you can select from a few predefined floor types. You can also create new floor types. In your residence you will use a predefined floor system for the first and second floors and then create a new type for the basement and garage.

Basement Floor, Slab on Grade:

Sketching floors is a lot like sketching roofs; you can select walls to define the perimeter and draw lines to fill in the blanks, and add holes, or cut-outs, in the floor object.

1. Open ex7-4.rvt and **Save As ex8-1.rvt**.

2. Switch to the *Basement Floor Plan* view.

Floor

3. Select **Home → Build → Floor** *(just the icon, not the down-arrow)*.

4. Click the **Edit Type** button on the *Properties Palette*.

5. Select **Concrete Slab – 4″** from the *Type* drop-down list near the top.

6. Click **Duplicate**.

7. Type **4″ Slab on Grade over Vapor Barrier**, then **OK**.

8. Click the **Edit** button next to the *Structure* parameter.

Here you could change the thickness of the slab, but you will leave it at 4″ for the basement.

Next you will add a vapor barrier and sand bed below the slab.

9. Insert a new layer:
    a. *Function:* **Membrane Layer**
    b. *Material:* **Vapor/Moisture Barriers – Vapor Retarder**
    c. *Thickness:* **0″**

NOTE: *Vapor barriers do have a thickness, of course (4mil, 6mil, etc). However, the thickness is typically ignored on drawings. A Membrane is the only layer which can have no thickness; that is, a zero value.*

10. Add another layer:
    a. *Function:* **Substrate [2]**
    b. *Material:* **Site - Sand**
    c. *Thickness:* **4″** (Figure 8-1.1).

NOTE: *The sand is sometimes placed over the vapor barrier. The sand helps to protect the vapor barrier until the rebar and concrete slab are in place. Additionally, the sand allows the concrete to cure more evenly with less chance of cupping. On the other hand, a vapor barrier directly below the slab helps prevent some floor finishes from delaminating due to moisture in the sand.*

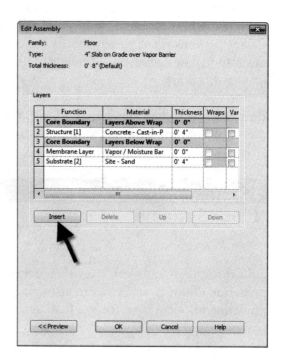

FIGURE 8-1.1 New floor system

TIP: *You can change the position of layers within a system. Simply select the row and then click the Up or Down button until positioned.*

11. Click **OK** to close the open dialog boxes.

12. Select the walls in the **Basement Plan** as shown in Figure 8-1.2.

    TIP: *Select the interior side of the wall. You can use the control arrows if needed, opposite of what you did for the roof.*

13. Click the **green check mark** on the *Ribbon*.

    TIP: *If you get any errors, see the next page.*

Common Errors Finishing a Floor Sketch:

If you get an error message when trying to finish a floor sketch, it is probably due to a problem with the sketched perimeter lines. Here are two common problems:

Perimeter not closed:

You cannot finish a floor if there is a gap, large or small, in the perimeter sketch. *FIX:* Sketch a line to close the loop.

Sketch lines – perimeter not closed because line is missing

Error message after clicking finish sketch

Perimeter lines intersect:

You cannot finish a floor if any of the sketch lines intersect. *FIX:* Use *Trim* to make it so all line endpoints touch.

Sketch lines – lines extend past each other; not good

Error message after clicking finish sketch

FIGURE 8-1.2 Basement floor plan; floor slab sketched

14. Click **No** when prompted to join the floor to the walls (Figure 8-1.3).

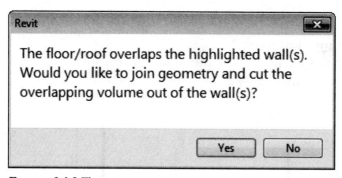

FIGURE 8-1.3 Floor prompt

You now have a floor at the basement level. You should see a stipple pattern representing the floor area. You would most likely want to turn that pattern off for a floor plan. You will do that next.

15. In the ***Basement Floor Plan*** view, type **VV**; this is the keyboard shortcut for *Visibility/Graphic Overrides*.

    TIP: *You may have to click within the drawing window before typing the keyboard shortcut for Revit to recognize it.*

16. In the *Visibility/Graphic Overrides* dialog, on the *Model Categories* tab and in the **Floors** row, click the empty cell in the **Projection/ Surface → Patterns** column (Figure 8-1.4).

17. With the word *Override* now showing, click the exact same location again.

FIGURE 8-1.4 Visibility/Graphics Overrides: Editing the floor surface pattern visibility

18. Uncheck **Visible**, which will make the floor surface pattern not visible in the current view (Figure 8-1.5).

19. Click **OK** to close the dialogs.

The stipple pattern is no longer visible. The *Visibility/Graphic Overrides* dialog now indicates that the surface pattern is hidden (Figure 8-1.6). Keep in mind, this override is only for the current view. If you create

FIGURE 8-1.5 Fill Pattern Graphics

another floor using the same 4″ concrete type you just created in the Level 1 floor plan view, it would have the stipple pattern. It would even show up if in another basement level floor plan, as it is possible to create more than one view which references the same *Level Datum*.

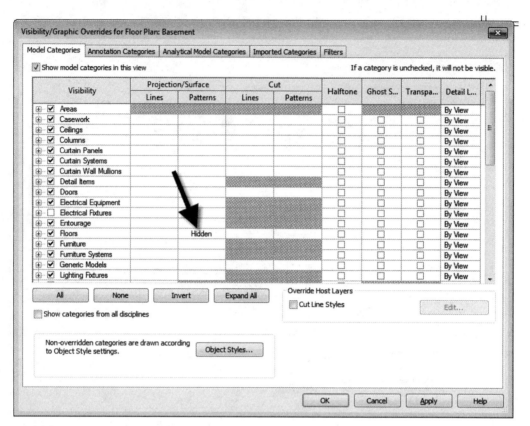

FIGURE 8-1.6 Visibility/Graphics Overrides

Garage Floor, Slab on Grade:

Now you will sketch the floor slab for the garage area. Because this floor will have vehicles parking on it, you will create a new slab type that is 6" thick.

20. Switch to the ***First Floor Plan*** view.

21. Select the ***Floor*** tool.

22. Using the floor type you just created as a starting point, create a new floor type named **6" Slab on Grade over Vapor Barrier**.

> ***TIP:*** *Properties Palette → Edit Type →*
> *Duplicate*

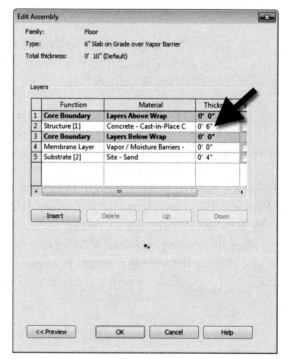

FIGURE 8.1-7 Changing the conc. slab thickness

23. Click the **Edit** button next to the *Structure* parameter.

24. Change the *Concrete* thickness from **4"** to **6"** (Figure 8-1.7).

25. Click **OK** to close the open dialog boxes.

26. With *Pick Walls* selected on the *Ribbon*, select the interior side of the four walls surrounding the garage (Figure 8.1-8).

27. Click the **green checkmark** to finish the floor. Click **No** when prompted to join the wall and the floor.

You now have a floor slab in the garage area. You will notice that the floor element has a stipple pattern, even though you turned that stipple pattern off in the *Basement* view. Remember: the visibility settings are controlled by view, not project-wide, although they can be. You will turn this off later.

Notice the **Span Direction** symbol identified in the image to the right. This can be ignored for this type of floor. It is meant to define the flute direction for a metal floor/roof deck, which your residential floors will not have.

> ***FYI:*** *The Span Direction button on the Ribbon, visible while in the Floor tool, will allow you to change the span direction by picking a different sketch line.*

FIGURE 8.1-8 First floor: floor slab sketched

When floors are created, the top of the floor aligns with the level (see image below). Each floor plan view is associated with a level (which cannot be changed), so the view in which you create the floor determines the default level the floor references. The referenced floor level can be changed at any time. The top of the floor will stay aligned with the level even if the floor thickness is changed. However, it is possible to select the floor and change its "Height Offset From Level" parameter to change the default behavior.

Top of floor aligns with level

First Floor (Wood Joists):

28. Use the floor type *Wood Joist 10" - Wood Finish* as a starting point to create a new floor type named **Wood Joist 14" - Wood Finish**.

29. Change the *Structure* settings per the following image (Figure 8-1.9).

    FYI: *This has all been covered previously.*

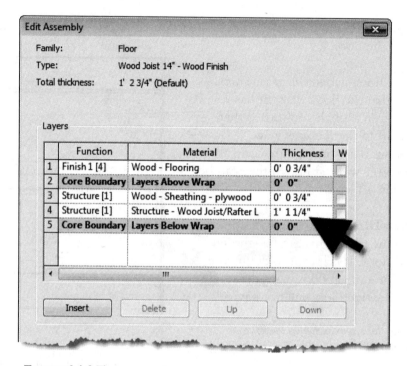

FIGURE 8.1-9 Floor properties

Creating the first and second floors will be a little more involved than were the basement and garage floors. This is because the upper floors require openings. For example, you need to define the openings for the stair. Revit makes the process very simple.

You should still be in the *Floor* tool.

30. On the *Options Bar*, check ***Extend into wall (to core)***.

    FYI: *The* Extend into wall (to core) *option will extend the slab under your wall core (wood stud and sheathing are in the core in our example) and go under the gypsum wall board. This is similar to the information presented at the end of the previous chapter.*

31. Select the exterior walls indicated in Figure 8-1.10. Select the exterior side of the wall; use the flip control arrows if needed.

FIGURE 8-1.10 First Floor – floor system sketched

Next you will define the hole in the floor for the stair that leads down to the basement. You will need to use the *Lines* option from the *Draw* panel to define this area.

32. While the *Floor* tool is still active, **Zoom In** to the stair area.

33. Select the **Rectangle** icon on the *Ribbon*; see image below.

34. Draw a rectangle defining the stair opening; use Revit's snaps to accurately pick the points as shown in **Figure 8-1.11**.

FIGURE 8-1.11 First Floor – sketching floor opening

FYI: This floor opening has a big problem. You will see this problem when you get to the building sections exercise later in this book.

35. Click the **green check mark** to finish the floor.

Next, you will get two prompts: one asks if you want the walls below, whose tops are set to terminate at the first floor, to attach to the new floor. The other prompt asks if you want the floor to attach to the exterior walls. You will answer **Yes** to both.

36. Click **Yes** to the prompt *"Would you like the walls that go up to this floor's level to attach to its bottom?"* (Figure 8-1.12). Also, click **OK** if prompted with a "highlighted walls are attached, but miss…" warning.

> *FYI: This will allow the walls to dynamically change if the floor elevation or thickness is changed.*

37. Click **Yes** for the prompt to join the walls that overlap the floor system (Figure 8-1.13).

FIGURE 8-1.12 Join walls below to new floor prompt

FIGURE 8-1.13 Join walls that overlap the new floor prompt

Now that the floor is placed, you should see a dense horizontal line pattern that represents the finished wood floor. This would be nice for presentation drawings, but like the basement, you will turn the floor hatch off so the floor plan is not too cluttered.

38. Change the first floor's *Visibility* to turn off the floor hatch.

Copy/Paste the First Floor to the Second:

That completes the first floor system. Next you will copy the floor you just created to the second floor. It would probably be easier to just create a floor from scratch, but you will get more practice editing existing elements.

39. Select the floor you just created, in the first floor plan view, and select **Modify | Floors → Clipboard → Copy to Clipboard** on the *Ribbon*. See *TIP* on next page.

TIP: *Selecting elements that overlap, like the exterior walls and the edge of floor system, may require the use of the* Tab *key. The only way to select a floor element is by picking its edge. Revit temporarily highlights elements when you move your cursor over them. But, because the floor edge may not have an "exposed" edge to select, you will have to toggle through your selection options for your current cursor location. With the cursor positioned over the edge of the floor, probably with an exterior wall highlighted, press the* Tab *key to toggle through the available options. A tooltip will display the elements. When you see* floors: floor:floor-name, *click the mouse; also watch the Status Bar.*

40. Pick **Modify → Clipboard → Paste → Aligned to Selected Levels**.

41. Select **Second Floor** and then **OK**.

42. Switch to the **Second Floor**.

You now have a copy of the first floor's "floor system" in the *Second Floor Plan* view (Figure 8-1.14); keep in mind that all the views are looking at a single 3D model. You will edit the sketch lines of the second floor slab to make the stair hole larger and remove a portion of the floor that extends past the East exterior wall.

TIP: *You can press Ctrl and select more than one.*

FIGURE 8-1.14 New floor added to level 2 using the paste aligned option

43. Select the floor element in the **Second Floor Plan** view.

   TIP: *The edge of the floor is "exposed" at the stair opening; this would be the easiest place to select the floor.*

Edit
Boundary

44. Click **Edit Boundary** from the *Ribbon*. See icon to right.

You are now in *Sketch* mode, where you can change the perimeter and holes for the selected floor element. You can select lines and delete them, sketch new lines, and use *Trim* to modify lines.

45. Modify the lines at the far right, using *Delete* and *Trim*, so your sketch looks like Figure 8-1.15.

46. *Stair opening: Move* the West vertical line **4'-10"** farther West; the horizontal sketch lines should automatically extend, as shown in Figure 8-1.15. The overall width of the stair opening should be 8'-0"; if not you should go back and double check your stair dimensions with Chapter 6, page 6-25.

47. Click the **green checkmark** to recreate the floor element.

FIGURE 8-1.15 Second floor: sketch lines modified

Now that Revit is recreating the floor, it notices the walls below and at the exterior so you get the "join" prompts.

48. Click **Yes** to the two "join" prompts, if you get them.

Your ***Second Floor Plan*** view should look like Figure 8-1.16.

FIGURE 8-1.16 Second Floor: sketch lines modified

FIGURE 8-1.17 3D view: cutaway view showing floor elements added

49. Change the second floor's *Visibility* to turn off the floor hatch.

Turning off Surface Pattern at the Source:

If you do not want a portion of your plan to show a surface pattern, you might want to remove the surface pattern associated with the floor system. That way you could leave the surface pattern setting turned on.

Basically you remove the surface pattern for the *Finish* layer in a floor system.

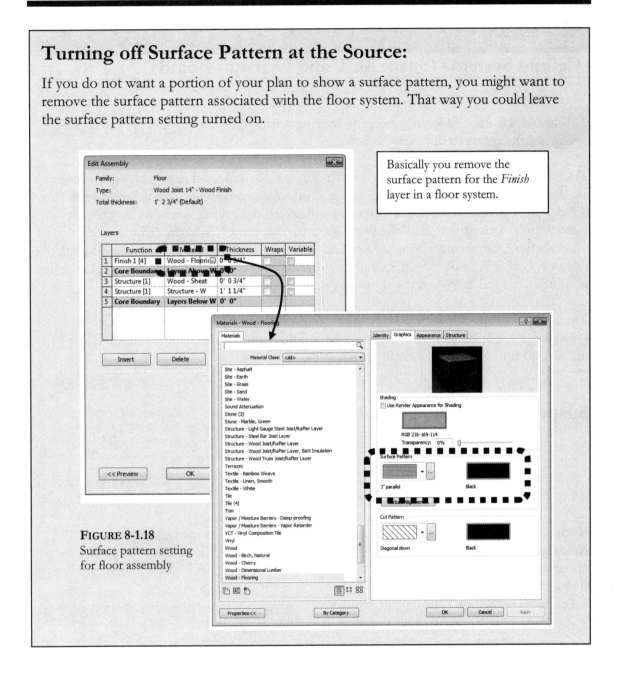

FIGURE 8-1.18
Surface pattern setting for floor assembly

50. Save your project as **ex8-1.rvt**.

Exercise 8-2:
Ceiling Systems (Susp. ACT and Gypsum Board)

This lesson will explore Revit's tools for drawing reflected ceiling plans. This will include drawing different types of ceiling systems.

Traditionally, residential projects do not typically include reflected ceiling plans. The ceilings are generally straightforward, with all required information coming from a *Room Finish Schedule* and *Sections*. However, in Revit you will sketch the ceiling profile in the ceiling plan views, similar to how you drew the floor systems. You want to add the ceilings so they show up in sections. So, seeing as you have ceiling plans, why not include them in the construction documents set? Your design intent will be clearer, and you can make sure the lighting design is coordinated and laid out the way you want it.

The use of suspended acoustical ceiling tile in residential projects is somewhat limited. However, it is occasionally used so it will be covered here. In this lesson you will add it to the second floor office and a family room in the basement.

Suspended Acoustical Ceiling Tile System:

1. Open ex8-1.rvt and **Save As ex8-2.rvt**.

2. Switch to the ***Second Floor Ceiling Plan*** view, from the *Project Browser*; ceiling plans are just below the floor plans.

Notice the doors and windows are automatically "turned off" in the ceiling plan views. Actually, the ceiling plan views have a cutting plane similar to floor plans, except they look up rather than down. You can see this setting by right-clicking on a view name in the *Project Browser* and selecting *Properties*, and then selecting **View Range**. The default value is 7'-6". You might increase this if, for example, you had 10'-0" ceilings and 8'-0" high doors. Otherwise, the doors would show because the 7'-6" cutting plane is below the door height (Figure 8-2.1).

FIGURE 8-2.1 Properties: View Range settings

3. Close the open dialog boxes and then select **Home → Build → Ceiling**.

Ceiling

You have four ceiling types, by default, to select from (Figure 8-2.2).

FIGURE 8-2.2 Ceiling: types

4. Select *Compound Ceiling:* **2'x4' ACT System**.

Next you will change the ceiling height. The default setting is 8'-0" above the current level. You will change the ceiling height to 8'-4"; this will give about 6½" of space above the ceiling to the bottom of the rafters for recessed light fixtures and any required wiring. This setting can be changed on a room by room basis; that is why it is an *Instance Parameter*.

5. In the *Properties Palette*, set the *Height Offset From Level* setting to **8'-4"** (Figure 8-2.3).

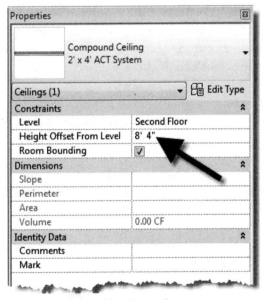

FIGURE 8-2.3 Ceiling: Properties

You are now ready to place ceiling grids. This process cannot get much easier, especially compared to 2D CAD programs.

6. Move your cursor anywhere within the office in the lower-right corner of the building. You should see the perimeter of the room highlighted.

7. Pick within the room; Revit places a ceiling grid in the room (Figure 8-2.4).

FYI: Skylights in roof

FYI: Line of roof ridge

2'x4' ACT added

FYI: Roof overhang

FIGURE 8-2.4: Second Floor Ceiling Plan view: 2'x4' suspended acoustical ceiling tile added to office

You now have a 2x4 ceiling grid at 8'-4" above the floor, the second floor in this case. Later in the book, when you get to the exercise on cutting sections, you will see the ceiling with the proper height and thickness.

Next, you will add the same ceiling system to the family room in the basement. But, you will notice the ceiling plan section in the *Project Browser* does not have a *Basement* view.

Many residential basements do not have any finished ceilings, so that view was not included in the template from which you started. Next you will create a view for this.

8. Select **View → Create → Plan Views → Reflected Ceiling Plan**.

9. Select the ***Basement*** view from this list and then click **OK** (see image to the right).

10. You are taken to the ***Basement Ceiling Plan*** view automatically.

Your view should look a little funny, no walls. You will have adjust the *View Range* settings.

11. Set the *View Range* to **6'-6"**.

You should now see the walls and doors. The doors show because the cut plane is lower than the top of the door. You will ignore that for now.

12. Use the **Ceiling** tool to place 2′x 4′ acoustic ceiling tile in the *Family Room*, the large room to the far East. See the following notes (Figure 8-2.5):
    a. You will probably get a symbol at the cross-hairs that indicates you cannot place a ceiling anywhere; the symbol is a circle with a slash through it. This has to do with the ceiling height.
    b. Via the *Properties Palette*, change the ceiling height to **7′-0″**.
    c. You should be able to place the ceiling system now.
    d. Revit automatically rotates and centers the ceiling grid within each room.

FIGURE 8-2.5: Basement Ceiling Plan view: 2′x4′ suspended acoustical ceiling tile added to Family Rm.

When you place a ceiling grid, Revit centers the grid in the room. The general rule-of-thumb is you should try to avoid reducing the tile size by more than half of a tile. You can see in Figure 8-2.5 that the East and West sides look OK. However, the North and South sides are small slivers. You will adjust this next.

Looking at Figure 8-2.6, you can see why it was not possible to place a ceiling until the ceiling height was lowered and why the walls did not show up; the foundation wall is only 7′-3″ above the basement floor. Thus, a floor cut plane of 7′-6″ would not show walls and an 8′-4″ ceiling could not find walls to form a perimeter to contain it.

FIGURE 8-2.6
Section at basement / foundation wall

13. Select **Modify** from the *Ribbon*.

14. **Select** the ceiling grid. Only one line will be highlighted.

15. Use the **Move** tool to move the grid 24" to the North (Figure 8-2.7).

FIGURE 8-2.7
Basement: Ceiling Grid moved

You should notice that only the grid moved, not the ceiling perimeter.

Modifying the Suspended Acoustical Ceiling Tile System:

Making modifications to the grid is relatively easy. Next, you will adjust the ceiling height and rotate the grid.

16. In the **Basement** view, select the ceiling grid in the *Family Room*.

17. Within the *Properties Palette*, change the height to **7'-2"**. *(Every inch counts!)*

18. Click **Apply** to accept the new height change (or just move your cursor back into the drawing area).

19. Again, with the grid still selected, use the **Rotate** tool from the *Ribbon* to rotate the grid **30 degrees**.

> **FYI:** *Notice, while in the Rotate command, the <u>Center of Rotation</u> icon appears, and like in the earlier lessons, this can be dragged to a different location if needed.*

TIP: *When using the Rotate tool you need to pick two points. The first point is your reference line. The second point is the number of degrees off that reference line. In this example, try picking your first point to the right as a horizontal line. Then move the cursor counter-clockwise until 30 degrees is displayed. You can also type the angle rather than clicking the second point.*

Your drawing should look similar to **Figure 8-2.8**. Notice how the perimeter of the room acts like a cropping window when you use *Move* or *Rotate* on a ceiling grid.

Deleting a Ceiling Grid:
When selecting a ceiling grid, Revit only selects one line. This does not allow you to delete the ceiling.

To delete: hover cursor over a ceiling grid line and press the TAB key until you see the ceiling perimeter highlight, then click the mouse. The entire ceiling will be selected. Press Delete.

FIGURE 8-2.8 Basement: Modified Ceiling

Next, you will look at drawing gypsum board ceiling systems. The process is identical to placing the grid system. Additionally, you will create a ceiling type.

Gypsum Board Ceiling System:

You will create a new ceiling type for a gypsum board (gyp. bd.) ceiling. To better identify the areas that have a gyp. bd. ceiling, you will set the ceiling type to have a stipple pattern. This will provide a nice graphical representation for the gyp. bd. ceiling areas. The ceiling you are about to create would lean more towards a commercial application. However, it will give you a better understanding of how to create custom ceilings. You will add this ceiling to a room in the basement; assume it is being installed below HVAC ductwork, to finish the room.

Materials

20. Select **Manage → Settings → Materials**. *This is the list of materials you select from when assigning a material to each layer in a wall system, etc.*

21. Select *Gypsum Wall Board* in the name list and then click the **Duplicate** button and enter the name: **Gypsum Ceiling Board**.

22. In the *Surface Pattern* area, pick the button and select **Gypsum-Plaster** from the list, and then click **OK** twice (Figure 8-2.9).

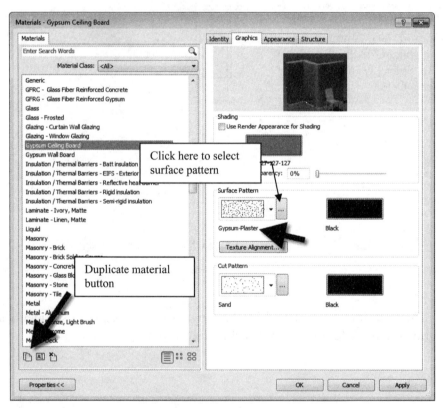

FIGURE 8-2.9 Materials dialog

The *Surface Pattern* setting is what will add the stipple pattern to the gyp. bd. ceiling areas. With this set to *none*, the ceiling has no pattern, like the basic ceiling type.

Thus, if you wanted "Carpet 1" finish to never have the stipple hatch pattern, you could change the surface pattern to none via the *Materials* dialog and not have to change each view's visibility override.

23. Select the ***Ceiling*** tool from the *Ribbon*.

Ceiling

24. Set the *Type Selector* to **GWB on Metal Stud**.

> *FYI: You are selecting this because it is similar to the ceiling you will be creating.*

25. Click the **Edit Type** button in the *Properties Palette*.

26. Click *Duplicate* and type the name **Susp GB on Metal Stud**.

27. Select **Edit** next to the *Structure* parameter.

28. Create a *Layer* and set the *Values* as follows (Figure 8-2.10):
    a. **1½" Mtl. Stud**
    b. **¾" Mtl. Stud**
    c. **Gypsum Ceiling Board** *(This is the material you created in Step 21.)*

29. Click **OK** two times.

FYI: *The ceiling assembly you just created represents a typical suspended gyp. bd. ceiling system. The metal studs are perpendicular to each other and suspended by wires, similar to an ACT (acoustical ceiling tile) system.*

You are now ready to draw a gypsum board ceiling.

30. Make sure **Susp GB on Metal Stud** is selected in the *Type Selector* on the *Properties Palette*.

31. Set the ceiling height to **7'-0"**.

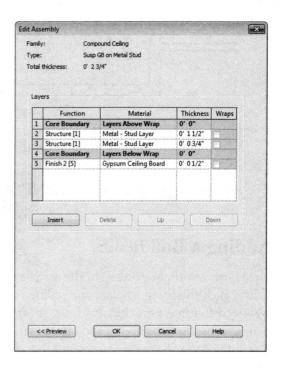

FIGURE 8-2.10 New ceiling – Edit assembly

32. Pick the lower left room as shown in **Figure 8-2.11**.

FIGURE 8-2.11 Gyp. Bd. Ceiling

You now have a gypsum board ceiling at 7'-0" above the basement floor slab.

Adding a Bulkhead:

Next, you will draw a ceiling in the area at the bottom of the steps. However, you cannot simply pick the room to place the ceiling because Revit would fill in the stair area. First, you will need to draw a bulkhead at the bottom of the steps. A bulkhead is a portion of wall that hangs from the floor above and creates a closed perimeter for a ceiling system to tie into. The bulkhead will create a perimeter that the *Ceiling* tool will detect for the proper ceiling placement.

33. While still in the *Basement Reflected Ceiling Plan* view, select the **Wall** tool.

FIGURE 8-2.12 Bulkhead (wall) properties

34. Set the *Type Selector* to **Interior – 4 1/2" Partition**

35. In the *Properties Palette* set the *Base Offset* to **7'-0"** (Figure 8-2.12).

This will put the bottom of the wall at 7'-0" above the current floor level, basement in this case.

36. Set the *Top Constraint* to: **Up to level: First Floor** (Figure 8-2.12).

   TIP: The next time you draw a wall you will have to change the Base Offset back to 0'-0" or your wall will be 7'-0" off the floor; this can be hard to remember!

37. **Draw the bulkhead**; make sure you snap to the adjacent walls (Figure 8-2.13).

Bulkhead added here; a wall with the bottom starting at 7'-0" above the basement floor

FIGURE 8-2.13 Bulkhead drawn

38. Select the **Ceiling** tool.

You could just pick within this room and Revit would automatically create a ceiling; however, you will look at another way to place a ceiling. Next you will sketch the perimeter of the ceiling, just like you did for the floor slabs in the previous lesson.

39. Select **Sketch Ceiling** from the *Ribbon*.

Sketch
Ceiling

40. Sketch a line around the perimeter of the room using *Snaps* (Figure 8-2.14).

> *TIP: Remember to use the Chain option.*

41. Click the **green check mark** to finish the sketch.

FIGURE 8-2.14 Sketching Ceiling

Your ceiling should look like Figure 8-2.15. You will see what is happening here a little better in the sections exercise.

FIGURE 8-2.15 Ceiling added at bottom of steps

Modifying a Floor System to Include the Ceiling:

Next you will modify the floor systems, already in place, to have gypsum board attached to the bottom of the joists. This is what is typically done in a residence, unless room is needed above the ceiling for ductwork.

42. Switch to the **Second Floor Plan** view (not the ceiling plan).

43. Select the floor.

> *TIP: Clicking near the stair opening may be the easiest way to select the floor.*

44. Via *Edit Type*, create a *Duplicate* floor from the one selected; name it: **Wood Joist 14″ – Wood Finish – Gyp Bd Ceiling**.

45. Edit the floor structure via *Type Properties* (Figure 8-2.16).
    a.   Insert a new *Layer* at the bottom of the floor assembly
    b.   Set the *Function* to: **Finish 1 [4]**
    c.   Set the *Material* to: **Gypsum Ceiling Board**
    d.   Set the *Thickness* to: ½″

Why Did You Create a New Floor Type?

You needed to create a new floor type for the second floor because the first floor does not need gypsum board on the underside. When you modify a *family type*, all instances of that type are changed throughout the project. This is very powerful when you actually want to change several instances of a type. However, if you modify a type and only want the selected one to change, you are in for a big surprise when you look at the other instances of that type elsewhere in your project, because they will all change. That is why you had to create a new floor type, because that same floor type is also placed on the first floor.

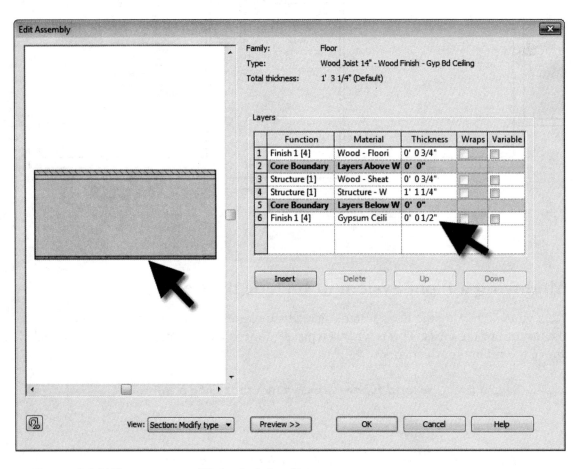

FIGURE 8-2.16 Floor system modified to include ceiling

46. Close the open dialog boxes.

Now switch to the *First Floor Ceiling Plan* (Figure 8-2.17) and notice that the gypsum ceiling board surface pattern is showing everywhere the floor occurs. If not, make sure the second floor system has been changed to the new type. That takes care of the ceiling for the first floor.

47. Switch to the *Second Floor Ceiling Plan* and add your **Susp GB on Metal Stud** at 8'-0" high to the remaining rooms (Figure 8-2.18).

> *FYI: Once a ceiling is placed you can select it and click Edit Boundary on the Ribbon. Then you can change the perimeter or add an enclosed area within the main perimeter to create a hole. This is how you would accommodate the skylights in the roof: by adding holes to the ceiling to let the light in.*

48. **Save** your project as **ex8-2.rvt**.

FIGURE 8-2.17 First floor ceiling plan: gypsum board added to bottom of floor structure

Real-Time Design Validation

Notice how the ceiling, which is a 3D object, covers the roof ridge line and skylights? This is very powerful in that you see all aspects of the design. If you could see ductwork in the view below, that would mean it was added to the model too low and needs to be raised or moved. Being able to see everything in context helps the designers validate their design solution.

FIGURE 8-2.18 Second Floor Ceiling Plan: gypsum board ceiling system suspended at 8'-0" AFF

Exercise 8-3:
Placing Light Fixtures

In this exercise, you will learn to load and place light fixtures in your reflected ceiling plans.

Loading Families:

Before placing fixtures, you need to load them into your project.

1. Select **Component** from the *Home* tab on the *Ribbon*.

2. Select **Load Family** on the contextual *Ribbon* (Figure 8-3.1).

FIGURE 8-3.1 Component tool active; contextual Ribbon options

3. Double-click the *Lighting Fixtures* folder, and then double-click **Troffer Light - 2x4 Parabolic.rfa** (Figure 8-3.2).

FIGURE 8-3.2 Load component

Placing Instances of Components:

You are now ready to place the fixtures in your ceiling plans.

4. With **Component** still selected, pick **Troffer Light – 2′ x 4′ Parabolic: 2′x4′ (2 Lamp) – 120 V** from the *Type Selector* drop-down on the *Properties Palette*.

5. On the ***Second Floor Ceiling Plan*** view, place fixtures as shown in **Figure 8-3.3**.

FIGURE 8-3.3 Light fixtures added to ceiling

You will have to use the *Move* command, or even better the *Align* tool, to move the fixture so it fits perfectly in the ACT grid.

6. Switch to the *Basement Ceiling Plan* view.

7. Now place another **2x4 light fixture** as shown in **Figure 8-3.4**.

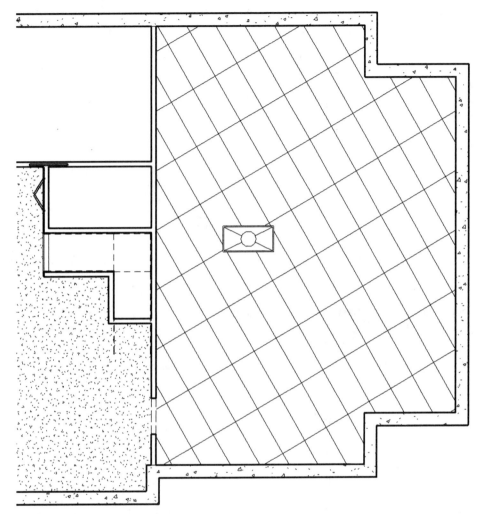

FIGURE 8-3.4 Basement ceiling plan; light fixture added

Notice the fixture does not automatically orient itself with the ceiling grid. There may be an occasion when you want this.

Also, notice the light fixture hides a portion of the ceiling grid. This is nice because the grid does not extend through a light fixture.

8. Use *Rotate* and *Move* to rotate the fixture to align with the grid (Figure 8-3.5). The *Align* tool will also work.

   TIP: You can use the normal Rotate *and* Move *tools in conjunction with the Snaps.*

FIGURE 8-3.5 Basement Ceiling Plan; light fixture moved/rotated into place

9. Once you have one fixture rotated, it is easier to use the *Copy* tool and the *Snaps* to add rotated light fixtures. **Copy** the light fixture to match the layout in **Figure 8-3.6**.

   TIP: Check Multiple *on the Options Bar when the Copy command is active.*

FIGURE 8-3.6 Basement Ceiling Plan; light fixture copied

10. **Save** your project as **ex8-3.rvt**.

These 2x4 light fixtures have *Rendering* settings already setup. That means the room will automatically have lights when you get to creating a photo-realistic rendering using this built-in feature!

The example image below shows a reflected ceiling plan with supply and return diffusers added. These are not used too often in residential work. They are loaded similar to the light fixture via component tool.

FIGURE 8-3.7 Example image; supply and return diffusers added

Reflected Ceiling Plan Symbols:

Revit provides many of the industry standard content necessary in drawing reflected ceiling plans (RCP). As shown in Figure 8-3.7, supply air diffusers are represented with an X and return air has a diagonal line. It is typical to have an RCP symbol legend showing each symbol and material pattern and listing what each one represents. The *Legend* feature makes this a snap!

Component Properties

If you want to adjust the properties of a component, such as a light fixture, you can browse to it in the *Project Browser* and right click on one of the *Types* listed. *Notice the right click menu also has the option to select all instances of the item in the drawing.* Select *Properties*. You will see the dialog below for the 2x4 (2 lamps)-120V.

You can also click *Duplicate* and add more sizes (e.g., a 4′x4′ light fixture).

You can also select an inserted component and look at the *Properties Palette* for additional properties for that particular instance.

Exercise 8-4:
Annotations

This short section will look at adding notes to your RCP.

Adding Annotations:

1. In the ***Basement Reflected Ceiling Plan*** view, select the **Annotate → Text → Text** tool from the *Ribbon*.

2. Pick **Text: 3/32″ Arial** from the *Type Selector* (Figure 8-4.1).

3. Select the **Leader** (Curved) button highlighted in **Figure 8-4.1**.

FIGURE 8-4.1 Text; Ribbon options

Next, you will add a note indicating that a room in the basement does not have a ceiling. First you will draw a leader, and then Revit will allow you to type the text.

4. Add the note "**NO CEILING - TYPICAL**" shown in **Figure 8-4.2**.

FIGURE 8-4.2 Text with Curved leader

Notice that immediately after adding the text or while it is selected, you see the *Move* icon, the *Rotate* icon and *Grips* to edit the arrow/leader.

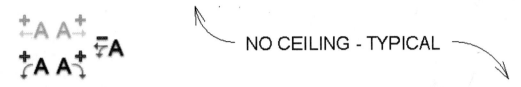

When the text is selected you can click the "add leader" tools on the *Ribbon* (shown on the left above) to add additional leaders.

Adding Text Styles to Your Project:

You can add additional text styles to your project. Some firms prefer a font that has a hand lettering look and others prefer something like the Arial font. These preferences can be saved in the template file so they are consistent and always available. Next, you will add a new style to your Revit project.

5. Click on the *Text* tool.

6. Next, click **Edit Type** in the *Properties Palette*.

7. Select **Duplicate** and enter **1/4″ OUTLINE TEXT** (Figure 8-4.3).

8. Next, make the following adjustments to the *Type Properties* (Figure 8-4.4).
    a. Text Font: **Swis721 BdOul BT**
    b. Text Size: ¼″

    NOTE: *You can use any Windows True-Type font. If you do not have this font, select another that best matches (Figure 8-4.5).*

FIGURE 8-4.3 New text name

The text size you entered in Step 9 is the size of the text when printed. Revit automatically scales the text, in each view, based on the *View Scale* setting. For example, if you are adding 3/32″ text to a ⅛″ floor plan view, the text placed will be 9″ tall. If you add text to a ¼″ plan view, the text will be 4½″ tall. When both the ¼″ and ⅛″ plan views are placed on a sheet, the text for each is 3/32″ tall. Here is what happens: adding text to the ¼″ plan causes the 3/32″ text to be scaled up 48 times, and when the plan view is placed on a *Sheet*, the entire view, including the text, is scaled down 1/48 times; thus, the text makes a full loop back to being 3/32″ tall.

If you change the *View Scale* of the drawing, the text size will automatically change, so the text is always the correct size when printing. It is best to set the drawing to the correct scale first, as changing the *View Scale* can create a lot of work, repositioning resized text that may be overlapping something or too big for a room.

9. Select **OK** to close the open dialog.

You should now have the new text style available in the *Element Type Selector* on the *Ribbon*.

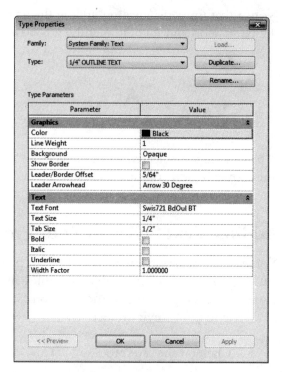

10. Use the new text style to create the text shown below (Figure 8-4.5).

> **TIP:** *Select the text only options on the Ribbon – i.e., No Leader.*

When typing text, you simply click somewhere in the view to complete the text string; pressing *Enter* just adds more lines.

11. Save as **ex8-4.rvt**.

FIGURE 8-4.4 New text properties

FIGURE 8-4.5 New text style added

Self-Exam:

The following questions can be used as a way to check your knowledge of this lesson. The answers can be found at the bottom of the page.

1. You must pick walls to define floor areas. (T/F)

2. Use the Ctrl key to cycle through the selection options. (T/F)

3. When you add a floor element in plan view, the floor does not show up right away in the other views, i.e., 3D, Sections, etc. (T/F)

4. You use the _____ feature; if you need to add a new product, like exterior plaster, so you can add it to wall types and other systems.

5. You have _____ different types of leader options with the *Text* tool (not including the 6 leader location icons).

Review Questions:

The following questions may be assigned by your instructor as a way to assess your knowledge of this section. Your instructor has the answers to the review questions.

1. It is not possible to create new text styles. (T/F)

2. You can add additional light fixture sizes to the family as required. (T/F)

3. The light fixtures automatically turn to align with the ceiling grid. (T/F)

4. You can adjust the ceiling height room by room. (T/F)

5. Revit allows you to model bulkheads by adjusting the bottom position of the wall. (T/F)

6. You can use any Windows True Type font in Revit. (T/F)

7. Use the _____ tool if the ceiling grid needs to be at an angle.

8. Use the _____ tool to adjust the ceiling grid location if a ceiling tile is less than half its normal size.

9. Use the _____ tool to adjust whether an element's surface pattern is displayed (i.e., the stipple for the gypsum board ceiling).

10. What is the current size of your project (after completing exercise 8-4)?

_____ MB.

SELF-EXAM ANSWERS:
1 – F, 2 – F, 3 – F, 4 – Material, 5 – 4

Notes:

Lesson 9
Residence: ELEVATIONS:

This lesson will cover interior and exterior elevations. The default template you started with already has the four main exterior elevations set up for you. You will investigate how Autodesk® Revit® Architecture generates elevations and the role the elevation tag plays in that process. Be sure to review the video on elevations which came with this book.

Exercise 9-1:
Creating and Viewing Exterior Elevations

Here you will look at setting up an exterior elevation and how to control some of the various options.

Setting up an Exterior Elevation:

Even though you already have the main exterior elevations set, you will go through the steps necessary to set one up. Many projects have more than four exterior elevations, so all exterior surfaces are elevated.

1. Open your project, ex8-4.rvt, and **Save As ex9-1.rvt**.

2. Switch to your *First Floor Plan* view.

3. Select **View → Create → Elevation** *(not the down-arrow)*.

4. Make sure the *Type Selector* is set to *Elevation:* **Building Elevation** and then place the elevation tag in plan view as shown in Figure 9-1.1.

   NOTE: As you move the cursor around the screen, the Elevation Tag automatically turns topoint at the building.

You now have an elevation added to the *Project Browser* in the *Elevations* section. **The first thing you should do after placing an elevation is rename it**; the default name is not very descriptive. These generic names would get very confusing on larger projects with dozens of views.

Add this ──────► elevation tag

FIGURE 9-1.1 Added elevation tag

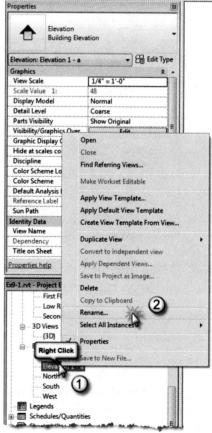

5. Right-click on the new view name, in the *Project Browser*, and select **Rename** (Figure 9-1.2).

6. Type: **South – Main Entry**.

The name should be fairly descriptive so you can tell where the elevation is just by the name in the *Project Browser*.

7. Double-click on **South –Main Entry** in the *Project Browser*.

The elevation may not look correct right away (Figure 9-1.3). You will adjust this in the next step. Notice, though, that an elevation was created simply by placing an *Elevation Tag* in plan view.

8. Switch back to the ***First Floor Plan*** view.

FIGURE 9-1.2 Renaming new view name

FIGURE 9-1.3 Initial elevation view

Next, you will study the options associated with the elevation tag. This, in part, controls what is seen in the elevation.

9. The elevation tag has two parts: the pointing triangle and the square center. Each part will highlight as you move the cursor over it. **Select the square center part.**

You should now see the symbol shown on the right.

View direction boxes:
The checked box indicates which way the elevation tag is looking. You can check, or uncheck, the other boxes. Do NOT do that at this time. Each checked box adds another view name to the *Project Browser.*

Rotation Control icon visible when Elevation Tag is selected

Rotation Control:
Clicking and dragging on this allows you to look perpendicular to an angled wall in plan, for example.

Interior Elevations:
When adding an interior elevation tag to the floor plan, you should select *Interior Elevation* from the *Type Selector*. This will use a different symbol to help distinguish the interior tags from the exterior tags in the plan views. Also, the interior and exterior views are separated in the *Project Browser*, making it easier to manage views as the project continues to develop.

10. Press the **ESC** key to unselect the elevation tag.

11. Select the "pointing" portion of the elevation tag.

Your elevation tag should look similar to Figure 9-1.4.

FIGURE 9-1.4 Selected elevation tag

The elevation tag, as selected in Figure 9-1.4, has several features for controlling how the elevation looks. Here is a quick explanation:

- **Cutting plane/extent of view line:** This controls how much of the 3D model is elevated from left to right (i.e., the width of the elevation).

- **Far clip plane:** This controls how far into the 3D model the elevation view can see.

- **Adjustment grips:** You can drag this with the mouse to control the features mentioned above.

12. Next you will take a look at the new elevation's *View Properties*. You can do this in one of the following ways:

    a. Select the "pointing" portion of the elevation tag (which should currently be selected based on the previous step).

    b. Select the view label (South – Main Entry in this example) in the Project Browser.

    c. Open the view, with nothing in the model selected.

You have several options in the *Properties Palette* (Figure 9-1.5). Notice the three options with check boxes next to them; these control the following:

- **Crop View**: This crops the width and height of the view in elevation.
  Adjusting the width of the cropping window in elevation also adjusts the "extent of view" control in plan view.

- **Crop Region Visible**: This displays a rectangle in the elevation view indicating the extent of the cropping window, described above.
  When selected in elevation view, the rectangle can be adjusted with the adjustment grips.

- **Far Clipping**: If this is turned off, Revit will draw everything visible in the 3D model, *within the "extent of view".*

FIGURE 9-1.5 South – Mail Entry Elev view properties

You will manipulate some of these controls next.

13. With the elevation tag still selected (as in Figure 9-1.4), drag the "cutting plane/ extent of view" line up **into** the main entry as shown in Figure 9-1.6.

FIGURE 9-1.6 Relocated cutting plane

14. Now switch to the elevation view **South – Main Entry**. Adjust the **Crop Region** so the entire roof is visible; click the *Crop Region* to select it and drag the top grip upward.

Your elevation should look similar to Figure 9-1.7.

The main entry wall and roof are now displayed in section because of the location of the *cutting plane* line in plan.

FIGURE 9-1.7 Elevation with cutting plane thru front entry

Notice that the roof is not fully visible. This is not related to the cropping window shown in Figure 9-1.7. Rather, it is related to the *Far Clip Plane* set in the plan view.

15. Adjust the *Far Clip Plane* in the **First Floor Plan** view so that the entire roof shows in the **South – Main Entry** view.

   TIP: Click on the grip and drag the Far Clip Plane *North until it is past the ridge line, which is at the middle of the building.*

Now when you switch back to the **South – Main Entry** elevation view, you should see the entire roof.

Next, you will adjust the elevation tag to set up a detail elevation for the main entry area.

16. In the **First Floor Plan** view, adjust the elevation tag to show only the main entry wall (Figure 9-1.8).
   • The cutting plane/extent of view line is moved South so it is outside of the building footprint.
   • Use the left and right grips to shorten the same line.

17. Switch to the **South – Main Entry** view to see the "detail" elevation you are setting up (Figure 9-1.9).

18. Make sure the **View Scale** is set to ½" = 1'-0" on the *View Control Bar* at the bottom of the screen.

Notice how the *Level Datum* tags have changed to a smaller size. *Undo* and try it again if you missed it. You did notice the levels were automatically added, right?

19. Click the **Hide Crop Region** icon on the *View Control Bar* to make the *Crop Region* disappear.

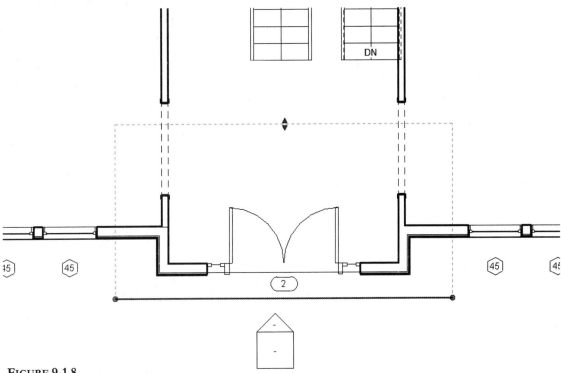

FIGURE 9-1.8
Main Entry wall detail elevation

Once you modify the view constraints in plan view (Figure 9-1.8) and you switch to the new elevation view, you can click on the *crop region* and use the grips to make the view wider. You might want to do this to make sure the roof overhang shows.

When you drag the *crop region* to the right, the *Level Datum* tags move so they do not overlap the elevation. This is another example of Revit taking the busy work out of designing a residence!

Crop region; visibility should be turned off in Step 19.

DETAIL ELEVATION:
A detail elevation like this might be used to dimension various items like the mail box, sign, special siding/ trim, etc. The scale would typically be larger than the full South elevation so you can fit more notes and dimensions.

This view might be placed on a sheet with the other elevations or any sheet where you can find room.

FIGURE 9-1.9 Main Entry wall detail elevation; View Scale is set to ¼″ = 1′-0″ so the level labels would be legible in this book

Many designers like to change the line weight around portions of the building which protrude out from the main elevation. This helps the builder and client to more easily read the drawings. However, Revit does not do this automatically. It can be done manually using the **Linework** tool on the *Modify* tab. When the tool is active you can select a line style from the *Ribbon* and then begin clicking lines in the model to override their default settings. These lines will adjust as the model is changed. Selecting **<by category>** for a line style and then clicking an overridden line will set it back to its original state. Give it a try!

20. **Save** your project as **ex9-1.rvt**.

Exercise 9-2:
Modifying the Project Model: Exterior Elevations

The purpose of this exercise is to demonstrate that changes can be made anywhere and all other drawings are automatically updated.

Modify an Exterior Elevation:

1. Open ex9-1.rvt and **Save As ex9-2**.

2. Open the **West** exterior elevation view. Adjust the start and end locations of the *Level Datum* lines to be closer to the edge of the building (Figure 9-2.1)

3. Using the **Ctrl** key, select the two double-hung windows on the right, two of the four windows in the garage wall.

You will delete the two selected windows and move the remaining two windows to the center of the wall.

4. Press the **Delete** key to erase the selected windows.

5. Select the remaining two windows and use the *Move* tool to approximately center them on the wall/roof ridge, keeping the vertical alignment unchanged (Figure 9-2.1). The next page will discuss how to center them more precisely.

FIGURE 9-2.1 Modifying windows on the West elevation

Now you will switch to the *First Floor Plan* view to see your changes.

6. Switch to the ***First Floor Plan*** view and zoom in on the Garage area (Figure 9-2.2).

Notice how the windows in plan have changed to match the modifications you just made to the exterior elevations? This only makes sense seeing as both the floor plan and the exterior elevation are projected 2D views of the same 3D model. Both views are directly manipulating the 3D model.

Also, notice that even the dimensions adjusted! Revit is all about reducing drafting time and maximizing design time. Step 5 had you approximately locate the windows; now you can select the windows in plan and type the exact dimension you want; 12'-3" centers them on the building.

FIGURE 9-2.2 Changes automatically made to the floor plan

Next, you will insert a window in elevation. This will demonstrate, first, that you can actually add a window in elevation not just plan view, and second, that the other views are automatically updated.

7. Switch to the **North** exterior elevation view.

8. Select the **Window** tool from the *Home* tab.

Notice, with the window selected for placement, you have the usual dimensions helping you accurately place the window. As you move the window around, you should see a dashed horizontal cyan colored line indicating the default sill height, although you can deviate from this in elevation views.

9. From the *Type Selector*, choose: *Double Hung with Trim:* **36"x48"**.

10. Place a window as shown in **Figure 9-2.3**; make sure the bottom of the window *Snaps* to the dashed, cyan colored, sill line.

> *TIP: The window should be about centered between the existing windows.*

FIGURE 9-2.3 Placing a window on the North elevation

If you laid out the interior walls as described in Lesson 5, you should get a warning message when inserting the window. This is because the interior wall between the kitchen and the living room conflicts with the exterior window. Revit is programmed to see that conflict and bring it to your attention. You can ignore this error because it is possible to build a wall up to the center of a window; some errors you cannot ignore because they will have a negative impact on Revit's functionality.

11. Click the "X" in the upper-right corner to ignore the wall/window conflict warning (Figure 9-2.4).

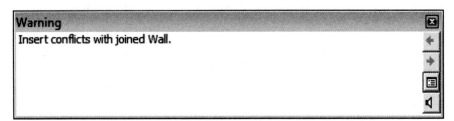

Warning
Insert conflicts with joined Wall.

FIGURE 9-2.4 Conflict warning

12. Switch to the ***First Floor Plan*** view to see the problem (Figure 9-2.5).

Interior wall conflicts with window just placed.

FIGURE 9-2.5 First Floor – kitchen area

13. While in plan view, select the new window and **Delete** it.

Why did the window location dimensions update in Figure 9-9.2 and not in Figure 9-2.5? The first had dimensions associated with the windows and the latter did not. When you dimension something in Revit, the witness lines "remember" what they are dimensioning to and move with that element. Also, notice how the window was tagged in elevation view, but not in plan view like the previously placed windows? The tag is only added in the view the element was placed in, but can be manually tagged in any view (even multiple times).

TIP: When working in the exterior elevation view, you can quickly see where the interior walls are simply by selecting the exterior wall (Figure 9-2.6).

Whenever something is selected, it turns blue and becomes transparent. Thus, the things behind the element are temporarily visible.

FIGURE 9-2.6 Transparent selections

Adding Shutters to the South Elevation:

Next you will add shutters to the South elevation. You will need to load a family from the online Revit Content website.

14. Switch back to the **North** elevation view and notice that the new window is gone, per your plan change.

15. Switch to the **Insert** tab on the *Ribbon*.

16. Using *Autodesk Seek*, search for **shutter (high-res)**; save it to your hard drive and then *Load* it.

    TIP: Refer to previous lessons for more instruction.

17. With the **Component** tool active and **Shutter (high-res): 18″ x 48″** selected in the *Type Selector*, place a shutter in elevation as shown in Figure 9-2.7 (upper-left window on North Elevation).

    TIP: If the shutter does not land in the correct spot, select it and use the arrow keys (on the keyboard) to nudge it into place, or use the Align tool per the tip below.

18. Use the same technique to place the remaining shutters shown in **Figure 9-2.8**.

19. Add shutters to the South elevation per **Figure 9-2.9**.

TIP: USING THE ALIGN TOOL
Don't forget about the Align tool. Simply drop your shutter somewhere near the window and use the Align tool to move it into place. After placing the shutter, click Align, select the edge of the window and then select the edge of the shutter to move the shutter into place. If the window moves, you picked in the wrong order – click Undo and try again. Also, immediately after you use Align you can click the Padlock to maintain a parametric relationship; meaning, if the window moves, even via a plan view, the shutters will move with it!

FIGURE 9-2.7 Placing a shutter on the North elevation

The shutter element has been set up so that it can only be placed on a wall (this is called a *wall hosted family*). If you move the cursor over a door or window, you get the (⊘) symbol; meaning it cannot be placed there.

FIGURE 9-2.8 (8) Shutters added to the North elevation

FIGURE 9-2.9 (4) Shutters added to the South elevation

20. **Save** your Project as ex9-2.rvt.

REMINDER: **ENTERING DIMENSIONS IN REVIT**

As your experience with Revit grows, you will want to learn some of the shortcuts to using the program. One of those shortcuts is how you enter dimensions when drawing. You probably already know, maybe by accident, that if you enter only one number (e.g., 48) and press Enter, Revit interprets that number to be feet (e.g., 48'-0"). So, if you want to enter 48", you may be typing 0'-48" or 48". Both work, but having to press the Shift key to get the inch symbol takes a little longer.

Here are some options for entering dimensions:

0 48	*Revit reads this as 48" (zero space forty-eight)*
48	*Revit reads this as 48'-0"*
5.5	*Revit reads this as 5'-6"*
0 5.5	*Revit reads this as 5 ½"*
2 0 1/4	*Revit reads this as 2'-0¼" (two space zero space fraction)*

Exercise 9-3:
Creating and Viewing Interior Elevations

Creating interior elevations is very much like exterior elevations. In fact, you use the same tool. The main difference is that you are placing the elevation tag inside the building, rather than on the exterior.

Adding an Interior Elevation Tag:

1. Open project ex9-2.rvt and **Save As ex9-3.rvt**.

2. Switch to the *First Floor Plan* view, if necessary.

3. Select the *Elevation* tool from the *View* tab.

In the next step you will place an elevation tag. Before clicking to place the tag, try moving it around to see how Revit automatically turns the tag to point at the closest wall.

4. Select *Elevation:* **Interior Elevation** and then place an elevation tag, looking East, or to the right, in the living room area (Figures 9-3.1a and b).

FIGURE 9-3.1B First floor: Elev tag added in Living Rm

FIGURE 9-3.1A Element Type Selector

REMEMBER: *The first thing you should do after adding an* Elevation Tag *is to give it an appropriate name in the* Project Browser *list.*

5. Change the name of the elevation to **Living Room - East**.

6. Switch to the ***Living Room – East*** view.

    TIP: Try double-clicking on the elevation tag, the pointing portion.

Initially, your elevation should look something like Figure 9-3.2; if not, you will be adjusting it momentarily so do not worry. You will adjust this view next. *Notice how Revit automatically controls the lineweights of things in section versus things in elevations.*

FIGURE 9-3.2 Living Room - East, initial view

7. Switch back to the ***First Floor Plan*** view.

8. Pick the "pointing" portion of the elevation tag, so you see the view options (Figure 9-3.3).

You should compare the two drawings on this page (Figures 9-3.2 and 9-3.3) to see how the control lines in the plan view dictate what is generated and visible in the elevation view, for both width and depth.

Revit automatically found the left and right walls, the floor and ceiling in the elevation view.

Notice the *Far Clip Plane* is also acceptable. If you cannot see the fireplace in the elevation view, that means the *Far Clip Plane* needs to be moved farther to the right.

FIGURE 9-3.3 Elevation tag selected

FYI: *The elevation tags are used to reference the sheet and drawing number so the client or contractor can find the desired elevation quickly while looking at the floor plans. This will be covered in a later lesson. It is interesting to know, however, that Revit automatically does this, fills in the elevation tag, when the elevation is placed on a sheet, and will update it if the elevation is moved.*

9. Switch back to the **Living Room - East** view.

Just to try adjusting the *crop region* to see various results; you will extend the top upward to see the second floor.

10. Select the *cropping region* and drag the top middle grip upward, to increase the view size vertically (Figure 9-3.4).

FIGURE 9-3.4 Living Room - East elevation: crop region selected and modified

Here you are getting a sneak peak ahead to the "sections" portion of this book. Notice that additional level datums where added automatically as the view grew to include more vertical information (i.e., second floor, roof).

11. Now select **Undo** to return to the previous view (Figure 9-3.2).

As you probably noticed, the interior elevation shows the *Foundation* level datum below the *First Floor* level datum. The *Foundation* level datum is not necessary in this view, so you will remove it from this view.

IMPORTANT: You cannot simply delete the level datum because it will actually delete all related views from the entire project (i.e., floor and ceiling plan views). This will delete any model elements that are hosted by that level (walls, doors, windows) and any tags, notes and dimensions in that view.

To remove a level datum, you select it and tell Revit to hide it in the current view. You will do this next.

12. Click on the horizontal line portion of the ***First Floor*** level datum.

13. Right-click and select **Hide in View → Elements** from the pop-up menu.

> *TIP: Selecting* Category *would make all level datum elements disappear from the current view.*

14. Adjust the bottom of the ***crop region*** to align with the *First Floor* level (horizontal line).

15. On the *View Control Bar*, set the ***View Scale*** to ¼"=1'-0".

Your elevation should look like Figure 9-3.5.

FIGURE 9-3.5 Living Room - East Elevation

You can leave the *crop region* on to help define the perimeter of the elevation. You can also turn it off, however, some lines that are directly under the *crop region* might disappear. You could use the *Detail Line* tool to manually define the perimeter, using a heavy line.

TIP: *If perimeter lines disappear when you print interior elevations, try unchecking* Hide Crop Regions *in the Print dialog, and turn off the ones you don't want to see.*

Turning off the View Name on the Elevation Tag:

The interior elevation tag currently has the view name showing (in plan view). You will turn this off as it is not required on the construction drawings.

16. Select **Manage → Settings → Additional Settings** (down-arrow)**→ Elevation Tags**

17. Set the *Type* to **½" Circle** (Figure 9-3.6).

18. Select **Elevation Mark Body_Circle: Filled Arrow** from the *Elevation Mark* drop-down list (Figure 9-3.6).

19. Click **OK** to close the dialog box.

The view name is now gone from the *elevation tags* in the floor plan view.

FIGURE 9-3.6 Adjusting the interior elevation tag

FYI: *If you right-click on an elevation view name in the Project Browser, you will notice you can* Duplicate *the view (via Duplicate View → Duplicate). This is similar to how a floor plan is duplicated with one major variation: when an elevation view is duplicated, Revit actually just copies another elevation tag on top of the one being duplicated in the plan view. This is because each elevation view requires its own elevation tag. If two views could exist based on one elevation tag, then Revit would not know how to fill in the drawing number and sheet number if both views are placed on a sheet.*

Adding Annotation:

Now you will add a note and dimensions to the interior elevation view.

20. Add the (2) dimensions and (1) text (3/32″ text style) with leader shown in Figure 9-3.7.

FIGURE 9-3.7 Living Room - East elevation: annotation added

21. On the *View Control Bar*, set the ***View Scale*** to ½″=1′-0″.

Notice the text and dimensions automatically resize to match the new scale. When space permits, most residential interior elevations are ½″ = 1′-0″.

22. Save your project as **ex9-3.rvt**.

Exercise 9-4:
Modifying the Project Model: Interior Elevations

This short exercise, similar to Exercise 9-2, will look at an example of Revit's parametric change engine. All drawings are generated from one 3D model.

Modify the Interior Elevations:

1. Open ex9-3.rvt and **Save As ex9-4.rvt.**

2. Open the ***Living Room - East*** elevation view.

You will move the windows and add an exterior door.

3. Select both of the windows on the right; use the **Ctrl** key to select multiple objects at one time.

4. Use the ***Move*** tool to move the windows 6″ to the right, or South.

5. Repeat the previous steps to *Move* the other two windows 6″ towards the left, or North.

6. In the *Living Room - East* elevation view, use the ***Door*** tool to place a **Single Entry 3: 32″ x 84″** door in the wall to the far left (North). See Figure 9-4.1.

FIGURE 9-4.1 Living Room - East - modified

You moved the windows out from the mantel so they provide a little more space between them. Revit allows you to design in all views!

You should notice, in Figure 9-4.1, that the door bottom is below the floor level; this is a problem only if your cursor was near the bottom of the wall when you clicked. You will fix it next.

7.   Select the new door in the *Living Room – East* view.

8.   In *Properties*, change the **level** from *Foundation* to **First Floor.**

The interior elevation should now look correct (Figure 9-4.2).

FIGURE 9-4.2 Living Room - East elevation: door height adjusted

Notice, back in the *Properties Palette* for the new door, a setting called *Sill Height.* This setting allows you to move the door vertically, relative to the specified level. For example, you might have a second floor door that opens onto a low roof, but the door needs to be 1'-0" above the second floor for this door to work correctly (roof insulation, flashing, etc.). You simply select the door and adjust its *Sill Height* to 1'-0", with the level set to *Second Floor,* via the *Properties Palette.*

Now it is time to see the effects to the plan views.

9.   Switch to the **First Floor Plan** view (Figure 9-4.3).

When placing a door in elevation, you may have to switch to plan view to verify the door swing is the way you want it. You can control the door swing in elevation: right-click and select "flip hand" or "flip facing".

In elevation, you can adjust many things this way. Some examples are: ceiling height, interior and exterior windows, wall locations, perpendicular to the current view, etc.

Notice that the door does not have a door tag like the other doors in the plan view. This is because the door was not placed in this view. You will learn how to add this tag later.

FIGURE 9-4.3 First Floor plan with changes

10. Save your project as **ex9-4**.

Exercise 9-5:
Design Options

This exercise will look at a feature called *Design Options*. This feature allows you to present two or more options for a portion of your design without having to save a copy of your project and end up having to maintain more than one project until the preferred design option is selected.

Design Options Overview:

A Revit project can have several design option studies at any given time; you might have an (A) entry porch options study, (B) a kitchen options study and a (C) master bedroom furniture layout options study in a project. Each of these studies can have several design options associated with them. For example, the entry porch study might have three options: 1. flat roof, 2. shed roof and 3. shed roof with a dormer type embellishment.

A particular study of an area within your project is called a *Design Option Set*, and the different designs associated with a *Design Options Set* are each called an *Option*. Both the *Design Options Set* and the *Options* can be named (see the examples below).

One of the *Options* in a *Design Option Set* is specified as the *Primary* option (the others are called *Secondary Options*); this is the option that is shown by default in all new and existing views. However, you can adjust the *Visibility* of a *View* to show a different option. Typically you would duplicate a *View*, adjust the *Visibility*, and *Rename* it to have each option at your finger-tips.

When the preferred design is selected, by you and/or the owner, you set that *Option* to *Primary*. Finally, you select a tool called *Accept Primary* which deletes the *Secondary Options* and the *Design Option Set*, leaving the *Primary Option* as part of the main building model.

Design Option Set

Option 1   Option 2

The following images (Figures 9-5.1a and b) is an overview of the *Design Options* dialog box and *Status Bar* tools. See Step 2 to access this dialog.

FIGURE 9-5.1A
Status Bar; Design Options tools

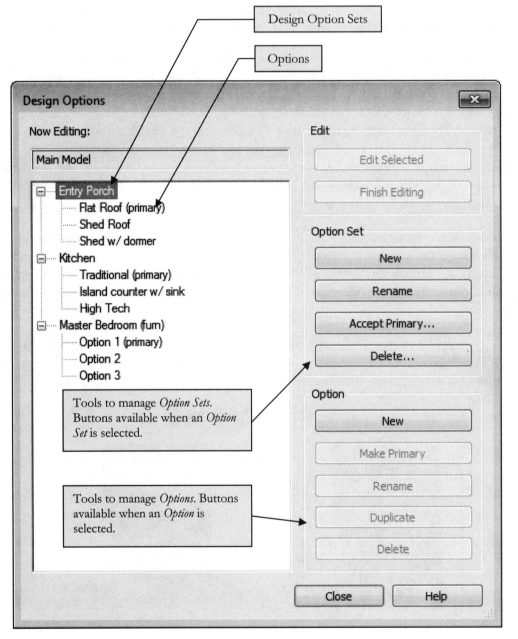

FIGURE 9-5.1B Design Options Dialog

Notes about the *Design Options* dialog box:

Edit buttons:

You can edit a *Design Option* by selecting an *Option* (in the window area on the left) and then clicking the **Edit Selected** button. Next you add, move and delete elements in that *Design Option*.

When finished editing a *Design Option*, you reopen the *Design Options* dialog and click the **Finish Editing** button.

If you are currently in an *Option Editing* mode, the *Now Editing* area in the *Design Options* dialog displays the *Option* name being modified; otherwise it displays *Main Model*.

Option Set buttons:

The **New** button is always available. You can quickly set up several *Option Sets*. Each time you create a new *Option Set*, Revit automatically creates a *Primary Option* named *Option 1*.

The other buttons are only available when an *Option Set* label is highlighted (i.e., selected) in the window list on the left.

The **Accept Primary** button causes the *Primary Option* of the selected set to become a normal part of the building model and deletes the set and secondary options. This is a way of "cleaning house," by getting rid of unnecessary information which helps to better manage the project and keeps the file size down.

Option buttons:

These buttons are only available when an *Option* (primary or secondary) is selected within an *Option Set*. You can quickly set up several *Options* without having to immediately add any content (i.e., walls, components, etc.) to them.

The **Make Primary** button allows you to change the status of a *Secondary Option* to *Primary*. As previously mentioned, the *Primary Option* is the *Option* that is shown by default in existing and new views. You can only have one *Primary* option in an *Option Set*.

The **Duplicate** button will copy all the elements in the selected *Option* into a new *Option*; this makes the file larger because you are technically adding additional content to the project. You can then use the copied elements (e.g., walls, furniture, etc.) as a starting point for the next design option. This is handy if the various options are similar.

Now you will put this introductory knowledge to use!

Setting up a Design Option Set:

In this exercise you will create two *Design Option Sets*; one for the Main Entry Roof and another for the windows above the Entry Door. You will create an alternate roof and window design for your project.

You could just create one *Design Option Set* and have two design options total. However, by placing the roof options in one *Option Set* and the windows in another, you actually get four design options total; you can mix and match the window and roof options.

Setting up Design Options in Your Project:

First you will set up the *Option Sets* and *Options*.

1. Open ex9-4.rvt and **Save As ex9-5.rvt**.

2. Click the **Design Options** icon on the *Status Bar* (Figure 9-5.1a).

You are now in the *Design Options* dialog box (Figure 9-5.2). Your dialog will look like this one, basically empty:

FIGURE 9-5.2 Design Options Dialog; initial view

3. In the *Option Set* area click **New**.

Notice an *Option Set* named *Option Set 1* has been created. Revit also automatically created the *Primary Option* named *Option 1* (Figure 9-5.3). Next you will rename the *Option Set* to something that is easier to recognize.

FIGURE 9-5.3 Design Options dialog; new option set created

4. Select the *Option Set* currently named *Option Set 1* and then click the **Rename** button in the *Option Set* area.

    WARNING! *Be sure you are not renaming the* Option, *but rather, the* Option Set.

5. In the *Rename* dialog type: **Entry Windows** (Figure 9-5.4).

6. Click **OK** to rename.

Giving the *Option Set* a name that is easy to recognize helps in managing the various options later, especially if you have several.

Next you will create a *Secondary Option* for the *Entry Windows* option set.

FIGURE 9-5.4 Rename Option Set dialog

7. With the *Entry Windows* option set selected, click **New** in the *Option* area (Figure 9-5.5).

Notice a secondary *Option* was created and automatically named *Option 2*. If you have descriptive names for the options in a set, you should apply them. In this example you can leave them as they are.

FIGURE 9-5.5
Design Options dialog; secondary option created

FIGURE 9-5.6
Design Options dialog

8. Create an *Option Set* for the roof (Figure 9-5.6):
    a. Name the set: ***Entry Roof***
    b. Create one secondary option

The basic thinking with the *Design Options* feature is that you set up the *Option Set* and *Option*s and then start drawing the elements related to the current *Option*. So, you select the *Option* from the drop-down list on the *Status Bar*, make the additions and modifications relative to that *Design Option*, and finally switch the drop-down back to *Main Model* to finish editing the option and then be able to make changes in the main model.

However, in your case, you want to move content already drawn to *Option 1*. Revit has a feature that allows you to move content to a *Design Option Set*, which means the content gets copied to the *Options* in the *Set* you select.

Entry Windows Design Option:

You are now ready to set up the different design options.

9. Close the *Design Options* dialog and switch to the **3D** view; adjust the view so you are looking at the main entry (South elevation).

Unfortunately, you cannot just select the windows and add them to a *Design Option Set* because they are hosted elements that require a wall to be inserted in. Therefore, you will also add the entry walls and door to the *Design Option Set*.

10. Select the three walls at the main entry, three windows and main entry door; orbit as required.

11. Click the **Add to Set** icon on the *Status Bar*.

12. Select *Entry Windows* from the dialog drop-down and then click **OK** (Figure 9-5.7).

The selected items are now in both *Option 1* and *Option 2* under the option set *Entry Windows*, because both options were selected in the previous dialog, Figure 9-5.7.

FIGURE 9-5.7 Add to Design Option Set Dialog

From this point forward you can only modify the entry windows, door and walls when in *Option 1* or *Option 2 Edit* mode. In which case, the tables are turned and you cannot edit the main building model; this is because *Active Only* is checked on the *Status Bar*.

13. In the **Design Options** drop-down list, on the *Status Bar*, select **Entry Windows: Option 2** as shown in the image below.

Now you should notice that the main building model is slightly grey and not editable; it is not editable because *Active Only* is selected on the *Status Bar*. You will change the windows per Figure 9-5.8.

14. Zoom in on the main entry, particularly the second floor window area in your *3D* view.

15. Select the three windows above the main entry door and change their type to **Double Hung with Trim: 16″ x 72″** from the *Type Selector*.

16. Make sure the window head (i.e., top) is at **7′-0″** via the *Properties Palette* for the selected windows.

17. Change the *Design Options* drop-down list, on the *Status Bar*, back to **Main Model**.

FIGURE 9-5.8 3D View: second floor windows modified

It now appears like all your changes disappeared, right? Well, if you recall from the introduction to this exercise, the *Primary Option* is displayed by default for all new and existing views. So when you finished editing *Entry Windows: Option 2* the *3D* view switched back to the *Primary Option*, which is currently set to *Option 1* (Figure 9-5.6).

Next, you will create a new view and adjust its *Visibility* to display *Option 2* of the *Entry Windows* options set.

First you will create a duplicate copy of the *3D* view.

18. In the *Project Browser*, under *3D Views*, right-click on the **{3D}** label.

19. Select **Duplicate View → Duplicate** from the pop-up menu.

You now have a copy of the *3D* view named *Copy of {3D}*.

20. **Rename** the new 3D view to *Entry Windows Option 2*.

21. Switch to your new view, if needed.

22. Select **View → Graphics → Visibility/Graphics** (or type **VV**).

23. Click on the **Design Options** tab at the top of the dialog.

24. Change the *Design Option* parameter for *Entry Windows* to **Option 2** (Figure 9-5.9).

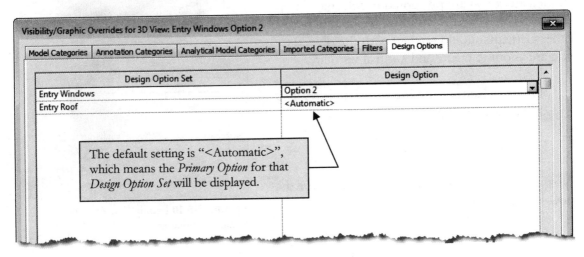

FIGURE 9-5.9 Visibility/Graphic Overrides dialog: modified Entry Windows design option visibility

25. Click **OK** to close the dialog.

Now, with the *Default 3D* view and the *Entry Windows:Option 2* view, you can quickly switch between design options. Both views could be placed on the same sheet and printed out for a design critique.

Entry Roof Design Option:

Now you will add an option for a roof over the entry door.

26. Select *Entry Roof:* **Option 2** from the *Design Options* drop-down list on the *Status Bar*.

You will add a roof shortly.

27. Switch to the **South** elevation view.

28. Zoom in to the area below the entry windows.

Next you will create an *in-place family* to represent a curved roof option over the entry area. Basically, you will create a solid by specifying a depth and then drawing a profile of the curved roof with lines.

29. Click **Home → Build → Component (down-arrow) → Model In-Place.**

Immediately, you are prompted to select a *Family Category*. This allows Revit to understand how other elements should interact with the object(s) you are about to create and control visibility.

30. Select **Roofs** from the *Family Category* list (Figure 9-5.10).

31. Click **OK.**

Now you are prompted to provide a name for the new *in-place family*.

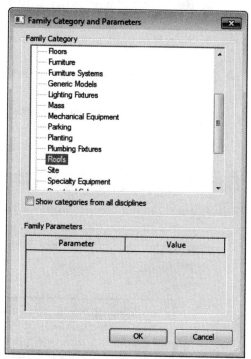

FIGURE 9-5.10 Family Category and Parameters dialog

32. For the family *Name*, type **Entry Roof** (Figure 9-5.11).

FIGURE 9-5.11 Family name prompt

You are now in a mode where you draw the *Entry Roof*. Notice that the *Ribbon* has changed to have special buttons on the *Home* tab which has all the tools needed to create a family. You are continuously in the *Model In-Place* mode until you select *Finish Model* (green check mark) or *Quit Model* (red x) from the *Ribbon*.

FIGURE 9-5.12 Form Ribbon; select Extrude

You will now select the type of solid you wish to create.

33. Select **Home → Forms → Extrusion**.

Finally, you are prompted to select a plane in which to start drawing the profile of the solid to be extruded. Even though the view is a 2D representation of a 3D model, Revit needs to know where you want the 3D solid created so it knows how to show it in other views (both 2D representations and 3D). You will select the entry wall as a reference surface to establish a working plane.

34. Select **Pick a Plane** and click **OK** (Figure 9-5.13).

FIGURE 9-5.13 Work Plane dialog; select Pick a Plane

35. Move the cursor near the edge of the entry wall and then click to select it.

TIP: If needed, click the Tab *key until a heavy line appears around the perimeter of the wall. Then click the mouse to select (Figure 9-5.14). Do not hold the Tab key down.*

Hover cursor here and press the Tab key until the wall is highlighted as shown.

(Entry Windows : Option 1) : Walls : Basic Wall : Exterior - Wood Shingle over Wood Siding on Wood Stud : Reference

FIGURE 9-5.14 South Elevation; select wall to establish work plane

Next, you will draw an arc to specify the bottom edge of the curved roof design option. Notice the *Ribbon* changed again to show tools related to drawing an extruded solid.

36. On the *Options Bar*, enter **2'-0"** for the **Depth** (Figure 9-5.15).

FYI: A negative number for the depth would cause the solid to project in towards the building from the work plane.

Depth 2' 0" ☑ Chain Offset: 0' 0" ☐ Radius: 1' 0"

37. Click the **Start – End – Radius Arc** icon from the *Draw* panel, on the contextual tab: *Modify | Create Extrusion*.

38. Pick the three points shown in Figure 9-5.15 to draw the arc. The angle 71.343° is not critical; get as close as possible. The ends of the arc are approximately straight up from the edge of the entry door below.

TIP: Try typing SO before clicking the third point to temporarily turn off the Snaps for one pick (SO = Snap Off).

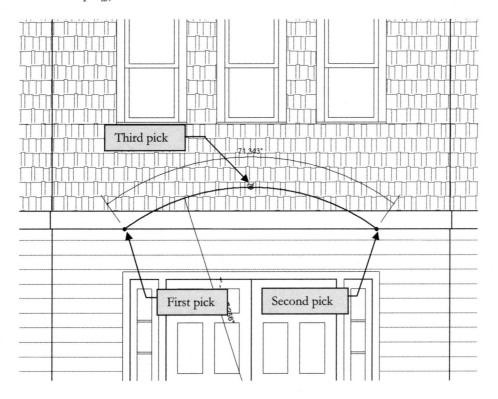

FIGURE 9-5.15 South Elevation; drawing arc to define roof

Now you will draw another arc 7¼″ above the previous one.

39. Press **Esc**; on the *Options Bar*, enter **0 7.25** for the *Offset*.

40. Draw another **Arc** picking the same three points; be sure to snap to the end points and midpoint of the previous arc (Figure 9-5.15).

Notice that an arc is drawn offset 7¼″ from the points you picked. If you pick the first two points in the other direction, the arc would be offset in the other direction, downward in this case.

Next, you will draw two short lines to connect the endpoints of the two arcs. This will create a closed area, which is required before finishing the sketch. Think of it this way: you need to completely define at least two dimensions before Revit can create the third.

41. Click the "straight line" icon on the *Draw* panel (see image on previous page); this will switch you from drawing arcs back to drawing straight line segments. Set the *Offset* back to **0"**.

42. Zoom in and sketch a short line on each end of the arc as shown in Figure 9-5.16; be sure to use your *Endpoint* snaps (type SE).

FIGURE 9-5.16 South elevation; two arcs and two short lines define roof profile

43. Click the **green checkmark** from the *Ribbon*.

> ***TIP:*** *If you get any warnings, it may be because one or more of the profile's corners do not create a perfect intersection; zoom in to see and use the Trim tool to close the corners. Delete any stray lines.*

You are still in the *Model In-Place Family* mode. Before you finish you will apply a material to the roof element.

44. Click the roof to select it.

45. In the *Properties Palette*, click in the *Material* value field and then click the "**...**" icon that appears.

The *Materials* dialog opens.

46. Select **Metal – Roofing** from the list of predefined *Materials*.

> ***FYI:*** *Notice the* Render Appearance *material is set to* Aluminum Anodized Dark Bronze *for* Metal – Roofing.

47. Click **OK** to close the *Materials* dialog.

You are now ready to finish the family.

48. From the *Ribbon* click **Finish Model**.   Finish Model

Next you will move the roof down a little. At this point, the only "mode" you are in is for editing the *Entry Roof: Option 2*.

49. Click on the roof to select it.

50. Use the arrow keys on the keyboard to nudge the roof element down until it looks similar to Figure 9-5.17.

FIGURE 9-5.17 South elevation; roof element moved to a lower position

Notice the arrow-grips on each end of the roof element when it is selected? Clicking one of these grips allows you to extend that solid perpendicular to the arrow. Try it; just *Undo* (Ctrl+Z) when you are done experimenting. It works better on rectilinear objects.

You are now ready to finish editing the current design option for the time being.

51. Set the *Design Options* drop-down back to **Main Model**.

As before, the option you were just working on was not the *Primary Option* in the *Entry Roof* design set, so the current view reverted back to *Entry Roof: Option 1*, which is the primary view.

You will create a 3D view that has *Option 2* set to be visible for both the *Entry Window* option set and the *Entry Roof* option set.

52. Right-click on the **Default 3D** view and click **Duplicate View → Duplicate**.

53. Rename the duplicated view to **Entry – Option 2**.

54. Switch to the new view (*Entry – Option 2*); you should already be in that view.

55. Click **Visibility/Graphics** from the *View* tab (or type **VV**).

56. On the *Design Options* tab, set both *Option Sets* to **Option 2** in the *Design Option* column.

57. Click **OK** to close the dialog.

FIGURE 9-5.18 Entry – Option 2 view with shadows on

You can now see a 3D view of your new entry roof option. The previous image has shadows turned on. This can provide a very dramatic result with almost no extra effort. The shadows can be useful while designing; however, you will probably have them turned off most of the time just to maintain system performance.

To turn on shadows, you simply click the *Shadows* toggle icon on the *View Control Bar* at the bottom of the screen.

Because the new entry roof element is a roof to Revit, you can attach walls to it, meaning a wall top would conform to the underside of the curved roof.

Another entry roof option might be a more traditional shed type porch roof like the one shown above. You might try adding this roof to the *Option 1* place holder. Simply sketch a roof by footprint, with only the South edge set to *Defines slope*.

58. **Save** your project as **ex9-5.rvt**.

TIP: *The Design Options feature can also be used to manage alternates, where both the base bid and the alternate(s) need to be drawn.*

Self-Exam:

The following questions can be used as a way to check your knowledge of this lesson. The answers can be found at the bottom of the page.

1. The plan is updated automatically when an elevation is modified, but not the other way around. (T/F)

2. You can use the *Elevation* tool to place both interior and exterior elevations. (T/F)

3. You can rename elevation views to better manage them. (T/F)

4. You have to resize the level datums and annotations after changing a view's scale. (T/F)

5. How do you enter 5½″ without entering the foot or inch symbol? _____

Review Questions:

The following questions may be assigned by your instructor as a way to assess your knowledge of this section. Your instructor has the answers to the review questions.

1. The visibility of the *crop region* can be controlled. (T/F)

2. You **have to** manually adjust the lineweights in the elevations. (T/F)

3. As you move the cursor around the building, during placement, the elevation tag turns to point at the building. (T/F)

4. There is only one part of the elevation tag that can be selected. (T/F)

5. You cannot adjust the "extent of view" using the *crop region*. (T/F)

6. What is the first thing you should do after placing an elevation tag?

    _____

7. Although they make the drawing look very interesting, using

    the _____ feature can cause Revit to run extremely slow.

8. With the elevation tag selected, you can use the _____ icon to adjust the tag orientation to look at an angled wall.

9. You need to adjust the _____ to see objects, in elevation, that are a distance back from the main elevation.

10. What feature allows you to develop different ideas? _____

Lesson 10
Residence: SECTIONS:

Sections are one of the main communication tools in a set of architectural drawings. They help the builder understand vertical relationships. Architectural sections can occasionally contradict other drawings, such as mechanical or structural drawings. One example is a beam shown on the section is smaller than what the structural drawings call for; this creates a problem in the field when the duct does not fit in the ceiling space. The ceiling gets lowered and/or the duct gets smaller, ultimately compromising the design to a certain degree.

Autodesk® Revit® Architecture takes great steps toward eliminating these types of conflicts. Sections, like plans and elevations, are generated from the 3D model. So it is virtually impossible to have a conflict between the architectural drawings. Many structural, mechanical and electrical engineers are starting to use Autodesk Revit Architecture for even greater coordination; this is helping to eliminate conflicts and redundancy in drawing.

The DVD has a video on sections you should take the time to review.

Exercise 10-1:
Specify Section Cutting Plane in Plan View

Similar to elevation tags, placing the section "graphics" in a plan view actually generates the section view. You will learn how to do this next.

Placing Section Marks:

1. Open ex9-5.rvt and **Save As ex10-1.rvt**.

2. Switch to the *First Floor Plan* view.

Section

   TIP: *You may also select the Section icon from the Quick Access Toolbar, which would be more convenient.*

3. Select **View → Create → Section**.

4. Draw a **Section** mark as shown in Figure 10-1.1. Start on the left side in this case. Use the *Move* tool if needed to accurately adjust the section after insertion. The section line should go through the stair landings (Figure 10-1.1).

FIGURE 10-1.1 Section mark (selected)

You can see that the *Far Clip Plane* location in the plan view is out past the building perimeter; this means you will see everything (Figure 10-1.1). Anything passing through the section line is in section; everything else you see is in elevation (Revit calls it "projection"). Also, you can see the roof is shown in section exactly where the section line is shown in plan. Figure 10-1.2 also shows the *crop region*.

The *Section* tool is almost exactly like the *Elevation* tool.

FIGURE 10-1.2 Longitudinal section view

Notice in the *Project Browser* that a new category has been created: *Sections (building Section)*. If you expand this category, you will see the new section view listed; it is called *Section 1*. You should always rename any new view right after creating it. This will help with navigation and when it comes time to place views on sheets for printing.

5. Rename section view *Section 1* to **Longitudinal Section**.

6. Switch to the new section view, **Longitudinal Section**.

   TIP: *Double-click on the section bubble head to open that view. The section needs to be unselected first; double-click on the blue part.*

7. Change the *View Properties* so the **Detail Level** is set to **Medium**.

Notice how the walls change to show more detail. You can set this on the *View Control Bar* at the bottom of the screen.

8. Zoom in on the portion of the section through the stairs.

You should notice an added level of detail in the section view.

You may also notice a big problem, as first mentioned on page 8-10; in Figure 10-1.3, the stair to the basement is obstructed by the first floor system. You will fix this soon.

The image below lists the additional terms related to the section mark graphics in the plan view, as compared to elevation tags.

A person would have to crawl to the basement

FIGURE 10-1.3 Section view – zoomed in

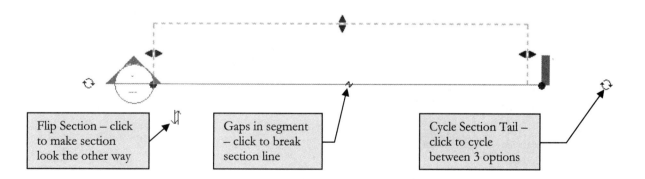

Flip Section – click to make section look the other way

Gaps in segment – click to break section line

Cycle Section Tail – click to cycle between 3 options

9. Create a **section** in the *First Floor Plan* as shown in **Figure 10-1.4**.

    TIP: You can use the control arrows to make the section look the other direction.

FIGURE 10-1.4 Plan view; Section tag (selected)

10. Rename the new section view to ***Cross Section 1*** in the *Project Browser*.

11. Switch to the ***Cross Section 1*** view.

12. Set the *Detail Level* to **Medium** and turn off the ***crop region*** visibility via the *View Control Bar* (Figure 10-1.5).

Revit automatically displays lines heavier for elements that are in section than for elements beyond the cutting plane and shown in elevation.

Also, with the *Detail Level* set to *Medium*, the walls and floors are hatched to represent the material in section.

FIGURE 10-1.5 Cross Section 1 view

Notice that the *Longitudinal Section* mark is automatically displayed in the *Cross Section 1* view. If you switch to the *Longitudinal Section* view, you will see the *Cross Section 1* mark. Keeping with Revit's philosophy of changing everything anywhere, you can select the section mark in the other section view and adjust its various properties, like its *Far Clip Plane.*

FYI: In any view that has a section mark in it, you can double-click on the round reference bubble to quickly switch to that section view. However, the section cannot be selected. The section head is dark blue when not selected.

Modifying the First Floor Stair Opening:

Next, you will fix the problem with the stair opening in the first floor system. Basically, you will switch to the *First Floor Plan* view and select the floor. Then you will click *Edit Boundary* from the *Ribbon* and modify the sketch so the stair opening is larger.

13. Switch to the **First Floor Plan** view.

14. Select the floor; use Tab if required to highlight the floor element for selection.

15. Click **Edit Boundary** on the *Ribbon* (see image below).

16. Use the *Line* and *Edit* tools, such as *Split* and *Trim*, to modify the sketch of the floor opening as shown in Figure 10-1.6.

17. Click the **green check mark** and choose **No** to the *attach walls* prompt.

18. Switch back to the **Longitudinal Section** view.

Notice the stair no longer has a problem (Figure 10-1.7).

19. **Save** your project as **ex10-1.rvt.**

FIGURE 10-1.6 Plan view – Floor, sketch edit

FIGURE 10-1.7 Longitudinal view – First floor element modified

Exercise 10-2:
Modifying the Project Model in Section View

Again, similar to elevation views, you can modify the project model in section view. This includes adjusting door locations and ceiling heights.

Modifying Doors in Section View:

In this section you will move a door and delete a door in section view.

1. Open ex10-1.rvt and **Save As ex10-2.rvt**.

2. Open *Cross Section 1* view.

Looking back to Figure 10-1.5, you should notice the wall below the basement stair still extends up through the stair. You will move the wall over in the section view and then note that the adjacent wall and ceilings all automatically adjust in other views.

3. Use the *Align* tool to make the wall align with the edge of the floor opening (Figure 10-2.1).

   TIP: Pick the edge of the floor first and then the face of the wall to align with the selected edge.

FIGURE 10-2.1 Cross Section 1 view; wall below stair moved

10-7

4. Switch to the *Basement Ceiling Plan* view.

Notice the wall below the stair moved South and the ceiling automatically adjusted as well (Figure 10-2.2).

As long as a wall that defines the perimeter of a ceiling does not get deleted or shortened so that the ceiling perimeter is no longer defined, Revit will automatically update the ceiling. If the perimeter does become undefined, you may have to edit it manually. **Avoid deleting objects** just to redraw them because "hosted" elements, such as lights and dimensions, will be deleted.

Next, looking at Figure 10-2.1, you see that the arched opening in the basement is too tall; you will make it shorter. This will require a new *Type* within the *Opening-Elliptical Arch* family.

5. Switch back to *Cross Section 1*.

6. **Select** the **arched opening** in the basement.

7. Click **Edit Type** on the *Properties Palette* and then **Duplicate**.

8. Enter **60″ x 80″** for the name.

9. Change the **Height** *Parameter* to **6′-8″** (Figure 10-2.3).

10. Click **OK** to close the open dialog box.

Your arched opening should now look like Figure 10-2.4 in *Cross Section 1* view. This change would not be apparent in a plan view because the only change was to the opening's height.

FIGURE 10-2.2 Basement Floor Plan view; notice changes

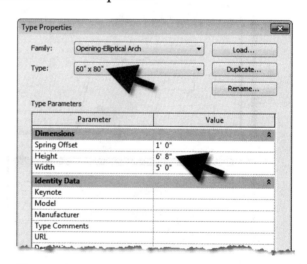

FIGURE 10-2.3 Changing the arched opening height

FIGURE 10-2.4 Cross Section 1 view; arched opening modified

Next you will adjust a ceiling height via your *Longitudinal Section* view.

11. Switch to ***Longitudinal Section*** view.

12. At the basement level, select the suspended acoustical ceiling tile system in the *Family Room* (lower right room).

Notice that while a ceiling is selected in a section view, a temporary dimension appears. This dimension allows you to directly change the ceiling height.

FYI: *The dimension may be overlapping a wall.*

13. Change the ceiling height to **6′-8″** using the temporary dimension. If required, adjust the witness lines to go from the top of the basement floor slab to the bottom of the ceiling.

Now, as you can see in the section view (Figure 10-2.5), the ceiling has lowered and there is more room for the recessed light fixtures shown; notice the lights lowered automatically.

FIGURE 10-2.5 Cross Section 1 view; ceiling height modified

Adding the Strip Footing Below the Foundation Wall:

A strip footing, in Revit, can be just a wall type set up as concrete. The width of the "wall" is set to be the width of your footing, as is the height. Revit provides a predefined wall and plan view in the residential template; this makes is very easy.

14. Switch to the plan view called **T.O. Footing**.

    FYI: T.O. means "Top Of"; i.e., "Top Of Footing".

15. Select the **Wall** tool and then select *Basic Wall: **24″ Footing*** from the *Type Selector*.

16. Set the *Location Line* to **Wall Centerline** and make sure the *Depth* is set to **B.O. Footing** (i.e., Bottom of Footing) on the *Options Bar*.

17. Select **Chain** on the *Options Bar*.

18. Start picking the intersection of wall centerlines, working around the perimeter of the building; also add a footing below the wall between the garage and the house. You want the 24″ footing to be centered on the foundation wall (Figure 10-2.6).

    TIP: Setting the Location Line to Wall Centerline is for the wall you are about to draw. Revit will automatically "snap" to the centers of walls previously drawn. Hover your cursor over the center of the wall until you see a dashed magenta/purple reference line, letting you know you are snapped to the center of the wall, and then move your cursor towards the end of that wall/purple reference line and click.

After drawing the footings, you will notice the interior side of the footing will disappear because it is below the basement floor slab; it is visible in the garage area because it is unexcavated.

Figure 10-2.6 T.O. Footing view; 24″ footing added

19. Switch back to the section view **Cross Section 1**.

As you can see (Figure 10-2.7), the footings have been added.

FIGURE 10-2.7 Cross Section 1 view (modified)

If you look at the properties for the 24"
footing wall type, you can see how the
wall was created relative to the *T.O.
Footing* view in which you drew it.

Notice the *Base* and *Top Constraints* are
selected. The *Base Constraint* is set to
B.O. Footing and the *Top Constraint* is set
to *Up to level: T.O. Footing*. Also notice
the *Unconnected Height* is grayed-out,
meaning you cannot change this
setting, which makes sense seeing as
you have defined both the top and
bottom of the wall.

The distance between the two levels is
1'-0", so the footing is 1'-0" high.

In *Cross Section 1* view, try clicking on
the *B.O. Footing* text (i.e., the -10'-3"
text) and change it to -11'-3" and notice
the footing size will automatically
change.

Figure 10-2.8 Properties for 24" Footing wall

If you try this, make sure you *UNDO* so that when
you finish this exercise your footing is only 1'-0"
thick (see image to the right).

Adding the Strip Footing Using the Foundation Tool on the Structure tab:

Revit offers another tool to add continuous strip footings below
your foundation wall. On the *Foundation* panel (on the *Structure* tab)
you can select the **Wall Foundation** tool. Then you simply select
foundation walls and Revit automatically places a footing, centered,
and directly under the wall. If you want to try this option, you can
delete a portion of footing and use the *Structure* tool to replace it. If
you try this, make sure you *Undo* before proceeding.

Modifying the Footing Linework in Plan View:

Revit has predefined settings for line styles and lineweights. Most of the time, the developers have selected settings that will be satisfactory to most designers, which is great because this saves much time. However, you will occasionally want to tweak these prescribed settings. As mentioned in the previous chapter, Revit makes this easy with the *Linework* tool on the *Modify* tab. Basically you select the *Linework* icon, select the desired setting from the *Type Selector* (e.g., lineweight or line style) and then select the lines to change. This change only applies to the current view.

You will try this next, switching the footing lines to dashed.

20. Switch back to the **T.O. Footing** view.

21. Select **Modify → View → Linework**.

22. Select **Hidden** from the *Line Style Panel* on the *Ribbon* (Figure 10-2.9).

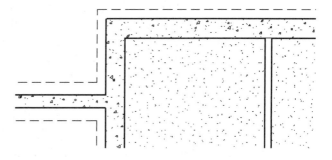

23. Click all the visible footing lines. Click Ctrl+Z if you pick another line by accident; that will *Undo* the previous pick.

Figure 10-2.9 Linework icon selected

The footing lines are now the hidden line style (i.e., dashed) in the current view (Figure 10-2.10).

24. Save your project as **ex10-2.rvt**.

FIGURE 10-2.10 Footing lines dashed

*FYI: The Linework tool will work on most lines generated by the model that are visible in a view. In the above example, the **Filter** feature of Revit might be more appropriate because you can set up a view to make all the walls with the word "footing" in the name be dashed; this is just one example of how Filter can be used. This will affect current walls and future walls that are visible in the current view. This filter can then be applied to other views if desired.*

Stepped Footings:

Foundation walls and footings often need to step on sloped sites and around utilities. This is a little more work to set up in Revit but is still very doable. You will not actually do this at this time, but the concept will be covered here to get you started in the right direction when the time comes that you need to implement this type of design.

Basically, you *Split* the footings where the steps occur and edit the vertical position of each section of footing. You do not need to Split the foundation wall; you will see why in a moment.

- In elevation or plan view, use the ***Split*** tool to break the footings up where each step needs to occur.

- Modify the *Base* and *Top Constraints* as required for each wall so they are in the correct position vertically (Figure 10-2.11).

FIGURE 10-2.11
Footing Split and heights adjusted

- In an elevation or section view, select the foundation wall and pick the **Edit Profile** button on the *Ribbon*.

- Use the ***Lines*** tool, on the *Ribbon*, and any of the edit tools (*Split, Trim, Mirror*, etc.) to redefine the perimeter of the wall in elevation. Modify the bottom magenta sketch line to follow the tops of the footings. Click **Finish Edit Mode** (i.e., green checkmark) when done (Figure 10-2.12).

FIGURE 10-2.12
Foundation wall modified
(via Edit Profile)

- Using the same technique as for the footing "wall" (i.e., *Edit Profile*), you can edit the profile of the footings so they appear correctly in elevation making sure the adjacent edges touch.

- When you **Finish Edit Mode** on the footings, you should see the footings join together and appear monolithic. If not, you can use the ***Join Geometry*** tool unless the edges do not touch perfectly, in which case you need to use *Edit Profile* again and fix the problem.

FIGURE 10-2.13
Footing "wall" modified
(via Edit Profile)

Exercise 10-3:
Wall Sections

So far in this lesson you have drawn building sections. Building sections are typically ⅛″ or ¼″ scale and light on the detail and notes. Wall sections are drawn at a larger scale and have much more detail. You will look at setting up wall sections next.

Setting up the Wall Section View:

1. Open ex10-2 and **Save As ex10-3.rvt**.

2. Switch to the **Cross Section 1** view.

3. From the *View* tab on the *Ribbon*, click the **Callout** tool and then select *Section:* **Wall Section** from the *Type Selector*.

Callout

4. Place a **Callout** tag as shown in Figure 10-3.1.

   TIP: *Pick in the upper left and then in the lower right to place the Callout tag; do not drag.*

   TIP: *You can use the* control grips *for the Callout tag to move the reference bubble if desired; for example, move it way from notes/dimensions.*

FIGURE 10-3.1 Cross Section 1 view with Callout added

Notice that a view was added in the *Sections (Wall Section)* category of the *Project Browser*. Because *Callouts* are detail references off of a section view, it is a good idea to keep the new callout view name similar to the name of the section.

Additionally, *Callouts* differ from section views in that the callout is not referenced in every related view. This example is typical, in that the building sections are referenced from the plans and wall sections are referenced from the building sections. The floor plans can get pretty messy if you try to add too much information to them.

5. Double-click on the reference bubble portion of the *Callout* tag to open the **Callout of Cross Section 1** view (Figure 10-3.2).

Notice, down on the *View Control Bar*, that the scale is set to ½″ = 1′-0″. This affects the elevation tags, text, datums and any annotation you add.

6. On the *View Control Bar* set:
   a) *View Scale* to ¾″ = 1′-0″
   b) *Detail Level* to **Fine**.

Notice the level datum's size changed.

If you zoom in on a portion of the *Callout* view, you can see the detail added to the view. The wall's interior lines are added and the materials in section are hatched (see Figure 10-3.4, at the second floor line).

You can use the *Detail Lines* tool to add more detailed information to the drawing. For example, you could show the truss, wall base, and flashing. Walls can be configured to have wall bases, which are set up as sweeps.

FIGURE 10-3.2 Callout of Cross Section 1

As before, you can turn off and adjust the *crop region*. If you set the *Detail Level* to **Coarse**, you get just an outline of your structure. The *Coarse* setting is more appropriate for building sections than wall sections. Figure 10-3.3 is an example of the *Coarse* setting.

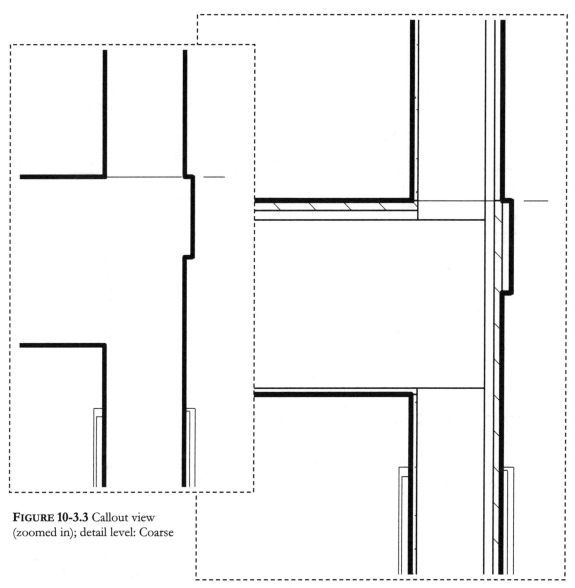

FIGURE 10-3.3 Callout view (zoomed in); detail level: Coarse

FIGURE 10-3.4 Callout view (zoomed in); detail level: Fine

Refining the Walls:

Now that the residence is more developed, you will modify various wall properties to make them more accurate to what they would be in the real world. Both the main building walls and the garage need a little attention.

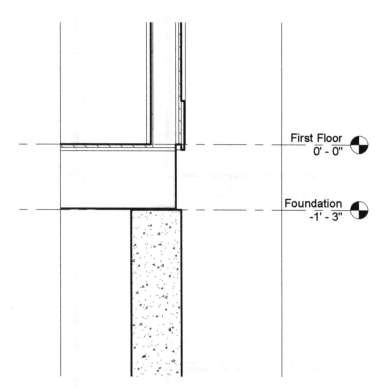

In the larger scale wall section you can see a few problems that need to be addressed.

A – The siding and sheathing need to extend down and over the edge of the flooring.

B – The top of the foundation wall needs to be modified to accommodate a 2x plate for the floor joists to bear on and attach to.

FIGURE 10-3.5 First floor condition in Wall Section view

7. In the wall section view, *Callout of Cross Section 1*, click to select the **Foundation** datum and then click to select the elevation text **-1'-3"** and change it to **-1'-4 ½"**.

You have now provided space for a continuous 2x board (which is 1 ½" high). This board will be added later.

Note that **all** of the foundation walls in the model have been changed by this one modification!

FIGURE 10-3.6 Top of foundation wall modified

Next you will adjust the sheathing and siding. Revit provides a way in which specific "layers" (i.e., the sheathing and siding in this example) can extend down farther than the rest of the wall (i.e., the wood studs and gypsum board). You will modify your exterior walls, except at the garage, so that the sheathing and siding extend down to the top of foundation wall. To do this you need to make one change within the wall type.

8. In the wall section view, select the exterior wall *Basic Wall:* **Exterior - Wood Shingle over Wood Siding on Wood Stud**.

9. Select **Edit Type** on the *Properties Palette* and then click **Edit** next to the *Structure* parameter.

10. Make sure the preview pane is displayed by clicking the **Preview** button in the lower left.

11. Below the preview pane, set the **View** to **Section: Modify type attributes** so the wall is shown in section (Figure 10-3.7).

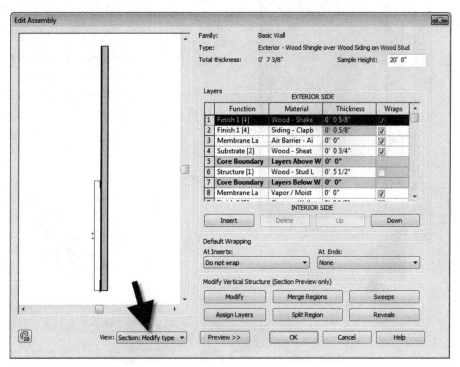

FIGURE 10-3.7 Wall structure – edit assembly

Next, you will zoom in on the bottom of the wall in the preview pane and unlock the bottom edge of the siding and sheathing layers. This will allow the unlocked material to extend up or down apart from the bottom location of the wall.

12. Click in the preview pane to make sure it is active and then scroll the wheel on your mouse to zoom in on the bottom of the wall; you can also press the wheel button while moving the mouse to pan.

13. Click the **Modify** button (Figure 10-3.8).

14. Click the bottom edge of the siding "layer" (Figure 10-3.8).

Be sure you have the bottom edge of the siding layer selected. You should see a padlock symbol above it. Next you will click that symbol to unlock it. As soon as you make this change you will have a new parameter associated with that wall type named *Base Extension Distance*, which is an *Instance Parameter*, allowing you to change this value on a wall-by-wall basis. Entering a positive number moves the sheathing and siding up that distance from the bottom of the wall and a negative number moves it down.

15. Click the padlock symbol so it is shown in the **unlocked** position.

FIGURE 10-3.8 Enabling base extension for selected wall type

You will repeat the previous two steps for the sheathing layer as well.

16. Click on the bottom edge of the sheathing layer.

17. Click the padlock symbol to unlock it.

> *FYI: Only one contiguous section of layers can be set up to move up and down like this. Contiguous means the layers have to touch each other.*

18. **Close** the open dialog boxes.

19. Switch to the *First Floor Plan* view.

In the next step you will select all the exterior walls except the three at the garage. In order to select the three walls at the front entry, you will need to uncheck an option on the *Status Bar*, you will do this next.

20. Uncheck **Exclude Options** on the *Status Bar* (lower right).

21. Hover your cursor over one of the exterior walls to highlight it, but do not click, and then press the **Tab** key, which will highlight all the exterior walls. Click to select the highlighted walls.

> *FYI: Alternately you can simply hold down the Ctrl key and individually pick each wall.*

22. Press the **Shift** key and select the four garage walls, one at a time while holding the Shift key down, to un-select them (if they are selected).

23. With all the exterior walls selected, except the four garage walls, draw your attention to the *Properties Palette*.

24. Set the *Base Extension Distance* to **-1'-4"**. Do not forget to add the negative sign at the beginning. See Figure 10-3.9.

This will make the sheathing and siding extend down 1'-4" below the bottom of the wall.

FIGURE 10-3.9 Base Extension Distance

25. Switch back to *Callout of Cross Section 1* to see the modified wall (Figure 10-3.10).

First Floor
0' - 0"

Foundation
-1' - 4 1/2"

FIGURE 10-3.10 Results of 'Base Extension Distance' modification

26. Switch back to plan view and enter the two *Entry Windows – Options* edit mode, via the *Status Bar*, so you can make the same change to the three entry walls located in the two design options for the entry windows. Refer to previous sections for more information on editing *Design Options*.

Wall Section at Garage:

Next you will set up a wall section view at the garage wall.

27. Switch to the *Longitudinal Section*.

28. Add a "wall section" type **Callout** at the garage wall (Figure 10-3.11).

29. Rename the new view to *Garage Wall Section*.

30. **Open** the *Garage Wall Section* view.

As you can see, the top of foundation wall is not correct for the garage area. The foundation wall typically comes up to the top of floor slab or 8-16" above that. You will make this change next.

FIGURE 10-3.11 Callout added to longitudinal section

31. Switch to the **_Basement Floor Plan_** and select the three foundation walls at the garage.

32. In *Properties Palette*, set the *Top Constraint* to **Up to level: First Floor.**

33. Switch back to the **_Garage Wall Section_** view.

As you can see in the figure below, the foundation wall and floor slab overlap each other. You will fix this next.

FIGURE 10-3.12
Garage Wall Section – edge of slab condition

34. Click **Modify → Geometry → Join**.   Join ▾

35. Select the foundation wall and then the floor slab.

Your wall section should now look like Figure 10-3.13. You can use the *Linework* tool if desired to edit any line styles or weights.

36. **Save** your project as **ex10-3.rvt**.

FIGURE 10-3.13
Garage Wall Section

TIP: The wall section in Figure 10-3.13 shows two level datums that are not required in this view (Low Roof and Foundation). You cannot delete them, but you can select them, right-click and then pick Hide in View → Elements *from the pop-up menu. Click* Reveal Elements *on the View Control Bar to see them again.*

Exercise 10-4:
Annotation and Detail Components

This exercise will explore adding notes, dimensions and detail components to your wall section.

Add Notes and Dimensions to Callout of Cross Section 1:

1. Open ex10-3.rvt and **Save As ex10-4.rvt**.

2. Switch to *Callout of Cross Section 1* view.

3. Click the *Hide Crop Region* icon on the *View Control Bar*.

4. Add the three dimensions as show in **Figure 10-4.1**.

> *TIP: Revit lets you dimension to the window opening even though you are not cutting directly through a window in the current view.*

These dimensions are primarily for the carpenters framing the stud wall. Typically, when a window opening is dimensioned in wood stud framing, the dimension has the suffix R.O. This stands for Rough Opening, clearly representing that the dimension identifies an opening in the wall. You will add the suffix next.

5. Select the dimension at the window opening.

6. Click directly on the blue dimension text (i.e., 4'-0").

7. Type **R.O.** in the *Suffix* field and then click **OK**.

FIGURE 10-4.1 Added dimensions

FIGURE 10-4.2 Selected dimension properties

FIGURE 10-4.3 Dimension with suffix

Figure 10-4.3 shows the dimension with the added suffix.

8. Use the same process to add the text "WINDOW BEYOND" in the *Below* field (Figure 10-4.4).

FIGURE 10-4.4 Text added below dimension

9. Turn the *crop region* back on for a moment.

10. Select the ***crop region***.

Notice the dashed line that shows around the *crop region*? It has its own set of positioning grips. This dashed lined area allows you to control the visibility of various elements in the current view, such as text. You will adjust the right-hand side so it will accommodate more text and notes.

11. Drag the control grips for the vertical dashed line on the right as per **Figure 10-4.5**.

12. Turn the *crop region* off again.

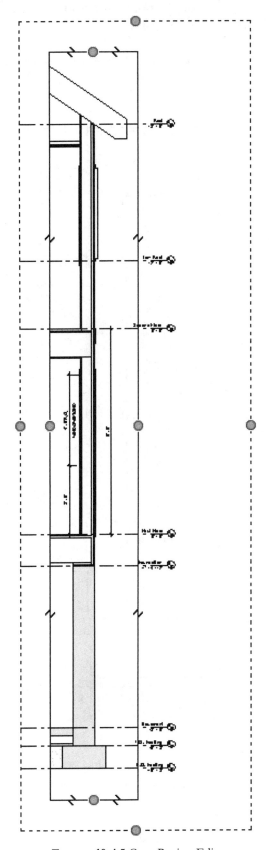

FIGURE 10-4.5 Crop Region Edits

13. Add the notes with leaders shown in Figure 10-4.6. (See Step 14.)

> *TIP: Select the Text tool and then one of the leader icons on the Ribbon (see image to right).*

FIGURE 10-4.6 Notes added to wall section

14. The text style should be set to **3/32″ Arial**; it may still be set to the last text style you used in this book: ¼″ Outline Text.

15. Select the text and use the grips and the justification buttons to make the text look like **Figure 10-4.6**.

Adding Detail Components:

Revit provides a way in which you can quickly add common 2D detail elements like dimensional lumber in section, anchor bolts, wall base profiles to "embellish" your sections. These are just a few loaded with your template file (Figure 10-4.7); many others can be created or downloaded from the internet.

Next, you will add just a few *Detail Components* so you have a basic understanding of how this feature is used.

You will add a 2x6 sill plate and double top plate. You will also add the batt insulation symbol in the stud cavity.

16. Select **Annotate → Detail → Component → Detail Component**.

17. From the *Type Selector*, pick *Dimension Lumber-Section:* **2 x 6**.

18. Add the sill plates as shown in Figure 10-4.8.

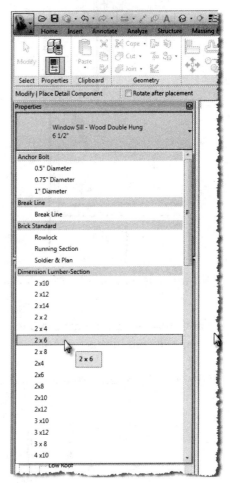

FIGURE 10-4.7
Detail Components; Type Selector open

TIP: When placing the 2x6 you will need to press the spacebar to Rotate, and then Move to properly position the element. The sill plate should be directly on the ¾" wood sheathing. Note that the horizontal line that extends through the sill plate is the level datum.

FIGURE 10-4.8 Callout of Cross Section 1 view; 2 x 6 sill plates added

Detail Components can be copied once you have placed one in the view. This saves the step of rotating the stud in this example.

19. Use **Copy** and **Snaps** to add the double top plate (Figure10-4.9).

FIGURE 10-4.9 Callout of Cross Section 1 view; 2 x 6 dbl. top plate added

Next you will add the batt insulation.

Insulation

20. Select **Annotation → Detail → Insulation**.

21. Pick the midpoint of the sill plate and the top plate to draw a line that represents the center of the batt insulation symbol, you can pick in either direction (Figure 10-4.10).

FIGURE 10-4.10 Callout of Cross Section 1 view; Insulation added

Next you will change the width of the insulation so it fits the space of the stud cavity (i.e., 5½″ wide).

22. Click **Modify** and then click to select the insulation just drawn.

23. Adjust the **Width** on the *Options Bar* to **5½″**.

24. This change can also be made via the *Instance Properties* dialog (Figure 10-4.11).

25. Click **OK** and then **Modify**.

FIGURE 10-4.11 Insulation properties

FIGURE 10-4.12
Insulation width changed

These tools we just used are on the *Annotate* tab of the *Ribbon* because they are 2D graphics and only show up in the current view.

Drawing some elements like this, rather than modeling them three-dimensionally, can save time and system resources. A file could get very large if you tried to model everything. Of course, every time you skip drawing in 3D, you increase the chance of error. It takes a little experience to know when to model and when not to model.

FYI: *Architectural text is typically all uppercase.*

Loading Additional Detail Components:

In addition to the *Detail Components* that are preloaded with the template file you started with, you can load more from the Revit content folder on your hard drive.

26. Select **Component** → **Detail Component** from the *Annotate* tab.

27. Click the **Load Family** button from the *Ribbon*.

28. Double-click on the ***Detail Components*** folder and then the following sub-folders: *Div 06-Wood* and *Plastic\064000-Architectural Woodwork\064600-Wood Trim*.

29. Double-click the file named ***Crown Molding-Section.rfa***.

You now have access to the newly imported crown molding. Take a minute to observe some of the other *Detail Components* that may be loaded into the project; for example, in the *Div 05-Metals\05200-Structural Steel Framing* folder you can load a steel beam family which has all the standard shapes contained within it as types (Figure 10-4.13).

26. Add the *Crown Molding* to the intersection between the wall and the ceiling using the **Component** tool on the *Annotate* tab (not the *Home* tab).

FIGURE 10-4.13 Load Detail Component dialog, wide flange beams selected

Using Repeating Details:

Many details and sections have components that occur multiple times, one right after another. Some examples are brick, siding and floor joists in section. Revit provides a tool, called *Repeating Details*, which can basically copy any *Detail Component* the required number of times to fill the space between two pick points you select with the mouse. The spacing of the *Detail Component* being copied has to be predefined when setting up the *Repeating Detail* style.

27.   Click **Annotate → Detail → Component → Repeating Detail**.

28.   From the *Type Selector*, select *Repeating Detail:* **Lap Siding 6"**.   Repeating Detail Component

For now, you will draw the siding off to one side just to test this feature. Make sure you are within the *crop window* area or you will not see the results.

29.   Pick two points similar to those shown in Figure 10-4.14.

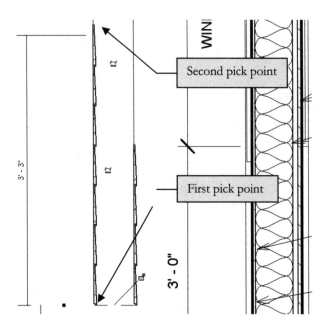

The example to the left shows two *Repeating Details* added. You can adjust them via the grips or the temporary dimensions.

FIGURE 10-4.14 Repeating Detail added: lap siding

30.   Try adjusting the length of the siding by selecting it and clicking on the dimension text.

One way to quickly study several *Repeating Details* is to download the sample file for repeating details from SEEK (Figure 10-4.15).

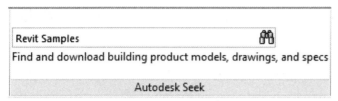

FIGURE 10-4.15 Search for Revit sample files on SEEK

FIGURE 10-4.16 Sample file downloaded from Revit content website

Once you download the file you can open it and examine how the repeating details work.

FIGURE 10-4.17 Type Properties dialog box

The sample file shows Brick, CMU, Lap Siding, Stone Wall (plan), Metal Deck, 2x Floor Framing, Concrete Pavers, Cut Stone, Brick Paver (Figure 10-4.16).

Selecting a *Repeating Detail* and opening its *Type Properties* dialog reveals the handful of settings associated with it (Figure 10-4.17).

31. **Delete** the *Lap Siding* repeating detail.

32. **Save** your project as **10-4.rvt**.

Self-Exam:

The following questions can be used as a way to check your knowledge of this lesson. The answers can be found at the bottom of the page.

1. The controls for the section mark, when selected, are similar to the controls for the elevation tag. (T/F)

2. *Detail Components* added in this lesson were 3D. (T/F)

3. The footings drawn in this lesson were a Revit wall type. (T/F)

4. The *crop region* is represented by a rectangle in the section view. (T/F)

5. Use the _____ tool to reference a larger section off a building section.

Review Questions:

The following questions may be assigned by your instructor as a way to assess your knowledge of this section. Your instructor has the answers to the review questions.

1. The visibility of the *crop region* can be controlled. (T/F)

2. It is not possible to draw a leader with out placing text. (T/F)

3. When a section mark is added to a view, all the other related views automatically get a section mark added to them. (T/F)

4. It is possible to modify elements such as doors, windows and ceilings in section views. (T/F)

5. You cannot adjust the "depth of view" using the *crop window*. (T/F)

6. What is the first thing you should do after placing a section mark?

   _____

7. If the text appears to be excessively large in a section view, the view's

   _____ _____ is probably set incorrectly.

8. The abbreviation R.O. stands for _____ _____.

9. Describe what happens when you double-click on the section bubble:

   _____.

10. Revit provides _____ different leader options within the *Text* command, not including the leader location options.

Lesson 11
Residence: INTERIOR DESIGN:

This lesson explores some interior design elements of a floor plan, such as toilet room layouts and kitchen cabinets. Additionally, you will look at placing furniture and guardrails into your project.

Exercise 11-1:
Bathroom Layouts

Bathroom layouts involve placing toilets, tubs and sinks. You will start with the half bath on the first floor.

1. Open ex10-4.rvt and **Save As ex11-1.rvt**.

The template you started with has everything you need to lay out this room. You will create the layout shown in Figure 11-1.1.

FIGURE 11-1.1 First Floor plan view: half bath layout

2. Switch to **_First Floor Plan_** view and zoom in on the half bath next to the garage, North of the dining room.

The first step will be to place the toilet.

3. With the *Component* tool selected on the *Home* tab, pick **Toilet-Domestic-3D** from the *Type Selector*. Click **No** when prompted to load a *Plumbing Fixture* tag.

4. **Place** the toilet in the middle of the room and then *Move* and *Rotate* into place utilizing *Snaps* (Figure 11-1.2).

   TIP: Press the spacebar to rotate the toilet before placing it.

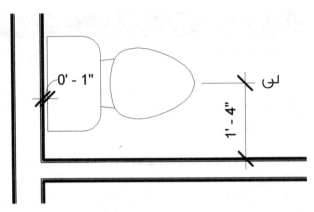

The toilet is 1″ out from the wall, which is typical for floor mounted – tank type toilets.

The overlapping letters, C and L, is the symbol for "centerline". This means that the middle of the toilet is 1′-4″ from the wall. Actually, if you were to add this dimension, Autodesk® Revit® Architecture would automatically add this symbol if the *Centerline Symbol* parameter is turned on in the properties of the dimension!

FIGURE 11-1.2 Toilet location

If you want to make sure the 1′-4″ dimension never changes, you can add the dimension shown and then click the padlock symbol to *Lock* that dimension. Then, anytime the wall moves, the toilet will move with it. If you want the constraint but do not want the dimension, you can delete the dimension and Autodesk® Revit® Architecture will ask you if you want to maintain the constraint after the dimension is deleted.

Next, you will add the sink. This consists of three separate components: a base cabinet, a countertop and a sink, which is similar to what you would have in the "real-world". First you will add the base cabinet.

5. Place a *Vanity Cabinet-Double Door Sink Unit*: **24″** using the *Component* tool (Figure 11-1.3).

   TIP: Use the spacebar to rotate.

   TIP: It is hard to tell which side is the front of the cabinet in plan view; the side the cursor is attached to is the back of the cabinet. If you add it incorrectly you will see the problem when you set up the interior elevation.

FIGURE 11-1.3 Vanity base cabinet added

Next, you will add the countertop. Autodesk Revit Architecture has one that even has a hole in it for the sink. You will have to adjust the length to fit your cabinet.

6. Using the *Component* tool, place the <u>*Vanity Counter Top w Round Sink Hole*</u>: **24″** depth in the middle of the room.

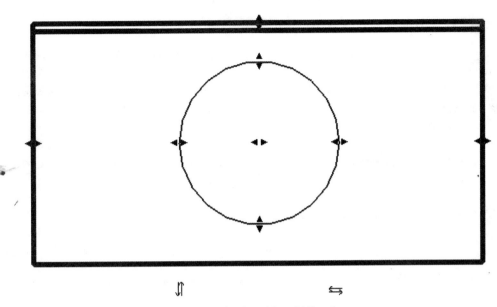

FIGURE 11-1.4 Vanity counter top temporarily placed in middle of room

FIGURE 11-1.5 Vanity counter top properties

You will notice that the counter top is 48″ long; you will change this to 24″ in a moment. When selected, you see several arrow-grips which allow you to graphically adjust the size of the selected element.

7. With the counter top selected, note the ***Properties Palette*** options.

8. Change the *Length* to **2′-0″** and the *Sink Location* to **1′-0″** (Figure 11-1.5).

9. Click **Apply**, or just move your cursor back into the drawing window.

The counter top is now the correct size for your base cabinet.

10. Use ***Move*** and ***Rotate*** to position the counter top over the vanity base cabinet; use **Snaps** for accuracy.

11. Again, using the *Component* tool, add <u>*Sink Vanity-Round:*</u> **19″ x 19″**. Press the spacebar to rotate the sink 90 degrees and then visually place the sink in the center of the hole in the countertop.

Your plan should now look like Figure 11-1.1, less the elevation tag which you will add next.

Interior Elevation View:

Next, you will set up an interior elevation view for the half bath. You will also add a mirror above the sink in elevation view. As you can see, the tasks in this book are building on previously learned material; refer back to previous chapters if you need a refresher. Using these features multiple times will help you to become more efficient and to better understand the tools.

12. Place an **Elevation** tag, with the *Type Selector* set to **Interior Elevation**, looking towards the "wet" wall, the wall with fixtures on it (Figure 11-1.6).

> ***FYI:*** *A "wet" wall is any wall that has plumbing fixtures on it and piping behind it.*

> ***TIP:*** *When placing the Elevation Tag, Revit turns the pointer to look at the closest wall, so you will have to place the tag close to the West wall (overlapping the plumbing fixtures) and then move the tag back as a separate step.*

13. Rename the new view to: **1/2 Bath** in the *Project Browser*.

FIGURE 11-1.6 Elevation tag added

14. Switch to the new view; click the *crop region* and drag the bottom up so the floor system does not show. Your view should look like Figure 11-1.7.

First Floor
0' - 0"

FIGURE 11-1.7 ½ Bath elevation

15. Change the *View Scale* to **½" = 1'-0"**.

16. Load the component **Mirror** from the Autodesk Seek library; it will be from the *Revit Architecture* **library** rather than a manufacturer such as Bradley Corp.

Mirror
Library Revit Architecture

17. Create a *Duplicate* of the mirror family just loaded and name the new *Type*: **24" x 36"**; Change the *Width* to **24"** and the *Height* to **36"**.

18. While in the *1/2 Bath* elevation view, place the mirror as shown in Figure 11-1.8.

19. Add the notes and dimensions shown in Figure 11-1.8.

> ***Tip:*** *As you are drawing the leaders, Revit will help you align your pick points vertically so the leaders and notes align; just watch for the dashed vertical reference line before picking your points.*

20. Using the same techniques just covered, lay out the two second floor bathrooms per **Figure 11-1.9**; use the tub loaded with the template.

    a. Make the larger vanity cabinet and counter top 4'-0" wide.

FIGURE 11-1.8 Interior elevation with mirror and notes added

FYI: *Keep in mind that many of the symbols that come with Revit, or any program for that matter, are not necessarily drawn or reviewed by an architect. The point is that the default values, such as mounting heights, may not meet ADA, national, state or local codes. Items such as accessible mirrors have a maximum height off the floor to the reflective surface that Revit's standard components may not comply with. However, as you apply local codes to these families, you can reuse them in the future.*

FIGURE 11-1.9 Second Floor Bath Rooms

21. **Save** your project as **ex11-1.rvt**.

Exercise 11-2:
Kitchen Layout

In this exercise you will look at adding kitchen cabinets and appliances to your project. As usual, Revit provides several predefined families to be placed into the project.

Placing Cabinets:

You will add base cabinets and appliances first.

1. Open ex11-1.rvt and **Save As ex11-2.rvt**.

2. Switch to the *First Floor Plan* view and zoom into the kitchen.

    FYI: As with other families (i.e., doors and windows), Revit loads several Types to represent the most valuable and useful sizes available. Cabinets typically come in 3" increments with different types (i.e., single or double door unit) having maximum and minimum sizes.

3. With the *Component* tool selected, place the families, cabinets **and appliances**, as shown in Figure 11-2.1; use *Snaps* for accuracy. Remember that the cursor is at the back of the cabinet when placing the component.

    FYI: Most of the specified families are already loaded into your project from your template you started with; the others can be loaded manually from the local or online libraries.

4. Select one of the base cabinets and click **Edit Type** from the *Properties Palette*.

Notice the height is 2'-10½" which, when combined with a 1½" standard counter top, gives you a 3'-0" surface.

Next, you will add the counter tops to the base cabinets. You will place three separate counter top elements (Figure 11-2.2). You will adjust the lengths of the counter tops to fit the cabinets below.

FIGURE 11-2.1 First Floor Plan View: base cabinets added to kitchen

5. Per the steps listed below, add the counter tops shown in Figure 11-2.2, using *Snaps* to accurately place them.

    a. Load the elements not currently loaded in your project from the *Casework\ Domestic Kitchen* folder.

    b. Place the bottom-right corner unit (use *Move, Mirror* and *Snaps*) and then, with the unit selected, drag one of the end grips back to align with the edge of the cabinet below.

    c. Load and place the other corner unit with the sink hole.
        i. Adjust the edge locations (use *Properties* for accuracy)
        ii. Adjust sink hole via *Properties Palette: Sink Location:* **5'-4"**

    d. Add the two straight counter tops as shown.

    e. Verify the *Height* is **3'-0"** via the *Properties Palette*.

FIGURE 11-2.2 First Floor Plan View: counter tops added

6. Select the counter top with the sink hole and go to the ***Properties Palette***.

7. Change the following (Figure 11-2.3):
   a. Sink Location to Wall: **5"**
   b. Sink Opening Depth: **1'-5"**
   c. Sink Opening Width: **3'-4"**

TIP: *Some settings are per instance (i.e., the settings in the palette to the left) and others are per type (i.e., clicking the* Edit Type *button – Type Parameters); the Instant Parameters only affect the selected item. So, if you place another instance of this family in the basement, the sink can be in a different location.*

FIGURE 11-2.3 Properties for Counter Top with Sink Hole: 24" Depth

8. Using the *Component* tool, add **Sink Kitchen-Double: 42″ x 21″** to your project – centered on the sink hole (Figure 11-2.4).

FIGURE 11-2.4 Sink placed in countertop, centered on hole

Placing Wall Cabinets:

Next you will add a couple wall cabinets to see how they work. They are similar to adding base cabinets, with the exception that they are dependent on walls (i.e., they are *wall hosted*). You can only place an upper cabinet on a wall, not in the middle of a room like you did with the base cabinets. The base cabinets are set up to sit on the floor and the upper cabinets are assigned a height above the floor, on the wall, via *Properties*.

9. Using the **Component** tool, add the upper cabinets as shown in **Figure 11-2.5**:

   a. Move the cursor close to a wall until you see the cabinet, which means Revit found a wall.

   b. Center the upper cabinet above the range, leaving an equal space on each side of the cabinet; these spaces will get a filler that matches the cabinets.

   c. The numbers (which represent the cabinet width) and X's in the cabinets are for clarity of this step only; you do not need to add these items.

   d. Use both single and double upper cabinets as necessary.

   e. If you have trouble adding the uppers at the pocket door location, add them to the right and move them into place.

The text box within the figure reads:

Use the *Measure* tool to figure out how wide each upper cabinet needs to be. First, add the corner units and then list the distance from the edge of the corner cabinet to the edge of the base cabinet below that the upper cabinet will align with, or to the window jamb.

FIGURE 11-2.5 First Floor plan view: upper cabinets added (X'S added for clarity in this image)

The heights of the cabinets will be adjusted when you get to the interior elevation view.

FYI: Wall cabinets are typically dashed in plan because they are above the floor plan cut plane.

Adding the Interior Elevation Tag:

10. Add an interior **Elevation Tag** as shown in Figure 11-2.6.

    TIP: Make sure you select Interior Elevation *from the Type Selector.*

11. Rename the new elevation view to ***Kitchen (east)***.

12. Select the **circle** portion of the symbol; the symbol should look like Figure 11-2.7 when selected correctly.

13. Click the *North* and *South* check-
    boxes as shown in Figure 11-2.7.

14. **Rename** the two new views to
    Kitchen (north) and ***Kitchen
    (south)***.

The single elevation tag in plan view is
associated with the three kitchen elevation
views.

15. Double-click the pointer portion
    of the elevation tag pointing
    towards the East to open that
    view.

16. Adjust the ***crop region*** so the floor
    system is not visible.

17. Set the *View Scale* to **½″ = 1′-0″**; your interior
    elevation view should look like **Figure 11-2.8**.

Depending on where, exactly, you placed the *Elevation
Tag*, you may see the side of the refrigerator or a section
through it, as in Figure 11-2.8. In this case you will
want to adjust the view so you see the cabinets beyond,
which is more important to show. You will switch back
to the plan view and adjust the views settings.

FIGURE 11-2.6 Elevation tag added to kitchen

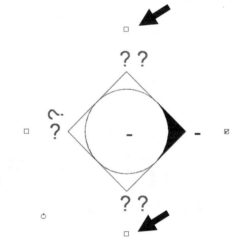

FIGURE 11-2.7 Elevation tag selected

18. Switch back to the ***First Floor Plan*** view.

19. Click, to select, the *East view's* pointer portion of the elevation tag so you see the
    Extent of View/Far Clip Plane lines.

FIGURE 11-2.8 Kitchen (east); initial view

20. Click and drag to adjust the location of the *Extent of View* line as shown in Figure 11-2.9; also adjust the *Far Clip Plane* if necessary.

Notice the *Extent of View* line has been moved to the east of the refrigerator and the *Far Clip Plane* is in the middle of the wall.

21. Switch back to the **Kitchen (east)** view and note the changes (Figure 11-2.10).

You will modify one more thing in this view before moving on. The height of the wall cabinets needs a little work (Figure 11-2.10); the corner wall cabinets are too short and the cabinet over the range is too tall. You can adjust these in either the plan or elevation view. You will adjust them in the elevation view so you can immediately see the changes.

FIGURE 11-2.9 First Floor; elev. tag selected

FIGURE 11-2.10 Kitchen (east) view; view settings adjusted

22. Select both **corner** upper cabinets and change their height to **2'-6"** and the Elevation to **4'-6"** (2'-6" + 4'-6" = 7'-0" to top). Make these changes via the *Properties Palette* and *Type Properties*.

23. Select the upper cabinet above the range and change its height to **15"** and the elevation so the top stays at 7'-0".

24. Search the **Web Library** for a range hood; load and then place it.

Range Hood
Library Revit Architecture

Your elevation should now look like Figure 11-2.11. Notice that the cabinets on the right and left, which are actually in section, have heavier lines than the cabinets which are in elevation. Again, Revit saves time by assuming the industry standard. However, you can use the *Linework* tool to change this if you so desire!

FIGURE 11-2.11 Kitchen (east) view; view settings adjusted

You will add notes and dimensions to the elevation.

25. Add the notes and dimensions per **Figure 11-2.12**.

26. Select the ***Linework*** tool from the *Modify* tab, and set the *Line Style* (on the *Ribbon*) to **Wide lines**. Select the perimeter lines so they stand out more.

FIGURE 11-2.12 Interior elevation with annotations

That is it for the East elevation! Next, you will take a quick look at the other two elevations you set up in the kitchen.

27. Switch to the ***Kitchen (north)*** view.

28. Adjust the *crop region* and the perimeter lines per the previous elevation (Figure 11-2.13).

29. Change the *View Scale* to **½″ = 1′-0″**.

You will notice right away that the windows are in conflict with the cabinets and the countertop does not extend over the dishwasher. Both of these required changes can be made in either the plan or the elevation; again, you will make changes in the elevation view so you can see the results.

First you will fix the windows. An error like this could easily be overlooked using a traditional CAD program because the exterior elevation and the interior elevations are separate/independent drawings files; so you could fix the height of the windows in the interior elevation, but forget to change the exterior elevation, where the windows are specified and ordered from. In Revit, it is not even possible to have one window be two different sizes in the same project file.

FIGURE 11-2.13 Kitchen (north); initial view

30. Select the *Section* line, right-click and pick **Hide in View → Elements**. You do not need to see that section mark here.

31. Select the two windows in the ***Kitchen (north)*** view.

32. Via *Properties*, create a new window *Type*, via *Edit Type* → *Duplicate*, named *Double Hung with Trim:* **36" x 42"**:
    a. Set the *Height* to **3'-6"** (from 4'-0") – *Type Parameter*
    b. See the *Sill Height* to **3'-6"** (From 3'-0") – *Instance Parameter*
    c. Click **OK** and then adjust the sill height for the selected windows to **3'-6"**.

Now the windows do not conflict with the countertop's backsplash. Next, you will adjust the counter top.

33. In the ***Kitchen (north)*** view, zoom in on the dishwasher area.

34. Select the **Counter Top** over the **15"** wide base cabinet, to the left of the dishwasher, and press the **Delete** key to erase it.

35. Using the ***Align*** tool, select the left-edge of the 15" wide base cabinet and then select the left edge of the countertop. The countertop should now align with the edge of the cabinets.

    FYI: *You must pick these items in the order specified.*

36. Edit the perimeter using the ***Linework*** tool and adjust the *Crop Region* to hide the floor.

Your modified *Kitchen (north)* should look like Figure 11-2.14.

FIGURE 11-2.14 Kitchen (north); modified view

37. Open *Kitchen (south)*.

38. Modify the *crop region* and the perimeter linework.

You cannot see the refrigerator doors; you now realize that the refrigerator was inserted backwards (Figure 11-2.15). You will fix this next.

FIGURE 11-2.15 Kitchen (south); initial view

39. Set the scale to ½" = 1'-0" and *Hide* the building section mark.

40. *Rotate* the refrigerator (in plan view) 180 degrees (if required – the door handles should be visible if facing the correct way).

41. Modify the upper cabinet above the refrigerator to be **12"** tall, with the top at **7'-0"**.

> *TIP: If this cabinet were used anywhere else in the project, you would have had to make a duplicate before changing the height; otherwise, all the cabinets would have changed as well, because it is a Type Parameter you are changing, not an Instance Parameter.*

Often, you have a portion of a wall that does not have very much on it, so it is not worth elevating. In the **Kitchen (south)** view you will crop a portion of the wall on the right.

42. Click the **crop region** and drag the right side of the *crop region* rectangle towards the left so only the portion of elevation shown in Figure 11-2.16 is visible.

Your **Kitchen (south)** view should now look like Figure 11-2.16.

FIGURE 11-2.16 Kitchen (south); modified view

The last things you will adjust are the lines in the cabinet elevations that indicate the swing of the cabinet door; these lines are typically dashed lines.

There are two ways to accomplish this. One way will only affect the current view (View → *Visibility/Graphics*) and the other will affect the entire project (Manage → *Settings* → *Object Styles*). You want this change to be applied everywhere, so you want to implement per the latter method.

43. Select **Manage → Settings → Object Styles**.

Object Styles

44. On the *Model* tab, click the plus symbol next to **Casework** in the *Category* column (Figure 11-2.17).

45. Change the **Line Pattern** for *Elevation Swing* to **Hidden 1/8″** (Figure 11-2.17).

46. Click **OK** to see the results in the three kitchen elevations.

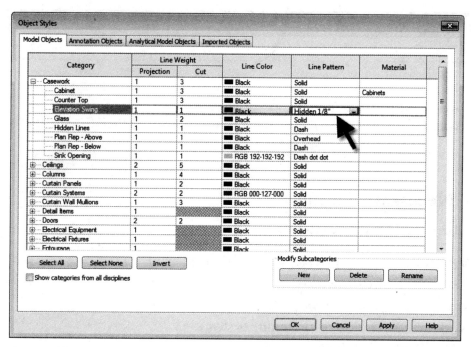

FIGURE 11-2.17 Object Styles dialog box; controls project wide graphics settings

That is it for the kitchen! With a little practice, you could design a kitchen in very short order.

47. **Save** your project as **ex11-2.rvt**.

TIP: The Woodwork Institute (http://www.wicnet.org/publications/casework.asp) has Revit families for most of the industry standard cabinets. You can download the cabinets from their website. You can even print out a small flyer that shows an image of each cabinet that can be downloaded.

Exercise 11-3:
Furniture

This lesson will cover the steps required to lay out furniture. The processes are identical to those previously covered for toilets and cabinets. First you will start with the office on the second floor.

Loading the Necessary Families:

1.   Open ex11-2.rvt and **Save As ex11-3.rvt**.

2.   Select the *Component* tool (on the *Home* tab) and load (via the *Load Family* icon) the following items into the current project:

> <u>**Local Files**</u> *(i.e., on your hard drive)*
> a.   **Work Station Desktops** (Furniture System)
> b.   **Chair-Breuer** (Furniture)
> c.   **Chair-Executive** (Furniture)
> d.   **Sofa-Pensi** (Furniture)
> e.   **Table-Round** (Furniture)
>
> <u>**Online Files**</u> *(i.e., Autodesk Seek on the internet)*
> f.   Search SEEK for **Copier-Floor**
>
> *TIP: You can type "copier" in SEEK and find a few options.*

TIP: You can set the View *mode for the* Open *dialog box, which is displayed when you click* Load from *Library. One option is* Thumbnail *mode; this displays a small thumbnail image for each file in the current folder. This makes it easier to see the many symbols and drawings that are available for insertion.*

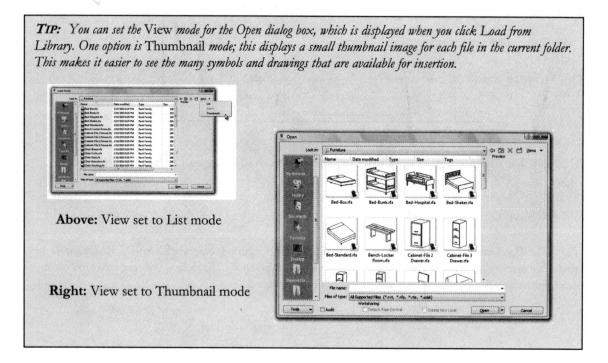

Above: View set to List mode

Right: View set to Thumbnail mode

Designing the Office Furniture Layout:

3. Switch to the *Second Floor* view.

4. Place the furniture as shown in Figure 11-3.1.

   TIP: Use Snaps to assure accuracy; use Rotate and Mirror as required.

FIGURE 11-3.1 Second Floor – Office furniture layout

Look at the properties for the desktop to see the *Desktop Height* setting which controls how high the surface is above the current floor.

You may want to browse through the component library and the web library for miscellaneous residential furniture. You can add dining room tables and chairs, bookshelves, washer and dryer, etc. Your instructor may require you to complete this suggested step. An example of a few items placed can be seen in Figure 11-3.2.

FIGURE 11-3.2 First Floor; one possible furniture layout

3D View of Office Layout:

Next, you will look at a 3D view of your office area. This involves adjusting the visibility of the roof and skylights.

5. Switch to the **Default 3D** view via the *QAT*.

6. Click anywhere in the drawing window to activate the view.

7. Type **VV** to access the *Visibility/Graphics Overrides* dialog box. Remember, these settings are only for the current view.

8. Uncheck the *Ceiling* and the *Roof* category then click **OK**.

The ceilings and roof should not be visible now. However, you should still see the light fixtures floating in space. You will make those disappear next.

9. Select one of the 2′ x 4′ light fixtures floating above the office.

10. Click the **Temorary Hide/Isolate** tool from the *View Control Bar*.

You should see the menu shown **Figure 11-3.3** show up next to the *Hide/Isolate* icon. This allows you to isolate an element, so it is the only thing on the screen. Or you can hide it, so the element is temporarily not visible.

FIGURE 11-3.3 Hide/Isolate popup menu

11. Click **Hide Category** in the menu (Figure 11-3.3).

> **FYI:** *This makes all the lights hide; you could leave it at* Hide Element *and select each light.*

12. Adjust your **3D** view to look similar to **Figure 11-3.4**; try looking at the room from other angles as well.

> **TIP:** *While pressing the Shift key, also press the wheel button on the mouse and drag the mouse around to "orbit" the model without selecting any icons. Also, selecting an object in the view makes the model pivot about the selected object.*

You will now restore the original visibility settings for the **3D** view. Notice the *Hide/Isolate* icon now has a colored background, which means something in the project is temporarily hidden from view.

13. Click the *Hide/Isolate* icon and then select ***Reset Temporary Hide/Isolate*** from the popup up menu.

14. Reset the **3D** view's visibility settings so the ceilings and roof are visible (type VV).

15. Click the *Home* icon via the ***ViewCube*** to reset the view (Figure 11-3.5).

16. **Save** your project as **ex11-3.rvt**.

FIGURE 11-3.4 3D view with ceiling/roof/lights hidden

> **FYI:** *Not all families found online are drawn in full 3D. Some may have been brought over from a CAD program where all the symbols are drawn in 2D only.*

Online Content:

A few locations on the internet provide additional content for use in Revit; some is free and some is not. Hopefully, product manufacturers will start providing content based on the products they make, making it easier for people to include that manufacturer's product in their project, both in the virtual and real projects.

You have already spent a little time looking at Revit's online content library (seek.autodesk.com). You should spend some more time there so you know what is generally available. This will help you to reduce duplicated effort.

As previously mentioned in this text, the Autodesk SEEK initiative is meant to facilitate the dissemination of high quality manufacturer Revit content, as well as content for other Autodesk products: AutoCAD, Inventor, etc. The screen shot below shows the seek.autodesk.com homepage. This site can be directly accessed from within Revit via the *Insert* tab and then the *Autodesk Seek* panel.

End user content can also be uploaded (to be shared with others) via **Application Menu →
Publish → Share with Autodesk Seek**.

FIGURE 11-3.5 Home icon next to ViewCube; Home icon is only visible when cursor is over ViewCube.

The following sites also contain content that can be downloaded:
- www.revitcity.com *(free content provided by other users)*
- http://www.turbosquid.com/revit *(buy, sell and trade other user's content)*

You should occasionally search the internet to see if additional content becomes available. You can do an internet search for "revit content"; make sure to include the quotation marks. Rendering content, such as that offered by www.archvision.com, will be covered in Chapter 13.

Exercise 11-4:
Adding Guardrails

This lesson will cover the steps required to lay out guardrails. The steps are simple; you select your style and draw its path.

Adding a Guardrail to the Second Floor Stair Area:

1. Open ex11-3.rvt and **Save As ex11-4.rvt**.

2. Switch to **Second Floor Plan** view.

3. Select **Home → Circulation → Railing**.

4. **Zoom** into the stair area.

At this point you will draw a line representing the path of the guardrail. The railing is offset to one side of the line, similar to walls. However, you do not have the *Location Line* option as you do with the *Wall* tool, so you have to draw the railing in a certain direction to get the railing to be on the floor and not hovering in space just beyond the floor edge.

5. Draw a line along the edge of the floor as shown in **Figure 11-4.1**.

   TIP: Select Chain *from the Options Bar to draw the railing with fewer picks.*

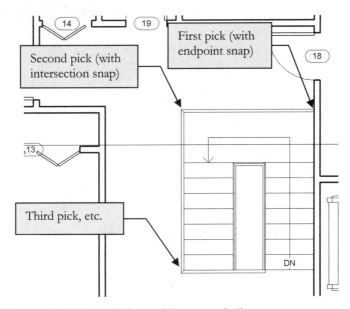

FIGURE 11-4.1 Second Floor: adding a guardrail

6. Click the **green checkmark** from the *Ribbon* to finish the railing.

The railing has now been drawn. In the next step you will switch to a 3D view and see how to quickly change the railing style. This will also involve changing the height of the railing. Most building codes require the railing height be 42″ when the drop to the adjacent surface is more than 30″; this is called a guardrail.

7. Switch to the **3D** view.

8. Turn off the ceilings and roof as previously reviewed (**TIP:** *Temp. Hide/Isolate*), and then zoom into the railing just added to the second floor. Notice the railing style shown in Figure 11-4.2.

9. Select the railing. You may have to use the *Tab* key to cycle through the various selection options.

10. With the railing selected, select the other railing type available in the *Type Selector* on the *Properties Palette*. When finished make sure *Railing:* **Handrail – Rectangular** is selected.

FIGURE 11-4.2 Added railing – 3D view

Modify Railing on the Properties Palette

When the alternate style was selected, your railing should have looked like Figure 11-4.3. Even the railing for the stair could be changed by a similar step. This style is too contemporary for this design so you will not use it at this time.

FYI: You can change the height via Type Properties.

Notice stair handrail buried within the wall; see discussion below.

FIGURE 11-4.3 Railing with alternate style

Editing the Sketch Lines for the Stair Railing:

You will notice, in the image above (Figure 11-4.3), that a portion of the railing added with the stair is buried in the wall. You will edit the railing sketch lines to remove this conflict.

FIGURE 11-4.4 Edit railing sketch lines

11. Switch to the *First Floor Plan* view.

12. Select the outer <u>railing</u> for the upper stair; use the *Tab* key to cycle through your selection options.

13. Click the **Edit Path** button on the *Modify | Railings* tab.

14. Delete the sketch lines on the north and east walls, shown dashed in Figure 11-4.4.

FYI: The railing added with the stair is simply a separate railing element that was atomically added with the stair.

15. Select the **green check mark** on the *Design Bar* when finished.

16. Reset the 3D view so the roof and ceiling elements are visible.

Switching back to the **3D** view, you notice the railing lines in the walls are gone (Figure 11-4.5). Revit is consistent in the way many 3D components are defined and edited with 2D sketch linework; editing the stringer extensions is a similar process. This consistency helps reduce the learning curve.

FIGURE 11-4.5 Railing conflict resolved

The *Railing* tool has the ability to create fairly complex railings. The image below shows the interface for setting up the baluster placement (Figure 11-4.6). This kind of advanced control is beyond the scope of this textbook.

FIGURE 11-4.6 Dialog to control baluster and newel post placement

Make sure to examine the railing sample file available on Autodesk's online content library (seek.autodesk.com – search for "Revit samples" and select the railing option). You can download this file, open it, select a railing and view its properties to see how it works.

FIGURE 11-4.7
Railing sample file downloaded
from Revit's website

You can *Copy/Paste* a railing style from this drawing into one of your project files. Then you select your railing and pick the newly imported one from the *Type Selector*. This process was done to achieve the image below (Figure 11-4.8). Notice the traditional balusters and newel post.

FIGURE 11-4.8 Optional railing configuration

17. **Save** your project as **ex11-4.rvt**.

Self-Exam:

The following questions can be used as a way to check your knowledge of this lesson. The answers can be found at the bottom of the page.

1. The bathroom fixtures are preloaded in the template file. (T/F)

2. You do not need to be connected to the internet when you want to download content from Autodesk's content site SEEK. (T/F)

3. Revit content may not always be in compliance with local codes. (T/F)

4. You can use *Crop Region* to crop a portion of wall that is blank. (T/F)

5. Click the _____ _____ tool to modify the path of a railing.

Review Questions:

The following questions may be assigned by your instructor as a way to assess your knowledge of this section. Your instructor has the answers to the review questions.

1. Revit provides several different styles of vanity cabinets for placement. (T/F)

2. Revit automatically adds a rail to every stair. (T/F)

3. It is not possible to draw dimensions on an interior elevation view. (T/F)

4. Cabinets typically come in 2" increments. (T/F)

5. Base cabinets automatically have a countertop on them. (T/F)

6. When you created a hole in a floor, Revit automatically adds a railing. (T/F)

7. You can use the _____ _____ to control element visibility.

8. What is the current size of your Revit Project? _____

9. What should you use to assure accuracy when placing cabinets? _____

10. You use the _____ tool to make various components temporarily invisible.

Lesson 12
Residence: SCHEDULES:

You will continue to study the powerful features available in Autodesk® Revit® Architecture. The ability to create parametric schedules is very useful; for example, you can delete a door number on a schedule and Autodesk Revit Architecture will delete the corresponding door from the plan. Be sure to watch the video on creating schedules located on the DVD.

Exercise 12-1:
Room and Door Tags

This exercise will look at adding room tags and door tags to your plans. As you insert doors, Autodesk Revit Architecture adds tags to them automatically. However, if you copy or mirror a door, or add one in elevation, you can lose the tag and have to add it.

Adding Rooms and Room Tags:

You will add a *Room* object, which will also add a *Room Tag* to the current view, to each room on your first floor plan. A *Room* object is not visible by default. It is an object which is used to calculate area, volume and store information about the room (i.e., the I in BIM... **B**uilding **I**nformation **M**odeling).

1. In the **First Floor** view, select **Home → Rom & Area → Room**.

Placing a *Room* is similar to placing a ceiling in the reflected ceiling plan; as you move your cursor over a room, the room perimeter highlights. When the room you want to place a *Room* element in is highlighted, you click to place it in that room. You are actually placing a *Room* and a *Room Tag*.

2. Place your cursor within the *Entry* area and place a *Room* (Figure 12-1.1). Make sure *"Tag on placement"* is highlighted on the *Ribbon*.

By default, Autodesk Revit Architecture will simply label the space 'Room' and number it '1.' You will change these to something different.

FIGURE 12-1.1 Room & Room Tag added to entry

FIGURE 12-1.2 Room tags – First Floor

3. Press **Esc** or select **Modify** to end the *Room* command.

4. Click on the **Room Tag** you just placed to select it.

5. Now click on the room name label to change it; enter **Entry**.

6. Now click on the room number to change it; enter **100**.

7. Add *Rooms/Room Tags* for each room on the first floor, incrementing each room number by 1 (Figure 12-1.2). Be sure to change the room names as well.

   TIP: During placement, pressing the spacebar will toggle the tag between horizontal and vertical orientation.

Second and Basement Floors:

8. Add *Rooms/Room Tags* to the *Second Floor*. The numbering should start with 200; do **not** change the room names (Figure 12-1.3).

9. Add *Rooms/Tags* to the *Basement Floor Plan*. The numbering should start with 1; **do** change the room names (Figure 12-1.4). Don't worry about the "00" prefix shown for the room numbers.

   FYI: Room tags can also be added to your building sections, as the Room element will now be there! When the Room element already exists, in plan or section, you use the Room Tag tool, not the Room command.

FIGURE 12-1.3 Second Floor – Room tags

FIGURE 12-1.4 Basement – Room tags

Adding Door Tags:

Next you will add *Door Tags* to any doors that are missing them. Additionally, you will adjust the door numbers to correspond to the room numbers.

Revit numbers the doors in the order they are placed into the drawing. This would make it difficult to locate a door by its door number if door number 1 was on the first floor and door number 2 was on the second floor, etc. Typically, a door number is the same as the room number the door swings into. For example, if a door swings into a room numbered 104, the door number would also be 104. If the room had two doors into it, the doors would be numbered 104A and 104B.

10. Switch to **First Floor Plan** view.

11. Select **Annotate → Tag → Tag By Category** from the *Ribbon* (Figure 12-1.5).

FIGURE 12-1.5 Annotate tab

Notice, as you move your cursor around the screen, Revit displays a tag for any element which can have a tag, when the cursor is over it. This includes walls, doors, windows, etc. When you click the mouse is when Revit actually places a tag.

12. **Uncheck** the **Leader** option on the *Options Bar.*

13. Place a **Door Tag** for each door that does not have a tag; do this for each level.

    TIP: *Press the spacebar to* Rotate *before clicking to place the tag.*

    TIP: *These should mainly be the doors in the Basement and the one added in elevation in the Living Room.*

14. **Renumber** all the *Door Tags* to correspond to the room they open into; do this for each level. Figure 12-1.6 is an example of the first floor and Figure 12-1.7 of the second floor.

    REMEMBER: *Click* Modify, *select the* Tag *and then click on the number to edit it*

TIP – TAG ALL *(Figure 12-1.5): This tool allows you to quickly tag all the elements of a selected category (e.g., doors) at one time. After selecting the tool, you select the category from a list and specify whether or not you want a leader. When you click OK, Revit tags all the untagged doors in that view. This helps to avoid not tagging a door. However, all doors will show up in a schedule whether they are tagged or not.*

FIGURE 12-1.6 First Floor; door tags

FIGURE 12-1.7 Second Floor; door tags

TIP: *The wall Instance Parameter, via the Properties Palette, must be set to "room bounding" for the Room tool to consider a wall as part of the perimeter within a particular room. For example, you could set a closet wall so it was not "room bounding" so Revit would ignore it when creating the Room, thus adding the closet square footage to the room total.*

15. **Save** your project as **ex12-1.rvt**.

Exercise 12-2:
Generate a Door Schedule

This exercise will look at creating a door schedule based on the information currently available in the building model (i.e., the *Room* and *Door* elements). The tags only report information stored within the element being tagged, so it is possible to delete a tag at any time without losing information. The tag can then be added later if required; tags are view specific.

Create a Door Schedule View:

A door schedule is simply another view of the building model. However, this view displays numerical data rather than graphical data. Just like a graphical view, if you change the view it changes all the other related views. For example, if you delete a door number from the schedule, the door is deleted from the plans and elevations.

1. Open ex12-1.rvt and **Save As ex12-2.rvt**.

2. Select **View → Create → Schedules → Schedules/Quantities**.

3. Select **Doors** under *Category* and then click **OK** (Figure 12-2.1).

FYI: The template you started with already has a door schedule set up and ready to go, so the first door you added was already scheduled. However, you will go through the steps of setting up a schedule so you understand how a schedule is created.

FIGURE 12-2.1 New Schedule dialog

You should now be in the *Schedule Properties* dialog where you specify what information is displayed in the schedule, how it is sorted, and the text format.

On the ***Fields*** tab, *Add* the information you want displayed in the schedule. Select the following (Figure 12-2.2):

a. Mark
b. Width
c. Height
d. Frame Material
e. Frame Type
f. Fire Rating

As noted in the dialog, the fields added to the list on the right are in the order they will be in the schedule view. Use the *Move Up* and *Move Down* buttons to adjust the order.

4. Do **NOT** click OK. You need to adjust one more thing.

FIGURE 12-2.2 Schedule Properties; Fields tab

TIP: *If you accidentally clicked* OK, *click the* Edit *button next to the Fields parameter in the Properties Palette.*

5. On the ***Sorting/Grouping*** tab, set the schedule to be sorted by the **Mark** (i.e., door number) in *Ascending* order (Figure 12-2.3).

TIP: *The* Formatting *and* Appearance *tabs allow you to adjust how the schedule looks. The formatting is not displayed until the schedule is placed on a sheet.*

6. Click the **OK** button to generate the schedule view.

You should now have a schedule similar to Figure 12-2.4.

FIGURE 12-2.3 Schedule Properties; Sorting tab

FIGURE 12-2.4 Door schedule view

Next, you will see how deleting a door number from the schedule deletes the door from the plan.

7. Switch to the **Door Schedule 2** view, under *Schedules/Quantities* in the *Project Browser*, if you are not already there.

Next, you will delete door *102* from the **Door Schedule** view; this was the door you added in an interior elevation, the exterior door in the *Living Room*.

8. Click in the cell with the number **102**.

9. Now click the **Delete** button from the *Ribbon* (Figure 12-2.5).

FIGURE 12-2.5 Ribbon panel for the door schedule view

You will get an alert. Revit is telling you that the actual door will be deleted from the project model (Figure 12-2.6).

10. Click **OK** to delete the door (Figure 12-2.6).

11. Switch back to the *First Floor* view and notice that door 102 has been deleted from the project model (Figure 12-2.7).

Revit

This will delete 1 instance(s).

Please note that you are not just removing rows from the schedule, but also deleting the associated elements and geometry from the project.

OK   Cancel

FIGURE 12-2.6 Revit alert message

FIGURE 12-2.7 First Floor plan view; door 102 has been removed

12. **Save** your project as **ex12-2.rvt**.

TIP: You can also change the door number in the schedule and the even the size; however, changing the size actually changes the door's Type Property which affects all the door instances of that type.

Exercise 12-3:
Generate a Room Finish Schedule

In this exercise you will create a room finish schedule. The process is similar to the previous exercise.

Create a Room Finish Schedule:

1. Open ex12-2.rvt and **Save As ex12-3.rvt**.

2. Select **View → Create → Schedules → Schedule/Quantities**.

3. Select **Rooms** under *Category* and then click **OK** (Figure 12-3.1).

4. In the **Fields** tab of the *Schedule Properties* dialog, add the following fields to be scheduled (Figure 12-3.2):
   a. Number
   b. Name
   c. Base Finish
   d. Floor Finish
   e. Wall Finish
   f. Ceiling Finish
   g. Area

FIGURE 12-3.1 New Schedule dialog

Area is not typically listed on a room finish schedule. However, you will add it to your schedule to see the various options Revit allows.

5. On the *Sorting/Grouping* tab, set the schedule to be sorted by the **Number** field.

6. On the *Appearance* tab, check **Bold** for the *Header Text* (Figure 12-3.3).

7. Select **OK** to generate the *Room Schedule* view.

FIGURE 12-3.2
Schedule Properties - Fields

FIGURE 12-3.3
Schedule Properties - Appearance

Place cursor here to resize the column

Room Schedule						
Number	Name	Base Finish	Floor Finish	Wall Finish	Ceiling Finish	Area
001	HALLWA					271 SF
002	Room					39 SF
003	FAMILY R					754 SF
004	SHOP					271 SF
005	MECH RM					80 SF
006	Room					36 SF
007	CRAFT					298 SF
100	ENTRY					282 SF
101	COAT CL					39 SF
102	LIVING RO					786 SF
103	KITCHEN					280 SF
104	MUD ROO					87 SF
105	Bath					38 SF
106	DINING					312 SF
107	GARAGE					749 SF
200	HALLWA					345 SF
201	Room					241 SF
202	Room					343 SF
203	Room					44 SF
204	Room					40 SF
205	Room					80 SF
206	Room					207 SF
207	Room					272 SF

FIGURE 12-3.4 Room Schedule view

Your schedule should look similar to the one to the left (Figure 12-3.4).

8. Resize the **Name** column so all the room names are visible. Place the cursor between *Name* and *Base Finish* and drag to the right until all the names are visible.

The formatting (i.e., Bold header text) will not show up until the schedule is placed on a sheet.

FYI: If you right-click on a column, you can select to hide it. Why add a column if you are just going to hide it? Well, for Revit to do calculations on data, the required parameters must be "in" the schedule, not just the project.

Modifying and Populating a Room Schedule:

Like the door schedule, the room schedule is a tabular view of the building model, so you can change the room name or number on the schedule or in the plans.

9. In the **Room Schedule** view, change the name for room **201** (lower right corner) to **OFFICE**.

> **TIP:** *Click on the current room name and then click on the down-arrow that appears. This gives you a list of all the existing names in the current schedule; otherwise you can type a new name.*

10. Switch to the **Second Floor Plan** view to see the updated *Room Tag*.

You can quickly enter finish information to several rooms at one time. You will do this next.

11. In the **Second Floor Plan** view, select the **Rooms** (not the *Room Tags*) for all bedrooms (three total); move the cursor near the *Room Tag* until you see the room highlight with an "X" (Figure 12-3.5).

> **REMEMBER:** *Hold the Ctrl key down to select multiple objects.*

FIGURE 12-3.5 Second Floor Plan – Rooms selected

The parameters listed here are the same as the *Fields* available for display in the *Room Schedule*. When more than one room is selected and a parameter is not the same (e.g., different names), that value field is left blank. Otherwise, the values are displayed for the selected room. Next, you will enter values for the finishes.

12. In the *Properties Palette*, change the *Name* field; enter **BEDROOM**.

13. Enter the following for the finishes (Figure 12-3.6):
    a. *Base Finish:* **Wood**
    b. *Ceiling Finish:* **GB**   *(Gb = gypsum board)*
    c. *Wall Finish:* **PAINT-1**
    d. *Floor Finish:* **CARPET-1**

FIGURE 12-3.6 Element Properties – Room Tags

14. Click **Apply**.

15. Switch back to the ***Room Schedule*** view to see the automatic updates (Figure 12-3.7).

You can also enter data directly into the *Room Schedule* view.

Hopefully, in the near future, Revit will be able to enter the finishes based on the wall's *Material* settings, as well as floor and ceiling types previously created in the project!

TIP: You can add fields and adjust formatting anytime by clicking on one of the edit buttons in the Properties Palette. This gives you the same options that were available when you created the schedule.

Room Schedule						
Number	Name	Base Finish	Floor Finish	Wall Finish	Ceiling Finish	Area
001	HALLWAY					271 SF
002	Room					39 SF
003	FAMILY ROOM					754 SF
004	SHOP					271 SF
005	MECH RM					80 SF
006	Room					36 SF
007	CRAFT ROOM					298 SF
100	ENTRY					282 SF
101	COAT CLOSET					39 SF
102	LIVING ROOM					786 SF
103	KITCHEN					280 SF
104	MUD ROOM					87 SF
105	Bath					38 SF
106	DINING					312 SF
107	GARAGE					749 SF
200	HALLWAY					345 SF
201	OFFICE					241 SF
202	BEDROOM	WOOD	CARPET-1	PAINT-1	GB	343 SF
203	Room					44 SF
204	Room					40 SF
205	Room					80 SF
206	BEDROOM	WOOD	CARPET-1	PAINT-1	GB	207 SF
207	BEDROOM	WOOD	CARPET-1	PAINT-1	GB	272 SF

FIGURE 12-3.7 Room Schedule; new data added

If you have trouble finding a room in the *Floor Plan* view, you can click the room number in the *Schedule* view and then click the **Highlight in Model** button on the *Ribbon*.

16. **Save** your project as **ex12-3.rvt**.

FYI: When the Room Tag *is selected, not the* Room *element, you can change its type from the Type Selector. The other option available, by default, is one without the square footage listed below the room number. For the cubic footage to show up, the* Area and Volumes Computations *dialog must be set to calculate volumes.*

GARAGE   **GARAGE**   **GARAGE**

107		107		107

749 SF   6739 CF

FIGURE 12-3.8 Room Tag options in current project

Self-Exam:

The following questions can be used as a way to check your knowledge of this lesson. The answers can be found at the bottom of the page.

1. Doors are automatically numbered based on the room number. (T/F)

2. The area for a room is calculated when a *Room*, and tag, is placed. (T/F)

3. Revit can tag all the doors not currently tagged on a given level with the *Tag All* tool. (T/F)

4. You can add or remove various fields in a door or room schedule. (T/F)

5. Click Delete on the *Ribbon* to delete a door from a schedule. (T/F)

Review Questions:

The following questions may be assigned by your instructor as a way to assess your knowledge of this section. Your instructor has the answers to the review questions.

1. You can add a door tag with a leader. (T/F)

2. You can add a fire rating by selecting a door, then *Properties Palette*. (T/F)

3. A door can be deleted from the door schedule. (T/F)

4. The schedule formatting only shows up when you place the schedule on a sheet. (T/F)

5. It is not possible to add the finish information (i.e., base finish, wall finish) to multiple rooms at one time. (T/F)

6. To modify the schedule view, click Edit in the *Properties Palette*. (T/F)

7. Use the _____ palette to adjust the various fields associated with each Room in a plan view.

8. Most door schedules are sorted by the _____ field.

9. You can select a different *Room Tag* via the *Type Selector*. (T/F)

10. A schedule is just another way of looking at the building information model, a tabular view of the project database. (T/F)

Notes:

Lesson 13
Residence: Photo-Realistic Rendering:

You will take a look at Autodesk® Revit® Architecture photo-realistic rendering abilities. Autodesk recently overhauled the rendering engine in Autodesk Revit Architecture completely, starting in the 2009 version, using their rendering technology known as mental ray®. This is similar technology to that used in their flagship rendering software, Autodesk 3ds Max®, which is used by the motion picture industry. The DVD has a video on rendering in Autodesk Revit Architecture.

Exercise 13-1:
Creating an Exterior Rendering

The first thing you will do is set up a view. You will use the *Camera* tool to do this. This becomes a saved view that can be opened at any time from the *Project Browser*. Several cameras can be added to a project.

Creating a Camera View:

1. Open the **First Floor** plan view and **Zoom to Fit** so that you can see the entire plan (or type ZF).

2. On the *QAT*, select the down-arrow next to the 3D view and then select **Camera**. See image to the right.

3. Click the mouse in the lower right corner of the screen to indicate the camera eye location (Figure 13-1.1).

   NOTE: *Before you click, Autodesk Revit Architecture tells you on the Status Bar it first wants the eye location, and you can set the eye level on the Options Bar.*

4. Next, click near the entry doors (Figure 13-1.1).

Autodesk Revit Architecture will automatically open a view window for the new camera. Take a minute to look at the view and make a mental note of what you see and do not see in the view (Figure 13-1.2).

5. Switch back to the **First Floor** plan view.

6. Adjust the camera, using its grips, to look similar to Figure 13-1.3.

   TIP: *If the camera is not visible in plan view, right click on the 3D view name in the Project Browser (3D View 1) and select Show Camera; do all this while still in the first floor plan view.*

FIGURE 13-1.1 Placing a Camera in plan view

FIGURE 13-1.2 Initial Camera view

FIGURE 13-1.3 Revised camera – plan

7. Now switch to **3D View 1** and adjust the **Crop Region** to look similar to **Figure 13-1.4**.

> ***FYI:*** *You may need to adjust the Camera location back in the plan view as well.*

This will be the view you render later in this exercise.

FIGURE 13-1.4 Revised camera – 3d View 1

Assigning Materials to Elements:

Materials are high quality images which represent the materials your building will be made of.

Typically, materials are added while the project is being modeled. For example, when you create a material, using the *Materials* command on the *Manage tab*, you can assign it to elements in the model at that time. Of course, you can go back and add or change it later. Next, you will change the material assigned for the brick chimney.

8. Switch to **First Floor** plan view.

9. Select the fireplace, not the mantle.

10. Click **Edit Type** on the *Properties Palette*.

11. Click on the **Exterior Material** *value*; notice the material selected for the exterior finish is **Masonry – Brick** (Figure 13-1.5).

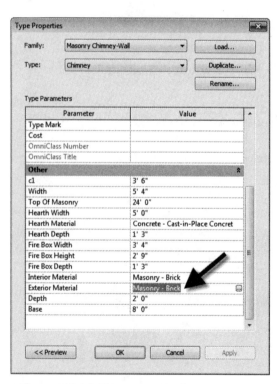

FIGURE 13-1.5 Chimney properties

12. Click the icon to the right of the label **Masonry – Brick**.

Now you will take a look that the definition of the material Masonry – Brick.

FYI: From the Manage *tab you can also select* **Materials**.

You are now in the *Materials* dialog. You should notice that a material is already selected. Next, you will select a different brick material.

FIGURE 13-1.6 Materials dialog

13. On the *Appearance* tab, notice the *Appearance Property Sets* tag appears on the left (Figure 13-1.6).

You can browse through the thumbnails and select any material in the list to be assigned to the *Masonry – Brick* material in Revit. The material does not have to be brick but would be confusing if something else where assigned to the *Masonry – Brick* material name.

14. Scroll down in the *Brick* category and select **Brick Non-Uniform Running Red**, and then click **OK** (Figure 13-1.6).

Notice the material preview is now updated.

15. Click **OK** to close the *Materials* and *Properties* dialog boxes.

Now, when you render, any object (wall, ceiling, etc.) that has the material "Masonry – Brick" associated with it, will have the red brick on them.

If you need more than one brick color, you simply create a new material in the *Material* dialog and assign that material to another element.

Project Location:

A first step in setting up a rendering is to specify the location of the project on the earth. This is important for accurate daylight studies.

16. Select **Manage → Project Location → Location**.

Location

17. In the *Project Address* field, enter **Minneapolis, MN**.

    a. You may also enter your location if you wish.

    b. It is even possible to enter the actual street address.

18. Press **Enter**.

FIGURE 13-1.8 Location Weather and Site dialog

You should now see an internet based map of your project location, complete with longitude and latitude (Figure 13-1.8).

19. Click **OK**.

Sun Settings:

Another step in preparing a rendering is to define the sun settings. You will explore the various options available.

20. Select **Manage → Settings → Additional Settings** (*drop-down list icon*) **→ Sun Settings**.

 Sun Settings

21. Make the following changes (Figure 13-1.9)

    a. Solar Study: **Still**
    b. **Uncheck** *Ground Plane at Level*.
    c. Select **Summer Solstice** on the left.
    d. Change the year to 2011.

FIGURE 13-1.9 Sun Settings dialog

22. Click **OK** to close the dialog

Setting Up the Environment:

You have limited options for setting up the building's environment. If you need more control than what is provided directly in Revit, you will need to use another program like Autodesk 3DS Max Design 2012, which is designed to work with Revit and can create extremely high quality renderings and animations; it even has daylighting functionality that helps to validate LEED® (Leadership in Environmental and Energy Design) requirements.

23. Switch to your camera view:
3D View 1.

24. Select the **Show Rendering Dialog** icon on
the *View Control Bar*, it looks like a teapot
(Figure 13-1.10).

FIGURE **13-1.10** Render dialog icon

*FYI: This icon is only visible when you are in a 3D view,
which is the same with the NavigationWheel and
ViewCube.*

The *Rendering* dialog box is now open (Figure 13-1.11).
This dialog box allows you to control the environmental
settings you are about to explore and actually create the
rendering.

25. In the *Lighting* section, click the
down-arrow next to *Scheme* to see
the options; select **Exterior: Sun
and Artifical** (Figure 13-1.12).

FIGURE **13-1.12** Lighting options

FIGURE **13-1.11** Rendering dialog

The lighting options are very simple choices; is your rendering an interior or exterior
rendering and is the light source *Sun, Artificial*, or both? You may have artificial lights, that is,
light fixtures like the ones you placed in the office, but still only desire a rendering solely
based on the light provided by the sun.

26. Also in the *Lighting* section, set the *Sun* to **Summer Solstice**.

*FYI: In the Sun Settings dialog box, Revit lets you set up various "scenes" which control time of day. Two
examples might be:*
- *Daytime, summer*
- *Nighttime, winter*

Looking back at Figure 13-1.9; you would click *Duplicate* and provide a name. This name
would then be available from the *Sun* drop-down list in the *Render* dialog box.

27. Click on the **Artificial Lighting** button.

You will now see a dialog similar to the one shown to the right (Figure 13-1.13).

You will see several 2x4 light fixtures. The light fixtures relate to the fixtures you inserted in the reflected ceiling plans. It is very convenient that you can place lights in the ceiling plan and have them ready to render whenever you need to (i.e., render and cast light into the scene!). Here you can group lights together so you can control which ones are on (e.g., exterior and interior lights).

FIGURE 13-1.13 Scene Lighting dialog

28. Click **Cancel** to close the *Artificial Lighting* dialog.

29. Click the down-arrow next to *Style* in the *Background* area (Figure 13-1.14).

30. Select **Sky: Few Clouds**.

31. Click the "**X**" to close the Rendering dialog box for now. Your settings will be saved.

FIGURE 13-1.14 Background style

Notice that for the background, one option is Image. This allows you to specify a photograph of the site, or one similar. It can prove difficult getting the perspective just right, but the end results can look as if you took a picture of the completed building.

Next, you will place a few trees into your rendering. You will adjust their exact location so they are near the edge of the framed rendering, so as not to cover too much of the building.

32. Switch to the **First Floor** plan view and select **Component** from the *Home* tab.

33. Pick **RPC Tree – Deciduous : Largetooth Aspen 25′** from the *Type Selector* on the *Properties Palette*.

> ***FYI:*** *If the tree is not listed in the Type Selector, click Load Family and load the* RPC Tree - Deciduous *tree family from the* Plantings *folder.*

34. Place four trees as shown in **Figure 13-1.15**; you will make one smaller in a moment.

FIGURE 13-1.15 First Floor – with trees added

35. Adjust the trees in plan view, reviewing the effects in the *3D View 1* view, so your 3D view is similar to Figure 13-1.16.

   TIP: Adjust the crop region if required.

36. In the **First Floor** plan view, select the tree that is shown smaller in **Figure 13-15**.

37. Click **Edit Type** on the *Properties Palette*.

38. Click **Duplicate** and enter the name: **RPC Tree – Deciduous : Largetooth Aspen 18′**.

39. Change the *Height* to **18′** (it is currently 25′) and then click **OK** to close the open dialog boxes.

The previous three steps allow you to have a little more variety in the trees being placed. Otherwise they would all be the same height, which is not very natural.

FIGURE 13-1.16 3D View 1 – with trees

The image above, and from here on out, will have the site added to it, which is based on the bonus chapter on the DVD. If you have time, **you are encouraged to add the site now**.

40. Open the **3D View 1** camera view.

41. Open the *Rendering* dialog.

42. Make sure the *Quality* is set to **Draft**.

> ***FYI:*** *The time to process the rendering increases significantly as the quality level and resolution are raised.*

43. Click **Render** from the *Rendering* dialog box.

You will see the following progress bar while Revit is processing the rendering (Figure 13-1.17).

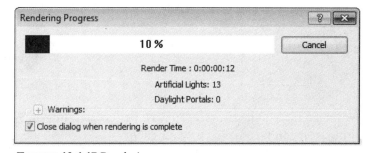

FIGURE 13-1.17 Rendering progress

After a few minutes, depending on the speed of your computer, you should have a rendered image similar to Figure 13-1.18 on the next page. You can increase the quality of the image by adjusting the quality setting in the *Render* dialog. However, these higher settings require substantially more time to generate the rendering. The last step before saving the Revit project file is to save the rendered image to a file.

FYI: Each time you make changes to the model, that are visible from that view, you will have to re-render the view to get an updated image. Depending on exactly how your view was set up, you may be able to see light from one of the light fixtures in the second floor office or see the stair and railing through the window, Revit can have the glazing in windows set to be transparent!

FIGURE 13-1.18 Rendered view

44. From the *Rendering* dialog select **Export**.

   FYI: The 'Save to Project' button saves the image within the Revit Project for placement on Sheets, this is convenient but does make the project size larger so you should delete the old ones when they are not needed anymore!

45. Select a *location* and provide a *file name*.

46. Set the *Save As* type: to **JPEG**.

47. Click **Save**.

The image file you just saved can now be inserted into MS Word or Adobe Photoshop for editing or it can be emailed to your client.

Design Options can also be Rendered:

You can render your design options in addition to the primary options. As mentioned before, you can copy a view and change its visibility settings to show specific design options or you can just change the settings for the current view. You will do that next.

48. In the **3D View 1** view, adjust the **View Properties** so the curved entry roof and taller entry windows are visible. Refer back to the *Design Options* section if necessary – page 9-25.

49. Switch to plan view and change the tree in front of the house to another option available from the *Type Selector* or the Library.

50. **Render** the image.

51. **Save** your project as **ex13-1.rvt**.

FIGURE 13-1.19 Rendered view

Notice the large tree casts shadows on the ground; you can also see reflections of the tree in the windows when the angle and lighting are right. Remember, the angle and location of the shadows are based on the time, date and location on the earth; if you change those settings, the shadows will change accordingly. You also need to set true North for the given site! This can be done via **Mange → Project Location → Rotate True North**.

As you can imagine, an image like this could really "sell" your design to the client. Revit makes the process to get to this point very easy compared to legacy CAD programs and techniques used prior to Revit.

Exercise 13-2:
Rendering an Isometric in Section

This exercise will introduce you to a view tool called *Section Box*. This tool is not necessarily related to renderings, but the two tools together can produce some interesting results.

Setting up the 3D View:

1. Open file ex13-1.rvt and **Save As ex13-2.rvt**.

2. Switch to the **Default 3D** view via the icon on the *QAT (not the 3D View 1 from Exercise 13-1)*.

3. Make sure nothing is selected so the *Properties Palette* shows the current view's properties. If something is selected, you can still see the current view's properties by selecting **3D View: {3D}** from the drop-down list below the *Type Selector*.

4. Activate the **Section Box** parameter and then click **Apply**.

You should see a box appear around your building, similar to Figure 13-2.1. When selected, you can adjust the size of the box with its grips. Anything outside the box is not visible. This is a great way to study a particular area of your building while in an isometric view. You will experiment with this feature next.

Section Box (shown selected)

Six grips to manipulate the Section Box – only visible while the *Section Box* is selected

FIGURE 13-2.1 3D view with Section Box activated

5. To practice using the **Section Box**, drag the grips around until your view looks similar to Figure 13-2.2.

   TIP: This may require the ViewCube tool as well, or hold Shift + drag the Wheel button on the mouse.

   a. Click and drag the grip from the top downward.

   b. Click and drag the grip for the East (right) face toward the West (left).

FIGURE 13-2.2 3D view with adjusted Section Box

Did you notice the grips look different? One grip looks like two arrows rather than a small square. You can still click on any part of the grip and drag it, but you can also single-click on one of the arrows to slightly adjust the section box in the direction the arrow points. This is similar to the nudge feature, when an element is selected and you use the arrows keys to move it just a little bit.

This creates a very interesting view of the First Floor plan. What client would have trouble understanding this drawing?

6. Now readjust the **Section Box** to look similar to **Figure 13-2.3**.

FIGURE 13-2.3 3D view

7. From the *Manage* tab, select **Sun Settings** and change the following *Sun* settings (Figure 13-2.4): **TIP:** *Set* Solar Study *to* Still *first and then click any named preset.*

    a. New name: **28 February 8am** (via Duplicate)

    b. Month: **2** (February)

    c. Day: **28**

    d. Time: **8:00am**

FYI: *Do not forget, without doing any rendering in Revit you can turn on the "real-time" shadows in any view. You can even turn on shadows in your 2D exterior elevation view (see below) for a great effect will little effort!*

FIGURE 13-2.4 Modified Sun Settings

8. Select the **Render** icon, select the *Scheme:*
   Exterior: Sun only, and then set *Sun* to:
   23 February 8am.

9. Set the *Background Style* to:
   Color.

10. Select the **Region** option and then adjust the
    "render region crop" that appears to indicate the
    area to be rendered.

    TIP: *This tool is nice for checking a material before rendering
    the entire building, which takes longer.*

The image will take a few minutes to render, again
depending on the speed of your computer. When
finished it should look similar to **Figure 13-2.5**. The
image looks much better on the screen or printed in
color.

As mentioned previously, you can increase the rendering quality settings to get much better
results, though it simply takes more time. Also, the higher quality images can be printed
larger without pixilation. If you have time, try changing the Quality to Medium or High and
the Resolution to 300dpi. Note the difference in the time to complete.

Adjusting an Element's Material:

As previously mentioned, most elements already have a material assigned to them. This is great because it allows you to quickly render your project to get some preliminary images. However, they usually need to be adjusted. You will do this next.

FIGURE 13-2.5 Rendered isometric view - draft settings selected

11. In the *Render* dialog, click the *Show Model* button at the bottom; the rendered view disappears. Close the *Render* dialog.

12. Select one of the cabinets in the kitchen.

13. Click the **Edit Type** button in the *Properties Palette*.

Notice the Cabinet Material parameter is set to **<By Category>** (Figure 13-2.6). You could change the material here for just the selected cabinet type; however, by setting a material to be *By Category* you can quickly change the material for all the cabinets at one time, without having to select every cabinet.

Sun Path

It is possible to turn on the feature called Sun Path. This shows the path of the sun over a day and a year. This is accessed from the View Control Bar while in a 3D view.

Once on, you can click and drag the sun along its daily or yearly path!

---

14. **Close** the *Type Properties* dialog.

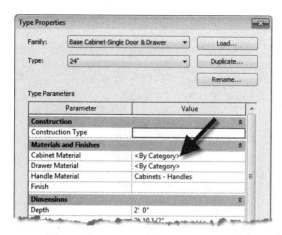

FIGURE 13-2.6 Cabinet properties

The next step will open the dialog box which controls color, line weight, line pattern and material, for both hatching and rendering representations. This is for the entire project, with the exception of any overrides added per view via VV.

15. Select **Manage → Settings → Object Styles**.

16. Expand the **Casework** category (Figure 13-2.7).

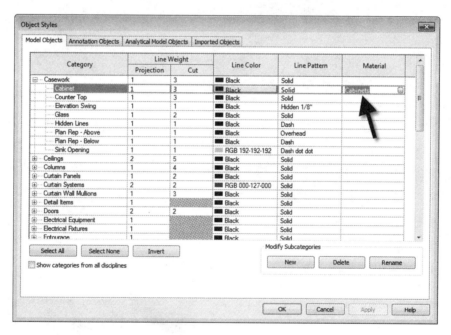

FIGURE 13-2.7 Object Styles dialog

The *Cabinet* subcategory has a material assigned to it called **Cabinets**.

17. Click on **Cabinets** in the *Material* column, and then click the "**...**" button that appears to the right.

You are now in the *Materials* dialog box, where you can create and edit *Materials*.

18. Select **Cabinets** from the *Name* list; it should already be selected (you may have to select the *Materials* tab to see this).

19. Change the *Appearance* material to:
    Cherry - Natural Low Gloss (Figure 13-2.8).

    TIP: Select the category label Wood *on the left first.*

FIGURE 13-2.8 Materials dialog – Render Appearance tab

20. Click **OK** to close the open dialog boxes.

21. You can now re-render the 3D view and see the results.

22. **Save** your project as ex **13-2.rvt**.

    TIP: While in the 3D view with the Section Box active, you can zoom in to an area, just like you can in other views, and render that enlarged area (just check the "Region" option in the Render dialog). The larger area will have more detail; for example, you can see the wood grain on the cabinets. Similarly, you can change the material for the counter top, faucet, dishwasher, etc.

Exercise 13-3:
Creating an Interior Rendering

Creating an interior rendering is very similar to an exterior rendering. This exercise will walk through the steps involved in creating a high quality interior rendering.

Setting Up the Camera View:

1. Open ex13-2.rvt and **Save As ex13-3.rvt**.

2. Open the **First Floor** plan view.

3. Select the **Camera** tool from the *QAT*.

4. Place the *Camera* as shown in **Figure 13-3.1**.

FIGURE **13-3.1** Camera placed – Kitchen

Revit uses default heights for the camera and the target. These heights are based on the current level's floor elevation plus the eye height of an average height person. These reference points can be edited via the camera properties.

Revit will automatically open the newly generated camera view. Your view should look similar to **Figure 13-3.2**.

FIGURE 13-3.2 Initial interior camera view

5. Using the **Crop Region** rectangle, modify the view to look like **Figure 13-3.3**; select it and then drag the grips.

6. Uncheck *Far Clip Active* in the *Properties Palette*. Copy the two trees in the back of the house into a position so they can be seen through the window over the sink.

    TIP: *You will have to switch to plan view to adjust the camera's depth of view to see the trees.* REMINDER: *If the camera does not show in plan view, right-click on the camera view label in the Project Browser, while in plan view, and select* Show Camera. *You may need to switch between the plan and camera views several times to adjust the trees so they are visible through the windows.*

7. Switch back to **First Floor** plan to see the revised *Camera* view settings.

Notice the field of view triangle is wider based on the changes to the **Crop Region** in the camera view (Figure 13-3.4).

FIGURE 13-3.3 Modified interior camera

Camera's depth of view line – adjust via center grip

FIGURE 13-3.4 Modified camera – First Floor

FIGURE 13-3.5 Camera properties

8. Select the *Camera*.

9. Make sure the **Eye Elevation** is **5'-6"** (Figure 13-3.5).

Notice the other settings for the camera, these are the properties for the 3D view itself; changing the *Target Elevation* would cause the camera to look up at the ceiling, or down at the floor depending on the value entered.

10. Click **Apply**.

The vertical lines are distorted due to the wide field of view, crop region. This is similar to what a camera with a 10-15mm lens would get in the finished building.

Creating the Rendering:

Next you will render the interior kitchen view.

11. Create a new item in *Sun Settings* dialog as shown below (Figure 13-3.6).

> *Name*: Kitchen
> *Azimuth*: 302.00
> *Altitude*: 34.00

FIGURE 13-3.6 Sun Settings

You just created a "fake" sun angle to make the rendering look better for presentation purposes. This may be useful if the exact north is not known or the designer wants to leverage a little artistic freedom.

12. Select **Show Rendering Dialog** from the *View Control Bar*.

13. Set the *Scheme* to **Interior: Sun only**.

14. Set the *Sun* to **Kitchen**, created on the previous page.

15. Click **Render** to begin the rendering process.

This will take several minutes depending on the speed of your computer. When finished, the view should look similar to **Figure 13-3.7**.

16. Click **Export** from the *Rendering* dialog box to save the image to a file on your hard drive. Name the file **Kitchen.jpg** (jpeg file format).

You can now open the *Kitchen.jpg* file in Adobe Photoshop or insert it into a MS Word type program, or equivalent, to manipulate or print.

To toggle back to the normal hidden view, select **Show the Model** from the *Rendering* dialog box.

There are many things you can do to make the rendering look even better. You can add interior light fixtures and props (e.g., pictures on the wall, items on the counter top, and lawn furniture in the yard). Once you add interior lights, you can adjust the Sun Setting to nighttime and then render a night scene.

> ***TIP:*** *Setting the Output to Printer rather than Screen allows you to generate a higher resolution image. Thus, between the Quality setting and the Output setting you can create an extremely high quality rendering, but it might take hours if not days to process!*

Revit also gives you the ability to set a material to be self-illuminating. This will allow you to make a button on the dishwasher look like it is lit up or, if applied to the glass on the range door, like the light in the oven is on! You can also set a lamp shade to glow when a light source has been defined under it so it looks more realistic.

FIGURE 13-3.7 Rendered view

You can quickly add another camera view to look at the other half of the kitchen. The ability to stretch the *Crop Region* allows you to create interesting views like the one below, which is really more like a panoramic view than a traditional camera view (Figure 13-3.8).

FIGURE 13-3.8 Another rendered view

17. **Save** your project as **13-3.rvt**.

Realistic Display Setting:

In addition to *Shade* and *Hidden Line* display settings you can also select *Realistic*. This will show the *Render Appearance* materials on your building without the need to do a full rendering. However, the shades and shadows are not nearly as realistic as a full rendering.

This is a great way to get an idea on how the materials look but you will find it best to minimize the use of this setting as Revit will run much slower.

Exercise 13-4:
Adding People to the Rendering

Revit provides a few free RPC people to add to your renderings; RPC stands for Rich Photorealistic Content. These are files from a popular company that provides 3D photo content for use in renderings (http://www.archvision.com). You can buy additional content in groupings such as college students, or per item. In addition to people, they offer items like cars, plants, trees, office equipment, etc.

Loading Content into the Current Project

1. Open ex13-3.rvt and **Save As 13-4.rvt**.

2. Switch to the **First Floor** plan view.

3. Select the **Component** tool from the *Home* tab.

4. Click the **Load Family** button on the *Ribbon*.

5. Browse to the **Entourage** folder and select both the **RPC Male** and **RPC Female** files, using the Ctrl key to select both at once, and click **Open** to load them.

6. Place one **Male** and one **Female**, specified via the *Type Selector*, as shown in **Figure 13-4.1**.

FIGURE **13-4.1** Kitchen – RPC people added

The line in the circle (Figure 13-4.1) represents the direction a person is looking. You simply *Rotate* the object to make adjustments. The image below shows the RPC people that can be placed in your project. Notice the two families each have multiple types.

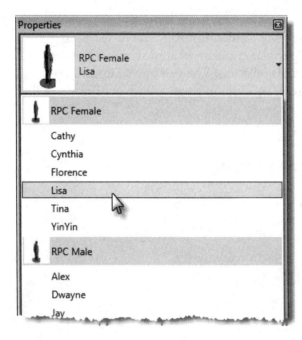

7. Switch to your interior kitchen camera view.

8. Set the *Quality* setting to **Medium**.

9. Set the *Scheme* to **Kitchen**.

10. Click **Render**.

Additional RPC content can be purchased from ArchVision via their website: www.archvision.com. They also have a yearly subscription option which provides hundreds of trees, cars and people to add to your renderings.

FIGURE 13-4.2 Type Selector – Properties Palette

FIGURE 13-4.3 Interior kitchen view with people added

Your rendering should now have people in it and look similar to **Figure 13-4.4**. Notice how the people cast shadows; remember the only light source is the sunlight coming through the two windows and the glass door. If you want to change the people, simply select them and pick from the *Type Selector*.

Adding people and other "props" gives your model a sense of scale and makes it look a little more realistic. After all, architecture is for people. These elements can be viewed from any angle. Try a new camera view from another angle to see how the people adjust to match the view and perspective; see Figure 13-4.3, front of the female model versus the side view below.

Try adding one of the RPC vehicles to the exterior and render the exterior of the building again.

FIGURE 13-4.4 Interior kitchen view with people added

11. **Save** your project as **ex13-4.rvt**.

FYI: As with other families or components, the more you add to your project, the bigger your project file becomes. It is a good idea to load only the items you need and delete the unused items via the Project Browser and the Purge Unused tool. Your project should be about 10.5MB at this point in the tutorial.

Self-Exam:

The following questions can be used as a way to check your knowledge of this lesson. The answers can be found at the bottom of the page.

1. Creating a camera adds a view to the *Project Browser* list. (T/F)

2. Rendering materials are defined in Revit's *Materials* dialog box. (T/F)

3. After inserting a light fixture, you need to adjust several settings before rendering to get light from the fixture. (T/F)

4. You can adjust the season, which affects how the trees are rendered. (T/F)

5. Use the _____ _____ tool to hide a large portion of the model.

Review Questions:

The following questions may be assigned by your instructor as a way to assess your knowledge of this section. Your instructor has the answers to the review questions.

1. Draft renderings can be printed very large with no pixilation. (T/F)

2. You cannot get accurate lighting based on day/month/location. (T/F)

3. Adding components, i.e. families, to your project does not make the project file bigger. (T/F)

4. Creating photo-realistic renderings can take a significant amount of time for your computer to process. (T/F)

5. The RPC people can only be viewed from one angle. (T/F)

6. The RPC components do not cast shadows (T/F).

7. Adjust the _____ _____ to make more of a perspective view visible.

8. You use the _____ tool to load and insert RPC people.

9. You can adjust the Eye Elevation of the camera via the camera's _____.

10. What is the file size of (completed) Exercise 13-4? _____ MB

Lesson 14
Residence: Construction Documents Set:

This lesson will look at bringing everything you have drawn thus far together onto sheets. The sheets, once set up, are ready for plotting. Basically, you place the various views you have created on sheets. The scale for each view is based on the scale you set while drawing that view, which is important to have set correctly because it affects the text and symbol sizes. When finished setting up the sheets, you will have a set of drawings ready to print, individually or all at once. The DVD has a video on creating sheets and sheet lists.

Exercise 14-1:
Setting up a Sheet

Creating a Sheet View:

1. Open ex13-4.rvt and **Save As** 14-1.rvt.

2. Select **View → Sheet Composition → Sheet**.

Next Autodesk® Revit® Architecture will prompt you for a *Titleblock* to use. The template file you started with has two *titleblock families* from which to choose: 11 x 17 and 22 x 34 (Figure 14-1.1).

3. Select the **D 22x34 Horizontal** titleblock and click **OK**.

That's it; you have created a new sheet that is ready to have views and/or schedules placed on it!

NOTE: *A new view shows up in the Project Browser under the heading:* Sheets. *Once you get an entire CD set ready, this list can be very long.*

Autodesk Revit Architecture also lets you create placeholder sheets which allow you to add sheets to the sheet index without the need to have a sheet show up in the *Project Browser*. This is helpful if a consultant, such as a food service designer, is not using Autodesk Revit Architecture. This feature allows you to add those sheets to the sheet index. Placeholder sheets can only be added in the sheet list schedule by using the *New Row* tool on the *Ribbon*. Once a placeholder sheet exists, it can be turned into a real sheet by selecting from the lower list in the dialog to the left.

FIGURE 14-1.1 Select a Titleblock

FIGURE 14-1.2 Initial Titleblock view

4. **Zoom in** to the sheet number area (lower right corner).

5. Adjust the text to look similar to **Figure 14-1.3**. Click on the text and edit it; make sure *Modify* is selected first.

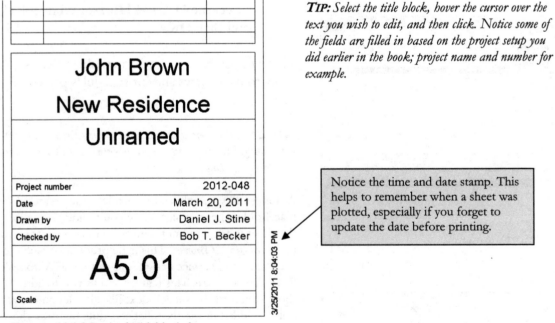

TIP: Select the title block, hover the cursor over the text you wish to edit, and then click. Notice some of the fields are filled in based on the project setup you did earlier in the book; project name and number for example.

Notice the time and date stamp. This helps to remember when a sheet was plotted, especially if you forget to update the date before printing.

FIGURE 14-1.3 Revised Titleblock data

6. **Zoom out** so you can see the entire sheet (type ZF).

7. With the sheet fully visible, click and drag the **Living Room - East** label, under *Elevations (Interior elevations)*, from the *Project Browser* onto the sheet view. Let go of the mouse button once it is within the drawing window; do not click yet.

You will see a box that represents the extents of the view you are placing on the current sheet. If the box is larger than the sheet, this means the *View Scale* is to a scale that is too large. You would need to open the view and adjust the *View Scale*.

8. Move the *Viewport* around until the box is in the upper-right corner of the sheet (this can be repositioned later at any time) and click to place.

Your view should look similar to **Figure 14-1.4**.

FIGURE 14-1.4 Sheet with Living Room view placed on it

9. Click the mouse in a white area, not on any lines, to deselect the *Living Room - East* view. Notice the extents box goes away.

FIGURE 14-1.5 Drawing title

10. **Zoom in** on the lower left corner to view the drawing identification symbol that Revit automatically added (Figure 14-1.5).

NOTE: Each drawing placed on a sheet automatically gets a number, starting with one. The next drawing you add will be number two.

The view name, from the *Project Browser*, is listed as the drawing title. This is another reason to rename the elevation and section views as you create them.

Also notice that the drawing scale is listed. Again, this comes from the *View Scale* setting for the *Living Room - East* view.

As you can see, if you added furniture to the living room, the furniture shows up; normally this would be turned off. You can turn these off using the same technique covered later in this chapter for the trees in the exterior elevations.

Setting up the Floor Plans:

Setting up floor plans is easy; actually, they are already set up from the template you started with.

11. From the *Sheets* section in the *Project Browser*, double-click on the sheet named **A1 – First Floor Plan** to open it.

As you can see, the floor plan is already set up on a sheet. Again, a few things can be turned off (i.e., trees, RPC People) per the techniques covered next. You would also want to move the exterior elevation tags closer to the building so they are within the title block, if they are not already.

12. Adjust the location of the plan view on the sheet if needed. Click and drag to move it.

13. Change the sheet number to **A2.01**, and then close the First Floor Plan, *Sheet*.

Setting up the Exterior Elevations:

Next you will set up the exterior elevations. Again, the sheets are already set up but the views have not been placed on the sheets like the floor plans have.

14. Open Sheet **A6 – Elevations**, and drag the *South* elevation view onto the sheet. Place the drawing near the bottom, and centered on the sheet.

Your drawing should look similar to Figure 14-1.6.

FIGURE 14-1.6 South exterior elevation

Next, you will turn off the trees in the *South* view. Normally you would turn them off in all views. However, you will only turn them off in the *South* view to show that you can control visibility per view on a sheet.

15. In the sheet view, click on the *South* exterior elevation view to select it; the outer extents rectangle is called the *viewport* (Figure 14-1.6).

16. Now **right-click** and select **Activate View** from the pop-up menu.

At this point you are in the viewport and can make changes to the project model to control visibility, which is what you will do next.

17. Turn on **View Cropping** and **Show Crop Region** on the *View Control Bar*; adjust the crop region to minimize the space needed by the view on the sheet. When finished, hide the crop region.

18. Make sure nothing is selected. With nothing selected in the view, the *Properties Palette* is displaying the activated view's properties, just as if you were in the view and not the sheet.

19. Click the **Edit** button next to *Visibility/Graphics Overrides*.

20. In the *Visibility* dialog **uncheck Planting**.

21. Close the open dialog box.

22. Right-click anywhere in the drawing area and select **Deactivate View** from the pop-up menu.

Now the trees are turned off for the *South* elevation, if you would have had another elevation view on this same sheet, the trees would still be visible for that view.

23. Add the **North** elevation to the **A7 – Elevations** *Sheet.*

> *TIP: You may need to switch to the North view and turn on the* Crop *and* Crop Display *icons on the* View Control Bar *to make the area placed on the sheet smaller so it will fit; when finished, turn off* Crop Display *but leave* Crop View *turned on. Or use the* Activate View *option just covered.*

Now you will stop for a moment and notice that Revit is automatically referencing the drawings as you place them on sheets.

24. Switch to **First Floor** (Figure 14-1.7).

Notice in Figure 14-1.7 that the number A6 represents the sheet number that the drawing can be found on. The number one (1) is the drawing number to look for on sheet A6. The empty tag is the enlarged elevation view you set up earlier in the book; it has not been placed on a sheet yet so it is not filled in.

FIGURE 14-1.7 First Floor – elevation tag filled-in

Setting up Sections:

25. Open *Sheet* **A8 – Building Sections** and place *Cross Section 1.*

26. Open *Sheet* **A9 – Building Sections** and place the *Longitudinal Section* view on the *Sheet.*

27. Switch to *First Floor* plan view and zoom into the area shown in Figure 14-1.9.

FIGURE 14-1.8 A9 – Building Sections sheet

Notice, again, that the reference bubbles are automatically filled in when the referenced view is placed on a sheet. If the drawing is moved to another sheet, the reference bubbles are automatically updated.

You can also see in Figure 14-1.8 that the reference bubbles on the building sections are filled in.

FIGURE 14-1.9 First Floor – Section ref's filled in

Set up the Remaining Sheets:

Next you set up sheets for the remaining views that have yet to be placed on a sheet, except for the 3D views.

28. Add the remaining views to the appropriate sheets; if one does not exist you can create a new sheet.

Question: On a large project with hundreds of views, how do I know for sure if I have placed every view on a sheet?

Answer: Revit has a feature, called *Browser Organization,* that can hide all the views that have been placed on a sheet. You will try this next.

Take a general look at the *Project Browser* to see how many views are listed.

29. Select **View → Window → User Interface** *(drop-down)* **→ Browser Organization…**

30. On the *Views* tab, click the checkbox next to **not on sheets** (Figure 14-1.10).

31. Click **OK**.

32. Notice the list in the *Project Browser* is now smaller (Figure 14-1.11).

FIGURE 14-1.10 Browser Organization dialog

The *Project Browser* now only shows drawing views that have not been placed onto a sheet. Of course, you could have a few views that do not need to be placed on a sheet, but this feature will help eliminate errors. Also notice the label at the top, *Views (not on sheets)*; this tells you what mode or filter the *Project Browser* is in.

Next you will reset the *Project Browser.*

33. Open *Browser Organization* again and check the box next to **all** and click **OK** to close the dialog box.

> *TIP: You can also select the title* Views *at the top of the Project Browser and toggle between filter types via the Type Selector.*

FIGURE 14-1.11 Project Browser

Sheets with Design Options:

Finally, you will set up a sheet to show the two *Design Options*.

34. Create a *Sheet* named **Entry Options** and number it **A100**.

35. Place both *Entry – Option 2* 3D views on the new sheet and change the scale to ⅛" = 1'-0".

    TIP: *Select the placed view and change the scale in the Properties Palette.*

36. **Save** your project as **ex14-1.rvt**.

Each 3D view has its *Visibility* modified to show the desired *Design Options*. When a view is placed on a sheet, those settings are preserved.

Figure 14-1.12 Entry Options Sheet; two views with Design Options added

Exercise 14-2:
Sheet Index

Revit has the ability to create a *Sheet List* (or sheet index) automatically. This feature uses the same schedule creation interface previously covered. Whenever a sheet is added or removed from the project, this *Sheet List* will automatically update. You can even use the *Sheet List* to make changes to the sheet. For example, if you noticed a few sheets were not all uppercase you could change them in the *Sheet List* and the sheet itself would update as it represents the same information. You will study this feature now.

Creating a Sheet List View

 Sheet List

1. Open ex14-1.rvt and **Save As** ex14-2.

2. Select **View → Create → Schedules** *(down-arrow)* **→ Sheet List**.

You are now in the *Sheet List Properties* dialog box. Here you specify which fields you want in the sheet index and how to sort the list (Figure 14-2.1).

3. Add **Sheet Number** and **Sheet Name** to the right (click *Add →*).

4. Click **OK**.

FIGURE 14-2.1 Sheet List Properties Dialog; sheet number and name added

Now you should notice that the *Sheet Names* are cut off because the column is not wide enough (Figure 14-2.2). You will adjust this next.

5. Move your cursor over the right edge of the *Sheet List* table and click-and-drag to the right until you can see the entire name (Figure 14-2.2).

Sheet List	
Sheet Number	Sheet Name
A2.01	First Floor
A2	Second Flo
A3	First Floor
A4	Second Flo
A5	Roof Plan
A6	Elevations
A7	Elevations
A8	Building Se
A9	Building Se
A10	Wall Sectio
A11	Wall Sectio
A12	Details
A13	Interior Elev
A14	Interior Det
A15	Schedules
C1	Site Plan
S0	Foundation
S1	First Floor
S2	Second Flo
S3	Roof Frami
A0	Basement
E0	Basement
E1	First Floor
E2	Second Flo
A5.01	Unnamed
A100	Entry Optio

FIGURE 14-2.2 Sheet List view; notice sheet names are cut off in right column

Sheet List	
Sheet Number	Sheet Name
A2.01	First Floor Plan
A2	Second Floor Plan
A3	First Floor Reflected Ceiling Plan
A4	Second Floor Reflected Ceiling Plan
A5	Roof Plan
A6	Elevations
A7	Elevations
A8	Building Sections
A9	Building Sections
A10	Wall Sections
A11	Wall Sections
A12	Details
A13	Interior Elevations
A14	Interior Details
A15	Schedules
C1	Site Plan
S0	Foundation Plan
S1	First Floor Framing Plan
S2	Second Floor Framing
S3	Roof Framing
A0	Basement Plan
E0	Basement Electrical Plan
E1	First Floor Electrical
E2	Second Floor Electrical
A5.01	Unnamed
A100	Entry Options

FIGURE 14-2.3 Sheet List view; sheet names are now visible

Adjusting Which Sheets Show Up in the List:

Looking at the *Sheet List* (Figure 14-2.3), you decide to remove the *Entry design options* sheet (i.e., sheet A100) from the list as it is not part of the construction document set.

As with other schedules, this is live data which is directly connected to the model. If you change a sheet number here, the number will change throughout the project. If you delete a number (i.e., a row), Revit will delete the sheet from the project.

You will look at the option that allows you to remove a sheet from the list without deleting the sheet.

6. Right-click on sheet **A100** in the sheet list and select **Delete Row(s)**. You will NOT actually delete this sheet, so <u>do not click **OK**</u>.

You will get a warning stating the sheet will be deleted and what you should do if you only want to remove the sheet from the *Sheet List*.

7. Click **Cancel**.

> Revit
>
> This will delete the 1 selected sheet(s).
>
> If you don't want to delete the sheets from the project, but only exclude them from the sheet list, you can edit the properties of each sheet that should not be listed and set Appears In Sheet List to No.
>
> OK   Cancel

8. Select *Sheet* **A100 – Entry Options** in the *Project Browser* and click **Properties**.

9. Uncheck **Appears In Sheet List** (Figure 14-2.4) and then click **Apply**.

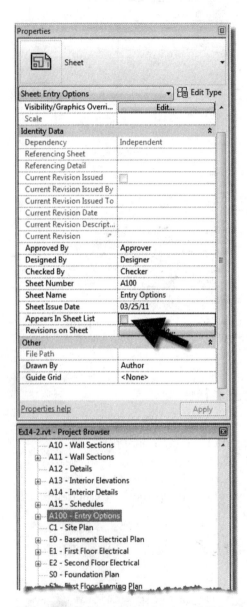

Notice the *Sheet* was removed from the *Sheet List* view, but is still in the project.

10. In the *Sheet List*, right-click on sheet **A13 Interior Elevations** and select **Delete Row(s)** from the menu.

11. Click **OK**.

Not only was the sheet removed from the *Sheet List*, it was also deleted from the project. However, any views placed on a sheet are not deleted from the project. Next, you will renumber a sheet via the *Sheet List*.

12. Click in the cell with the sheet number **A5.01** and change the number to read **A13**.

Now an existing sheet has been renumbered and so has all the detail, elevation and section bubbles that point to this sheet.

13. In the *Properties Palette*, click the **Edit...** button next to **Sorting/Grouping**.

14. Set *Sort By* to **Sheet Number**.

15. Click **OK** to close the open dialog box.

Now the sheets should be sorted correctly, including the sheet you just renumbered.

FIGURE 14-2.4 Properties for sheet A100

TIP: It is possible to create a custom parameter and sort the sheets using the information entered there. This allows you to place the sheets in any order you wish. Usually the "C" (i.e., civil) sheets are before the "A" (i.e., architectural) sheets. So, for example, all the "C" sheets could have the value "02" entered in the custom parameter, and the "A" sheets could all have the value "03" entered. Then, in sorting and grouping, you would sort by your custom parameter and then by sheet number. You can create the custom parameter on the Fields *tab in the* Sheet List *schedule (Figure 14-2.1) by clicking the* Add Parameter *button.*

Setting up a Title Sheet:

Now you will create a title sheet to place your sheet index on.

16. Create a new sheet:
    a. *Number:* **T1**
    b. *Name:* **Title Sheet**

17. From the *Schedules/Quantities* category of the *Project Browser,* place the view named ***Sheet List*** on the *Title Sheet* via drag-and-drop.

18. With the schedule selected on the sheet, drag the column grips so each row is only one line. (Figure 14-2.5).

19. Create a new text style named **1″ Arial**, and adjust the settings accordingly.

> ***TIP:*** *Select the* Text *tool, click* Edit Type *and then* Duplicate.

Sheet List	
Sheet Number	Sheet Name
A0	Basement Plan
A2	Second Floor Plan
A2.01	First Floor Plan
A3	First Floor Reflected Ceiling Plan
A4	Second Floor Reflected Ceiling Plan
A5	Roof Plan
A6	Elevations
A7	Elevations
A8	Building Sections
A9	Building Sections
A10	Wall Sections
A11	Wall Sections
A12	Details
A13	Unnamed
A14	Interior Details
A15	Schedules
C1	Site Plan
E0	Basement Electrical Plan
E1	First Floor Electrical
E2	Second Floor Electrical
S0	Foundation Plan
S1	First Floor Framing Plan
S2	Second Floor Framing
S3	Roof Framing
T1	Title Sheet

FIGURE 14-2.5 Adjusting column width

20. Add large text across the top of the sheet that reads "NEW RESIDENCE FOR JOHN BROWN" (Figure 14-2.6).

Next, you will place one of your rendered images that you saved to file, which is a raster image. If you have not created a raster image, you should refer back to Lesson 13 and create one now. Otherwise, you can use any BMP or JPG file on your hard drive if necessary.

If you used the *Save to Project* feature, you can simply drag one of the images listed under *Renderings* from the *Project Browser.* The interior kitchen rendering was added to the title sheet using this method. Here you can see Revit has added a *Drawing Title* tag beneath the image, which would allow you to reference this image from another location.

21. Select **Insert → Import → Image**.

22. Browse to your JPG or BMP raster image file, select it and click **Open** to place the Image.

Image

23. Click on your *Title Sheet* to locate the image; use the corner grips to resize the image.

Your sheet should look similar to Figure 14-2.6.

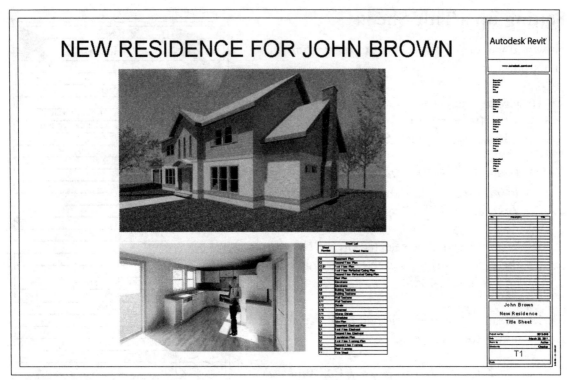

FIGURE 14-2.6 Sheet View: Title Sheet with drawing list, text and image added

24. Select **Insert → Import → Manage Images**.

You are now in the *Raster Image* dialog which gives you a little information about the image and allows you to delete it from the project (Figure 14-2.7).

FYI: You can delete a view from a Sheet without deleting the view from the project. Also, you can only place a view on one sheet; you would have to duplicate the view in order to have that view repeated.

TIP: You can use the standard modification tools on raster images (e.g., Move, Copy, Rotate and Resize). You can also control the draw order to make sure your leaders pointing at the image show up.

25. Click **OK** to close the ***Manage Images*** dialog.

FIGURE 14-2.7 Manage Images dialog

Exporting a 3D DWFx File:

The *3D DWFx* file is an easy way to share your project file with others without the need to give them your editable Revit file or the need for the recipient to have Revit installed.

> **NOTE:** *You can download Revit, from Autodesk's website, and run it in viewer mode. It's free – full Revit with no save functionality.*

The 3D DWFx file is much smaller in file size than the original Revit file. Also, *Autodesk Design Review* is a free DWF viewer which can be downloaded for free from www.autodesk.com.

26. Switch to your **Default 3D** view.

You must be in a 3D view for the 3D DWF feature to work. If you are not in a 3D view, you will get 2D DWF files:

27. Select **Application Menu → Export → DWF**.

 DWF/DWFx
Creates DWF or DWFx files.

28. Click the **Next** button in the lower right (Figure 14-2.8); specify a file name and location for the DWF file and then click **Save**.

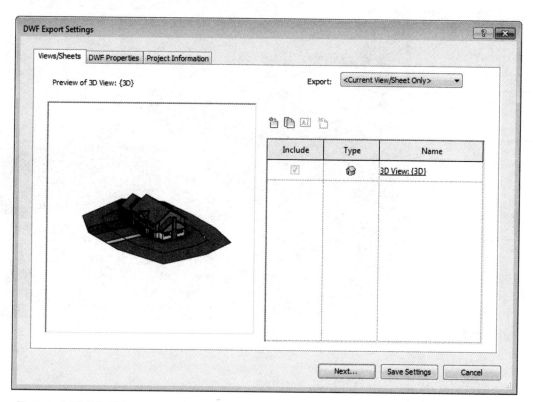

FIGURE 14-2.8 DWF export options

That's all you need to do to create the file. Now you can email it to the client or a product representative to get a cost estimate on windows, for example.

The 3D DWF file is a meager 300Kb whereas the Revit project file is 11 MB. Your file sizes will vary slightly based on factors like the number of families loaded. In many cases, networks and servers are set up so they cannot receive large files via email, so the 3D DWF is very useful.

The DWF viewer should have been installed with Revit. You can access it from *Start → All Programs → Autodesk → Autodesk Design Review 2012*. You can zoom, orbit and select objects. Notice the information displayed on the left when the front door is selected (see image below). Also notice, under the *Windows* heading; the sizes and quantities are listed.

> ***TIP:*** *Autodesk Design Review 2012 is a free download from Autodesk. This is their full-featured DWF viewer and markup utility!*

This DWF file can also be used in conjunction with **Autodesk Quantity Takeoff** to develop cost estimates for your project. See Autodesk's website for more information.

FIGURE 14-2.9 3D DWF in Autodesk Design Review

29. **Save** your project as **ex14-2.rvt.**

The assignment:

Using the information learned in previous sections, sketch the two-dimensional elevations on the grid provided. Don't forget to add the slope arrows in the roof plan view.

Also, make sure you use the proper line weights: heavy lines for the perimeter of masses that are closer and lighter lines for items that are "deeper" into the view.

Tear out each page, add your name and date in the space provided and turn them in to your instructor. You might want to make copies of the page for practice and then turn in the final version on the original page from the book.

The first exercise is shown completed so you know what is expected. You may have light reference lines, but must be distinct from the actual drawings being created.

This section will not incorporate any roof overhangs. Additionally, all roof slopes are to be 12/12, which is a 45 degree line in elevation.

Remember that the following is how the view names are related between architectural drawings and mechanical drawings:

> Roof plan = top view
> South elevation = front view
> East elevation = side view

Notes:

Exercise A3-1

Sketch the *Roof Plan* (top), *South elevation* (front) and *East elevation* (side) of the building shown. Use the provided 5'x5' grid space. See pages A-12 and 13 for typical information needed to complete this problem. <u>This problem is completed as an example.</u>

Notes:

Appendix A
Engineering Graphics:

This appendix is meant to complement the lessons learned in this book. Several exercises are provided to help the student learn to make to most out of both digital and "analog" design techniques and develop a three-dimensional vocabulary.

Appendix A-1:
Introduction

What is Engineering Graphics?

Engineering Graphics is the philosophy and process of describing and documenting three-dimensional objects via 2D drawings. The academic study of this concept is often limited to mechanical parts (e.g., gears, bolts, nuts, etc.). Furthermore, within the mechanical engineering world, many specific standards have been developed to document these mechanical parts so they can be manufactured by machine shops. Many of these standards are not really applicable to architectural design and documentation so they will not be covered in this appendix; rather, just the applicable, fundamental concepts of engineering graphics (related to architecture) will be studied by the reader.

Appendix A-2:
Engineering Graphics

The simple object below describes the standard views used to describe the 2D drawings that are created for a 3D object. Looking at the 2D elevations below and then at the 3D object above you should be able to visualize how each represents the object under consideration. Of course, things can get more difficult with complex objects.

The exercises on the following pages are provided as a way to help you to think three-dimensionally; for some it just comes naturally and for others it takes a little practice. One thing you will find interesting with the exercises that follow is that totally different-looking objects can have identical 2D views (i.e., the linework for the top elevation is exactly the same).

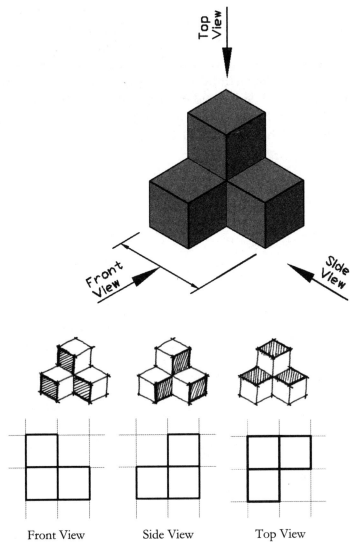

Front View   Side View   Top View

DIRECTIONS: Match the small top, front and side views with the proper isometric view (i.e., the two large views). Write the *view type* (top, front or side) and the *isometric name* that view corresponds to (one example shown on this page). Place a star on duplicate views for both isometric views.

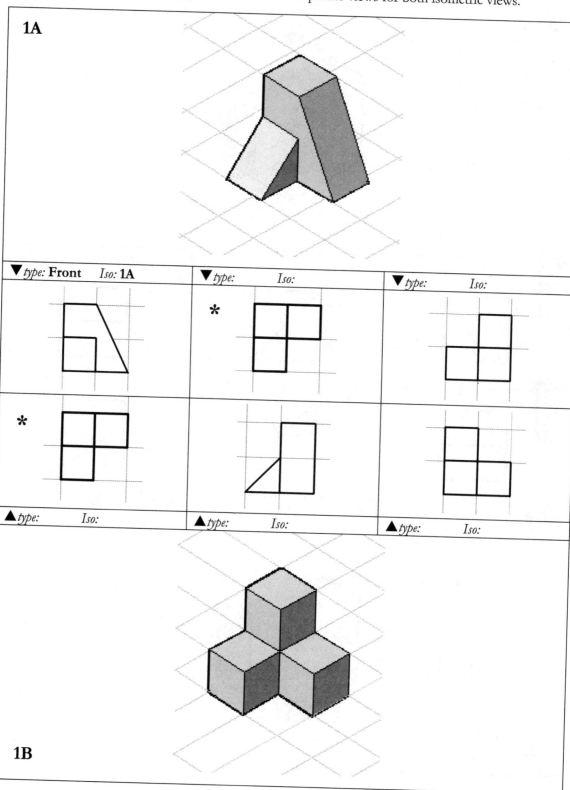

1A

▼*type:* **Front**   *Iso:* **1A**   ▼*type:*   *Iso:*   ▼*type:*   *Iso:*

▲*type:*   *Iso:*   ▲*type:*   *Iso:*   ▲*type:*   *Iso:*

1B

DIRECTIONS: Match the small top, front and side views with the proper isometric view (i.e., the two large views). Write the *view type* (top, front or side) and the *isometric name* that view corresponds to.

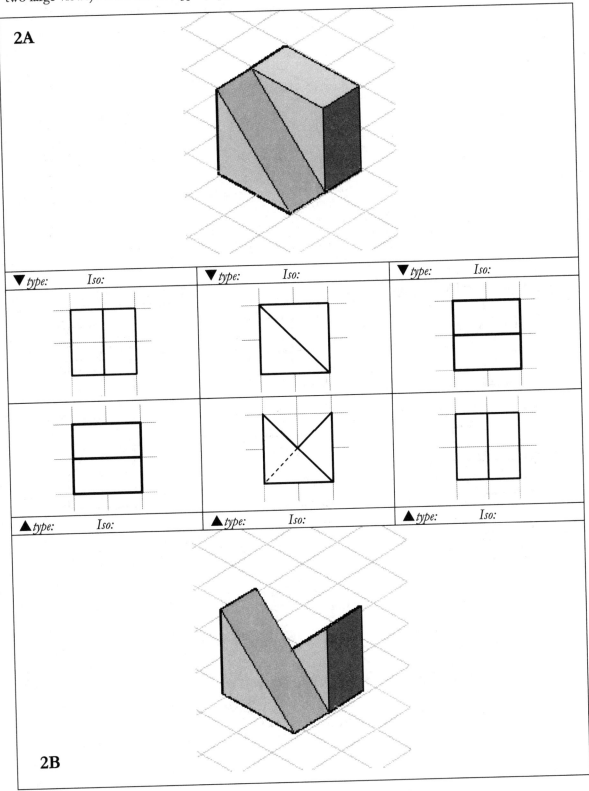

DIRECTIONS: Match the small top, front and side views with the proper isometric view (i.e., the two large views). Write the *view type* (top, front or side) and the *isometric name* that view corresponds to.

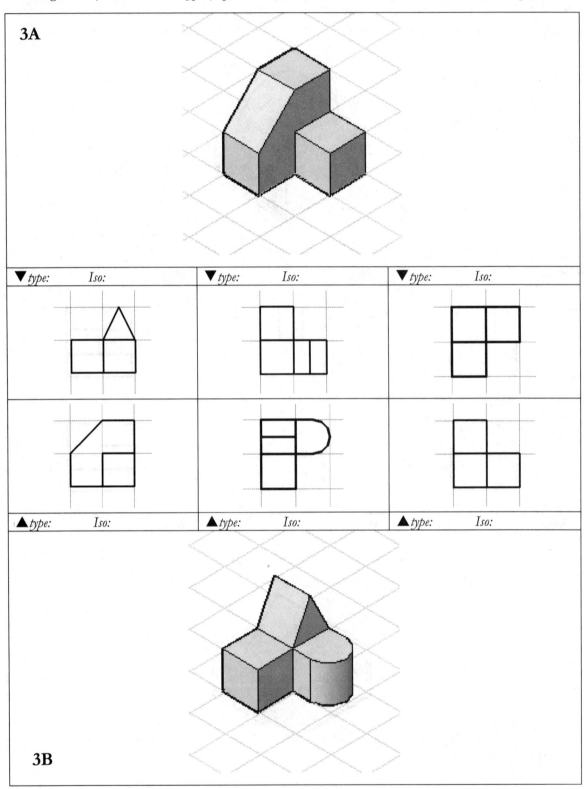

DIRECTIONS: Match the small top, front and side views with the proper isometric view (i.e., the two large views). Write the *view type* (top, front or side) and the *isometric name* that view corresponds to.

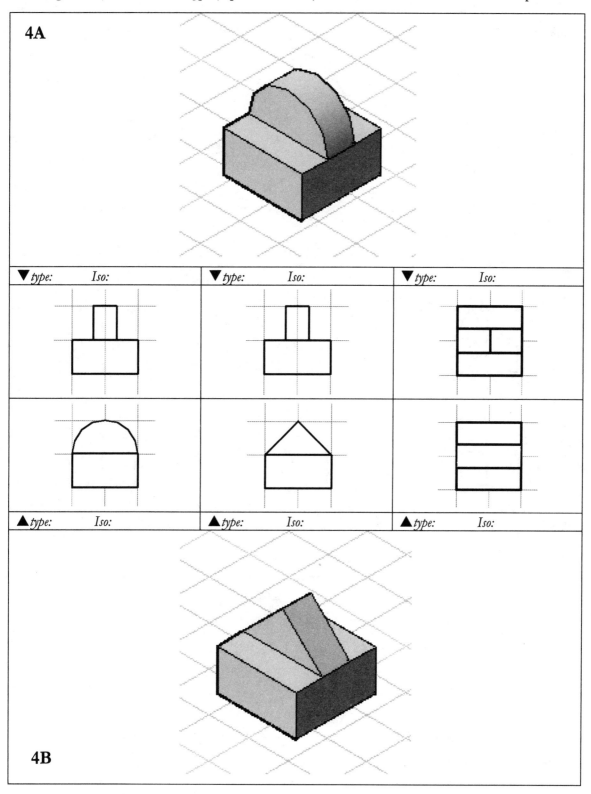

DIRECTIONS: Match the small top, front and side views with the proper isometric view (i.e., the two large views). Write the *view type* (top, front or side) and the *isometric name* that view corresponds to.

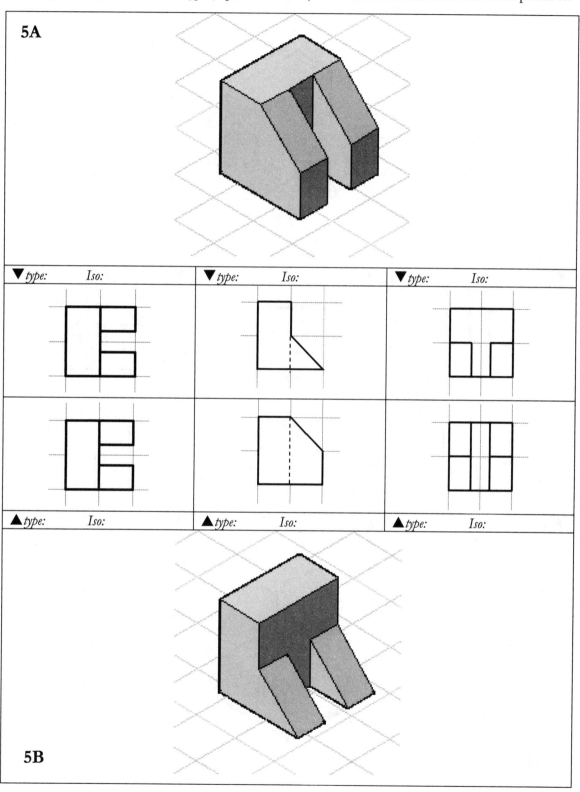

DIRECTIONS: Match the small top, front and side views with the proper isometric view (i.e., the two large views). Write the *view type* (top, front or side) and the *isometric name* that view corresponds to.

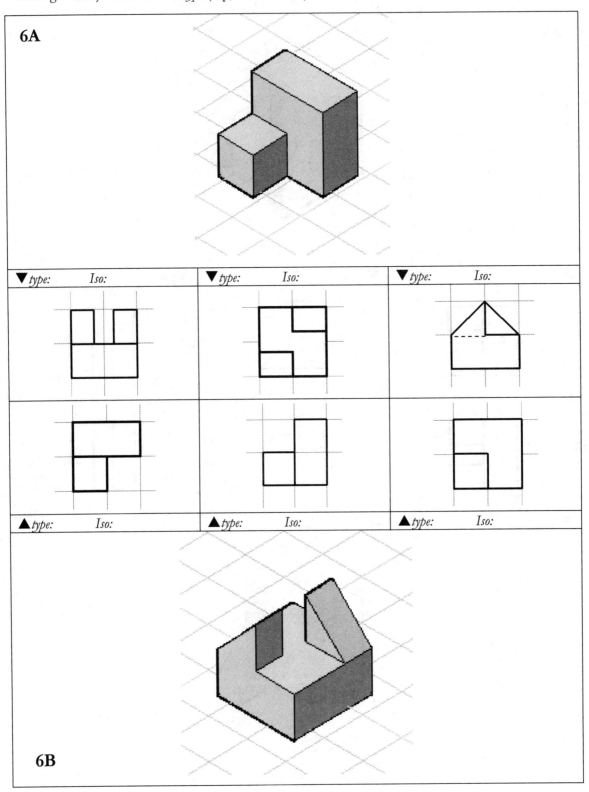

6A

▼ type: Iso: ▼ type: Iso: ▼ type: Iso:

▲ type: Iso: ▲ type: Iso: ▲ type: Iso:

6B

DIRECTIONS: Match the small top, front and side views with the proper isometric view (i.e., the two large views). Write the *view type* (top, front or side) and the *isometric name* that view corresponds to.

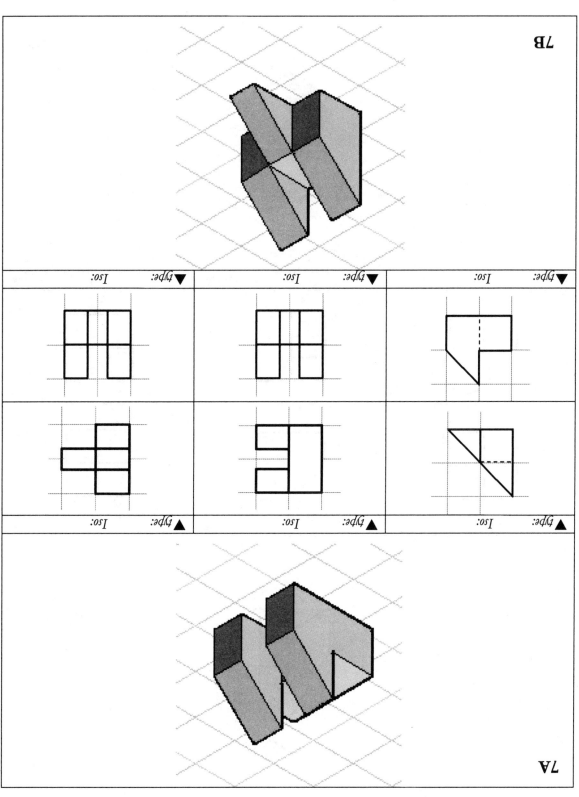

▲ *Type:* _____ *Iso:* _____

▲ *Type:* _____ *Iso:* _____

▲ *Type:* _____ *Iso:* _____

▼ *Type:* _____ *Iso:* _____

▼ *Type:* _____ *Iso:* _____

▼ *Type:* _____ *Iso:* _____

7A

7B

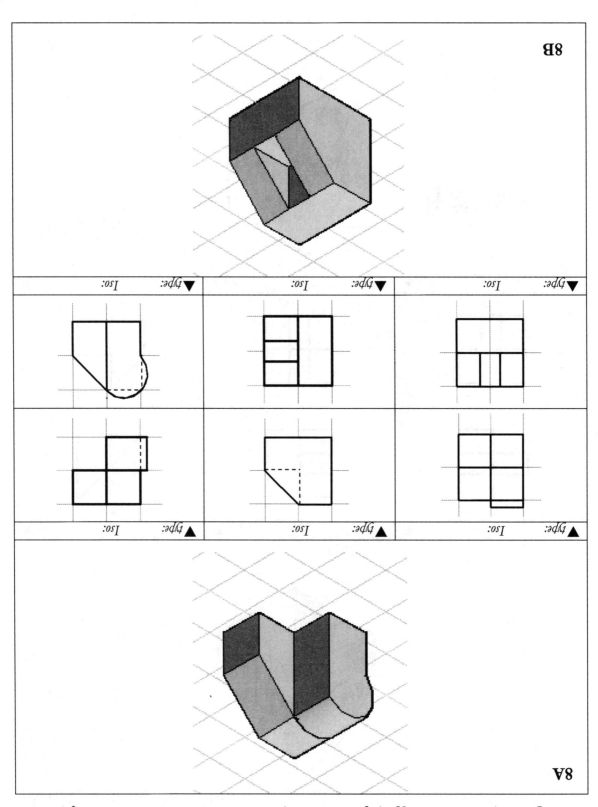

DIRECTIONS: Match the small top, front and side views with the proper isometric view (i.e., the two large views). Write the view *type* (top, front or side) and the *isometric name* that view corresponds to.

Appendix A-3:
Orthographic Projection

Introduction

In this section of the appendix, you will spend some time sketching various building forms. This will give you practice drawing various lines (i.e., weights and styles). The lines drawn will help convey the depth of the image.

Below is an example of a three-dimensional image that will be presented in the subsequent exercises in the appendix. The assignment will be to sketch two-dimensional views of the South and East elevations, plus the Roof Plan (examples of which can be found on the next page).

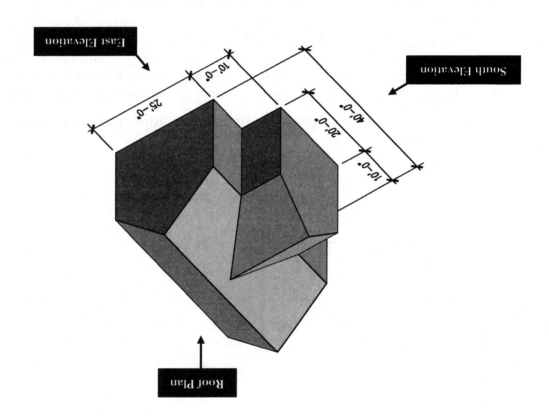

The next page begins a short overview of the process for sketching this assignment.

The image in the upper left represents the East elevation and the one to its right is the South elevation. The lower right image represents the Roof Plan (roof plans are covered in the Roof Study Workbook found on the DVD).

Finally, the dashed lines with arrows show information that can only be derived from another view (at least without having to do any math).

The most common way to draw two-dimensional views of a 3D object is by using the orthographic projection method. The image above shows an overview of how this method works. The dimensions shown represent the "given" information and the dashed lines show how information from one view can be projected onto another view. The 45 degree line simply represents the mirror plane utilized to project the line around a 90 degree corner.

Using the Orthographic Projection Method

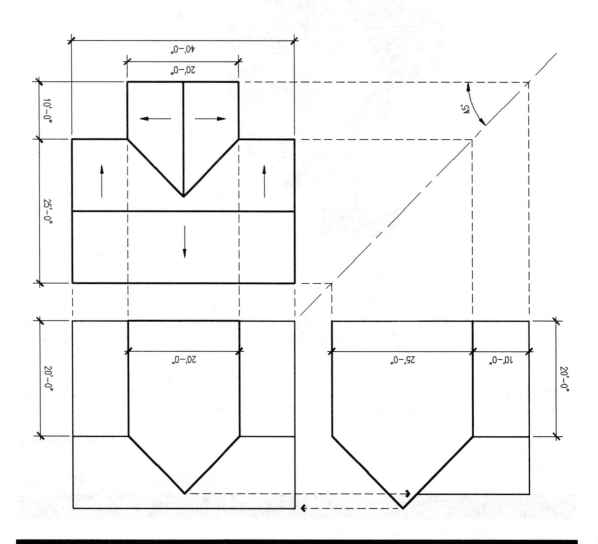

The first step is to sketch the Roof Plan. You have all the information you need in the three-dimensional image provided. You should notice that the roof is a simple gable with a smaller cross-gable at the South elevation. Also, even if the dimensions where not provided, you could determine the cross-gable end is not as wide (in plan view) as the main gable end, which is because the ridgelines do not align.

Remember that the intersecting roof surfaces (which are the same slope) form a 45 degree line. Another thing to remember is that *North* should be upward for the Roof Plan. The last step would be to add the slope arrows.

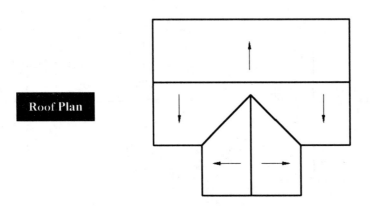

Next, one could begin to sketch either of the required elevations. You will start with the South elevation.

The image on the next page shows step-by-step how the South elevation might be drawn. This process is completely manual, but you can derive all the vertical lines by projecting lines up from the Roof Plan; all of the vertical lines can simply "connect the dots". The only exception is the ridgeline for the main roof; not enough information has been provided to draw that line. This is where Orthographic Projection comes into play. By sketching the East elevation you will establish the ridgeline and then be able to project it back to the South elevation (this requires the floor line of the two elevations to align with each other).

NOTE: *Two additional pieces of information, which will be provided for the upcoming exercises, are that all the roof slopes are to be 12/12 (which is a 45 degree line) and the walls are 20'-0" tall.*

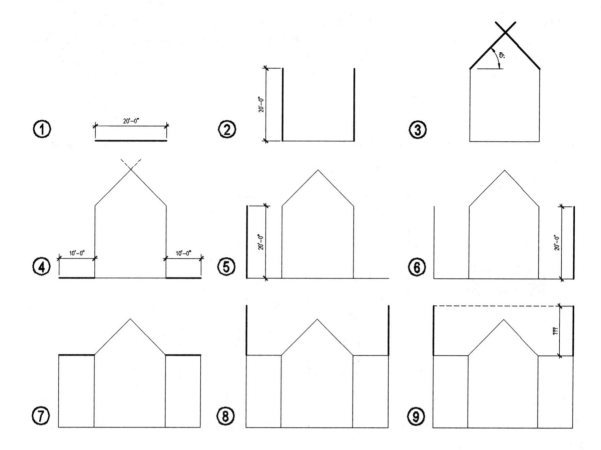

Sketching the South Elevation

The image above shows a detailed example of how one might sketch the South elevation for the three-dimensional image previously provided. The process is simplified by projecting lines up from the roof plan and using the provided grid (which is 5"x5").

Below is one possible step-by-step example of how one might draw the East elevation. Again, many of these lines can be drawn by projecting lines for the roof plan and the South elevation.

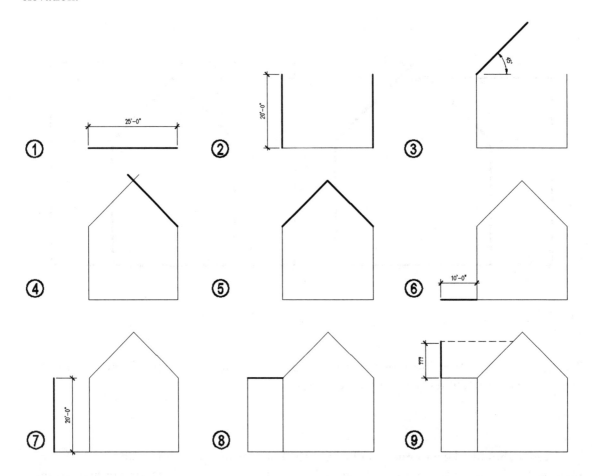

Sketching the East Elevation
The image above shows a detailed example of how one might sketch the East elevation for the three-dimensional image previously provided. Again, one ridgeline is derived by projecting the roof up, at the correct pitch, until it intersects the opposite side. However, the other ridgeline is not possible to locate directly. Information from the South elevation is required to complete this elevation. The final steps are covered next.

Now that you have both the East and South elevations drawn, you can use Orthographic Projection to complete both drawings.

It is now possible to project the known ridgeline from the East elevation to the previously unknown ridgeline in the South elevation (and visa versa).

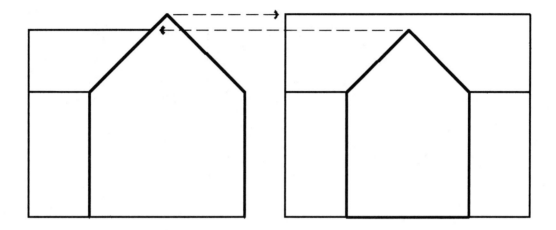

The concept just covered may seem overly simplistic, but the same simple principles are used to develop much more complicated designs!

The reader should take a moment and notice the line weights in the image above. As previously covered in this workbook, the gable end in the East view has heavier lines so the fact that that part of the building is closer to the viewer is graphically clarified. The same is also true for the South elevation.

Exercise 14-3:
Printing a Set of Drawings

Revit has the ability to print an entire set of drawings, in addition to printing individual sheets. You will study this now.

Printing a Set of Drawings:

1. **Open ex14-2.rvt.**

2. Select **Application Menu → Print → Print**.

3. In the *Print Range* area, click the option **Selected views/sheets** (Figure 14-3.1).

4. Click the **Select...** button within the *Print Range* area.

FIGURE 14-3.1 Print dialog box

You should now see a listing of all *Views* and *Sheets* (Figure 14-3.2).

Notice at the bottom you can show both *Sheets* and *Views*, or each separately. Because you are printing a set of drawing you will want to see only the sheets.

FIGURE 14-3.2 Set tool for printing

5. **Uncheck** the **Views** option.

The list is now limited to just *Sheets* that have been set up in your project.

6. Select all the drawing sheets except **A100**.

7. Click **OK** to close the ***View/ Sheet Set*** dialog.

8. IF YOU ACTUALLY WANT TO PRINT A FULL SET OF DRAWINGS, you can do so now by clicking OK. Otherwise click **Cancel**.

9. You do not need to save the file at this time.

> ***FYI:*** *Once you have selected the sheets to be plotted and click OK, you are prompted to save the list. This will save the list of selected drawings to a name you choose. Then, the next time you need to print those sheets, you can select the name from the drop-down list at the top (Figure 14-3.2). On very large projects (e.g., 20 floor plan sheets) you could have a Plans list saved, a Laboratory Interior Elevations list saved, etc.*

If you have software on your computer to create PDF files, you can check the "combine sheets" option in the *Print* dialog (14-3.3). Many design firms create a multi-sheet PDF file to send to a print shop so they can produce the final printed sheets for the contractors to bid from. It is also possible to do the same thing with a multi-sheet DWF file, but fewer people have Autodesk's Design Review installed than Adobe's PDF Reader. However, both viewers are free; the PDF format is used by virtually everyone, not just the design industry.

Good Luck!

You should now have a basic understanding of the Revit Architecture software. **Gook luck with your future Revit projects!** Be sure to visit *www.augi.com* to share knowledge with other Revit users.

Be sure to check out the Family creation and site design chapters located on the DVD.

Self-Exam:

The following questions can be used as a way to check your knowledge of this lesson. The answers can be found at the bottom of the page.

1. You have to manually fill in the reference bubbles after setting up the sheets. (T/F)

2. You cannot control the visibility of objects per *viewport*. (T/F)

3. It is possible to see a listing of only the views that have not been placed on a sheet via the *Project Browser*. (T/F)

4. You only have to enter your name on one titleblock, not all. (T/F)

5. Use the _____ tool to create another drawing sheet.

Review Questions:

The following questions may be assigned by your instructor as a way to assess your knowledge of this section. Your instructor has the answers to the review questions.

1. You need to use a special tool from the *Ribbon* to edit text in the titleblock. (T/F)

2. The template you started with has two titleblocks to choose from. (T/F)

3. You only have to enter the project name on one sheet, not all. (T/F)

4. The scale of a drawing placed on a sheet is determined by the scale set in that view's *Properties*. (T/F)

5. You can save a list of drawing sheets to be plotted. (T/F)

6. Use the _____ _____ tool to edit the model from a sheet view.

7. The reference bubbles will not automatically update if a drawing is moved to another sheet. (T/F)

8. On new sheets, the sheet number on the titleblock will increase by one from the previous sheet number. (T/F)

9. DWF files can consist of an entire set of drawings which a client/owner can view with a free download, similar to Adobe PDF files. (T/F)

10. It is not possible to remove a sheet from the *Sheet List* without deleting that sheet from the project. (T/F)

Notes:

Exercise A3-2

Sketch the *Roof Plan* (top), *South elevation* (front) and *East elevation* (side) of the building shown. Use the provided 5'x5' grid space. See pages A-12 and 13 for typical information needed to complete this problem.

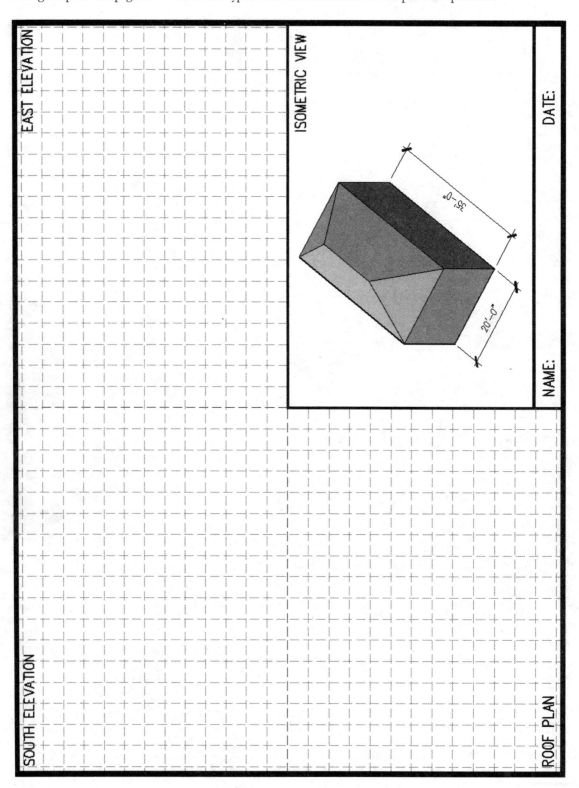

EAST ELEVATION

ISOMETRIC VIEW

DATE:

NAME:

35'-0"

20'-0"

SOUTH ELEVATION

ROOF PLAN

Notes:

Exercise A3-3

Sketch the *Roof Plan* (top), *South elevation* (front) and *East elevation* (side) of the building shown. Use the provided 5'x5' grid space. See pages A-12 and 13 for typical information needed to complete this problem.

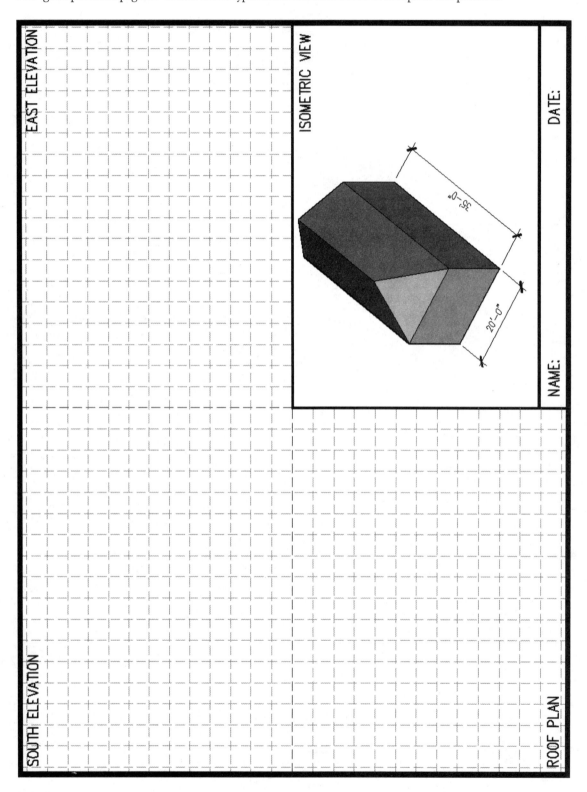

EAST ELEVATION

SOUTH ELEVATION

ISOMETRIC VIEW

35'-0"

20'-0"

NAME:

DATE:

ROOF PLAN

Notes:

Exercise A3-4

Sketch the *Roof Plan* (top), *South elevation* (front) and *East elevation* (side) of the building shown. Use the provided 5'x5' grid space. See pages A-12 and 13 for typical information needed to complete this problem.

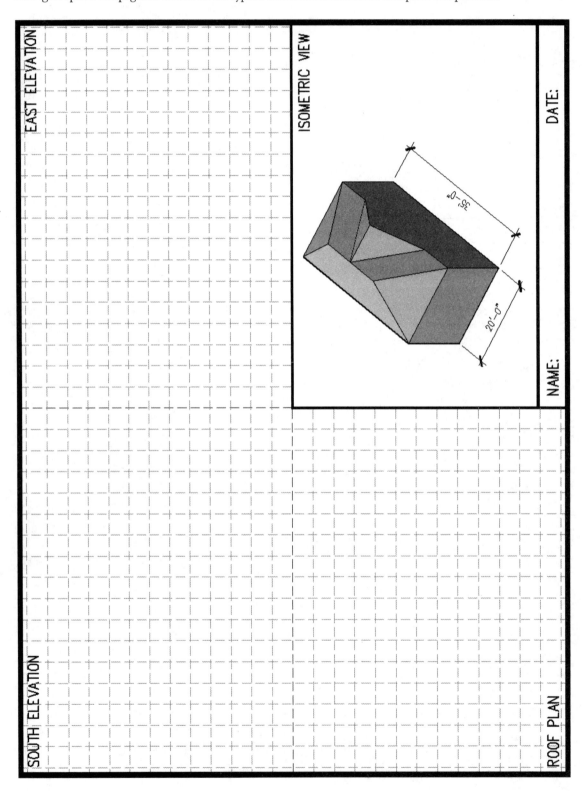

EAST ELEVATION

ISOMETRIC VIEW

35'-0"

20'-0"

DATE:

NAME:

SOUTH ELEVATION

ROOF PLAN

Notes:

Exercise A3-5

Sketch the *Roof Plan* (top), *South elevation* (front) and *East elevation* (side) of the building shown. Use the provided 5'x5' grid space. See pages A-12 and 13 for typical information needed to complete this problem.

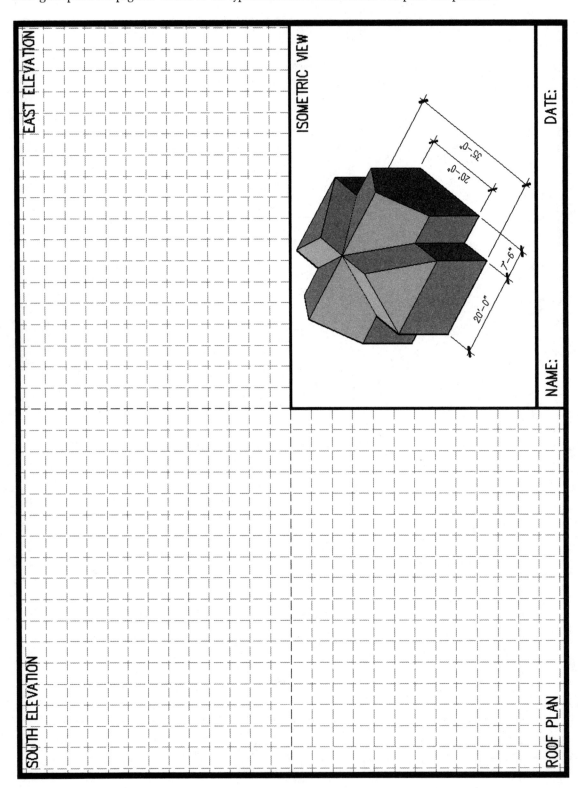

EAST ELEVATION

ISOMETRIC VIEW

35'-0"

20'-0"

7'-6"

20'-0"

DATE:

NAME:

SOUTH ELEVATION

ROOF PLAN

Notes:

Exercise A3-6

Sketch the *Roof Plan* (top), *South elevation* (front) and *East elevation* (side) of the building shown. Use the provided 5'x5' grid space. See pages A-12 and 13 for typical information needed to complete this problem.

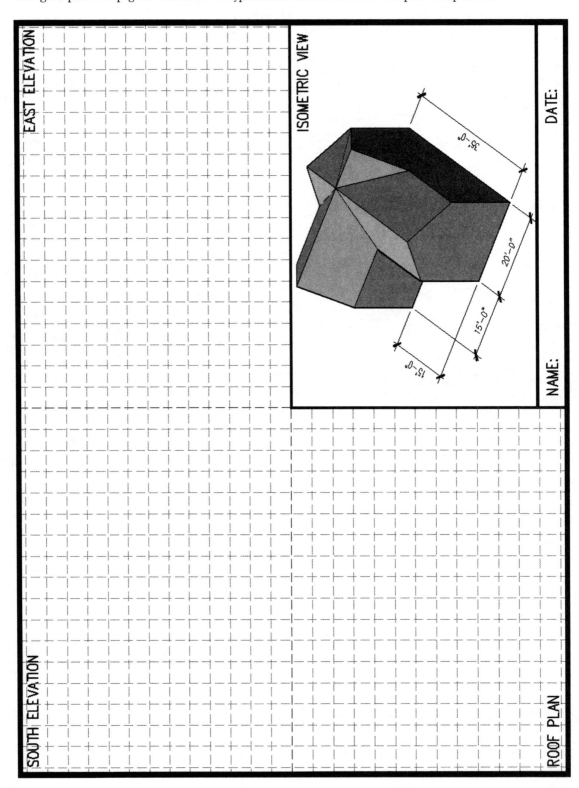

EAST ELEVATION

ISOMETRIC VIEW

35'-0"

20'-0"

15'-0"

15'-0"

DATE:

NAME:

SOUTH ELEVATION

ROOF PLAN

Notes:

Exercise A3-7

Sketch the *Roof Plan* (top), *South elevation* (front) and *East elevation* (side) of the building shown. Use the provided 5'x5' grid space. See pages A-12 and 13 for typical information needed to complete this problem.

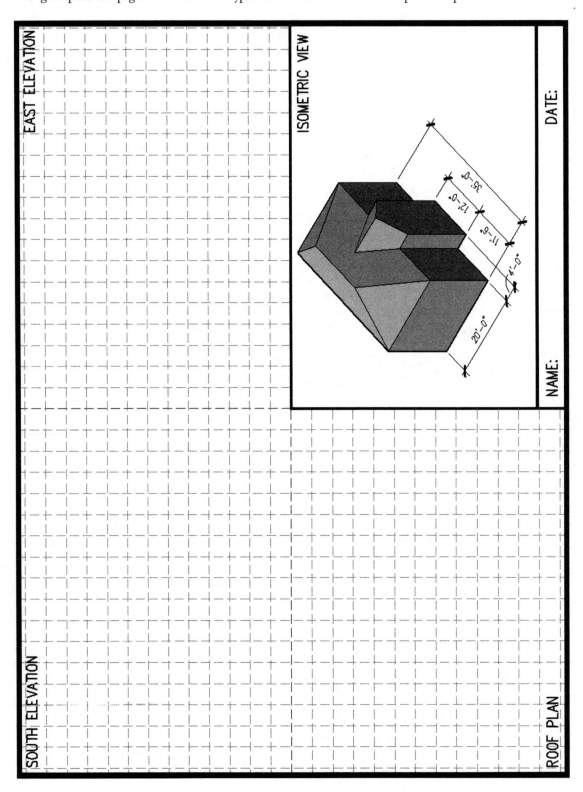

EAST ELEVATION

ISOMETRIC VIEW

35'-0"

12'-0"

11'-6"

4'-0"

20'-0"

DATE:

NAME:

SOUTH ELEVATION

ROOF PLAN

Notes:

Exercise A3-8

Sketch the *Roof Plan* (top), *South elevation* (front) and *East elevation* (side) of the building shown. Use the provided 5′x5′ grid space. See pages A-12 and 13 for typical information needed to complete this problem.

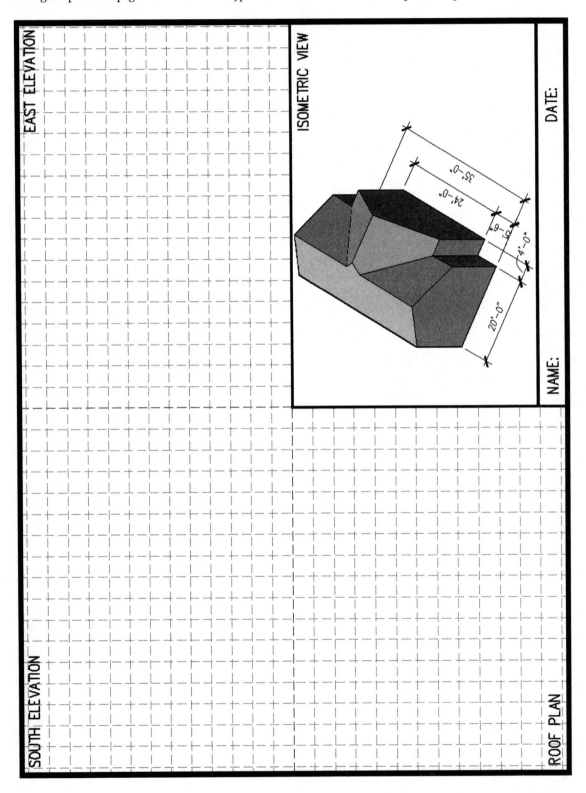

EAST ELEVATION

ISOMETRIC VIEW

DATE:

NAME:

SOUTH ELEVATION

ROOF PLAN

35'-0"

24'-0"

9'-6"

4'-0"

20'-0"

Notes:

Exercise A3-9

Sketch the *Roof Plan* (top), *South elevation* (front) and *East elevation* (side) of the building shown. Use the provided 5'x5' grid space. See pages A-12 and 13 for typical information needed to complete this problem.

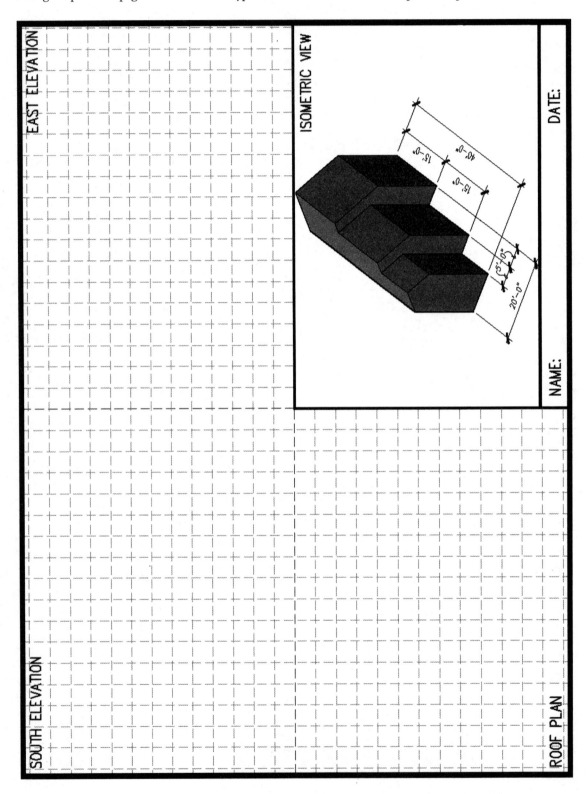

EAST ELEVATION

ISOMETRIC VIEW

SOUTH ELEVATION

ROOF PLAN

DATE:

NAME:

Notes:

Exercise A3-10

Sketch the *Roof Plan* (top), *South elevation* (front) and *East elevation* (side) of the building shown. Use the provided 5'x5' grid space. See pages A-12 and 13 for typical information needed to complete this problem.

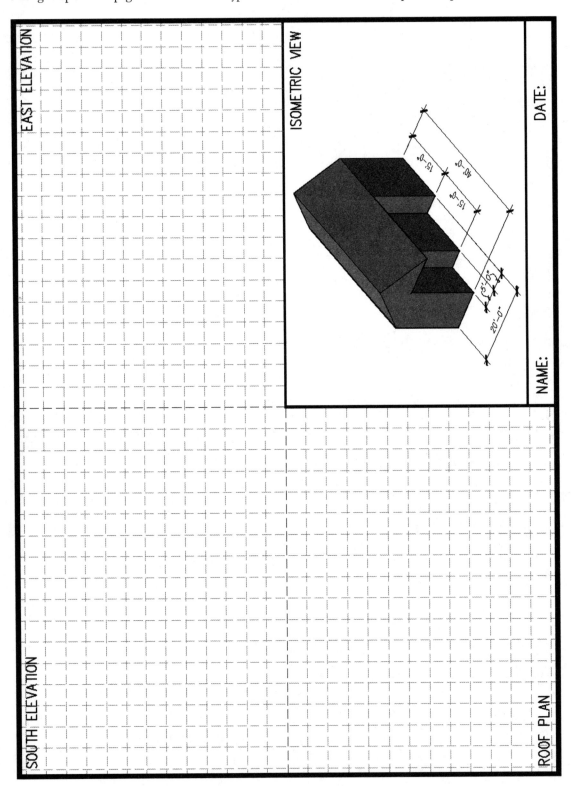

EAST ELEVATION

ISOMETRIC VIEW

15'-0"
40'-0"
15'-0"
5'-0"
20'-0"

DATE:

NAME:

SOUTH ELEVATION

ROOF PLAN

Notes:

Appendix B
Autodesk® Revit® Architecture Certification Exam:

This appendix will cover the certification exam that is offered by Autodesk to help users prove their level of knowledge. This can be helpful when seeking an increase in salary from your current employer or to be listed on your resume.

Appendix B-1:
Introduction and Overview

In the competitive world in which we live it is important to stand out to potential employers and prove your capabilities. One way to do this is by passing the Autodesk Certification Exam. A candidate who passes this exam has credentials from the makers of the software that you know how to use their software. This can help employers narrow down the list of potential interviewees when looking for candidates.

When the exam is successfully passed a certificate signed by the CEO of Autodesk, Carl Bass, can be printed out and displayed at your desk or included with your resume; see example below. You also have access to an Autodesk logo for use on business cards or on flyers promoting your work; two examples are shown below as well. This author uses the professional logo in the front of books and in presentations.

Autodesk offers two exams for Autodesk Revit Architecture; Certified Associate and Certified Professional.

- *Certified Associate*: This is an entry level exam to verify you have a basic understanding of the Revit user interface and functionality. The exam consists of 30 questions, many of which are multiple choice and some are matching or point and click (hotspot). The test is taken on a computer at any Autodesk Certification Center. The test must be completed in less than 60 minutes. You can check the required passing score at http://www.autodesk.com/certification and opening the document "Summary of Test Information". At the time of this printing, the cost for this exam is $75 (students: $25).

- *Certified Professional*: This is an intermediate level exam to prove you have a firm understanding of Revit Architecture's features. Before taking this exam, the associate exam must have been taken and successfully passed. Not only is this exam computer based, but it is also a hands-on Revit test. That is, you actually use the Revit Architecture software. There are twenty questions which have to be answered in 90 minutes. You can check the required passing score at http://www.autodesk.com/certification and opening the document "Summary of Test Information". At the time of this printing, the cost for this exam is $125 (students: $50).

Before taking the associate exam, you can prepare by working through this textbook and taking the assessment test online from home, work or school. One single assessment is available covering both exams. Note the following:

- *Associate Assessment Test*: This is a 67 question test. A time limit of 90 minutes is given but you can pause the test and restart it as often as you wish. At the time of this printing, the cost for this test is $20. Your computer must be Microsoft Windows based and have Internet Explorer 5.5 or higher.

- *Professional Assessment Test*: This test has 20 questions and a time limit of 90 minutes. You must have Autodesk Revit Architecture 2012 installed on your computer to answer the questions on the test; you can download the trial version if needed. At the time of this printing, the cost for this test is $30. Your computer must be Microsoft Windows based and have Internet Explorer 5.5 or higher.

Autodesk recommends how much time you should study and practice before taking each exam, the following highlights their recommendations:

- *Associate Exam*: A training session, plus 100 hours of hands on experience. Much of this requirement can be achieved by working through this book.

- *Professional Exam*: A training session such as this book, plus 400 hours of hands on experience.

FYI: This textbook may not cover every Revit concept or feature that could be asked on the exam. See the exam objectives on the next page.

Be sure to manage your time while taking the test. Quickly go through the test and answer the questions that are easy to you, skipping the ones you are not immediately sure of. The exam software allows you to view a list of questions you have not answered or have marked. Once you have answered all the easy questions you can, then go back and think through those which remain. Do not exit the exam until you are completely finished, as you will not be able to re-enter the exam after that point.

Once the exam is finished you will immediately see your score. If you failed, you should note the objective areas where you missed questions and study those areas more before taking the test again. Be sure to print your score report and take it with you to study.

The following table shows you which chapter in this textbook you can study to gain knowledge that relates to the Associates certification exam.

Exam Section	Exam Objective	Chapter in this book
Revit Architecture Basics	- Describe the different types of building elements. - Describe project templates.	Chapters 1 and 5
Starting a Design	- Create a floor plan view and place building elements in it. - Describe levels and their uses.	Chapters 2 and 5
The Basics of the Building Model	- Describe wall properties. - Describe compound walls.	Chapters 5 and 6
Loading Additional Building components	- Load component families and add components in a project.	Chapters 5 and 11
Viewing the Building Model	- Describe view properties. - Describe object visibility settings. - Describe the characteristics of a section view. - Describe 3D view types.	Chapter 1, 9, 10 and 13
Using Dimensions and Constraints	- Describe permanent dimensions. - Describe constraints and the types of constraints.	Chapters 3 and 5
Developing the Building Model	- Describe floors. - Add and modify ceilings in a building model. - Describe roofs. * Create and modify curtain walls. - Create stairs and railings.	Chapters 1, 5, 6 and 7
Detailing and Drafting	- Describe callouts. - Describe text. - Describe tags. - Create detail views. - Describe drafting views.	Chapters 3, 4 and 10
Construction Documentation	- Describe the properties of schedules. - Describe rooms. * Describe legends.	Chapters 12 and 14
Presenting the Building Model	- Describe drawing sheets. - Describe titleblocks. * Describe revision clouds. - Describe renderings.	Chapters 13 and 14

* topics not covered in this text due to the residential and introductory focus. Refer to the Revit *Help System* for more information on these topics.

Resources:
- Autodesk Certification Site: www.autodesk.com/certification
- Autodesk Authorized Training Center (ATC): www.autodesk.com/atc
- Online Testing Service: http://autodesk.starttest.com

Exercise B-2:
Certification Exam Sample Test

This section is provided to help you test your Revit knowledge before paying to take the associates assessment test or the certification exam. The answers to the questions will be on the last page. Keep in mind these questions are meant to aid in preparing to take the associates exam and not the professional exam, as the latter is a hands-on software exam.

The questions are made up by the author and should not be memorized, thinking the same questions might be asked on the exam. These questions are similar in that they relate to the exam objectives listed on the previous page and are in the format described on the Autodesk website; multiple choice. You are provided 30 questions, equal to the actual exam. It is recommended that you time yourself so that you only have one hour.

It is recommended that you wait to take this sample test until you have completed all the tutorials in this book and on the DVD.

Directions: Answer the following questions in 60 minutes or less:

TIP: The software helps you answer the question in the correct way. That is, if you are expected to select only one answer you can only select one; this looks like a circle. If you are expected to select all that apply, you select one or more square boxes:

        ○ = Select only one answer
        ☐ = Select all that apply

1. Which of the following is NOT a valid *Model Graphics Style*?
   - ☐ Shading with Edges
   - ☐ Realistic
   - ☐ Cartoon
   - ☐ Consistent Colors

2. How do you sort a schedule?
   - ○ Cut and Paste the rows
   - ○ Fields tab > Add Parameter
   - ○ Sorting/Grouping tab > Sort By
   - ○ Appearance tab > Sorting

3. What can you send a client or contractor that does not require them to have Revit and is a much smaller file; but only requires a free download to view?
   - ○ DXF file
   - ○ Word file (DOCx)
   - ○ DWF or DWFx file
   - ○ Excel file (XLSx)

4. Which are TRUE about a titleblock in Revit?
   - ☐ "Sheet number" must be unique
   - ☐ Are found on sheets
   - ☐ Project title automatically appears on all sheets
   - ☐ "Drawn by" field must be unique

5. Which TWO things are true about renderings
   - ☐ Renderings never take more than 5 minutes
   - ☐ Shadows are always created
   - ☐ The sun always casts light
   - ☐ The final rendering is not saved automatically

6. A *Room* has to be created in each level 1 plan you which to see a room tag in. For example: Level 1 Floor Plan, Level 1 Ceiling Plan, Level 1 Finish Plan.
   - o True
   - o False

7. What is NOT possible with the *Text* tool?
   - o Add a leader with no text
   - o Center justify the text
   - o Change the style
   - o Add multiple leaders

8. Which are true about *Detail Views*?
   - ☐ The *View Scale* can be adjusted
   - ☐ They update geometry when the model updates
   - ☐ They are 2D drawings
   - ☐ A different text tool is needed to add notes, compared to a model view

9. While sketching a stair, you can
   - o not adjust the stair width
   - o stop the sketch short of the specific level
   - o end up with various size risers
   - o not use snaps

10. Which are true about railings?
    - ☐ Added automatically with stairs
    - ☐ Can adjust height on options bar while sketching path
    - ☐ Automatically added to edge of interior floor openings
    - ☐ style can be changed, when selected, via the *Type Selector*

11. Select the item that can be loaded into the project from a file
    - o Wall
    - o Door
    - o Floor
    - o Roof

12. Which TWO views are automatically created when a level is added to a project
    - ☐ Floor plan
    - ☐ Detail view
    - ☐ 3D view
    - ☐ Ceiling plan

13. It is not possible to adjust the location of a ceiling grid once it is placed in the model.
    - ☐ True
    - ☐ False

14. Rows can be manually added to a schedule for items not found in the model.
    - o True
    - o False

15. Curtain walls can only have a consistent grid pattern.
    - o True
    - o False

16. Which are true statements about walls?
    - ☐ Tops can conform to underside of roof above
    - ☐ Corners and intersections automatically clean up with others of same type
    - ☐ Most detail shown while in *Coarse* detail level setting
    - ☐ Show heaver when they pass through the cut plane

17. Select the statements that are true about doors.
    - ☐ Doors may be placed in an elevation view
    - ☐ Doors can only be deleted in plan views
    - ☐ Doors are floor hosted
    - ☐ Doors can be deleted from the schedule

18. When a ceiling is added, the top of the ceiling is placed a distance from the floor that is specified in the *Properties Palette*.
    - o True
    - o False

19. Select the various constraints
    - ☐ Equality
    - ☐ Alignment
    - ☐ Pin
    - ☐ Length
    - ☐ Shared Parameter
    - ☐ Locked Dimension

20. Which statement is true about camera views?
    - ☐ The eye elevation cannot be adjusted
    - ☐ The target elevation can be adjusted
    - ☐ You cannot adjust how far into the model you see
    - ☐ Camera views can only be created form the *Ribbon*

21. If you delete a locked dimension you have the option to keep the constraint.
    - o True
    - o False

22. Which key do you use to be able to select elements which are overlapped?
    - ☐ Caps Lock
    - ☐ Alt
    - ☐ Tab
    - ☐ F6

23. Which are window family *Type Parameters*?
    - ☐ Window Sill
    - ☐ Width
    - ☐ Height
    - ☐ Type Mark

24. Where are newly created views listed?
    - o Options Bar
    - o Application Menu
    - o Ribbon
    - o Project Browser

25. You need to change the *Type Selector* to get different line options while using the *Detail Line* tool.
    - o True
    - o False

26. Which are components of the User Interface?
    - ☐ Options Bar
    - ☐ Application Menu
    - ☐ View Control Bar
    - ☐ Project Browser
    - ☐ Door Family

27. Which Statements are true about grid lines?
    - ☐ Two grids can have the same number
    - ☐ Show up automatically in elevation and section views
    - ☐ Start and end points will automatically align if drawn correctly
    - ☐ Grid heads and display on either end or both

28. Which statements are true about the rendering dialog?
    - ☐ The quality can be adjusted
    - ☐ Render time and quality are directly proportional
    - ☐ An image can be selected for the background
    - ☐ You can specify the season, summer, sprint, winter or fall.

29. A callout can be added in a plan, elevation or section view.
- ☐ True
- ☐ False

30. The default template is the preferred starting point for most projects.
- ☐ True
- ☐ False

ANSWERS:

1. Which of the following is NOT a valid *Model Graphics Style*?
   - o Shading with Edges
   - o Realistic
   - o Cartoon
   - o Consistent Colors

2. How do you sort a schedule?
   - o Cut and Paste the rows
   - o Fields tab > Add Parameter
   - o Sorting/Grouping tab > Sort By
   - o Appearance tab > Sorting

3. What can you send a client or contractor that does not require them to have Revit and is a much smaller file; but only requires a free download to view?
   - o DXF file
   - o Word file (DOCx)
   - o DWF or DWFx file
   - o Excel file (XLSx)

4. Which are TRUE about a titleblock in Revit?
   - ☐ "Sheet number" must be unique
   - ☐ Are found on sheets
   - ☐ Project title automatically appears on all sheets
   - ☐ "Drawn by" field must be unique

5. Which TWO things are true about renderings
   - o Renderings never take more than 5 minutes
   - o Shadows are always created
   - o The sun always casts light
   - o The final rendering is not saved automatically

6. A *Room* has to be created in each level 1 plan you which to see a room tag in. For example: Level 1 Floor Plan, Level 1 Ceiling Plan, Level 1 Finish Plan.
   - o True
   - o False

7. What is NOT possible with the *Text* tool?
   - o Add a leader with no text
   - o Center justify the text
   - o Change the style
   - o Add multiple leaders

8. Which are true about *Detail Views*?
   - ☐ The View Scale can be adjusted
   - ☐ They update geometry when the model updates
   - ☐ They are 2D drawings
   - ☐ A different text tool is needed to add notes, compared to a model view

9. While sketching a stair, you can
   - o not adjust the stair width
   - o stop the sketch short of the specific level
   - o end up with various size risers
   - o not use snaps

10. Which are true about railings?
    - o Added automatically with stairs
    - o Can adjust height on options bar while sketching path
    - o Automatically added to edge of interior floor openings
    - o style can be changed, when selected, via the *Type Selector*

11. Select the item that can be loaded into the project from a file
    - o Wall
    - o Door
    - o Floor
    - o Roof

12. Which TWO views are automatically created when a level is added to a project
    - ☐ Floor plan
    - ☐ Detail view
    - ☐ 3D view
    - ☐ Ceiling plan

13. It is not possible to adjust the location of a ceiling grid once it is placed in the model.
    - o True
    - o False

14. Rows can be manually added to a schedule for items not found in the model.
    - o True
    - o False

15. Curtain walls can only have a consistent grid pattern.
    - o True
    - o False

16. Which are true statements about walls?
    - ☐ Tops can conform to underside of roof above
    - ☐ Corners and intersections automatically clean up with others of same type
    - ☐ Most detail shown while in *Course* detail level setting
    - ☐ Show heaver when they pass through the cut plane

17. Select the statements that are true about doors.
    - ☑ Doors may be placed in an elevation view
    - ☐ Doors can only be deleted in plan views
    - ☐ Doors are floor hosted
    - ☑ Doors can be deleted from the schedule

18. When a ceiling is added, the top of the ceiling is placed a distance from the floor that is specified in the *Properties Palette*.
    - ○ True
    - ○ False

19. Select the various constraints
    - ☑ Equality
    - ☑ Alignment
    - ☑ Pin
    - ☑ Length
    - ☐ Shared Parameter
    - ☑ Locked Dimension

20. Which statement is true about camera views?
    - ○ The eye elevation cannot be adjusted
    - ○ The target elevation can be adjusted
    - ○ You cannot adjust how far into the model you see
    - ○ Camera views can only be created form the *Ribbon*

21. If you delete a locked dimension you have the option to keep the constraint.
    - ○ True
    - ○ False

22. Which key do you use to be able to select elements which are overlapped?
    - ○ Caps Lock
    - ○ Alt
    - ○ Tab
    - ○ F6

23. Which are window family *Type Parameters*?
    - ☑ Window Sill
    - ☑ Width
    - ☑ Height
    - ☑ Type Mark

24. Where are newly created views listed?
    - ○ Options Bar
    - ○ Application Menu
    - ○ Ribbon
    - ○ Project Browser

25. You need to change the *Type Selector* to get different line options while using the *Detail Line* tool.
    - ○ True
    - ○ False

26. Which are components of the User Interface?
    - ☑ Options Bar
    - ☑ Application Menu
    - ☑ View Control Bar
    - ☑ Project Browser
    - ☐ Door Family

27. Which statements are true about grid lines?
    - ☐ Two grids can have the same number
    - ☑ Show up automatically in elevation and section views
    - ☑ Start and end points will automatically align if drawn correctly
    - ☑ Grid heads and display on either end or both

28. Which statements are true about the rendering dialog?
    - ☑ The quality can be adjusted
    - ☑ Render time and quality are directly proportional
    - ☑ An image can be selected for the background
    - ☐ You can specify the season, summer, sprint, winter or fall.

29. A callout can be added in a plan, elevation or section view.
    - ○ True
    - ○ False

30. The default template is the preferred starting point for most projects.
    - ○ True
    - ○ False

INDEX

Sections *Sample image from page 14-7*

Renderings *Sample image from page 13-29*

3D Views *Sample image from page 13-15*

Interior Elevations *Sample image from page 9-23*